OXFORD **READERS**

The Mind

Daniel N. Robinson is Distinguished Research Professor at Georgetown
University and occasional visiting lecturer in philosophy at the University
of Oxford where he is visiting Senior Member of Linacre College. He is past-
President of the division of History of Psychology and of the Division of
Theoretical and Philosophical Psychology of the American Psychological
Association. His many books include *An Intellectual History of Psychology*
(3rd edn.), *Aristotle's Psychology,* and *Wild Beasts & Idle Humours: The Insanity
Defense from Antiquity to the Present.*

D0095930

OXFORD **READERS**

The Oxford Readers series represents a unique interdisciplinary resource, offering authoritative collections of primary and secondary sources on the core issues which have shaped history and continue to affect current events.

The Mind

Edited by Daniel Robinson

Oxford · New York
OXFORD UNIVERSITY PRESS
1998

Oxford University Press, Great Clarendon Street, Oxford OX2 6DP

Oxford New York

Athens Auckland Bangkok Bogota Bombay Buenos Aires
Calcutta Cape Town Dar es Salaam Delhi Florence Hong Kong Istanbul
Karachi Kuala Lumpur Madras Madrid Melbourne Mexico City
Nairobi Paris Singapore Taipei Tokyo Toronto Warsaw
and associated companies in
Berlin Ibadan

Oxford is a registered trade mark of Oxford University Press

British Library Cataloguing in Publication Data
Data available

Library of Congress Cataloging-in-Publication Data
The mind / edited by Daniel Robinson.
(Oxford readers)
Includes bibliographical references and index.
1. Philosophy of mind. 2. Mind and body.   I. Robinson, Daniel N., 1937–
  II. Series.
BD418.3.M55 1998   128'.2–dc21   98–11810
ISBN 0–19–289308–4 (Pbk.)

10 9 8 7 6 5 4 3 2 1

Typeset by The Spartan Press Ltd
Printed in Great Britain by
Biddles Ltd,
Guildford and King's Lynn

Foreword

Truth be told, we are really less in 'the decade of the brain' than in the third century of continuing research and theory on mind/brain relations. Nonetheless, the subject now asserts itself with special vigour. Modern technology has provided not only artificial versions of what seems to be highly developed 'intelligence', but also high-fidelity imaging techniques for visualizing the human brain in action. Ever more detailed correlational research presents striking evidence of the relationship between mind and brain. Ever more powerful computers and sophisticated programming lead many to doubt that human cognitive prowess is unique. When one of the world's great chess masters is vanquished by IBM's Deeper Blue, the privileged place long occupied by human intelligence appears less secure.

It is not surprising, therefore, that there would be a proliferation of texts, anthologies, and even personal perspectives on the venerable subject of the mind, with a wide and growing readership attentive to fast-breaking news from 'cognitive neuroscience'. Why, then, still another entry? First, although rich, various, and instructive, many of the works now intended for a general readership feature thinking so current—so *au courant* as to neglect the very history of debate that might permit more discerning assessments of this very thinking. It is worth remembering that in such matters technical progress is likely to outpace refinements in perspective; indeed, technical advances are likely to shape perspective. Consider only the telephone switchboard theories of brain function that were dominant thirty or forty years ago.

Those inclined to defend indifference to the past contend that the issue is a scientific one, the central terms of which were simply unknown in ancient or medieval times or even a century ago. What Aristotle or Kant thought about the mind is not likely to be any more informing than what they thought about gravitation or energy. But such a dismissal begs the question: *is* the issue of mind one that science is to settle? Such a dismissal also prejudges the extent to which past thinkers might even contribute to a clarification of the scientific aspects of the issue. Plato, Aristotle, Descartes, and Locke were ignorant of neurophysiological facts and principles now widely known, but this finally may have little bearing on whether their arguments for or against a given theory of mind retain their initial force. As the present collection should make clear, their understanding still repays attention and can provide useful critical resources to those who would weigh the claims now on offer in the busy market-place of neurocognitive ideas.

In emphasizing technical developments, including the intricacies (and not infrequent opacity) of analytical philosophy, the current literature has also tended to ignore the wider range of conceptions of the mental. Conceptions of mind drawn from the clinic, the surgery, the law courts, and the aesthetic imagination often reveal dimensions of mental life generally unexamined within philosophy of mind. The present volume is intended to redress the perceived imbalance and supplement a literature that is otherwise generous and usefully provocative.

In choosing items of this collection I have tried to draw attention to the continuity of issues and theories within that larger culture of thought in which the 'brain sciences' find their proper place. This is the culture that includes philosophy, neurology, psychiatry and psychology, evolutionary biology, jurisprudence, aesthetics—contexts in which 'mind' is considered in its various and vexing manifestations. In light of page limitations and the commitment to breadth of coverage, little more can be offered than an introduction to these several realms of thought.

Readers will note that some entries are very brief and others rather extensive. Some sections are nearly twice as populous as others. It is in the very nature of the subject, not to mention the larger aims of the volume, that attempts at greater symmetry would be futile and misdirected. In both science and philosophy, the subject of 'mind' has been dominated by the mind/body problem. That problem has received different and important treatments from different schools of philosophy and different scientific disciplines. Any fair sampling of the diverse literature must result in a section of greater bulk than that reserved for, say, 'spectator' theories of mind. It is not that the latter are less interesting or important; only that they can be conveyed in fewer pages composed by fewer writers.

The collection is intended for the non-specialist. Accordingly, introductions to each major section strive to anticipate likely gaps and sources of confusion. Terms that have a special (a specialist's) meaning are defined. Foundational arguments, theories, and modes of enquiry that have grown up around the subject are summarized. In this regard, I worry that there may be too little for those approaching the subject for the first time, and far too much for those who have been carefully following it all along. To repair such defects suggested readings follow at the end of the book, with entries to serve both novices and the already ordained. This much said, the patient reader is warned that the seas are choppy.

Contents

....

I. The Transcendent Mind

II. The Mind as Spectator

III. Mind, Brain, and Modules

IV. The Evolution of Mind

V. Mind and Self: Divided, Constructed, and Multiplied

VI. Epilogue: The Mind of the Poets

The Mind

Section 1

The Transcendent Mind

INTRODUCTION

> No mind? No matter.
> No matter; never mind.

These eight words yield a most economical summary of various philosophical positions that have been taken on the question of the nature of mind. Selections in this section are drawn from books and essays defending the proposition that the mind and mental life are real, that they are distinct from matter and are not reducible to anything that is merely physical. The mind *transcends* the plane of the physical. Here, then, is one 'solution' to the problem of mind; one among many. But what is it that makes 'mind' problematical? A sketch of the more influential solutions will reveal the nature of the problem.

Any number of labels (and not a few libels) have been attached to philosophers and scientists who have attempted to explain the mind and mental life. Arguments for and against various 'solutions' to the problem of mind are so diverse and subtle that some sort of taxonomy becomes necessary just to keep the house in order. At the most fundamental level, the major categories are *ontological*, revealing just how many kinds or types of basic 'stuff' theorists require to develop and defend a given solution. Ontological questions are questions about what has real existence, what really *is*. One such question is whether or not there really are 'minds' and 'mental events' at all! If one resists the temptation to make reality any more complicated than it already is, one might strive to limit the fundamental constituents of reality to a single type. One might insist, therefore, in the absence of any compelling argument to the contrary, that there is only one kind of 'stuff' in the universe, and that is a material or physical or matter–energy kind of stuff. Thus, *No mind!* Those who take this position are referred to as ontological *monists*, and more specifically *materialist*-monists.

At a common-sense level there seems to be no doubt, however, but that we do have minds and a mental life, and that what we take to be the 'mental' has little or nothing in common with what we take to be matter or energy. One doesn't think of electrons or quarks as being sweet or melodic or pensive. Accordingly, and given the indubitable reality of our thoughts, feelings, sensations, and memories, there seems to be a good common-sense argument for some form of ontological *dualism*. On this account, any complete description of reality must avail itself of two different kinds of 'stuff', one physical and one mental. The question that then arises addresses the nature of the relationship between the two. Is the mental caused by the physical? Are the two merely correlated? Are the influences two-way or one-way?

Again, at a common-sense level, the popular choice would probably be *two-way dualist interactionism*. When one's mind is devoted to cheerful themes one's physical health is enhanced, whereas morbid obsessions typically lead to illness. Similarly, a blinding headache makes clear thinking and sustained attention difficult if not impossible. Mind and body influence each other or else there would be nothing to either psychosomatic medicine or meditation.

Common sense, alas, is rarely sufficient unto the purposes of metaphysics! Its limitations become obvious once we demand a definition of 'mental' and 'physical', and then ask how such entities, thus defined, could possibly have any influence on each other at all. What, after all, do we mean by something being 'mental' if not *non-physical*? Something is mental insofar as it has no weight, has no shape or extension in space, cannot be halved or quadrupled, makes no sound, etc. And something is physical insofar as it requires force to accelerate it, displaces anything into whose space it moves, can be cut into pieces, and is audible when it makes contact with things like itself. If things of this latter sort are to have some sort of influence or effect on things of the former sort, there must be a point of impact; some place or locus at which the two meet. But an 'idea' or 'memory' is not *here* or *there*. It cannot be touched by a probe or weighed on a balance.

Common-sense varieties of dualism, therefore, face the challenge posed by two radically different ontologies which, nonetheless, are presumed to stand in some sort of causal relationship. The prevailing view in today's 'brain sciences' is that events described as 'mental' are either brain events under a set of 'folk' descriptions, or are causally produced by brain events. The first of these positions is sometimes called *eliminative materialism*; a materialism committed to the scientific elimination of the mental in just the way that science eliminates witches and goblins. Akin to this view is the so-called *identity thesis*, according to which mentalistic terms and states just are (are identical to) events in the brain. The 'identity' thus conceived is that which obtains between, for example, 'heat' and 'mean kinetic energy'. The second theory is known as *epiphenomenalism* and was given currency in the previous century by Thomas Henry Huxley. We can take it as asserting, *No matter: Never mind*. In later sections of this volume these terms and their defenders will be discussed and illustrated. It is sufficient here to note that only eliminative materialism and the identity thesis escape the challenge just noted. If it is implausible to regard entities drawn from such radically different ontological domains as the mental and the physical having any effect on each other, then one way out of the labyrinth is simply to reject the dualist's ontology and commit oneself to monism.

There is more than one species of monism, however. Competing with monistic materialism is the intriguing if counter-intuitive theory of monistic *idealism*. This position matches up with, *No mind? No matter!* The most famous argument for this view was developed by George Berkeley early in the eighteenth century. He set out to put an end, once and for all time, to radical materialism and what he took to be its sceptical consequences. Berkeley's subtle argument is presented in this section. In its skeletal form it appears as follows:

1. Take the word *idea* to refer to any and every element of conscious experience, including all perceptions, sensations, sentiments, etc.
2. It is thus contradictory to claim to *know* that of which one has no idea.
3. An idea can only be like another idea and surely not like any physical object; to have an awareness of the moon is not to have anything like the moon itself in one's mind.
4. All (allegedly) material entities are but a constellation of attributes: size, shape, colour, hardness, taste . . .
5. But all attributes are the contents of perceptions.
6. Strip away all attributes of anything and there is nothing left.
7. Thus, *to be is to be perceived* ('*Esse est percipi*').

Accordingly, No mind? No matter.

If the nuances of Berkeley's *immaterialism* are philosophically original, the general thesis is not. The ancient *Upaniṣads*, composed before the birth of philosophy itself, already record a sense of the mind's special nature in its intellectual or comprehending achievements. The selection offered in this Section is from the *Brihad-Aranyaka*: King Janaka questions the wise one about the source of light when neither sun nor moon nor candle nor even speech can lead us. It is then the unseizable soul (*Atman*) that shows us the way. By its light what the senses report can be made knowledge.

Pythagoras and his disciples had reached a similar conclusion if by a different route. On the Pythagorean understanding, the ultimate grounding of the physical universe cannot itself be physical. The manifest order and arrangement of the heavens and of the plant and animal forms express relationships at once perfect and abstract. The ultimate grounding, then, is mathematical. There is a cosmic mind or soul capable of generating physical reality but according to a scheme which is not itself physical and which cannot be comprehended by anything that is itself lacking in mind as such. Consider the *tetraktys*, the first four positive integers 1, 2, 3, 4, arranged in a triangle:

```
          ★

       ★     ★

    ★     ★     ★

 ★     ★     ★     ★
```

The first affords the necessary condition for a point; the second, a line; the third, a surface; the fourth for a solid. It is by way of the *tetraktys* that the cosmic soul actually produces the world of material things, but things finally grounded in *number*. The famous Pythagorean prayer of thanks includes the passage, 'By him that transmitted to our soul the Tetraktys . . .', which links the mind to number.

The concept of the mind as transcendent is indeed venerable. Though it has well served the aims and teachings of the world's spiritual leaders, it is a metaphysically durable concept quite apart from its religious implications. To keep the metaphysics and the theology in their proper places, it is important to define 'transcendent' with some care. The term suggests height and elevation, but it might be more faithful to its meaning within philosophical discourse to understand it as implying separation. Mind is a thing apart; neither dependent on nor reducible to matter; not sharing matter's features or fate.

However, if mind is separated from the realm of matter—and if the senses are material organs—then at least three daring conclusions become tenable. First, there must be knowledge that is independent of experience, for all experience is but the exercise of the senses. Second, this non-sensory knowledge must be about that which itself is non-material for a knowledge of material things comes about through their action on the (material) sense organs. Finally, being immaterial, mind as such may be 'embodied' without itself being a body; its functions within a body are, in principle, separable from that body.

All three of these conclusions are developed in a number of Plato's dialogues. Under the influence of Pythagorean thought, Plato distinguished between the fluctuating ephemera of the material world and the enduring truths of mathematics. If the whole point of philosophy is the search for truth, then the mere flotsam of daily experience can be little more than a distraction. What is eternally true of the rectilinear triangle is not anything about a physical three-sided figure, for such a thing must ultimately undergo degradation and disappearance. Moreover, no matter how carefully such a thing is drawn or made, it will never perfectly match the mathematical ideal. Rather, the *true form* of the rectilinear triangle is given by the Pythagorean theorem itself: $a^2 + b^2 = c^2$. Needless to say, Pythagoras did not discover such relationships by swanning around Samos and Crotona and measuring three-sided figures! Truths of this sort are not the result of visual sensations or experiences of any kind. These are eternal truths, possessed rather than discovered by the mind. It is in virtue of the mind's own rational character that it shares in the rational character of all that is true. On this understanding, the 'discovery' of what is true is by way of a special kind of self-discovery. The command to 'Know thyself' implies something more subtle and less personal than one might assume.

In Plato's *Republic* Socrates equates perception with the illusory knowledge of those trapped in a cave and staring at a wall on which shadowy forms are projected. Like the soul itself, such persons are imprisoned and are hostage to mere appearances. In the *Theataetus*, where he is asked to comment on Protagoras's famous maxim according to which *man is the measure of all things*, Socrates asks why we don't regard the dog-faced baboon as the measure of all things; or, for that matter, any creature with keen senses. Again, the sensory world is relegated to the category of the base, the changing, the illusory. True knowledge must transcend all this, and becomes possible only if the mind itself is of a transcendent nature.

Selections in this volume are drawn from Plato's *Meno* and *Phaedo*. Meno is a young Athenian who has recently returned from his travels and meets Socrates by chance. He is accompanied by a servant, born and raised in Meno's house, but uneducated; a 'barbarian'. Taking a leaf from the Sophists, Meno taunts Socrates for his famous search for truth: if one knows what one is looking for, there's no need to conduct a search, and if one doesn't know what one is looking for, there's no basis even for initiating a search. Socrates answers the challenge by engaging the uneducated boy in a series of questions about a figure Socrates draws in the earth. It becomes clear from the boy's answers that he understands the Pythagorean theorem, now expressed as 'the double space is the square of the diagonal'. As the boy had never been taught this, it must have been within him all along. Indeed, Socrates says, if he had ever acquired such knowledge 'he could not have acquired it in this life'. Knowledge of this sort is possessed by an immortal soul and can be recalled or recovered through philosophical guidance of the sort Socrates has given to Meno's servant.

In the *Phaedo* Socrates explains to Cebes that corporeal things, like the body, are 'burdensome, heavy, earthly and visible'. The soul is weighed down and dragged into the visible world as a result of its unwilling incarceration in the body. Those who have lived the wrong sort of life have souls which, on the death of the body, retain something of the visible, material world and thereupon 'flit about' as if in a dark graveyard, only again to become imprisoned in the body of one who has lived a comparably dissolute life. Only those who have lived the philosophical life can liberate their souls completely for an eternal life in communion with the gods.

Aristotle, far more the biologist and natural scientist than was Plato, his teacher for nearly twenty years in the Academy, composed an entire treatise on the soul, reserving whole sections to the perceptual, emotional, and intellectual operations of the mind. Consistently, Aristotle adopted the perspective of the natural scientist, except when considering the abstract rational powers of the human soul (mind). Whether or not his conclusions on this point establish Aristotle as a dualist or transcendentalist remains open to scholarly debate. In the selection provided here he declares, for example, that the part of the soul associated with thinking and judging has no existence until it engages in such activities. What is proposed, then, is that 'mind' is a term for an activity, not some separate immaterial entity. So he regards it as unreasonable to think of mind as an organ or as mixed with bodily organs. But mind is also capable of thinking itself (*kai autos de auton tote dunatai noein*), and this is surely a power not possessed by any other kind of activity. Moreover, as that 'place of forms' (*topon eidon*), the mind is able to receive an infinite variety of information from the external world, and this would not be possible if mind itself had some determinate physical nature. Earlier, in Book II of *On the Soul*, Aristotle had already equivocated on the extent to which reason and deliberation can be explained in the same way as sensation: 'But in the case of the mind and the thinking faculty nothing is yet clear; it seems to be a distinct kind of soul, and it alone admits of being separated, as the immortal from the perishable' (*On the Soul*, 413^{b}25–30).

And in Book I of the same treatise he is found going so far as to say that 'thought seems to be an independent substance implanted within us and to be incapable of being destroyed' (408^{b}18). In all, then, Aristotle resists any theory that would reduce all of mental life to physical processes or to the operation of any of the organs of the body.

There is more to Aristotle's transcendentalist theory than this, however. When we turn to Book XII (passages included in this section) of his *Metaphysics* we learn that the human mind shares at least episodically the transcendent features of the divine mind. Having attributed to the 'unmoved mover' the creative power behind 'the sensible universe and the world of nature', Aristotle is prepared to confer on abstract human thought a comparably divine power. The life of the unmoved mover, he says, 'is like the best which we temporarily enjoy' in those moments when our thoughts are of that which is best. 'If, then, the happiness which God always enjoys is as great as that which we enjoy sometimes, it is marvellous.'

Among the writers of the early modern and medieval eras the nature of mind took on added significance. The belief that we are made in the image of God lent itself directly to the view that human rational and discursive powers were the true mark of the divine. The later Stoic philosophers (e.g. Chrysippus) had concluded that language itself formed a unique class of beings who, by sharing this power, occupied a common household from which all non-linguistic beings were excluded. The Platonic and Stoic influence on Christianity expresses itself most clearly in psychological treatises concerning language and thought. Selected here are passages from Augustine and Aquinas.

In Augustine's treatise on free will (*De Libero Arbitrio*), the mind's essential character is again found to be equated with abstract mathematical truths. In Book II of that work (portions excerpted here) Augustine and Evodius examine the particular senses, noting that it is by sight that we can know visible things but that it is not by sight that we can know we are seeing. That is, these senses can convey information about objects in the external world but not information about themselves—about the very act of sensation—for this requires yet another sense. There must be some other inner sense by which we know we are seeing rather than hearing, hearing rather than touching, etc. Augustine claims that this inner sense is possessed by animals as well as human beings.

A question that arises in the course of their conversation is whether two persons can have the same experience. In the course of the discussion it is noted that two persons can see the same thing or hear the same sound or smell the same odour at the same time, but that they cannot touch precisely the same place simultaneously. Augustine then contrasts experiences that leave the object unchanged with those that result in the incorporation of the object into oneself. When Augustine and Evodius see and hear the same things, the objects of these experiences are not changed by the act of perception. But when either of them *tastes* or *smells* something, the sensations are individually incorporated into each of them and not possessed in common. What, then, about reason? 'Does each of us have his own?' asks Augustine.

Even though one has one's own sense of sight, there are not two suns seen by two observers. Material things that are incorporated into oneself are not 'common property', but the objects of sight and hearing are. We might then ask whether the objects of reason are of the common or of the private sort. Augustine asks Evodius if he can think of anything that is common to all who think, and Evodius replies that many such things answer to this description, but chiefly *number*. At this point Augustine offers a brief disquisition on the abstract nature of number, its transcendent (non-sensory) nature, concluding: 'We see it by an inner light of which the bodily sense knows nothing'. Evodius, sensing a parallel now between wisdom and number, wonders whether the two are really the same. Augustine, in the manner of a true Pythagorean, allows that they are, but that an understanding of this is not granted 'even to all souls, but only to rational souls'.

Less in the tradition of Plato than of Aristotle, Thomas Aquinas is led to the same conclusions reached by Augustine regarding the immateriality of the soul. Selections here from the *Summa Theologica* address two fundamental questions: first, whether the soul is something subsistent, meaning whether its operation or existence depends upon its *subsisting* in something else. And second, whether the soul is composed of matter and form. Thomas Aquinas answers the first question by arguing that the intellectual operations of the soul must be at once incorporeal and subsistent. As the intellectual operation of the soul is that by which we can know all corporeal things, it itself cannot be corporeal. Metaphorically speaking, Thomas notes that to a sick man's tongue everything seems bitter. The point is that a corporeal mind would impart to all it comprehended its own particular corporeal attributes. Indeed, the intellectual soul cannot even be caused to know particular things by way of the body for, in that case, 'the determinate nature of that organ would likewise impede knowledge of all bodies'. Translating this into contemporary terms, we might say that if our knowledge of visible things were determined by the corporeal properties of the visual system, all that we would experience would be the electrical discharges of the optic nerve fibres or of cells in the visual cortex or some such. Finally, if the intellectual soul were corporeal, it could only comprehend particular things, just as one body is influenced by another specific body. But the intellect comprehends universals, and this is possible only because intellect itself has a transcendent nature.

Although he would regard his own efforts as liberating philosophy from what he took to be the dead-ends of scholasticism, René Descartes actually patterns much of his own analysis of the mental on both Thomistic and Augustinian templates. Before considering this (in connection with Descartes's *Sixth Meditation*), it is instructive to examine his commitment to accept no proposition as true unless it attains undiminished clarity and logical force. Thus we find him, in the *Second Meditation*, offering that (in)famous argument needed to establish his own existence. The 'Cogito ergo sum' would lead more than one critic to chide Descartes for needing to *deduce himself!* His happy conclusion, however, was not part of an argument based on a doubted self-existence. Rather, he was searching for a standard against which to test all other claims; a standard capable of defeating the sceptic's thesis that all knowledge is but self-deception. Descartes's method here is just this very sceptical attitude, preparing him to reject any and every idea lacking in requisite clarity and in logical force. But the one truth that must survive even the most devious of divine perpetrators of confusion is this: to be deceived, an entity must be a *thinking* thing; a *res cogitans*. Descartes's vulnerability to deception itself clearly and indubitably establishes his real being.

In his *Fifth Meditation* (not included here), Descartes finds within himself 'countless ideas of things . . . [with] their own true and immutable natures'. These cannot be illusory creations of his fancy, for various formal properties of some such things can be established with mathematical rigour and logical certainty. In selections presented here from the *Sixth Meditation*, in which Descartes distinguishes between the mental and the physical, the echo of Augustine is again pronounced. He begins with a comparison of imagination and understanding—like the comparison Augustine made between perception and cognition—and uses the same example as Augustine had; viz. a chiliagon. Such a thousand-sided figure can be the subject of understanding (or cognition in Augustine's terms), but not of imagination (or perception, as Augustine would have it). That is, one can see and imagine a three- or four-sided figure, but not one with a thousand sides. One can understand or comprehend chiliagons not by way of a sensory or *passive* faculty but only through the operation of that *active* faculty that is the mind itself. Still, the chiliagon is not an invention. Such entities, writes Descartes, 'may not all exist in a way that exactly corresponds with my sensory grasp of them, for in many cases the grasp of the senses is very obscure and confused. But at least they possess all the properties . . . which, viewed in general terms, are comprised within the subject-matter of pure mathematics.'

Later in the *Sixth Meditation*, we find Descartes now arguing for the uniqueness of mind; its indivisibility, the unity of self-consciousness, its survival even as much of the body is destroyed or amputated. Though linked in some ways to the functions of the brain (chiefly by way of the pineal gland!), the mind has an independent existence and is able to comprehend abstract truths for which there is no material or physical corollary. Mind, then, transcends the plane of matter and grasps what the senses cannot reach. The goodness of God is revealed again in the providential arrangement of body and mind such that, for example, injury to the foot results in brain activities that inform the mind it is the foot and not some other part that has been attacked. But far from materializing mind such findings simply underscore the difference between mind and matter.

Against the more telling criticisms advanced by his contemporaries—chiefly Pierre Gassendi—Descartes defended the 'cogito' argument and the conclusion that all he could be certain of regarding himself is that he is a *thinking* thing. A dualist to the end, he is found satisfied in his 'Fifth Set of Replies' that his 'clear and distinct concept of this thinking substance . . . contains none of the things that belong to the concept of a corporeal substance'.

Berkeley's immaterialist thesis has already been briefly considered. The selection appearing in this Section is from Part I of his *A Treatise Concerning the Principles of Human Knowledge*. Berkeley has as his chief target in these pages John Locke's distinction between primary and secondary qualities. As we shall note in Section II of this collection, Locke had attempted to develop an essentially Newtonian theory of mind according to which simple ideas are formed out of elementary sensations, and more complex ideas out of simpler ones. Satisfied that the mind is 'furnished' solely by experience, Locke addressed the ageless sceptical question as to whether our knowledge of the external world is valid. Experience is mediated by the senses, such that what we are conscious of is whatever the senses have reported, rather than the objects themselves which have stimulated the senses. The question that thereupon arises is whether the perceived object faithfully conveys the attributes of the actual object.

In considering this question, Locke distinguished between the 'primary' and the 'secondary' qualities of objects. There are some qualities or attributes of bodies which the processes of perception do not alter or transform. These are 'primary' and include such attributes as shape and hardness. Oak is hard and is perceived as such; triangles are three-sided and are perceived as such. But there are other qualities of bodies which, though they reliably yield specific perceptual outcomes, are not directly conveyed by the perception itself. Colour is illustrative. Whatever it is in a body that gives rise to the perception of 'blue' is not itself blue. As we would say today, there are no 'blue quanta'. Locke dubbed these attributes 'secondary qualities'. What we find Berkeley insisting, however, is that *all* qualities of bodies are 'secondary', in that all qualities are *perceived*. Indeed, *Esse est percipi*.

Berkeley's thesis has lent itself to a range of interpretations, the tersest being Dr Johnson kicking a stone when asked by Boswell to comment on it. In this, however, Johnson made the common mistake of assuming that Berkeley was denying the existence of stones or of trees unheard when falling in the forest. Without hoping to put an end to Berkeley scholarship, I would say that Berkeley should be understood as he wished to be; viz. as an opponent of scepticism and a critic of materialist theories of mind. No man who nearly kills himself testing the curative powers of tar water, or who journeys to the American colonies to raise funds for a college to be founded in Bermuda, or who contributes originally to the geometric optics and theories of depth perception can be said to be doubtful about the existence of a material world. What Berkeley denies is that such a world can exist *independently* of the perceiving mind. All that is physical or material dependently exists or *subsists* in the mind that apprehends it. Otherwise, there would be bodies without attributes, a notion that Berkeley declares to be unintelligible. *No mind? No matter!* Returning to the problem of labels, one might wonder whether Berkeley is best cast as a monistic idealist (for he does finally conclude that real existence attaches only to 'ideas and spirits'). Might his acceptance of a dependently subsisting material world qualify him as some odd sort of dualist; a kind of reverse-epiphenomenalist? Let the reader decide.

If Berkeley's solution to the problem of mind seems counter-intuitive, Leibniz's may seem simply incredible. Yet, it provides a philosophically and logically coherent means by which to preserve the uniqueness of both the physical and the mental without calling on one to interact causally with the other. Selections here are drawn from Leibniz's *Monadology* and his *New Essays on Human Understanding*. The concept of the 'monad' is elusive but important, for it is at the foundation of Leibniz's metaphysics. The

Newtonian ontology is reducible to physical corpuscles, too small to see but nonetheless having mass and extension. Leibniz argues against this on the grounds that anything that is extended cannot be ultimate, for it is divisible. The ultimate constituent of reality must be indivisible: simple, without parts or pieces, having no windows or entry points by which to become occupied. As such, it is not composed and thus has no beginning—or end. In the parlance of modern cosmology, one might think of the monad as what was present before the Big Bang.

The evidence for monads cannot be sensory, of course, for if it were then monads would, indeed, be physical entities. The only monadic entity for which we have evidence is mind itself. That is, at least one type of monad is that with self-consciousness. The world of matter is a world of *phenomena*; the appearances created by extended things. But the world of self-consciousness is the world of reality, not appearances. It follows that events external to the monad can be presented to it, though self-consciousness does not entail that such presentations will be consciously experienced. Rather, there are gradations of consciousness, ranging from the unconscious to the clearly apprehended. 'Mind' is immersed in nothing less than the universe itself, of which it has awareness of only a tiny sample. For Descartes, the ultimate reality that is immunized against the claims of scepticism is the *res cogitans*. For Leibniz it is a monadic entity which may be *unconscious* of all but itself.

In no. 17 of the *Monadology* Leibniz illustrates the difference between matter and mind by inviting us into a machine capable of producing thought and perception but made so large that we could walk about within it. (Imagine the brain thus enlarged so that each neuron is large relative to our own size.) Nowhere, says Leibniz, in the operations of such a machine would we see anything that had any of the properties of a perception or thought. Nothing in the nature of figure and motion, nothing by way of purely mechanical causes can render perception intelligible.

The *New Essays* were written as a critical reply to Locke's *Essay Concerning Human Understanding*. Leibniz develops his criticism through an extended conversation between Philalethes (who has just returned from England and who has been impressed by Locke's essentially atomistic-physical theory of mind) and Theophilus, who is given Leibniz's own views. Philalethes is readily identified as holding to a materialist-dualist theory, for he notes that, in the past, he and Theophilus have disagreed, Theophilus taking Descartes's position and Philalethes that of Pierre Gassendi. We shall consider Gassendi in a later section. He was famous for his revival of the atomism of Democritus and Lucretius and, as noted, for his critique of Cartesian psychology and physics.

In the first chapter of the *New Essays* Leibniz is found defending a theory of innate ideas (*contra* Locke), and identifying the essential power of mind as *rational*. The logical certainties of which no one harbours the slightest doubt could not be the gift of experience, for all that we know by experience is what is merely contingently true, never necessarily true. It is Leibniz's thesis that nothing but confusion would arise from the mere exercise of the senses, unless there were already in place an active, organizing, rational power operating outside the domain of natural causation. For Leibniz, material entities are subject to the determinative laws of efficient causation, whereas the mind operates within the realm of final causation. Put another way, physical events are explained in the language of *causes*; mental (moral) events in the language of *reasons*.

What, then, is the nature of the relationship between the two? It cannot be causal, for then the mental would be indistinguishable from the physical. Rather, each—the physical and the mental—must honour its own mode of being, answerable to its own mode of determination; the physical by way of efficient causation, and the mental by way of intelligible ends and purposes (*final* causes). Each has its own history to unfold, timed by its own clock. Leibniz says it is as if two pendulums were started at the same time and marked off the same time. One who observed the perfect phase-relations between the two might be misled into thinking one was *causing* the other. Actually, the two are perfectly correlated, their histories meted out in parallel trajectories owing to a *pre-established harmony* that is part of the divine scheme of things.

Leibniz's solution to the problem of mind—to the 'mind/body' problem—is called *psychophysical parallelism*. It requires a strict ontological separation of the (monadic) mental and the physical, but also a strict correlation between events taking place in their respective ontological domains. This seems so bizarre that Philalethes cannot make heads or tails of it. Leibniz clarifies the argument in a number of places and offers an instructive illustration in the chapter on Perception (ch. IX). Here the Molyneux question is put forth and Locke's answer is rejected. Molyneux has asked whether a man born blind, but having learned how to distinguish a cube and a sphere tactually, would be able to distinguish them visually were he to gain sight. Locke, true to his empiricistic psychology, insisted that he would be unable to tell them apart until he had sufficient experience with each at the level of visual perception. Leibniz, however, true to his rationalist psychology, argues otherwise. Setting aside what the man might do 'on the spot, when . . . dazzled and confused by the strangeness', the man would readily identify each from the fact that the sphere was lacking in the cube's eight sides and the cube was lacking in the sphere's uniformity. Thus, one who is blind and another who is paralysed—one who cannot see and another who cannot feel objects—must reach precisely the same geometries, based on the same ideas, 'even though they have no images in common'. It is not sensations that the mind possesses in rendering the world intelligible, though the mind makes use of these. Sensations are the outcome of causal material sequences. Knowledge is grounded in mental events internal to the mind itself. The pre-established harmony of a providential God ensures that the mental and the physical will not contradict each other, but neither will they cause each other. The pre-established harmony assures that the universe as presented to each monad is *the same* as that presented to others.

A more carefully developed argument for the non-empirical, non-material essence of mind is offered by Immanuel Kant in his *Critique of Pure Reason*. The selection here is from Sections 1 and 2 of 'The Transcendental Aesthetic', in which Kant establishes the non-empirical grounding of all experience. By 'aesthetic' in this context, Kant is referring to all of the principles of sensibility as such; i.e. the conditions by which anything can be the subject of experience. The *transcendental* aesthetic examines the non-empirical grounding of all experience; not an examination of what is seen or heard or felt, but a metaphysical enquiry into the formal conditions that must obtain if there is to be experience of any kind whatever.

Kant credited David Hume with awakening him from his dogmatic slumbers. Hume, to be considered later in this volume, developed the empiricistic theory of mind more fully than had Locke and rendered it less vulnerable to rationalistic critiques. On Hume's account, there can be no factual knowledge prior to the relevant experience, and this applies even to such basic concepts as causation. Hume argued that the concept of causation was reducible to experiences that have been 'constantly conjoined'. We take X as the cause of Y whenever the two have been reliably associated in our past experiences. The sensed necessity between causes and their effects is just a measure of their nearly unfailing correlation in the past.

Although Kant accepted that all knowledge arises from experience, he denied that knowledge is *grounded* in experience. For there to be experience at all necessarily there must be the 'pure intuitions' of time and space. By 'pure' Kant means that which cannot be given in experience and which, therefore, cannot be 'empirical'. By 'intuition' Kant refers to the very *form* or *mode* of representation. All sensations of any kind occur within the framework of time and space. Thus, time and space are the necessary preconditions for experience itself, though neither is given in the experience. Absent these inherent, formal powers there could be neither experience nor the very *unity of experience* on which all understanding depends. The mind, then, though furnished by experience, is not a passive receptacle, nor is its understanding hostage to the evidence provided by the senses.

Though influenced by Leibniz, Kant did not accept an essentially contingent character of Leibniz's explanation of the rational forms of knowledge. As he understood Leibniz, Kant found psychophysical parallelism to be one of an indefinitely numerous set of possibilities by which the mental and the physical are linked. Thanks to the goodness of the Creator, there is this perfect correspondence (parallelism) between the two, but this surely could have been otherwise. But, as Kant argues, 'a man cannot dispute with anyone regarding that which depends merely on the mode in which he is himself organized' (*Critique of Pure Reason*, B168). The basis on which Kant finally rejects Leibniz's solution, then, is that it ties the framework of all knowledge to the manner in which a providential deity has constituted the human frame. What Kant calls 'a kind of *preformation-system* of pure reason' is seen to lack that very *necessity* of the categories of the understanding which Kant so laboriously developed and defended.

Various though the arguments and assumptions are, the selections here all have a common ground in the conviction that mind as such is not a material entity nor subject to the laws that operate at the level of matter. In its rational powers it transcends the sphere of matter and renders intelligible what would otherwise be the mere flotsam of the cosmos if, absent mind, there could be even so much as flotsam.

1 The Upaniṣads

Janaka of Videha exclaimed: 'I'll give you a thousand cows together with bulls and elephants!'

Yājñavalkya replied: 'My father believed that one should never accept a gift before giving instruction. Let's hear what else they have told you.'

'"*Brahman* is hearing." That's what Gardabhīvipīa Bhāradvāja told me,' said Janaka.

'Bhāradvāja told you "*Brahman* is hearing?" Why, that's like someone telling that he has a father, or a mother, or a teacher! He probably reasoned: "What could a person who cannot hear possibly have?" But did he tell you what its abode and foundation are?'

'He did not tell me that.'

'Then it's a one-legged *brahman*, Your Majesty.'

'Why don't you tell us that yourself, Yājñavalkya?'

'Hearing itself is its abode, and space is its foundation. One should venerate it as limitless.'

'What constitutes the limitless, Yājñavalkya?'

'The quarters themselves, Your Majesty,' he replied. 'Therefore, towards whichever quarter a man may travel, Your Majesty, he will never reach its limit, for the quarters are limitless. And the quarters, Your Majesty, are the same as hearing. So clearly, Your Majesty, the highest *brahman* is hearing. When a man knows and venerates it as such, hearing never abandons him, and all beings flock to him; he becomes a god and joins the company of gods.'

Janaka of Videha exclaimed: 'I'll give you a thousand cows together with bulls and elephants!'

Yājñavalkya replied: 'My father believed that one should never accept a gift before giving instruction. Let's hear what else they have told you,' said Janaka.

' "*Brahman* is the mind." That's what Satyakāma Jābāla told me.'

'Jābāla told you "*Brahman* is the mind?" Why, that's like someone telling that he has a father, or a mother, or a teacher! He probably reasoned: "What could a person who has no mind possibly have?" But did he tell you what its abode and foundation are?' [. . .]

[. . .] 'What looks like a person in the left eye, on the other hand, is his wife Virāj. Their meeting place is the space within the heart, their food is the red lump in the heart, and their garment is the mesh-like substance within the heart. The path along which they travel is the vein that goes up from the heart. The veins called Hitā that are located in the heart are as fine as a hair split a thousandfold. Along them the sap flows continuously. In some ways, therefore, this person eats food that is more refined than does the bodily self (*ātman*).

'The vital functions (*prāṇa*) of this person that are on his front side constitute the eastern quarter; the vital functions on his right side constitute the southern quarter; the vital functions at his back constitute the western quarter; the vital functions on his left side constitute the northern quarter; the vital functions on his upper side constitute the zenith; the vital functions on his bottom side constitute the nadir; and all his vital functions together constitute all the quarters.

'About this self (*ātman*), one can only say "not——, not——." He is ungraspable, for he cannot be grasped. He is undecaying, for he is not subject to decay. He has nothing sticking to him, for he does not stick to anything. He is not bound; yet he neither trembles in fear nor suffers injury. [. . .]'

One day Yājñavalkya paid a visit to Janaka, the king of Videha, thinking to himself, 'I won't tell him.' But once, when the two were engaged in a discussion about the daily fire sacrifice, Yājñavalkya had granted Janaka of Videha a wish. The wish he chose was the freedom to ask any question at will, and Yājñavalkya had granted it to him. So it was the king who now put the question to him first.

'Yājñavalkya, what is the source of light for a person here?'

'The sun, Your Majesty, is his source of light,' he replied. 'It is by the light of the sun that a person sits down, goes about, does his work, and returns.'

'Quite right, Yājñavalkya. But when the sun has set, Yājñavalkya, what then is the source of light for a person here?'

'The moon is then his source of light. It is by the light of the moon that a person sits down, goes about, does his work, and returns.'

'Quite right, Yājñavalkya. But when both the sun and the moon have set, Yājñavalkya, what then is the source of light for a person here?'

'A fire is then his source of light. It is by the light of a fire that a person sits down, goes about, does his work, and returns.'

'Quite right, Yājñavalkya. But when both the sun and the moon have set, Yājñavalkya, and the fire has died out, what then is the source of light for a person here?'

'The voice is then his source of light. It is by the light of the voice that a person sits down, goes about, does his work, and returns. Therefore, Your Majesty, when someone cannot make out even his own hand, he goes straightway towards the spot from where he hears a voice.'

'Quite right, Yājñavalkya. But when both the sun and the moon have set, the fire has died out, and the voice is stilled, Yājñavalkya, what then is the source of light for a person here?'

'The self (*ātman*) is then his source of light. It is by the light of the self that a person sits down, goes about, does his work, and returns.'

[From *Brihad-Aranyaka*, Second and Third Brahmana, *Upaniṣads*, trans. Patrick Olivelle (Oxford: Oxford University Press, 1996), 55, 57–8.]

PYTHAGORAS

2   Fragments from the Doxographers

Aetius, *Plac.* i. 3; *Dox.* 280. And again from another starting-point, Pythagoras, son of Mnesarchus, a Samian, who was the first to call this matter by the name of philosophy, assumed as first principles the numbers and the symmetries existing in them, which he calls harmonies, and the elements compounded of both, that are called geometrical. And again he includes the Monad and the Indefinite Dyad among the first principles; and for him one of the first principles tends toward the creative and form-giving cause, which is intelligence, that is God, and the other tends toward the passive and material cause, which is the visible universe. And he says that the starting-point of Number is the Decad; for all Greeks and all barbarians count as far as ten, and when they get as far as this they return to the monad. And again, he says, the power of ten is in four and the tetrad. And the reason is this: if anyone from the monad adds the numbers in a series as far as four, he will fill out the number ten [i.e., $1 + 2 + 3 + 4 = 10$], but if he goes beyond the number of the tetrad, he will exceed ten. Just as if one should add one and two and should add to these three and four, he will fill out the number ten; so that according to the monad number [actually] is in the ten, but potentially in the four.

Wherefore the Pythagoreans were wont to speak as though the greatest oath were the Tetrad:

> By him that transmitted to our soul the Tetraktys,
> The spring and root of ever-flowing nature.

And our soul, he says, is composed of the Tetrad, for this is intelligence, understanding, opinion, and sense, from which things come every art and science, and we ourselves become reasoning beings. The Monad, however, is intelligence, for intelligence sees according to the Monad. As for example, men are made up of many parts, and part by part they are devoid of sense and comprehension and experience, yet we perceive that man as one alone, whom no being resembles, possessing these qualities; and we perceive that a horse is one, but part by part it is without experience. For these are forms and classes according to monads. Wherefore, assigning this limit with reference to each one of these, they speak of a reasoning being and a neighing being. On this account then the Monad is intelligence by which we perceive these things. And the Indefinite Dyad is fittingly science, for all proof and persuasion is part of science, and further every syllogism brings together what is questioned out of some things that are agreed upon, and easily proves something else; and science is the comprehension of these things, wherefore it would be the Dyad. And opinion as the result of comprehending them is fittingly the Triad, for opinion has to do with many things, and the Triad is quantity, as 'The thrice-blessed Danaoi.' On this account then he includes the Triad . . . And their sect is called Italic because Pythagoras taught in Italy, having left Samos, his fatherland, of dissatisfied with the tyranny of Polycrates.

i. 7; *Dox.* 302. Pythagoras held that one of the first principles, the Monad, is God and the Good, which is the origin of the One, and is itself Intelligence, but the Indefinite Dyad is a daimon and bad, surrounding which is the mass of matter.

i. 8; *Dox.* 307. Divine spirits (*daimones*) are psychical beings, and heroes are souls separated from bodies; good heroes are good souls, bad heroes are bad souls.

i. 9; *Dox.* 307. The followers of Thales and Pythagoras and the Stoics held that matter is variable and changeable and transformable and is in a state of flux, the whole through the whole.

i. 10; *Dox.* 309. Pythagoras asserted that the so-called forms and ideas exist in numbers and their harmonies, and in what are called geometrical objects, apart from bodies.

i. 11; *Dox.* 310. Pythagoras and Aristotle asserted that the first causes are immaterial, but that other causes involve a union or contact with material substance [so that the world is material].

[From 'Fragments from the Doxographers', in *The Pythagorean Sourcebook and Library*, ed. and trans. K. S. Guthrie (Grand Rapids, Mich.: Phanes Press, 1987), 307–8.]

Socrates. Tell me, boy: here we have a square of four feet [ABCD], have we not? You understand?

Boy. Yes.

Socrates. And here we add another square [DCFE] equal to it?

Boy. Yes.

Socrates. And here a third [CHGE], equal to either of them?

Boy. Yes.

Socrates. Now shall we fill up this vacant space [BIHC] in the corner?

Boy. By all means.

Socrates. So here we must have four equal spaces?

Boy. Yes.

Socrates. Well now, how many times larger is this whole space than this other?

Boy. Four times.

Socrates. But it was to have been only twice, you remember?

Boy. To be sure.

Socrates. And does this line [BD], drawn from corner to corner, cut in two each of these spaces?

Boy. Yes.

Socrates. And have we here four equal lines [BD, DF, FH, HB] containing this space?

Boy. We have.

Socrates. Now consider how large this space [BDFH] is.

Boy. I do not understand.

Socrates. Has not each of the inside lines cut off half of each of these four spaces?

Boy. Yes.

Socrates. And how many spaces of that size are there in this part?

Boy. Four.

Socrates. And how many in this [ABCD]?

Boy. Two.

Socrates. And four is how many times two?

Boy. Twice.

Socrates. And how many feet is this space [BDFH]?

Boy. Eight feet.

Socrates. From what line do we get this figure?

Boy. From this.

Socrates. From the line drawn corner-wise across the four-foot figure?

Boy. Yes.

Socrates. The professors call it the diagonal: so if the diagonal is its name, then according to you, Meno's boy, the double space is the square of the diagonal.

Boy. Yes, certainly it is, Socrates.

Socrates. What do you think, Meno? Was there any opinion that he did not give as an answer of his own thought?

Meno. No, they were all his own.

Socrates. But you see, he did not know, as we were saying a while since.

Meno. That is true.

Socrates. Yet he had in him these opinions, had he not?

Meno. Yes.

Socrates. So that he who does not know about any matters, whatever they be, may have true opinions on such matters, about which he knows nothing?

Meno. Apparently.

Socrates. And at this moment those opinions have just been stirred up in him, like a dream; but if he were repeatedly asked these same questions in a variety of forms, you know he will have in the end as exact an understanding of them as anyone.

Meno. So it seems.

Socrates. Without anyone having taught him, and only through questions put to him, he will understand, recovering the knowledge out of himself?

Meno. Yes.

Socrates. And is not this recovery of knowledge, in himself and by himself, recollection?

Meno. Certainly.

Socrates. And must he not have either once acquired or always had the knowledge he now has?

Meno. Yes.

Socrates. Now if he always had it, he was always in a state of knowing; and if he acquired it at some time, he could not have acquired it in this life. Or has someone taught him geometry? You see, he can do the same as this with all geometry and every branch of knowledge. Now, can anyone have taught him all this? You ought surely to know, especially as he was born and bred in your house.

Meno. Well, I know that no one has ever taught him.

Socrates. And has he these opinions, or has he not?

Meno. He must have them, Socrates, evidently.

Socrates. And if he did not acquire them in this present life, is it not obvious at once that he had them and learnt them during some other time?

Meno. Apparently.

Socrates. And this must have been the time when he was not a human being?

Meno. Yes.

Socrates. So if in both of these periods—when he was and was not a human being—he has had true opinions in him which have only to be awakened by questioning to become knowledge, his soul must have had this cognisance throughout all time? For clearly he has always either been or not been a human being.

Meno. Evidently.

Socrates. And if the truth of all things that are is always in our soul, then the soul must be immortal; so that you should take heart and, whatever you do not happen to know at present—that is, what you do not remember—you must endeavour to search out and recollect?

From *Meno*, trans. W. R. M. Lamb (London: William Heinemann, 1924), 84D–86B,
pp. 315–21.

PLATO

4 Phaedo

'Consider, then, the matter in another way. When the soul and the body are joined together, nature directs the one to serve and be ruled, and the other to rule and be master. Now this being the case, which seems to you like the divine, and which like the mortal? Or do you not think that the divine is by nature fitted to rule and lead, and the mortal to obey and serve?'

'Yes, I think so.'

'Which, then, does the soul resemble?'

'Clearly, Socrates, the soul is like the divine and the body like the mortal.'

'Then see, Cebes, if this is not the conclusion from all that we have said, that the soul is most like the divine and immortal and intellectual and uniform and indissoluble and ever unchanging, and the body, on the contrary, most like the human and mortal and multiform and unintellectual and dissoluble and ever changing. Can we say anything, my dear Cebes, to show that this is not so?'

'No, we cannot.'

'Well then, since this is the case, is it not natural for the body to meet with speedy dissolution and for the soul, on the contrary, to be entirely indissoluble, or nearly so?'

'Of course.'

'Observe,' he went on, 'that when a man dies, the visible part of him, the body, which lies in the visible world and which we call the corpse, which is naturally subject to dissolution and decomposition, does not undergo these processes at once, but remains for a considerable time, and even for a very long time, if death takes place when the body is in good condition, and at a favourable time of the year. For when the body is shrunk and embalmed, as is done in Egypt, it remains almost entire for an incalculable time. And even if the body decay, some parts of it, such as the bones and sinews and all that, are, so to speak, indestructible. Is not that true?'

'Yes.'

'But the soul, the invisible, which departs into another place which is, like itself, noble and pure and invisible, to the realm of the god of the other world in truth, to the good and wise god, whither, if God will, my soul is soon to go,—is this soul, which has such qualities and such a nature, straightway scattered and destroyed when it departs from the body, as most men say? Far from it, dear Cebes and Simmias, but the truth is much rather this:—if it departs pure, dragging with it nothing of the body, because it never willingly associated with the body in life, but avoided it and gathered itself into itself alone, since this has always been its constant study—but this means nothing else than that it pursued philosophy rightly and really practised being in a state of death: or is not this the practice of death?'

'By all means.'

'Then if it is in such a condition, it goes away into that which is like itself, into the invisible, divine, immortal, and wise, and when it arrives there it is happy, freed from error and folly and fear and fierce loves and all the other human ills, and as the initiated say, lives in truth through all after time with the gods. Is this our belief, Cebes, or not?'

'Assuredly,' said Cebes.

'But, I think, if when it departs from the body it is defiled and impure, because it was always with the body and cared for it and loved it and was fascinated by it and its desires and pleasures, so that it thought nothing was true except the corporeal, which one can touch and see and drink and eat and employ in the pleasures of love, and if it is accustomed to hate and fear and avoid that which is shadowy and invisible to the eyes but is intelligible and tangible to philosophy—do you think a soul in this condition will depart pure and uncontaminated?'

'By no means,' said he.

'But it will be interpenetrated, I suppose, with the corporeal which intercourse and communion with the body have made a part of its nature because the body has been its constant companion and the object of its care?'

'Certainly.'

'And, my friend, we must believe that the corporeal is burdensome and heavy and earthly and visible. And such a soul is weighed down by this and is dragged back into the visible world, through fear of the invisible and of the other world, and so, as they say, it flits about the monuments and the tombs, where shadowy shapes of souls have been seen, figures of those souls which were not set free in purity but retain something of the visible; and this is why they are seen.'

'That is likely, Socrates.'

'It is likely, Cebes. And it is likely that those are not the souls of the good, but those of the base, which are compelled to flit about such places as a punishment for their former evil mode of life. And they flit about until through the desire of the corporeal which clings to them they are again imprisoned in a body. And they are likely to be imprisoned in natures which correspond to the practices of their former life.'

'What natures do you mean, Socrates?'

'I mean, for example, that those who have indulged in gluttony and violence and drunkenness, and have taken no pains to avoid them, are likely to pass into the bodies of asses and other beasts of that sort. Do you not think so?'

'Certainly that is very likely.'

'And those who have chosen injustice and tyranny and robbery pass into the bodies of wolves and hawks and kites. Where else can we imagine that they go?'

'Beyond a doubt,' said Cebes, 'they pass into such creatures.'

'Then,' said he, 'it is clear where all the others go, each in accordance with its own habits?'

'Yes,' said Cebes, 'of course.'

'Then,' said he, 'the happiest of those, and those who go to the best place, are those who have practised, by nature and habit, without philosophy or reason, the social and civil virtues which are called moderation and justice?'

'How are these happiest?'

'Don't you see? Is it not likely that they pass again into some such social and gentle species as that of bees or of wasps or ants, or into the human race again, and that worthy men spring from them?'

'Yes.'

'And no one who has not been a philosopher and who is not wholly pure when he departs, is allowed to enter into the communion of the gods, but only the lover of knowledge. It is for this reason, dear Simmias and Cebes, that those who truly love wisdom refrain from all bodily desires and resist them firmly and do not give themselves up to them, not because they fear poverty or loss of property, as most men, in their love of money, do; nor is it because they fear the dishonour or disgrace of wickedness, like the lovers of honour and power, that they refrain from them.'

[From *Phaedo*, trans. H. N. Fowler (Cambridge, Mass.: Harvard University Press, 1938), 79B–83B, pp. 279–87.]

ARISTOTLE

5 On the Soul

It is necessary then that mind, since it thinks all things, should be uncontaminated, as Anaxagoras says, in order that it may be in control, that is, that it may know; for the intrusion of anything foreign hinders and obstructs it. Hence the mind, too, can have no characteristic except its capacity to receive. That part of the soul, then, which we call *mind* (by mind I mean that part by which the soul thinks and forms judgements) has no actual existence until it thinks. So it is unreasonable to suppose that it is mixed with the body; for in that case it would become somehow qualitative, *e.g.*, hot or cold, or would even have some organ, as the sensitive faculty has; but in fact it has none. It has been well said that the soul is the place of forms, except that this does not apply to the soul as a whole, but only in its thinking capacity, and the forms occupy it not actually but only potentially. But that the perceptive and thinking faculties are not alike in their impassivity is obvious if we consider the sense organs and sensation. For the sense loses sensation under the stimulus of a too violent sensible object; *e.g.*, of sound immediately after loud sounds, and neither seeing nor smelling is possible just after strong colours and scents; but when mind thinks the highly intelligible, it is not less able to think of slighter things, but even more able; for the faculty of sense is not apart from the body, whereas the mind is separable. But when the mind has become the several groups of its objects, as the learned man when active is said to do (and this happens, when he can exercise his function by himself), even then the mind is in a sense potential, though not quite in the same way as before it learned and discovered; moreover the mind is then capable of thinking itself.

Since magnitude is not the same as the essence of magnitude, nor water the same as the essence of water (and so too in many other cases, but not in all, because in some cases there is no difference), we judge flesh and the essence of flesh either by different faculties, or by the same faculty in different relations; for flesh cannot exist without its matter, but like 'snub-nosed' implies a definite form in a definite matter. Now it is by the sensitive faculty that we judge hot and cold, and all qualities whose due proportion constitutes flesh; but it is by a different sense, either quite distinct, or related to it in the same way as a bent line to itself when pulled out straight, that we judge the essence of flesh. Again, among abstract objects 'straight' is like 'snub-nosed,' for it is always combined with extension; but its essence, if 'straight' and 'straightness' are not the same, is something different; let us call it duality. Therefore we judge it by another faculty, or by the same faculty in a different relation. And speaking generally, as objects are separable from their matter so also are the corresponding faculties of the mind.

One might raise the question: if the mind is a simple thing, and not liable to be acted upon, and has nothing in common with anything else, as Anaxagoras says, how will it think, if thinking is a form of being acted upon? For it is when two things have something in common that we regard one as acting and the other as acted upon. And our second problem is whether the mind itself can be an object of thought. For either mind will be present in all other objects (if, that is, mind is an object of thought in itself and not in virtue of something else, and what is thought is always identical in form), or else it will contain some common element, which makes it an object of thought like other things. Or there is the explanation which we have given before of the phrase 'being acted upon in virtue of some common element,' that mind is potentially identical with the objects of thought but is actually nothing, until it thinks. What the mind thinks must be in it in the same sense as letters are on a tablet which bears no actual writing; this is just what happens in the case of the mind. It is also itself thinkable, just like other objects of thought. For in the case of things without matter that which thinks and that which is thought are the same; for speculative knowledge is the same as its object. (We must consider why mind does not always think.) In things which have matter, each of the objects of thought is only potentially present. Hence while material objects will not have mind in them (for it is apart from their matter that mind is potentially identical with them) mind will still have the capacity of being thought.

From On the Soul, Bk. III, ch. 4, sect. IV, trans. W. Hett (Cambridge, Mass.: Harvard
University Press, 1936), 165–9.

ARISTOTLE

6   Metaphysics

There is something which is eternally moved with an unceasing motion, and that circular motion. This is evident not merely in theory, but in fact. Therefore the 'ultimate heaven' must be eternal. Then there is also something which moves it. And since that which is moved while it moves is intermediate, there is something which moves without being moved; something eternal which is both substance and actuality.

Now it moves in the following manner. The object of desire and the object of thought move without being moved. The primary objects of desire and thought are the same. For it is the apparent good that is the object of appetite, and the real good that is the object of the rational will. Desire is the result of opinion rather than opinion that of desire; it is the act of thinking that is the starting-point. Now thought is moved by the intelligible, and one of the series of contraries is essentially intelligible. In this series substance stands first, and of substance that which is simple and exists actually. (The one and the simple are not the same; for one signifies a measure, whereas 'simple' means that the subject itself is in a certain state.) But the Good, and that which is in itself desirable, are also in the same series; and that which is first in a class is always best or analogous to the best.

That the final cause may apply to immovable things is shown by the distinction of its meanings. For the final cause is not only 'the good *for something*,' but also 'the good which is *the end of some action*.' In the latter sense it applies to immovable things, although in the former it does not; and it causes motion as being an object of love, whereas all other things cause motion because they are themselves in motion. Now if a thing is moved, it can be otherwise than it is. Therefore if the actuality of 'the heaven' is primary locomotion, then in so far as 'the heaven' is moved, in this respect at least it is possible for it to be otherwise; *i.e.* in respect of place, even if not of substantiality. But since there is something—X—which moves while being itself unmoved, existing actually, X cannot be otherwise in any respect. For the primary kind of change is locomotion, and of locomotion circular locomotion; and this is the motion which X induces. Thus X is necessarily existent; and *qua* necessary it is good, and is in this sense a first principle. For the necessary has all these meanings: that which is by constraint because it is contrary to impulse; and that without which excellence is impossible; and that which cannot be otherwise, but is absolutely necessary.

Such, then, is the first principle upon which depend the sensible universe and the world of nature. And its life is like the best which we temporarily enjoy. It must be in that state always (which for us is impossible), since its actuality is also pleasure. (And for this reason waking, sensation and thinking are most pleasant, and hopes and memories are pleasant because of them.) Now thinking in itself is concerned with that which is in itself best, and thinking in the highest sense with that which is in the highest sense best. And thought thinks itself through participation in the object of thought; for it becomes an object of thought by the act of apprehension and thinking, so that thought and the object of thought are the same, because that which is receptive of the object of thought, *i.e.* essence, is thought. And it actually functions when it possesses this object. Hence it is actuality rather than potentiality that is held to be the divine possession of rational thought, and its active contemplation is that which is most pleasant and best. If, then, the happiness which God always enjoys is as great as that which we enjoy sometimes, it is marvellous; and if it is greater, this is still more marvellous.

From *Metaphysics*, Bk. XII, ch. vii, sects. 2–12, trans. H. Tredennick (Cambridge, Mass.: Harvard University Press, 1936), 145–51.

AUGUSTINE

7 On Free Choice of the Will

Augustine. Well then, tell me this. Can you think of anything that is common to all who think? I mean something that they all see with their own reason or mind, that is present to all but is not converted to the private use of those to whom it is present, as food and drink are, that remains unchanged and intact whether they see it or not? Or do you perhaps think that nothing like this exists?

Evodius. Actually, I see that there are many such things, but it will suffice to mention just one. The order and truth of number is present to all who think, so that those who make calculations try to grasp it by their own reason and understanding. Some can grasp it more easily than others can, but it offers itself equally to all who are capable of grasping it; unlike food, it is not transformed into a part of the one who perceives it. It is not at fault when someone makes a mistake; it remains true and complete, but the less one sees it, the greater is one's mistake.

Augustine. Quite right. Your quick reply shows that you are well acquainted with this subject. But suppose that someone told you that numbers are like images of visible things, that they are stamped on the soul, not by their own nature, but by the things that we perceive by the bodily senses. How would you respond? Would you agree?

Evodius. Not at all. Even if numbers were perceived by the bodily senses, it would not follow that I could also perceive the rules of addition and subtraction by the bodily senses. It is by the light of the mind that I refute someone who makes a mistake in adding or subtracting. Moreover, when I perceive something with the bodily sense, such as the earth and sky and the other material objects that I perceive in them, I don't know how much longer they are going to exist. But I do know that seven plus three equals ten, not just now, but always; it never has been and never will be the case that seven plus three does not equal ten. I therefore said that this incorruptible truth of number is common to me and all who think.

Augustine. Your reply is perfectly true and quite certain, so I make no objection. But you will easily see that numbers are not perceived by the bodily senses if you notice that each number is named on the basis of how many times it contains one. For example, if it contains one twice, it is called 'two', if three times, 'three', and if ten times, 'ten'. For any number at all, its name will be the number of times that it contains one. But anyone who thinks correctly will surely find that one cannot be perceived by the bodily senses. Anything that is perceived by such a sense is clearly not one but many, for it is a material object and therefore has countless parts. I won't even go into the minute and less complex parts, for any material object, however small, surely has a right and a left, a top and a bottom, a near side and a farther side, ends and a middle. We must admit that these parts are present in any material object, however tiny, and so we must concede that no material object is truly and simply one. And yet we could not enumerate so many parts unless we had some knowledge of what one is. For if I look for one in material objects and know that I have not found it, I must surely know what I was looking for and what I did not find there; indeed, I must know that it cannot be found there, or rather, that it is not there at all. And yet, if I did not know one, I could not distinguish many parts in material objects. So where did I come to know this *one* that is not a material object? Wherever it was, I did not come to know it through the bodily senses; the only things we know through the bodily senses are material objects, which we have found are not truly and simply one. Moreover, if we do not perceive *one* by the bodily sense, then we do not perceive *any number* by that sense, at least of those numbers that we grasp by the understanding. For every single one of them gets its name from the number of times that it contains one, which is not perceived by the bodily sense. The two halves of any material object together constitute the whole, but each half can in turn be divided in half. Thus, those two parts are in the object, but they are not strictly speaking two. But the number that is called 'two' contains twice that which is strictly speaking one. Thus, its half—that which is strictly speaking one—cannot be further subdivided, because it is simply and truly *one*.

After one comes two, which is two times one; but it does not follow that after two comes two times two. The next number is three, and then comes four, which is two times two. This order extends to all numbers by a fixed and unchangeable law. Thus, the first number after one (which is the first of all numbers) is two, which is two times one. The second number after two (which is the second number) is two times two—since the first number after two is three and the second number is four, which is two times two. The third number after three (which is the third number) is two times three—since the first number after three is four, the second number is five, and the third number is six, which is two times three. And the fourth number after the fourth number is twice that number; for the first number after four (which is the fourth number) is five, the second number is six, the third number is seven, and the fourth number is eight, which is two times four. And in all the rest you will find the same order that we found in the first two: however far any number is from the beginning, its double is in turn that far after it.

So we see that this order is fixed, secure, and unchangeable for all numbers. But how do we see this? No one perceives all the numbers by any bodily sense, for there are infinitely many of them. So where did we learn that this order extends to all of them? By what image or phantasm do we see so confidently this indisputable truth about number, which extends through infinitely many numbers? We see it by an inner light of which the bodily sense knows nothing.

For those inquirers to whom God has given the ability, whose judgment is not clouded by stubbornness, these and many other such examples suffice to show that the order and truth of numbers has nothing to do with the senses of the body, but that it does exist, complete and immutable, and can be seen in common by everyone who uses reason. Now there are many other things that are present generally and publicly, as it were, to those who use reason, and these things remain inviolate and unchangeable even though they are perceived separately by the mind and reason of each person who perceives them. Nonetheless, I do not object to the fact that the order and truth of number struck you most forcibly when you undertook to answer my question. It is no accident that Scripture associates number with wisdom: 'I went around, I and my heart, that I might know and consider and seek after wisdom and number,' [Ecclesiastes 7: 25].

But then how do you think we ought to regard wisdom itself? Do you think that each human being has his own personal wisdom? Or, on the contrary, is there one single wisdom that is universally present to everyone, so that the more one partakes of this wisdom, the wiser one is?

Evodius. I am not yet altogether certain what you mean by 'wisdom', since I see that people have different views about what counts as wise in speech or action. Those who serve in wars think that they are acting wisely. Those who despise the military and devote their care and labor to farming think more highly of what they do, and call it wise. Those who are clever in thinking up money-making schemes consider themselves wise. Those who neglect or renounce all of this, and everything that is temporal, and devote all of their energy to searching for the truth so that they might come to know themselves and God, judge that their own actions are truly wise. Those who do not wish to give themselves up to the leisure of seeking and contemplating the truth but instead busy themselves with the tedious duties of looking after the interests of human beings, and work to ensure that human affairs are justly regulated and governed, think that they are wise. And then again, those who do both, who spend some of their time in contemplating the truth and some of their time in the tedious duties that they think are owed to human society, regard themselves as the winners in the competition for wisdom. I won't even mention the countless sects, each of which holds that its own adherents are superior to everyone else, and that they alone are wise. Therefore, since we have agreed to answer only on the basis of what we clearly know, and not on the basis of what we merely believe, I cannot answer your question unless, in addition to believing, I know by reason and reflection what wisdom is.

Augustine. But don't you think that wisdom is nothing other than the truth in which the highest good is discerned and acquired? All the different groups you mentioned seek good and shun evil; what divides them is that each has a different opinion about what is good. So whoever seeks what ought not to be sought is in error, even though he would not seek it unless he thought it was good. On the other hand, those who seek nothing at all, or who seek what they ought to seek, cannot be in error. Therefore, insofar as all human beings seek a happy life, they are not in error [. . .] And whatever is done wisely cannot rightly be considered separate from wisdom.

Evodius. Exactly.

Augustine. So, just as there are true and unchangeable rules of numbers, whose order and truth you said are present unchangeably and in common to everyone who sees them, there are also true and unchangeable rules of wisdom. When I asked you about a few of these rules one by one, you replied that they are true and obvious, and you conceded that they are present in common to be contemplated by all who are capable of seeing them.

Evodius. I am quite certain of that. But I would very much like to know whether wisdom and number are both included in one single class. For as you have pointed out, wisdom and number are associated with each other even in Holy Scripture. Or perhaps one derives from the other or is contained in the other; for example, perhaps number derives from wisdom or is contained in wisdom. I wouldn't dream of saying that wisdom is derived from number or is contained in number. I don't know how that could be, for I have certainly known my share of mathematicians (or whatever you call those who are highly skilled at computation), but I have known very few who are wise—perhaps none at all—and wisdom strikes me as being far nobler than number.

Augustine. You have touched on a point that often astonishes me as well. For when I contemplate within myself the unchangeable truth of numbers and their lair (so to speak) and inner sanctuary or realm—or whatever else we might call their dwelling-place and home—I am far removed from material objects. I may, perhaps, find something that I can think about, but nothing that I can express in words. So in order to be able to say anything at all, I return in fatigue to familiar things and talk in the customary way about what is right in front of me. The same thing happens to me when I think as carefully and intently as I can about wisdom. So, given the fact that both wisdom and number are contained in that most hidden and certain truth, and that Scripture bears witness that the two are joined together, I very much wonder why most people consider wisdom valuable but have little respect for number. They are of course one and the same thing. Nevertheless, Scripture says of wisdom that 'it reaches from end to end mightily and disposes all things sweetly,' [Wisdom 8:1]. Perhaps the power that 'reaches from end to end mightily' is number, and the power that 'disposes all things sweetly' is wisdom in the strict sense, although both powers belong to one and the same wisdom.

Every material object, however mean, has its numbers; but wisdom was granted, not to material objects or even to all souls, but only to rational souls, as if it set up in them a throne from which to dispose all the things, however lowly, to which it gave numbers. But wisdom gave numbers to everything, even to the lowliest and most far-flung things. Thus, since we perceive the numbers that are stamped upon them, we can easily make judgments about material objects as things ordered lower than ourselves. Consequently, we come to think that numbers themselves are also lower than we are, and we hold them in low esteem. But when we begin to look above ourselves again, we find that numbers transcend our minds and remain fixed in the truth itself. And since few can be wise, but even fools can count, people marvel at wisdom but disparage number. But the learned and studious, as they separate themselves more and more from earthly filth, come to see ever more clearly that wisdom and number are united in the truth itself, and they regard both as precious. In comparison with that truth, they consider everything else worthless—not just the silver and gold that human beings covet, but their very selves.

It should not surprise you that people honor wisdom and denigrate numbers, simply because it is easier to count than to be wise. For you see that they consider gold more precious than lamplight—and yet, in comparison with light, gold is a ridiculous trifle. People give greater honor to what is vastly inferior, simply because even a beggar has a lamp to light, while few have gold. I don't mean to imply that wisdom is inferior to number, for they are the same thing; but one needs an eye that can perceive that fact. Consider this analogy: light and heat are both perceived consubstantially, as it were, in the same fire; they cannot be separated from each other. Yet the heat affects only the things that are nearby, while the light is radiated far and wide. In the same way, the power of understanding that inheres in wisdom warms the things that are closest to it, such as rational souls; whereas things that are further off, such as material objects, are not touched by the heat of wisdom, but they are flooded with the light of numbers. This matter may still be unclear to you; after all, no visible image can be perfectly analogous to something invisible. Nonetheless, you should notice this one point, which will suffice to answer the question that we set out to consider, and which is obvious even to lowly minds like ours. Even if we cannot be certain whether number is a part of wisdom or is derived from wisdom, or whether wisdom itself is a part of number or is derived from number, or whether both are names for a single thing, it is certainly clear that both are true, and indeed unchangeably true.

So you cannot deny the existence of an unchangeable truth that contains everything that is unchangeably true. And you cannot claim that this truth is yours or mine or anyone else's; it is present and reveals itself in common to all who discern what is unchangeably true, like a light that is public and yet strangely hidden. But if it is present in common to all who reason and understand, who could think that it belongs exclusively to the nature of any one of them? I'm sure you remember what we discussed earlier about the bodily senses. The things that we perceive in common by the sense of the eyes and ears, such as colors and sounds that both of us see or hear, do not belong to the nature of our eyes or ears; rather, they are present in common for both of us to perceive. So you would never say that the things that you and I both perceive, each with his own mind, belong to the nature of my mind or of yours. When two people see the same thing with their eyes, you cannot say that they are seeing the eyes of one or the other of them, but some third thing at which both of them are looking.

Evodius. That is quite obviously true.

Augustine. Well then, what do you think of this truth we have been discussing for so long, in which we see so many things? Is it more excellent than our minds, or equal to them, or even inferior to them? If it were inferior, we would make judgments *about* it, not *in accordance with* it, just as we make judgments about material objects because they are below us. We often say, not just that they *are* a certain way, but that they *ought to be* that way. The same is true of our souls: we often know, not merely that they *are* a certain way, but that they *ought to be* that way. We make such judgments about material objects when we say that something is not as white as it ought to be, or not as square, and so on. But we say that a soul is less capable than it ought to be, or less gentle, or less forceful, depending on our own character. We make these judgments *in accordance with* the inner rules of truth, which we perceive in common; but no one makes judgments *about* those rules. When someone says that eternal things are better than temporal things, or that seven plus three equals ten, no one says that it ought to be so. We simply recognize that it is so; we are like explorers who rejoice in what they have discovered, not like inspectors who have to put things right.

Furthermore, if this truth were equal to our minds, it too would be changeable. For our minds see the truth better at some times than at others, which shows that they are indeed changeable. But the truth makes no progress when we see it better and suffers no setback when we see it less. It remains whole and undefiled, giving the joy of its light to those who turn toward it but inflicting blindness on those who turn away. Why, we even make judgments about our own minds in accordance with that truth, while we can in no way make judgments about it. We say that a mind does not understand as much as it ought to, or that it understands just as much as it ought to. And the more a mind can be turned toward the unchangeable truth and cleave to it, the more it ought to understand.

Therefore, since the truth is neither inferior nor equal to our minds, we can conclude that it is superior to them and more excellent than they are.

But I had promised, if you recall, that I would prove that there is something more sublime than our mind and reason. Here it is: the truth itself. Embrace it, if you can; enjoy it; 'delight in the Lord, and he will give you the desires of your heart,' [Psalm 37:4]. What more can you desire than happiness? And what greater happiness can there be than to enjoy the unshakable, unchangeable, and most excellent truth?

[From On Free Choice of the Will, trans. T. Williams (Cambridge, Mass.: Hackett Publishing Co., 1993), Bk. II, pp. 44–55.]

THOMAS AQUINAS

8   Summa Theologica

Whether the human soul is something subsistent?

We proceed thus to the Second Article:—

Objection 1. It would seem that the human soul is not something subsistent. For that which subsists is said to be *this particular thing*. Now *this particular thing* is said not of the soul, but of that which is composed of soul and body. Therefore the soul is not something subsistent.

Obj. 2. Further, everything subsistent operates. But the soul does not operate, for, as the Philosopher says, *to say that the soul feels or understands is like saying that the soul weaves or builds*. Therefore the soul is not subsistent.

Obj. 3. Further, if the soul were something subsistent, it would have some operation apart from the body. But it has no operation apart from the body, not even that of understanding; for the act of understanding does not take place without a phantasm, which cannot exist apart from the body. Therefore the human soul is not something subsistent.

On the contrary, Augustine says: *Whoever understands that the nature of the mind is that of a substance and not that of a body, will see that those who maintain the corporeal nature of the mind are led astray because they associate with the mind those things without which they are unable to think of any nature*—i.e., imaginary pictures of corporeal things. Therefore the nature of the human mind is not only incorporeal, but it is also a substance, that is, something subsistent.

I answer that, It must necessarily be allowed that the principle of intellectual operation, which we call the soul of man, is a principle both incorporeal and subsistent. For it is clear that by means of the intellect man can know all corporeal things. Now whatever knows certain things cannot have any of them in its own nature, because that which is in it naturally would impede the knowledge of anything else. Thus we observe that a sick man's tongue, being unbalanced by a feverish and bitter humor, is insensible to anything sweet, and everything seems bitter to it. Therefore, if the intellectual principle contained within itself the nature of any body, it would be unable to know all bodies. Now every body has its own determinate nature. Therefore it is impossible for the intellectual principle to be a body. It is also impossible for it to understand by means of a bodily organ, since the determinate nature of that organ would likewise impede knowledge of all bodies; as when a certain determinate color is not only in the pupil of the eye, but also in a glass vase, the liquid in the vase seems to be of that same color.

Therefore the intellectual principle, which we call the mind or the intellect, has essentially an operation in which the body does not share. Now only that which subsists in itself can have an operation in itself. For nothing can operate but what is actual, and so a thing operates according as it is; for which reason we do not say that heat imparts heat, but that what is hot gives heat. We must conclude, therefore, that the human soul, which is called intellect or mind, is something incorporeal and subsistent.

Reply Obj. 1. *This particular thing* can be taken in two senses. Firstly, for anything subsistent; secondly, for that which subsists and is complete in a specific nature. The former sense excludes the inherence of an accident or of a material form; the latter excludes also the imperfection of the part, so that a hand can be called *this particular thing* in the first sense, but not in the second. Therefore, since the human soul is a part of human nature, it can be called *this particular thing* in the first sense, as being something subsistent; but not in the second, for in this sense the composite of body and soul is said to be *this particular thing*.

Reply Obj. 2. Aristotle wrote those words as expressing, not his own opinion, but the opinion of those who said that to understand is to be moved, as is clear from the context. Or we may reply that to operate through itself belongs to what exists through itself. But for a thing to exist through itself, it suffices sometimes that it be not inherent, as an accident or a material form; even though it be part of something. Nevertheless, that is rightly said to subsist through itself which is neither inherent in the above sense, nor part of anything else. In this sense, the eye or the hand cannot be said to subsist through itself; nor can it for that reason be said to operate through itself.

Hence the operation of the parts is through each part attributed to the whole. For we say that man sees with the eye, and feels with the hand, and not in the same sense as when we say that what is hot gives heat by its heat; for heat, strictly speaking, does not give heat. We may therefore say that the soul understands just as the eye sees; but it is more correct to say that man understands through the soul.

Reply Obj. 3. The body is necessary for the action of the intellect, not as its organ of action, but on the part of the object; for the phantasm is to the intellect what color is to the sight. Neither does such a dependence on the body prove the intellect to be non-subsistent, or otherwise it would follow that an animal is non-subsistent simply because it requires external sensibles for sensation. [. . .]

Whether the soul is composed of matter and form?

We proceed thus to the Fifth Article:—

Objection 1. It would seem that the soul is composed of matter and form. For potentiality is opposed to actuality. Now, whatsoever things are in actuality participate in the First Act, which is God. It is by participation in God that all things are good, beings, and living things, as is clear from the teachings of Dionysius. Therefore, whatsoever things are in potentiality participate in the first potentiality. But the first potentiality is primary matter. Therefore, since the human soul is, after a manner, in potentiality (which appears from the fact that sometimes a man is potentially understanding), it seems that the human soul must participate in primary matter, as a part of itself.

Obj. 2. Further, wherever the properties of matter are found, there matter is. But the properties of matter are found in the soul—namely, to be a subject, and to be changed. For the soul is subject to science, and virtue; and it changes from ignorance to knowledge and from vice to virtue. Therefore there is matter in the soul.

Obj. 3. Further, things which have no matter have no cause of their being, as the Philosopher says in *Metaph.* viii. But the soul has a cause of its being, since it is created by God. Therefore the soul has matter.

Obj. 4. Further, what has no matter, and is only a form, is a pure act, and is infinite. But this belongs to God alone. Therefore the soul has matter.

On the contrary, Augustine proves that the soul was made neither of corporeal matter, nor of spiritual matter.

I answer that, The soul has no matter. We may consider this question in two ways. First, from the notion of a soul in general, for it belongs to the notion of a soul to be the form of a body. Now, either it is a form in its entirety, or by virtue of some part of itself. If in its entirety, then it is impossible that any part of it should be matter, if by matter we understand something purely potential; for a form, as such, is an act, and that which is purely potential cannot be part of an act, since potentiality is repugnant to actuality as being its opposite. If, however, it be a form by virtue of a part of itself, then we shall call that part the soul, and that matter, which it actualizes first, we shall call the *primary animal.*

Secondly, we may proceed from the specific notion of the human soul, inasmuch as it is intellectual. For it is clear that whatever is received into something is received according to the condition of the recipient. Now a thing is known in as far as its form is in the knower. But the intellectual soul knows a thing in its nature absolutely: for instance, it knows a stone absolutely as a stone; and therefore the form of a stone absolutely, as to its proper formal notion, is in the intellectual soul. Therefore the intellectual soul itself is an absolute form, and not something composed of matter and form. For if the intellectual soul were composed of matter and form, the forms of things would be received into it as individuals, and so it would only know the individual; just as it happens with the sensitive powers which receive forms in a corporeal organ. For matter is the principle by which forms are individuated. It follows, therefore, that the intellectual soul, and every intellectual substance which has knowledge of forms absolutely, is exempt from composition of matter and form.

Reply Obj. 1. The First Act is the universal principle of all acts, because It is infinite, *precontaining all things* in its power, as Dionysius says. Therefore It is participated in by things, not as a part of themselves, but by diffusion of Its processions. Now as potentiality is receptive of act, it must be proportionate to act. But the acts received which proceed from the First Infinite Act, and are participations thereof, are diverse, so that there cannot be one potentiality which receives all acts, in the same way that there is one act from which all participated acts are derived; for then the receptive potentiality would equal the active potentiality of the First Act. Now the receptive potentiality in the intellectual soul is other than the receptive potentiality of primary matter, as appears from the diversity of the things received by each. For primary matter receives individual forms; whereas the intellect receives absolute forms. Hence the existence of such a potentiality in the intellectual soul does not prove that the soul is composed of matter and form.

Reply Obj. 2. To be a subject and to be changed belong to matter by reason of its being in potentiality. Just as, therefore, the potentiality of the intellect is one thing and the potentiality of primary matter another, so in each is there a different manner of subjection and change. For the intellect is subject to knowledge, and is changed from ignorance to knowledge, by reason of its being in potentiality with regard to the intelligible species.

Reply Obj. 3. The form causes matter to be, and so does the agent; and so, the agent causes matter to be in so far as it changes it to the actuality of the form. A subsistent form, however, does not owe its being to some formal principle, nor has it a cause changing it from potentiality to act. So after the words quoted above, the Philosopher concludes that in things composed of matter and form *there is no other cause but that which moves from potentiality to act; while whatsoever things have no matter are truly beings in themselves.*

Reply Obj. 4. Everything participated is compared to the participator as its act. But whatever created form be supposed to subsist *per se*, must have being by participation, for *even life*, or anything of that sort, *is a participator of being*, as Dionysius says. Now participated being is limited by the capacity of the participator; so that God alone, Who is His own being, is pure act and infinite. But in intellectual substances, there is composition of actuality and potentiality, not, indeed, of matter and form, but of form and participated being. Therefore some say that they are composed of that *whereby they are* and that *which they are;* for being itself is that by which a thing is.

[From *Summa Theologica*, ed. A. C. Pegis (New York: Random House, 1943), i. 684–6, 689–91.]

RENÉ DESCARTES

9 Meditations

Second Meditation
The nature of the human mind, and how it is better known than the body

So serious are the doubts into which I have been thrown as a result of yesterday's meditation that I can neither put them out of my mind nor see any way of resolving them. It feels as if I have fallen unexpectedly into a deep whirlpool which tumbles me around so that I can neither stand on the bottom nor swim up to the top. Nevertheless I will make an effort and once more attempt the same path which I started on yesterday. Anything which admits of the slightest doubt I will set aside just as if I had found it to be wholly false; and I will proceed in this way until I recognize something certain, or, if nothing else, until I at least recognize for certain that there is no certainty. Archimedes used to demand just one firm and immovable point in order to shift the entire earth; so I too can hope for great things if I manage to find just one thing, however slight, that is certain and unshakeable.

I will suppose then, that everything I see is spurious. I will believe that my memory tells me lies, and that none of the things that it reports ever happened. I have no senses. Body, shape, extension, movement and place are chimeras. So what remains true? Perhaps just the one fact that nothing is certain.

Yet apart from everything I have just listed, how do I know that there is not something else which does not allow even the slightest occasion for doubt? Is there not a God, or whatever I may call him, who puts into me the thoughts I am now having? But why do I think this, since I myself may perhaps be the author of these thoughts? In that case am not I, at least, something? But I have just said that I have no senses and no body. This is the sticking point: what follows from this? Am I not so bound up with a body and with senses that I cannot exist without them? But I have convinced myself that there is absolutely nothing in the world, no sky, no earth, no minds, no bodies. Does it now follow that I too do not exist? No: if I convinced myself of something then I certainly existed. But there is a deceiver of supreme power and cunning who is deliberately and constantly deceiving me. In that case I too undoubtedly exist, if he is deceiving me; and let him deceive me as much as he can, he will never bring it about that I am nothing so long as I think that I am something. So after considering everything very thoroughly, I must finally conclude that this proposition, *I am, I exist*, is necessarily true whenever it is put forward by me or conceived in my mind.

But I do not yet have a sufficient understanding of what this 'I' is, that now necessarily exists. So I must be on my guard against carelessly taking something else to be this 'I', and so making a mistake in the very item of knowledge that I maintain is the most certain and evident of all. I will therefore go back and meditate on what I originally believed myself to be, before I embarked on this present train of thought. I will then subtract anything capable of being weakened, even minimally, by the arguments now introduced, so that what is left at the end may be exactly and only what is certain and unshakeable.

What then did I formerly think I was? A man. But what is a man? Shall I say 'a rational animal'? No; for then I should have to inquire what an animal is, what rationality is, and in this way one question would lead me down the slope to other harder ones, and I do not now have the time to waste on subtleties of this kind. Instead I propose to concentrate on what came into my thoughts spontaneously and quite naturally whenever I used to consider what I was. Well, the first thought to come to mind was that I had a face, hands, arms and the whole mechanical structure of limbs which can be seen in a corpse, and which I called the body. The next thought was that I was nourished, that I moved about, and that I engaged in sense-perception and thinking; and these actions I attributed to the soul. But as to the nature of this soul, either I did not think about this or else I imagined it to be something tenuous, like a wind or fire or ether, which permeated my more solid parts. As to the body, however, I had no doubts about it, but thought I knew its nature distinctly. If I had tried to describe the mental conception I had of it, I would have expressed it as follows: by a body I understand whatever has a determinable shape and a definable location and can occupy a space in such a way as to exclude any other body; it can be perceived by touch, sight, hearing, taste or smell, and can be moved in various ways, not by itself but by whatever else comes into contact with it. For, according to my judgement, the power of self-movement, like the power of sensation or of thought, was quite foreign to the nature of a body; indeed, it was a source of wonder to me that certain bodies were found to contain faculties of this kind.

But what shall I now say that I am, when I am supposing that there is some supremely powerful and, if it is permissible to say so, malicious deceiver, who is deliberately trying to trick me in every way he can? Can I now assert that I possess even the most insignificant of all the attributes which I have just said belong to the nature of a body? I scrutinize them, think about them, go over them again, but nothing suggests itself; it is tiresome and pointless to go through the list once more. But what about the attributes I assigned to the soul? Nutrition or movement? Since now I do not have a body, these are mere fabrications. Sense-perception? This surely does not occur without a body, and besides, when asleep I have appeared to perceive through the senses many things which I afterwards realized I did not perceive through the senses at all. Thinking? At last I have discovered it—thought; this alone is inseparable from me. I am, I exist—that is certain. But for how long? For as long as I am thinking. For it could be that were I totally to cease from thinking, I should totally cease to exist. At present I am not admitting anything except what is necessarily true. I am, then, in the strict sense only a thing that thinks; that is, I am a mind, or intelligence, or intellect, or reason—words whose meaning I have been ignorant of until now. But for all that I am a thing which is real and which truly exists. But what kind of a thing? As I have just said—a thinking thing.

What else am I? I will use my imagination. I am not that structure of limbs which is called a human body. I am not even some thin vapour which permeates the limbs—a wind, fire, air, breath, or whatever I depict in my imagination; for these are things which I have supposed to be nothing. Let this supposition stand; for all that I am still something. And yet may it not perhaps be the case that these very things which I am supposing to be nothing, because they are unknown to me, are in reality identical with the 'I' of which I am aware? I do not know, and for the moment I shall not argue the point, since I can make judgements only about things which are known to me. I know that I exist; the question is, what is this 'I' that I know? If the 'I' is understood strictly as we have been taking it, then it is quite certain that knowledge of it does not depend on things of whose existence I am as yet unaware; so it cannot depend on any of the things which I invent in my imagination. And this very word 'invent' shows me my mistake. It would indeed be a case of fictitious invention if I used my imagination to establish that I was something or other; for imagining is simply contemplating the shape or image of a corporeal thing. Yet now I know for certain both that I exist and at the same time that all such images and, in general, everything relating to the nature of body, could be mere dreams (and chimeras). Once this point has been grasped, to say 'I will use my imagination to get to know more distinctly what I am' would seem to be as silly as saying 'I am now awake, and see some truth; but since my vision is not yet clear enough, I will deliberately fall asleep so that my dreams may provide a truer and clearer representation.' I thus realize that none of the things that the imagination enables me to grasp is at all relevant to this knowledge of myself which I possess, and that the mind must therefore be most carefully diverted from such things if it is to perceive its own nature as distinctly as possible.

But what then am I? A thing that thinks. What is that? A thing that doubts, understands, affirms, denies, is willing, is unwilling, and also imagines and has sensory perceptions.

This is a considerable list, if everything on it belongs to me. But does it? Is it not one and the same 'I' who is now doubting almost everything, who nonetheless understands some things, who affirms that this one thing is true, denies everything else, desires to know more, is unwilling to be deceived, imagines many things even involuntarily, and is aware of many things which apparently come from the senses? Are not all these things just as true as the fact that I exist, even if I am asleep all the time, and even if he who created me is doing all he can to deceive me? Which of all these activities is distinct from my thinking? Which of them can be said to be separate from myself? The fact that it is I who am doubting and understanding and willing is so evident that I see no way of making it any clearer. But it is also the case that the 'I' who imagines is the same 'I'. For even if, as I have supposed, none of the objects of imagination are real, the power of imagination is something which really exists and is part of my thinking. Lastly, it is also the same 'I' who has sensory perceptions, or is aware of bodily things as it were through the senses. For example, I am now seeing light, hearing a noise, feeling heat. But I am asleep, so all this is false. Yet I certainly *seem* to see, to hear, and to be warmed. This cannot be false; what is called 'having a sensory perception' is strictly just this, and in this restricted sense of the term it is simply thinking. [. . .]

Sixth Meditation
The existence of material things, and the real distinction between mind and body

It remains for me to examine whether material things exist. And at least I now know they are capable of existing, in so far as they are the subject-matter of pure mathematics, since I perceive them clearly and distinctly. For there is no doubt that God is capable of creating everything that I am capable of perceiving in this manner; and I have never judged that something could not be made by him except on the grounds that there would be a contradiction in my perceiving it distinctly. The conclusion that material things exist is also suggested by the faculty of imagination, which I am aware of using when I turn my mind to material things. For when I give more attentive consideration to what imagination is, it seems to be nothing else but an application of the cognitive faculty to a body which is intimately present to it, and which therefore exists.

To make this clear, I will first examine the difference between imagination and pure understanding. When I imagine a triangle, for example, I do not merely understand that it is a figure bounded by three lines, but at the same time I also see the three lines with my mind's eye as if they were present before me; and this is what I call imagining. But if I want to think of a chiliagon, although I understand that it is a figure consisting of a thousand sides just as well as I understand the triangle to be a three-sided figure, I do not in the same way imagine the thousand sides or see them as if they were present before me. It is true that since I am in the habit of imagining something whenever I think of a corporeal thing, I may construct in my mind a confused representation of some figure; but it is clear that this is not a chiliagon. For it differs in no way from the representation I should form if I were thinking of a myriagon, or any figure with very many sides. Moreover, such a representation is useless for recognizing the properties which distinguish a chiliagon from other polygons. But suppose I am dealing with a pentagon: I can of course understand the figure of a pentagon, just as I can the figure of a chiliagon, without the help of the imagination; but I can also imagine a pentagon, by applying my mind's eye to its five sides and the area contained within them. And in doing this I notice quite clearly that imagination requires a peculiar effort of mind which is not required for understanding; this additional effort of mind clearly shows the difference between imagination and pure understanding.

Besides this, I consider that this power of imagining which is in me, differing as it does from the power of understanding, is not a necessary constituent of my own essence, that is, of the essence of my mind. For if I lacked it, I should undoubtedly remain the same individual as I now am; from which it seems to follow that it depends on something distinct from myself. And I can easily understand that, if there does exist some body to which the mind is so joined that it can apply itself to contemplate it, as it were, whenever it pleases, then it may possibly be this very body that enables me to imagine corporeal things. So the difference between this mode of thinking and pure understanding may simply be this: when the mind understands, it in some way turns towards itself and inspects one of the ideas which are within it; but when it imagines, it turns towards the body and looks at something in the body which conforms to an idea understood by the mind or perceived by the senses. I can, as I say, easily understand that this is how imagination comes about, if the body exists; and since there is no other equally suitable way of explaining imagination that comes to mind, I can make a probable conjecture that the body exists. But this is only a probability; and despite a careful and comprehensive investigation, I do not yet see how the distinct idea of corporeal nature which I find in my imagination can provide any basis for a necessary inference that some body exists. [. . .]

The first observation I make at this point is that there is a great difference between the mind and the body, inasmuch as the body is by its very nature always divisible, while the mind is utterly indivisible. For when I consider the mind, or myself in so far as I am merely a thinking thing, I am unable to distinguish any parts within myself; I understand myself to be something quite single and complete. Although the whole mind seems to be united to the whole body, I recognize that if a foot or arm or any other part of the body is cut off, nothing has thereby been taken away from the mind. As for the faculties of willing, of understanding, of sensory perception and so on, these cannot be termed parts of the mind, since it is one and the same mind that wills, and understands and has sensory perceptions. By contrast, there is no corporeal or extended thing that I can think of which in my thought I cannot easily divide into parts; and this very fact makes me understand that it is divisible. This one argument would be enough to show me that the mind is completely different from the body, even if I did not already know as much from other considerations.

My next observation is that the mind is not immediately affected by all parts of the body, but only by the brain, or perhaps just by one small part of the brain, namely the part which is said to contain the 'common' sense. Every time this part of the brain is in a given state, it presents the same signals to the mind, even though the other parts of the body may be in a different condition at the time. This is established by countless observations, which there is no need to review here.

I observe, in addition, that the nature of the body is such that whenever any part of it is moved by another part which is some distance away, it can always be moved in the same fashion by any of the parts which lie in between, even if the more distant part does nothing. For example, in a cord ABCD, if one end D is pulled so that the other end A moves, the exact same movement could have been brought about if one of the intermediate points B or C had been pulled, and D had not moved at all. In similar fashion, when I feel a pain in my foot, physiology tells me that this happens by means of nerves distributed throughout the foot, and that these nerves are like cords which go from the foot right up to the brain. When the nerves are pulled in the foot, they in turn pull on inner parts of the brain to which they are attached, and produce a certain motion in them; and nature has laid it down that this motion should produce in the mind a sensation of pain, as occurring in the foot. But since these nerves, in passing from the foot to the brain, must pass through the calf, the thigh, the lumbar region, the back and the neck, it can happen that, even if it is not the part in the foot but one of the intermediate parts which is being pulled, the same motion will occur in the brain as occurs when the foot is hurt, and so it will necessarily come about that the mind feels the same sensation of pain. And we must suppose the same thing happens with regard to any other sensation.

My final observation is that any given movement occurring in the part of the brain that immediately affects the mind produces just one corresponding sensation; and hence the best system that could be devised is that it should produce the one sensation which, of all possible sensations, is most especially and most frequently conducive to the preservation of the healthy man. And experience shows that the sensations which nature has given us are all of this kind; and so there is absolutely nothing to be found in them that does not bear witness to the power and goodness of God. For example, when the nerves in the foot are set in motion in a violent and unusual manner, this motion, by way of the spinal cord, reaches the inner parts of the brain, and there gives the mind its signal for having a certain sensation, namely the sensation of a pain as occurring in the foot. This stimulates the mind to do its best to get rid of the cause of the pain, which it takes to be harmful to the foot. It is true that God could have made the nature of man such that this particular motion in the brain indicated something else to the mind; it might, for example, have made the mind aware of the actual motion occurring in the brain, or in the foot, or in any of the intermediate regions; or it might have indicated something else entirely. But there is nothing else which would have been so conducive to the continued well-being of the body. In the same way, when we need drink, there arises a certain dryness in the throat; this sets in motion the nerves of the throat, which in turn move the inner parts of the brain. This motion produces in the mind a sensation of thirst, because the most useful thing for us to know about the whole business is that we need drink in order to stay healthy. And so it is in the other cases.

It is quite clear from all this that, notwithstanding the immense goodness of God, the nature of man as a combination of mind and body is such that it is bound to mislead him from time to time. For there may be some occurrence, not in the foot but in one of the other areas through which the nerves travel in their route from the foot to the brain, or even in the brain itself; and if this cause produces the same motion which is generally produced by injury to the foot, then pain will be felt as if it were in the foot. This deception of the senses is natural, because a given motion in the brain must always produce the same sensation in the mind; and the origin of the motion in question is much more often going to be something which is hurting the foot, rather than something existing elsewhere. So it is reasonable that this motion should always indicate to the mind a pain in the foot rather than in any other part of the body. [. . .]

Again, what reason have you for saying that I 'did not need all this apparatus' to prove I existed? These very words of yours surely show that I have the best reason to think that I have not used enough apparatus, since I have not yet managed to make you understand the matter correctly. When you say that I 'could have made the same inference from any one of my other actions' you are far from the truth, since I am not wholly certain of any of my actions, with the sole exception of thought (in using the word 'certain' I am referring to metaphysical certainty, which is the sole issue at this point). I may not, for example, make the inference 'I am walking, therefore I exist', except in so far as the awareness of walking is a thought. The inference is certain only if applied to this awareness, and not to the movement of the body which sometimes—in the case of dreams—is not occurring at all, despite the fact that I seem to myself to be walking. Hence from the fact that I think I am walking I can very well infer the existence of a mind which has this thought, but not the existence of a body that walks. And the same applies in other cases. [. . .]

I do not accept your statement that the mind grows and becomes weak along with the body. You do not prove this by any argument. It is true that the mind does not work so perfectly when it is in the body of an infant as it does when in an adult's body, and that its actions can often be slowed down by wine and other corporeal things. But all that follows from this is that the mind, so long as it is joined to the body, uses it like an instrument to perform the operations which take up most of its time. It does not follow that it is made more or less perfect by the body. Your inference here is no more valid than if you were to infer from the fact that a craftsman works badly whenever he uses a faulty tool that the good condition of his tools is the source of his knowledge of his craft.

[From *Meditations on the First Philosophy*, in *The Philosophical Writings of Descartes*, ed. and trans. J. Cottingham, R. Stoothoff, and D. Murdoch (Cambridge: Cambridge University Press, 1984), ii. 16–19, 50–1, 59–61, 243–5.]

GEORGE BERKELEY

10   Of the Principles of Human Knowledge

It is evident to any one who takes a survey of the objects of human knowledge, that they are either ideas actually imprinted on the senses, or else such as are perceiv'd by attending to the passions and operations of the mind, or lastly ideas formed by help of memory and imagination; either compounding, dividing, or barely representing those originally perceiv'd in the aforesaid ways. By sight I have the ideas of light and colours with their several degrees and variations. By touch I perceive hard and soft, heat and cold, motion and resistance, [&c.] and of all these more and less either as to quantity or degree. Smelling furnishes me with odors; the palate with tastes, and hearing conveys sounds to the mind in all their variety of tone and composition. And as several of these are observ'd to accompany each other, they come to be marked by one name, and so to be reputed as one thing. Thus, for example, a certain colour, taste, smell, figure and consistence having been observ'd to go together, are accounted one distinct thing, signified by the name *apple*. Other collections of ideas constitute a stone, a tree, a book and the like sensible things; which as they are pleasing or disagreeable excite the passions of love, hatred, joy, grief, [&c.]

But besides all that endless variety of ideas or objects of knowledge, there is likewise something which knows or perceives them, and exercises divers operations, as willing, imagining, remembering [&c.] about them. This perceiving, active being is what I call *mind, spirit, soul* or *my self*. By which words I do not denote any one of my ideas, but a thing intirely distinct from them, wherein they exist, or, which is the same thing, whereby they are perceiv'd, for the existence of an idea consists in being perceiv'd.

That neither our thoughts, nor passions, nor ideas formed by the imagination, exist without the mind, is what every body will allow. And [to me it is] no less evident that the various sensations or ideas imprinted on the sense, however blended or combin'd together (that is whatever objects they compose) cannot exist otherwise than in a mind perceiving them. I think an intuitive knowledge may be obtain'd of this, by any one that shall attend to what is meant by the term *exist* when apply'd to sensible things. The table I write on, I say, exists, *i.e.* I see and feel it, and if I were out of my study I shou'd say it existed, meaning thereby that if I was in my study I might perceive it, or that some other spirit actually does perceive it. There was an odor, *i.e.* it was smelt; there was a sound, *i.e.* it was heard; a colour or figure and it was perceiv'd by sight or touch. This is all that I can understand by these and the like expressions. For as to what is said of the absolute existence of unthinking things without any relation to their being perceiv'd, that [is to me] perfectly unintelligible. Their *esse* is *percipi*, nor is it possible they shou'd have any existence, out of the minds or thinking things which perceive them.

It is indeed an opinion strangely prevailing amongst men, that houses, mountains, rivers and in a word all sensible objects have an existence natural or real, distinct from their being perceiv'd by the understanding. But with how great an assurance and acquiescence soever, this principle may be entertained in the world: yet whoever shall find in his heart to call it in question may, if I mistake not, perceive it to involve a manifest contradiction. For what are the foremention'd objects but the things we perceive by sense, and what, [I pray you,] do we perceive besides our own ideas or sensations, and is it not plainly repugnant that any one of these or any combination of them shou'd exist unperceiv'd.?

If we throughly examine this tenet, it will, perhaps, be found at bottom to depend on the doctrine of *abstract ideas*. For can there be a nicer strain of abstraction then to distinguish the existence of sensible objects from their being perceiv'd, so as to conceive them existing unperceiv'd? Light and colours, heat and cold, extension and figures, in a word the things we see and feel what are they but so many sensations, notions, ideas or impressions on the sense, and is it possible to separate, even in thought, any of these from perception? For my part I might as easily divide a thing from it self. I may, indeed, divide in my thoughts or conceive apart from each other those things which, perhaps, I never perceiv'd by sense so divided. Thus I imagine the trunk of a human body without the limbs, or conceive the smell of a rose without thinking on the rose it self. So far I will not deny I can abstract, if that may properly be called *abstraction*, which extends only to the conceiving separately such objects, as it is possible may really exist or be actually perceived asunder. But my conceiving or imagining power does not extend beyond the possibility of real existence or perception. Hence as it is impossible, for me to see or feel any thing without an actual sensation of that thing, so is it impossible for me to conceive in my thoughts any sensible thing or object distinct from the sensation or perception of it. [In truth the object and the sensation are the same thing, and cannot therefore be abstracted from each other.]

Some truths there are so near and obvious to the mind that a man need only open his eyes to see 'em. Such I take this important one to be, *viz.* that all the choir of heaven and furniture of the earth, in a word all those bodies which compose the mighty frame of the world, have not any subsistence without a mind, that their [*esse*] is to be perceiv'd or known; that consequently so long as they are not actually perceiv'd by me, or do not exist in my mind or that of any other created spirit, they must either have no existence at all, or else subsist in the mind of some eternal spirit: it being perfectly unintelligible and involving all the absurdity of abstraction, to attribute to any single part of them an existence independent of a spirit. [To make this appear with all the light and evidence of an axiom, it seems sufficient if I can but awaken the reflexion of the reader, that he may take an impartial view of his own meaning, and turn his thoughts upon the subject it self, free and disengaged from all embarras of words and prepossession in favour of received mistakes.]¹

From what has been said, ['tis evident,] there is not any other substance than *spirit* or that which perceives. But for the fuller [demonstration of this point, let it be consider'd, the sensible qualities are colour, figure, motion, smell, taste &c. *i.e* the ideas perceiv'd by sense. Now for an idea to exist in an unperceiving thing is a manifest contradiction, for to have an idea is all one as to perceive, that therefore wherein colour, figure, [&c.] exist must perceive them; hence 'tis clear there can be no unthinking substance or *substratum* of those ideas.

But say you, thô the ideas themselves do not exist without the mind, yet there may be things like them whereof they are copies or resemblances, which things exist without the mind, in an unthinking substance. I answer an idea can be like nothing but an idea, a colour, or figure, can be like nothing but another colour or figure. If we look but [never] so little into our thoughts, we shall find it impossible for us to conceive a likeness except only between our ideas. Again, I ask whether those suppos'd originals or external things, of which our ideas are the pictures or representations, be themselves perceivable or no? If they are, then they are ideas and we have gain'd our point; but if you say they are not, I appeal to any one whether it be sense, to assert a colour is like something which is invisible; hard or soft, like something which is intangible, and so of the rest.

Some there are who make a distinction betwixt *primary* and *secondary* qualities: by the former, they mean extension, figure, motion, rest, solidity or impenetrability and number: by the latter they denote all other sensible qualities as colours, sounds, tastes, [&c.] The ideas we have of these they acknowlege not to be the resemblances, of any thing existing without the mind or unperceiv'd, but they will have our ideas of the primary qualities to be patterns or images of things which exist without the mind, in an unthinking substance which they call *matter*. By matter, therefore, we are to understand an inert, senseless substance, in which extension, figure, motion, [&c.] do actually subsist, but it is evident from what we have already shewn, that extension, figure and motion are only ideas existing in the mind, and that an idea can be like nothing but another idea, and that consequently neither they nor their archetypes can exist in an unperceiving substance. Hence it is plain, that the very notion of what is called *matter* or *corporeal substance*, involves a contradiction in it. [Insomuch that I shou'd not think it necessary to spend more time in exposing its absurdity. But because the tenet of the existence of matter seems to have taken so deep a root in the minds of philosophers, and draws after it so many ill consequences, I chuse rather to be thought prolix and tedious, than omit any thing that might conduce to the full discovery and extirpation of that prejudice.]

10. They who assert that figure, motion, and the rest of the primary or original qualities do exist without the mind, in unthinking substances, do at the same time acknowlege that colours, sounds, heat, cold, [&c.] do not, which they tell us are sensations existing in the mind alone, that depend on and are occasion'd by the different size, texture, motion, [&c.] of the minute particles of matter. This they take for an undoubted truth, which they can demonstrate beyond all exception. Now if it be certain, that those original qualities are inseparably united with the other sensible qualities, and not, even in thought, capable of being abstracted from them, it plainly follows that they exist only in the mind. But I desire any one to reflect and try, whether he can by any abstraction of thought, conceive the extension and motion of a body, without all other sensible qualities. For my own part, I see evidently that it is not in my power to frame an idea of a body extended and

[moving], but I must withal give it some colour or other sensible quality which is acknowleg'd to exist only in the mind. In short, extension, figure, and motion, abstracted from all other qualities, are inconceivable. Where therefore the other sensible qualities are, there must these be also, *i.e.* in the mind and no where else. [. . .]

But thô it were possible that solid, figur'd moveable substances may exist without the mind, corresponding to the ideas we have of bodies, yet how is it possible for us to know this? Either we must know it by sense or by reason. As for our senses, by them we have the knowlege only of our sensations, ideas, or those things that are immediately perceiv'd by sense, call 'em what you will: but they do not inform us that things exist without the mind, or unperceiv'd, like to those which are perceiv'd. This the materialists themselves acknowlege. It remains therefore that if we have any knowlege at all of external things, it must be by reason, inferring their existence from what is immediately perceiv'd by sense. But [I do not see] what reason can induce us to believe the existence of bodies without the mind, from what we perceive, since the very patrons of matter themselves do not pretend, there is any necessary connexion betwixt them and our ideas. I say it is granted on all hands (and what happens in dreams, frenzys and the like puts it beyond dispute) that it is possible we might be affected with all the ideas we have now, thô [there were] no bodies [existing] without resembling them. Hence it is evident the supposition of external bodies is not necessary for the producing our ideas: since it is granted they are produced sometimes, and might possibly be produced always in the same order, we see them in at present, without their concurrence. [. . .]

Before we proceed any farther, it is necessary [we] spend some time in answering objections which may probably be made against the principles [we have] hitherto laid down. In doing of which, if I seem too prolix to those of quick apprehensions, I [desire I may be excused,] since all men do not equally apprehend things of this nature; and I am willing to be understood by every one. First, then, it will be objected that by the foregoing principles, all that is real and substantial in nature is banish'd out of the world: and instead thereof a chimerical scheme of ideas takes place. All things that exist, exist only in the mind, that is, they are purely notional. What therefore becomes of the sun, moon and stars? What must we think of houses, rivers, mountains, trees, stones; nay, even of our own bodies? Are all these but so many chimeras and illusions on the fancy? To all which, and whatever else of the same sort may be objected, I answer, that by the principles premis'd, we are not deprived of any one thing in nature. Whatever we see, feel, hear, or any wise conceive or understand, remains as secure as ever, and is as real as ever. There is a *rerum natura*, and the distinction between realities and chimeras retains its full force. This is evident from *Sect.* xxix, xxx and xxxiii, where we have shewn what is meant by *real things* in opposition to *chimeras*, or ideas of our own framing; but then they both equally exist in the mind, and in that sense are alike *ideas*.

I do not argue against the existence of any one thing that we can apprehend, either by sense or reflexion. That the things I see with [my] eyes and touch with my hands do exist, really exist, I make not the least question. The only thing whose existence we deny, is that which philosophers call matter or corporeal substance. And in doing of this, there is no damage done to the rest of mankind, who, I dare say, will never miss it. The atheist, indeed, will want the colour of an empty name to support his impiety; and the philosophers may possibly find, they have lost a great handle for trifling and disputation. [But that's all the harm that I can see done.]

If any man thinks [we detract] from the existence or reality of things, he is very far from understanding what has been premis'd in the plainest terms I cou'd think of. Take here an abstract of what has been said. There are spiritual substances, minds or human souls which will or excite ideas in themselves at pleasure: but these are faint, weak, and unsteady in respect of others they perceive by sense, which being impress'd upon them according to certain rules or laws of nature, speak themselves the effects of a mind more powerful and wise than human spirits. These latter are said to have more *reality* in them than the former: by which is meant that they are more affecting, orderly and distinct, and that they are not fictions of the mind perceiving them. And in this sense, the sun that I see by day is the real sun, and that which I imagine by night is the idea of the former. In the sense here given of *reality*, 'tis evident that every vegetable, star, mineral, and in general each part of the mundane system, is as much a *real being* by our principles as by any other. Whether others mean any thing by the term *reality* different from what I do, I intreat them to look into their own thoughts and see.

[From *A Treatise Concerning the Principles of Human Knowlege* (Dublin, 1710), Part I, pp. 27–33, 37, 46–7.]

G. W. LEIBNIZ

11   **The Monadology**

1. The Monad, of which we will speak here, is nothing else than a simple substance, which goes to make up composites; by simple, we mean without parts.

2. There must be simple substances because there are composites; for a composite is nothing else than a collection or *aggregatum* of simple substances.

3. Now, where there are no constituent parts there is possible neither

extension, nor form, nor divisibility. These Monads are the true Atoms of nature, and, in fact, the Elements of things.

4. Their dissolution, therefore, is not to be feared and there is no way conceivable by which a simple substance can perish through natural means.

5. For the same reason there is no way conceivable by which a simple substance might, through natural means, come into existence, since it can not be formed by composition.

6. We may say then, that the existence of Monads can begin or end only all at once, that is to say, the Monad can begin only through creation and end only through annihilation. Composites, however, begin or end gradually.

7. There is also no way of explaining how a Monad can be altered or changed in its inner being by any other created thing, since there is no possibility of transposition within it, nor can we conceive of any internal movement which can be produced, directed, increased or diminished there within the substance, such as can take place in the case of composites where a change can occur among the parts. The Monads have no windows through which anything may come in or go out. The Attributes are not liable to detach themselves and make an excursion outside the substance, as could *sensible species* of the Schoolmen. In the same way neither substance nor attribute can enter from without into a Monad.

8. Still Monads must needs have some qualities, otherwise they would not even be existences. And if simple substances did not differ at all in their qualities, there would be no means of perceiving any change in things. Whatever is in a composite can come into it only through its simple elements and the Monads, if they were without qualities, since they do not differ at all in quantity, would be indistinguishable one from another. For instance, if we imagine *a plenum* or completely filled space, where each part receives only the equivalent of its own previous motion, one state of things would not be distinguishable from another.

9. Each Monad, indeed, must be different from every other. For there are never in nature two beings which are exactly alike, and in which it is not possible to find a difference either internal or based on an intrinsic property.

10. I assume it as admitted that every created being, and consequently the created Monad, is subject to change, and indeed that this change is continuous in each.

11. It follows from what has just been said, that the natural changes of the Monad come from an internal principle, because an external cause can have no influence upon its inner being.

12. Now besides this principle of change there must also be in the Monad a manifoldness which changes. This manifoldness constitutes, so to speak, the specific nature and the variety of the simple substances.

13. This manifoldness must involve a multiplicity in the unity or in that which is simple. For since every natural change takes place by degrees, there

must be something which changes and something which remains unchanged, and consequently there must be in the simple substance a plurality of conditions and relations, even though it has no parts.

14. The passing condition which involves and represents a multiplicity in the unity, or in the simple substance, is nothing else than what is called Perception. This should be carefully distinguished from Apperception or Consciousness, as will appear in what follows. In this matter the Cartesians have fallen into a serious error, in that they treat as nonexistent those perceptions of which we are not conscious. It is this also which has led them to believe that spirits alone are Monads and that there are no souls of animals or other Entelechies, and it has led them to make the common confusion between a protracted period of unconsciousness and actual death. They have thus adopted the Scholastic error that souls can exist entirely separated from bodies, and have even confirmed ill-balanced minds in the belief that souls are mortal.

15. The action of the internal principle which brings about the change or the passing from one perception to another may be called Appetition. It is true that the desire (l'appetit) is not always able to attain to the whole of the perception which it strives for, but it always attains a portion of it and reaches new perceptions.

16. We, ourselves, experience a multiplicity in a simple substance, when we find that the most trifling thought of which we are conscious involves a variety in the object. Therefore all those who acknowledge that the soul is a simple substance ought to grant this multiplicity in the Monad, and Monsieur Bayle should have found no difficulty in it, as he has done in his *Dictionary*, article 'Rorarius.'

17. It must be confessed, however, that Perception, and that which depends upon it, are inexplicable by mechanical causes, that is to say, by figures and motions. Supposing that there were a machine whose structure produced thought, sensation, and perception, we could conceive of it as increased in size with the same proportions until one was able to enter into its interior, as he would into a mill. Now, on going into it he would find only pieces working upon one another, but never would he find anything to explain Perception. It is accordingly in the simple substance, and not in the composite nor in a machine that the Perception is to be sought. Furthermore there is nothing besides perceptions and their changes to be found in the simple substance. And it is in these alone that all the internal activities of the simple substance can consist.

[From *The Monadology*, trans. G. Montgomery, rev. A. R. Chandler, in *The Rationalists: René Descartes, Benedict de Spinoza, Gottfried Wilhelm Freiherr von Leibniz* (Garden City, NY: Doubleday & Co., 1960), 455–7.]

Philalethes. But suppose that truths can be imprinted on the understanding without being perceived by it: I do not see how they can differ, so far as their origin is concerned, from ones which the understanding is merely capable of coming to know.

Theophilus. The mind is capable not merely of knowing them, but also of finding them within itself. If all it had was the mere capacity to receive those items of knowledge—a passive power to do so, as indeterminate as the power of wax to receive shapes or of a blank page to receive words—it would not be the source of necessary truths, as I have just shown that it is. For it cannot be denied that the senses are inadequate to show their necessity, and that therefore the mind has a disposition (as much active as passive) to draw them from its own depths; though the senses are necessary to give the mind the opportunity and the attention for this, and to direct it towards certain necessary truths rather than others. The fundamental proof of necessary truths comes from the understanding alone, and other truths come from experience or from observations of the senses. Our mind is capable of knowing truths of both sorts, but it is the source of the former; and however often one experienced instances of a universal truth, one could never know inductively that it would always hold unless one knew through reason that it was necessary.

Philalethes. But if the words *to be in the understanding* have any positive content, do they not signify *to be perceived and comprehended by the understanding?*

Theophilus. They signify something quite different to us. It suffices that what is 'in the understanding' can be found there, and that the sources or fundamental proofs of the truths we are discussing are only 'in the understanding'. The senses can hint at, justify and confirm these truths, but can never demonstrate their infallible and perpetual certainty.

Philalethes. However, all those who will take the pains to reflect with a little attention on the operations of the understanding, will find that this ready assent of the mind to some truths depends on the faculty of the human mind.

Theophilus. Yes indeed. But what makes the exercise of the faculty easy and natural so far as these truths are concerned is a special affinity which the human mind has with them; and that is what makes us call them innate. So it is not a bare faculty, consisting in a mere possibility of understanding those truths: it is rather a disposition, an aptitude, a preformation, which determines our soul and brings it about that they are derivable from it.

Philalethes. But truths are subsequent to the ideas from which they arise, are they not? And ideas all come from the senses.

Theophilus. Intellectual ideas, from which necessary truths arise, do not come from the senses; and you acknowledge that some ideas arise from the mind's reflection when it turns in on itself. Now, it is true that explicit knowledge of truths is subsequent (in temporal or natural order) to the explicit knowledge of ideas; as the nature of truths depends upon the nature of ideas, before either are explicitly formed, and truths involving ideas which come from the senses are themselves at least partly dependent on the senses. But the ideas that come from the senses are confused; and so too, at least in part, are the truths which depend on them; whereas intellectual ideas, and the truths depending on them, are distinct, and neither the ideas nor the truths originate in the senses; though it is true that without the senses we would never think of them. [. . .]

Philalethes. A further problem is to know whether any purely material being thinks or not. Perhaps we shall never be capable of knowing this, despite the fact that we have the ideas of matter and thinking, because it is impossible for us, by the contemplation of our own ideas, without revelation, to discover whether Omnipotence has not given to some suitably disposed systems of matter a power to perceive and think, or has joined and fixed to matter so disposed a thinking immaterial substance.

Theophilus. There is no doubt that this question is incomparably more important than the preceding one. For a start, I grant you, sir, that when people have only confused ideas of *thought* and of *matter*, which is usually all they do have, it is no wonder that they cannot see how to resolve such questions. Similarly, as I remarked a little while back [p. 375], if someone has ideas of the angles of a triangle only in the way in which these ideas are commonly had, he will never come upon the discovery that they are always equal to two right angles. It should be borne in mind that matter, understood as a complete being (i.e. 'secondary matter', in contrast with 'prime matter' which is something purely passive and therefore incomplete), is nothing but an aggregate or the result of one; and that any real aggregate presupposes simple substances or *real unities*. If one also bears in mind what constitutes the nature of those real unities, namely perception and its consequences, one is transported into another world, so to speak: from having existed entirely amongst the phenomena of the senses, one comes to occupy the intelligible world of substances. And this knowledge of the inner nature of matter shows well enough what it is naturally capable of. And it shows that whenever God gives matter organs suitable for the expression of reasoning, it will also be given an immaterial substance which reasons; this is because of that harmony which is yet another consequence of the nature of substances. There cannot be matter without immaterial substances, i.e. without unities: that should put an end to the question of whether God is free to give or not to give immaterial substances to matter; and if the correspondence or harmony which I have just spoken of did not obtain amongst these substances, God would not be acting according to the natural order. To speak of sheerly 'giving' powers is to return to the bare faculties of the Scholastics, and to entertain a picture of little subsistent beings which can fly in and out like pigeons with a dovecote. It is unwittingly to turn them into substances. Primary powers are what make up the substances themselves; derivative powers, or 'faculties' if you like, are merely 'ways of being'—and they must be derived from substances, and are not derivable from matter considered as wholly mechanical, i.e. abstractly considered as merely that incomplete being which is prime matter or the purely passive. I believe you agree, sir, that it is not within the power of a bare machine to give rise to perception, sensation, reason. So these must stem from some other substantial thing. To maintain that God acts in any other way, and gives things accidents which are not 'ways of being' or modifications arising from substances, is to have recourse to miracles.

Philalethes. On the subject of the natural capacities of matter, I still have one objection. Body as far as we can conceive is able only to strike and affect body, and motion is able to produce nothing but motion, so that when we allow it to produce pleasure or pain, or the idea of a colour or sound, it seems that we are obliged to renounce our reason, go beyond our own ideas, and attribute it wholly to the good pleasure of our Maker. What reason shall we find, then, to conclude that perception does not occur in matter in that same way? I can see pretty well what reply this is open to.

Theophilus. You are correct in predicting, sir, that I will deny that matter can produce pleasure, pain or sensation in us. It is the soul that produces these in itself, in conformity with what happens in matter. Now, given my view, nothing unintelligible happens, except that we cannot sort out everything which has a part in our confused perceptions; they are expressions of the details of what happens in bodies, and even have about them something infinite. As for 'the good pleasure of our Maker', it should be said that he conducts himself in accordance with the natures of things, in such a way that he produces and conserves in them only what is suitable to them and can be explained through their natures; explained in a general way, at least, for often the details are beyond us, just as we lack the diligence and the power to arrange the grains in a mountain of sand according to their shapes, although apart from their sheer multiplicity there is nothing difficult to understand about that. If on the other hand that knowledge were inherently beyond us, and if we could not even conceive of a general explanation for the relations between soul and body, and if, finally, God gave things *accidental powers which were not rooted in their natures* and were therefore out of reach of reason in general; that would be a back door through which to re-admit 'over-occult qualities' which no mind can understand, along with inexplicable 'faculties'—those helpful little goblins—which come forward like gods on the stage to do on demand anything that a philosopher wants of them, without ways or means. But to attribute their origin to God's 'good pleasure'—that appears hardly worthy of him who is the supreme reason, and with whom everything is orderly, everything is connected. This good pleasure would indeed be neither good nor pleasure if God's power did not perpetually run parallel to his wisdom. [. . .]

Philalethes. Here is a problem for you, which the learned and worthy Mr Molyneux sent to the distinguished Mr Locke: 'Suppose a man born blind, and now adult, and taught by his touch to distinguish between a cube, and a sphere of the same metal, and nighly of the same bigness, so as to tell, when he felt one and t'other, which is the cube, which the sphere. Suppose then the cube and sphere placed on a table, and the blind man to be made to see. *Quaere*, whether by his sight, before he touched them, he could now distinguish, and tell, which is the globe, which the cube.'

Theophilus. I believe that if the blind man knows that the two shapes which he sees are those of a cube and a sphere, he will be able to identify them and to say without touching them that this one is the sphere and this the cube.

Philalethes. I am afraid I have to include you among the many who have given Mr Molyneux the wrong answer. The answer which this acute and judicious proposer gives is negative. For, he says, though this blind man has obtained the experience of how a globe, how a cube affects his touch, he does not yet know that what affects his touch so or so must affect his sight so or so, or that a protuberant angle in cube, that presses his hand unequally, will appear to his eye as it does in the cube.

Theophilus. If you will just consider my reply, sir, you will see that I have included in it a condition which can be taken to be implicit in the question: namely that it is merely a problem of telling which is which, and that the blind man knows that the two shaped bodies which he has to discern are before him and thus that each of the appearances which he sees is either that of a cube or that of a sphere. Given this condition, it seems to me past question that the blind man whose sight is restored could discern them by applying rational principles to the sensory knowledge which he has already acquired by touch. I am not talking about what he might actually do on the spot, when he is dazzled and confused by the strangeness—or, one should add, unaccustomed to making inferences. My view rests on the fact that in the case of the sphere there are no distinguished points on the surface of the sphere taken in itself, since everything there is uniform and without angles, whereas in the case of the cube there are eight points which are distinguished from all the others. If there were not that way of discerning shapes, a blind man could not learn the rudiments of geometry by touch, nor could someone else learn them by sight without touch. However, we find that men born blind are capable of learning geometry, and indeed always have some rudiments of a natural geometry; and we find that geometry is mostly learned by sight alone without employing touch, as could and indeed must be done by a paralytic or by anyone else to whom touch is virtually denied. These two geometries, the blind man's and the paralytic's, must come together, and agree, and indeed ultimately rest on the same ideas, even though they have no images in common. Which shows yet again how essential it is to distinguish *images* from *exact ideas* which are composed of definitions.

But to return to the man born blind who begins to see, and to what he would judge about the sphere and the cube when he saw but did not touch them: as I said a moment ago, I reply that he will know which is which if he is told that, of the two appearances or perceptions he has of them, one belongs to the sphere and the other to the cube. But if he is not thus instructed in advance, I grant that it will not at once occur to him that these paintings of them (as it were) that he forms at the back of his eyes, which could come from a flat painting on the table, represent bodies. That will occur to him only when he becomes convinced of it by the sense of touch or when he comes, through applying principles of optics to the light rays, to understand from the evidence of the lights and shadows that there is something blocking the rays and that it must be precisely the same thing that resists his touch. He will eventually come to understand this when he sees the sphere and the cube rolling, with consequent changes in their appearances and in the shadows they cast; or when, with the two bodies remaining still, the source of the light falling on them is moved or the position of his eyes changes. For these are pretty much the means that we do have for distinguishing at a distance between a picture or perspective representing an object and the real object.

[From *New Essays on Human Understanding*, ed. and trans. P. Remnant and J. Bennett (Cambridge: Cambridge University Press, 1982), Bk. I, ch. 1, 5 pp.]

IMMANUEL KANT

13   Critique of Pure Reason: The Transcendental Aesthetic

Section I.—*Of Space*

METAPHYSICAL EXPOSITION OF THIS CONCEPTION

By means of the external sense (a property of the mind), we represent to ourselves objects as without us, and these all in space. Therein alone are their shape, dimensions, and relations to each other determined or determinable. The internal sense, by means of which the mind contemplates itself or its internal state, gives, indeed, no intuition of the soul as an object; yet there is nevertheless a determinate form, under which alone the contemplation of our internal state is possible, so that all which relates to the inward determinations of the mind is represented in relations of time. Of time we cannot have any external intuition, any more than we can have an internal intuition of space. What then are time and space? Are they real existences? Or, are they merely relations or determinations of things, such, however, as would equally belong to these things in themselves, though they should never become objects of intuition; or, are they such as belong only to the form of intuition, and consequently to the subjective constitution of the mind, without which these predicates of time and space could not be attached to any object? In order to become informed on these points, we shall first give an exposition of the conception of space. By exposition, I mean the clear, though not detailed, representation of that which belongs to a conception; and an exposition is metaphysical, when it contains that which represents the conception as given *à priori*.

1. Space is not a conception which has been derived from outward experiences. For, in order that certain sensations may relate to something without me (that is, to something which occupies a different part of space from that in which I am); in like manner, in order that I may represent them not merely as without of and near to each other, but also in separate places, the representation of space must already exist as a foundation. Consequently, the representation of space cannot be borrowed from the relations of external phenomena through experience; but, on the contrary, this external experience is itself only possible through the said antecedent representation.

2. Space then is a necessary representation *à priori*, which serves for the foundation of all external intuitions. We never can imagine or make a representation to ourselves of the non-existence of space, though we may easily enough think that no objects are found in it. It must, therefore, be considered as the condition of the possibility of phenomena, and by no means as a determination dependent on them, and is a representation *à priori*, which necessarily supplies the basis for external phenomena.

3. Space is no discursive or, as we say, general conception of the relations of things, but a pure intuition. For in the first place, we can only represent to ourselves one space, and when we talk of divers spaces, we mean only parts of one and the same space. Moreover these parts cannot antecede this one all-embracing space, as the component parts from which the aggregate can be made up, but can be cogitated only as existing in it. Space is essentially one, and multiplicity in it, consequently the general notion of spaces, of this or that space, depends solely upon limitations. Hence it follows that an *à priori* intuition (which is not empirical) lies at the root of all our conceptions of space. Thus, moreover, the principles of geometry—for example, that 'in a triangle, two sides together are greater than the third,' are never deduced from general conceptions of line and triangle, but from intuition, and this *à priori* with apodictic certainty.

4. Space is represented as an infinite given quantity. Now every conception must indeed be considered as a representation which is contained in an infinite multitude of different possible representations, which, therefore,

comprises these under itself; but no conception, as such, can be so conceived, as if it contained within itself an infinite multitude of representations. Nevertheless, space is so conceived of, for all parts of space are equally capable of being produced to infinity. Consequently, the original representation of space is an intuition *à priori*, and not a conception.

TRANSCENDENTAL EXPOSITION OF THE CONCEPTION OF SPACE

By a transcendental exposition, I mean the explanation of a conception, as a principle, whence can be discerned the possibility of other synthetical *à priori* cognitions. For this purpose, it is requisite, firstly, that such cognitions do really flow from the given conception; and, secondly, that the said cognitions are only possible under the presupposition of a given mode of explaining this conception.

Geometry is a science which determines the properties of space synthetically, and yet *à priori*. What, then, must be our representation of space, in order that such a cognition of it may be possible? It must be originally intuition, for from a mere conception, no propositions can be deduced which go out beyond the conception, and yet this happens in geometry. (Introd. V.) But this intuition must be found in the mind *à priori*, that is, before any perception of objects, consequently, must be pure, not empirical, intuition. For geometrical principles are always apodictic, that is, united with the consciousness of their necessity, as, 'Space has only three dimensions.' But propositions of this kind cannot be empirical judgments, nor conclusions from them. (Introd. II.) Now, how can an external intuition anterior to objects themselves, and in which our conception of objects can be determined *à priori*, exist in the human mind? Obviously not otherwise than in so far as it has its seat in the subject only, as the *formal* capacity of the subject's being affected by objects, and thereby of obtaining immediate representation, that is, intuition; consequently, only as the *form of the external sense* in general.

Thus it is only by means of our explanation that the possibility of geometry, as a synthetical science *à priori*, becomes comprehensible. Every mode of explanation which does not show us this possibility, although in appearance it may be similar to ours, can with the utmost certainty be distinguished from it by these marks.

CONCLUSIONS FROM THE FOREGOING CONCEPTIONS

1. Space does not represent any property of objects as things in themselves, nor does it represent them in their relations to each other; in other words, space does not represent to us any determination of objects such as attaches to the objects themselves, and would remain, even though all subjective conditions of the intuition were abstracted. For neither absolute nor relative

determinations of objects can be intuited prior to the existence of the things to which they belong, and therefore not *à priori*.

2. Space is nothing else than the form of all phenomena of the external sense, that is, the subjective condition of the sensibility, under which alone external intuition is possible. Now, because the receptivity or capacity of the subject to be affected by objects necessarily antecedes all intuitions of these objects, it is easily understood how the form of all phenomena can be given in the mind previous to all actual perceptions, therefore *à priori*, and how it, as a pure intuition, in which all objects must be determined, can contain principles of the relations of these objects prior to all experience.

It is therefore from the human point of view only that we can speak of space, extended objects, etc. If we depart from the subjective condition, under which alone we can obtain external intuition, or, in other words, by means of which we are affected by objects, the representation of space has no meaning whatsoever. This predicate (of space) is only applicable to things in so far as they appear to us, that is, are objects of sensibility. The constant form of this receptivity, which we call sensibility, is a necessary condition of all relations in which objects can be intuited as existing without us, and when abstraction of these objects is made, is a pure intuition, to which we give the name of space. It is clear that we cannot make the special conditions of sensibility into conditions of the possibility of things, but only of the possibility of their existence as far as they are phenomena. And so we may correctly say that space contains all which can appear to us externally, but not all things considered as things in themselves, be they intuited or not, or by whatsoever subject one will. As to the intuitions of other thinking beings, we cannot judge whether they are or are not bound by the same conditions which limit our own intuition, and which for us are universally valid. If we join the limitation of a judgment to the conception of the subject, then the judgment will possess unconditioned validity. For example, the proposition, 'All objects are beside each other in space,' is valid only under the limitation that these things are taken as objects of our sensuous intuition. But if I join the condition to the conception, and say, 'all things, as external phenomena, are beside each other in space,' then the rule is valid universally, and without any limitation. Our expositions, consequently, teach the *reality* (*i.e.* the objective validity) of space in regard of all which can be presented to us externally as objects, and at the same time also the *ideality* of space in regard to objects when they are considered by means of reason as things in themselves, that is, without reference to the constitution of our sensibility. We maintain, therefore, the *empirical reality* of space in regard to all possible external experience, although we must admit its *transcendental ideality;* in other words, that it is nothing, so soon as we withdraw the condition upon which the possibility of all experience depends, and look upon space as something that belongs to things in themselves.

But, with the exception of space, there is no representation, subjective and referring to something external to us, which could be called objective *à priori*. For there are no other subjective *representations* from which we can deduce synthetical propositions *à priori*, as we can from the intuition of space. Therefore, to speak accurately, no ideality whatever belongs to these, although they agree in this respect with the representation of space, that they belong merely to the subjective nature of the mode of sensuous perception; such a mode, for example, as that of sight, of hearing, and of feeling, by means of the sensations of color, sound, and heat, but which, because they are only sensations, and not intuitions, do not of themselves give us the cognition of any object, least of all, an *à priori* cognition. My purpose, in the above remark, is merely this: to guard anyone against illustrating the asserted ideality of space by examples quite insufficient, for example, by color, taste, etc.; for these must be contemplated not as properties of things, but only as changes in the subject, changes which may be different in different men. For in such a case, that which is originally a mere phenomenon, a rose, for example, is taken by the empirical understanding for a thing in itself, though to every different eye, in respect of its color, it may appear different. On the contrary, the transcendental conception of phenomena in space is a critical admonition, that, in general, nothing which is intuited in space is a thing in itself, and that space is not a form which belongs as a property to things; but that objects are quite unknown to us in themselves, and what we call outward objects, are nothing else but mere representations of our sensibility, whose form is space, but whose real correlate, the thing in itself, is not known by means of these representations, nor ever can be, but respecting which, in experience, no inquiry is ever made.

Section II.—Of Time

METAPHYSICAL EXPOSITION OF THIS CONCEPTION

1. Time is not an empirical conception. For neither coexistence nor succession would be perceived by us, if the representation of time did not exist as a foundation *à priori*. Without this presupposition we could not represent to ourselves that things exist together at one and the same time, or at different times, that is, contemporaneously, or in succession.

2. Time is a necessary representation, lying at the foundation of all our intuitions. With regard to phenomena in general, we cannot think away time from them, and represent them to ourselves as out of and unconnected with time, but we can quite well represent to ourselves time void of phenomena. Time is therefore given *à priori*. In it alone is all reality of phenomena possible. These may all be annihilated in thought, but time itself, as the universal condition of their possibility, cannot be so annulled.

3. On this necessity *à priori* is also founded the possibility of apodictic

principles of the relations of time, or axioms of time in general, such as, 'Time has only one dimension,' 'Different times are not coexistent but successive' (as different spaces are not successive but coexistent). These principles cannot be derived from experience, for it would give neither strict universality, nor apodictic certainty. We should only be able to say, 'so common experience teaches us,' but not it must be so. They are valid as rules, through which, in general, experience is possible; and they instruct us respecting experience, and not by means of it.

4. Time is not a discursive or, as it is called, general conception, but a pure form of the sensuous intuition. Different times are merely parts of one and the same time. But the representation which can only be given by a single object is an intuition. Besides, the proposition that different times cannot be coexistent, could not be derived from a general conception. For this proposition is synthetical, and therefore cannot spring out of conceptions alone. It is therefore contained immediately in the intuition and representation of time.

5. The infinity of time signifies nothing more than that every determined quantity of time is possible only through limitations of one time lying at the foundation. Consequently, the original representation, time, must be given as unlimited. But as the determinate representation of the parts of time and of every quantity of an object can only be obtained by limitation, the *complete* representation of time must not be furnished by means of conceptions, for these contain only partial representations. Conceptions, on the contrary, must have immediate intuition for their basis.

TRANSCENDENTAL EXPOSITION OF THE CONCEPTION OF TIME

I may here refer to what is said above, where, for the sake of brevity, I have placed under the head of metaphysical exposition, that which is properly transcendental. Here I shall add that the conception of change, and with it the conception of motion, as change of place, is possible only through and in the representation of time; that if this representation were not an intuition (internal) *à priori*, no conception, of whatever kind, could render comprehensible the possibility of change, in other words, of a conjunction of contradictorily opposed predicates in one and the same object, for example, the presence of a thing in a place and the non-presence of the same thing in the same place. It is only in time, that it is possible to meet with two contradictorily opposed determinations in one thing, that is, after each other. Thus our conception of time explains the possibility of so much synthetical knowledge *à priori*, as is exhibited in the general doctrine of motion, which is not a little fruitful.

[From *Critique of Pure Reason*, trans. J. M. D. Meiklejohn (New York: Willey Book Co., 1781), 23–9.]

Section 2

The Mind as Spectator

INTRODUCTION

There are several senses of 'spectator' that might figure in accounts of any 'spectator' theory of mind, and the different senses are not compatible. As employed here the term refers to theories that take the contents of mental life to be provided by either direct or mediated contact with an external world which is knowable only in virtue of experience itself. The term, then, draws attention to the mental as *formed* from the outside, its operations thereupon limited to the grist of experience.

'Spectator' refers to one who looks at or examines something, but 'spectator' theories of mind have been advanced which differ on the question of just what it is that the spectator is looking at. The major theories fall into the general categories of *direct realism* and *representational realism*, one version of the latter being *phenomenalism*. The direct realist insists, often on quasi-Darwinian or providentialist grounds, that the practical demands of life require a knowledge of the world as it is, and that creatures prone to delusions would not survive the unforgiving minute. Accordingly, though sensory organs and mechanisms are interposed between the external world and any awareness of it, the latter is not of the sensory responses to but of the actual features of the external world. One sees what is there.

The representational realist takes the interposing sensory organs and processes as creating objects of experience that may be physically unlike the actual sources of stimulation, but sufficiently faithful as coded representations of reality to serve the interests of the creature. Human colour vision is most sensitive to light in the region of wavelengths centred on 555 nanometres. Human colour vision is blind to light in the ultraviolet region. But the honey bee is most sensitive in just this region. Human and bee purposes are served by their respective representations of the external world, but these representations are radically different experientially.

Phenomenalism is just such a representational or mediational theory. The external world is known only in the form of *phenomena* and never as in itself it really is. This does not amount to scepticism, however, for an unembarrassed naturalistic orientation allows the phenomenalist to assert that the phenomena match up with the needs of the percipient in such a way as to allow practical success.

In this section these several accounts of mind and mental content are featured. What they have in common is loyalty to the view that knowledge arises from experience, that hidden powers need not be invoked to account for it, and that the relationship between knowledge and the facts of the external world is foundational for all of the practical affairs of human and animal life. However, there are significant points of separation and departure to be noted as well, some of them leading to the conclusion that the very concept of 'mind' as something distinct from these very practical engagements is in the nature of a myth. We can pick up the line of descent as regards these different theories with Aristotle.

Aristotle made clear in a number of places, and notably in both the *Posterior Analytics* and the *Metaphysics*, that 'scientific' understanding cannot be won through merely perceptual processes; he also accorded to perception a central role in learning, memory, and general knowledge. Moreover, he strongly resisted that feature of Plato's psychology which invested the mind with innate knowledge. As Aristotle understood what might be called 'the *Meno* problem', it arises from different senses of knowing. Smith and Jones might both know that the triangle they perceive contains 180 degrees. Smith knows this because he has used a measuring device and has discovered that there are three 60-degree angles within the triangle. Jones, however, knows because he understands that *all* triangles circumscribe 180 degrees. What Smith knows is chiefly the gift of perception by which particulars enter the mind. What Jones knows is a form of *scientific* knowledge (*episteme*) which requires the capacity for abstract and deliberative rationality. Children and non-human animals, on Aristotle's account, can know what Smith knows, but not what Jones knows.

This, however, is not to depreciate perceptual sources of knowledge. Consider the opening lines of Aristotle's most profound philosophical treatise:

All men by nature desire to know. An indication of this is the delight we take in our senses; for even apart from their usefulness they are loved for themselves; and above all others the sense of sight . . . The reason is that this, most of all the senses, makes us know and brings to light many differences between things. (*Metaphysics*, Book I (A))

This section begins with passages taken from Aristotle's *Posterior Analytics*. Here 'the Meno problem' is tackled, Aristotle acknowledging something of a conundrum: we cannot follow the sort of demonstrative argument that establishes, for example, the Pythagorean theorem unless we already possess such 'primitive, immediate principles' on which all demonstrative arguments depend. If we (the soul) always possess them, an absurdity arises, for we end up knowing something profound though it nonetheless 'escapes notice'! And if we don't possess them, there is nothing in experience that will provide them, for they are, alas, *primitive* and *immediate*. In the selection included here

Aristotle is seen to begin with the particular facts gleaned by perception. By this process the external world is presented to mind, including the mind of animals, for sensation is part of the very definition of 'animal'. Some animals also possess the power of memory, such that individual percepts can be retained and combined, though even these have very little of connected experience. Human beings, however, are able to join memories in rich combinations to yield bona fide *experiences*, and from the multiplication of such experiences arises understanding itself. The universal concept is developed out of the particulars.

Aristotle reserves this abstract form of understanding only to those with developed rationality; only to normal, adult human beings. But knowledge is a different matter and comes about through perceptual processes able to furnish the mind with the facts of the external world. As summarized in the selection of On the Soul (Book III, ch. 7), Aristotle's theory of thinking is very much a 'spectator' theory. 'To the thinking soul images serve as if they were contents of perception', he says, going on to claim that, 'the soul never thinks without an image'. It should not be thought that 'image' refers to a picture (except when thoughts are of what is visible); only that thought is about *something*, and the contents of thought inevitably are representations of what has been experienced or, based on past experience, what might plausibly be expected.

Both Thomas Aquinas and William of Ockham advance a 'spectator' theory of the mind, at least as the first stage in the acquisition of knowledge. Reprinted here are portions of Question 84, Articles 7, 8 and Question 88, Articles 1, 2 of the *Summa Theologica*. In the first selection the question is whether we are able to know things without the aid of those *phantasms* arising from sensory encounters with the world. The term 'phantasm' refers to the mental representation of what the senses report. Phantasms are what the spectator witnesses on the mind's screen. What is at stake is of vital importance to Christian teaching for, if we can know only by way of phantasms, then we cannot know that which is immaterial—and this means we cannot know 'truth, and God, and the angels'. Thomas's reply, citing Aristotle on the same matter, is that in this life soul and body are united and therefore all mental representations must be by way of sense-generated phantasms. What we can know of the essence (*quiddity*) of a thing is the essence of its corporeality. In Article 8 Thomas leaves no doubt but that, without the sensitive powers, the judgement of the intellect must be impaired. The intellect is superior to the senses, but its objects are what is found in sensibles.

In Articles 1 and 2 of Question 88 Thomas then examined the claim that soul can understand 'what is above itself'; viz. immaterial entities. The adversary is found asserting that like is known by like and, as the mind is more like the immaterial, it must have direct knowledge of what is immaterial.

Moreover, the senses deceive and are corruptible, whereas the intellect is not; so, the intellect should be able to fathom uncorrupted immaterial entities. Thomas acknowledges that this is consistent with Plato's teaching but rejects it on Aristotelian grounds and on the basis of experience itself. Simply stated, our contact with the external world is by way of the senses, and the mind is thus furnished only by that which the senses are able to record.

Aristotle states that not Socrates but those who came after him came to regard the 'true forms' as really existing apart from individual things. By the medieval period, the question of the existence of such entities would fuel the controversy between Realists and Nominalists. Contrary to what the terms suggest to the modern reader, the Realists were those who accorded ontological standing to *universals*. Nominalists, on the other hand, argued that universals were but class-names having only a *nominal* existence. There is no really existing universal rectilinear triangle of which sensible ones are but instances. There are only actual right-angle triangles, all of them collectively *named* 'rectilinear'.

Perhaps the most influential Nominalist of the period was William of Ockham. In denying the reality of universals, he relied on a version of the 'spectator' theory of mind. The universal, he argues, is something of *a picture in the mind* formed out of many individual experiences. But as such the universal does not have a mental existence either, for the mind is able to frame any number of fictions. We can imagine the chimera, but there are no chimeras. As different portions of a picture can be rearranged to depict what has never occurred, so also can the mind assemble fictions from perceived facts. What is known is the particular. There is no universal 'human nature' in Socrates apart from all of the particulars constitutive of the individual Socrates.

A defender and disciple of the emerging scientific age, Thomas Hobbes had journeyed to meet the great Galileo and also established his credentials as a leading mechanistic theorist in his critique of Descartes's mind/body dualism, as will be seen in the next section. Galileo's method of *resolution and composition* provided the model of scientific reasoning for Hobbes's *Leviathan*, in which fear of violent death serves as a natural impulse resulting in the voluntary surrender of certain rights to that sovereign who is able to protect life itself. Part I of *Leviathan* begins with the chapter 'Of Sense' from which the pages in this Section are drawn. Hobbes leaves no doubt about the source of 'the Thoughts of man', whether considered *Singly* or in a '*Trayne*'. Hobbes attaches himself firmly to the old Scholastic chestnut according to which 'nothing is in the intellect which is not first in the senses', the very maxim to which Leibniz offered the ageless rationalist reply: nothing but the intellect itself; *nisi intellectus ipse*.

It is to John Locke that one turns for the most influential of the modern 'spectator' theories of mind. His *Essay Concerning Human Understanding* is the *locus classicus* for modern empiricistic theories of knowledge and for one of the earliest sustained critiques of the notion of innate ideas. It was during a period of self-exile in Holland that Locke read deeply in the works of Descartes. At about the same time Ralph Cudworth, Henry More, and other 'Cambridge Platonists' had revived and embellished ancient versions of transcendentalist philosophy, and these writers, too, must have been the unnamed targets of Locke's critique.

The *Essay* appeared in 1690, thirty years after the founding of the Royal Society (of which Locke was Fellow) and toward the close of what may have been the most productive century in the history of science; the century of Kepler, Galileo, Descartes, Newton, Leibniz, Boyle, Hooke, Huygens, Wren—the list could be extended by another half-page. But the veritable emblem of the age was Newton, who not only established his scientific and mathematical genius in a dozen different ways, but who also laid down the principles by which scientific research and theory are to be developed. It was Locke's intention to lay the foundations for a science of the mind—a science of human understanding—based on the principles of Newtonian science. In this he cast himself, as he said in the introduction to the *Essay* as but an 'under labourer', clearing a path others might follow.

What was this Newtonian science? Its ontology was corpuscular, but Newton's science was also and even more importantly a *method*, a mode of thought about how complex problems are to be approached, and it was this feature of his work that had the most general effect on his contemporaries and on the century of Enlightenment that followed. One illustration might be useful. Kepler's laws of planetary motion were based on exhaustive observational data compiled by Tycho Brahe. But Newton's approach to the problem of explaining planetary motion begins not with such a profusion of observations; rather, he begins with the idealized and utterly simplified case of a mass revolving around a gravitational force. The elliptical trajectory predicted and explained in the ideal case then is applied to the domain of real motions recorded by Brahe and others. Newton even distinguished between the true or actual dynamics unearthed by the reductive approach and the comparable but measurably different data obtained from observations. The latter yield quantities described by Newton as 'hypothetical'—by which he means *approximate*. (His famous 'Hypothesis non fingo' is perhaps better understood as his refusal to traffic in approximations rather than any reluctance to theorize).

Locke's method of analysis is also reductive. The welter of conscious ideation at any given moment is beyond our descriptive and analytical powers. The proper scientific approach to mind, however, calls for an understanding of the macroscopic complexities by way of elementary simplicities. Thus does Locke take the basic *datum* of mental life to be the *elementary sensation*. In the passages included in this section from Book II ('Of

Ideas') of Locke's *Essay*, the theory of innate ideas is rejected. Rather, 'All ideas come from sensation or reflection'.

The Lockian mind begins as 'white paper, void of all characters, without any ideas'. The answer to the question of how, then, it comes to possess such rich stores of knowledge, is given in the single word, EXPERIENCE. It is through direct sensory commerce with the external world that we come to have the ideas of '*yellow, white, heat, cold, soft, hard*'. In the discussion of Berkeley in section I the Lockian distinction was noted between primary and secondary qualities of things. Sensation is the mind's source of both. Some sensations convey the actual (primary) qualities of the external object; e.g. its hardness. Other sensations are of qualities not in the object as such but brought about by the effect the object's primary qualities have on the sense organs themselves; e.g., corpuscular interactions between light and the visual sense, resulting in the sensation of yellow.

In addition to sensation, which supplies the mind, there is that power or faculty by which the mind is able to consider its own operations such that other ideas are brought about 'which could not be had from things without'. This set of internal operations gives rise to '*perception, thinking, doubting, believing, reasoning, knowing, willing*'—collectively, a species of what Locke calls *internal sense* and which he dubs *reflection*. All ideas originate in the actions of the external and the internal sense, in the processes of sensation and reflection.

Our ideas, however, are far richer than anything that might be found in such elementary sensations as 'yellow' or 'sweet'. Locke's theory of mind supposes that elementary sensations form ensembles that constitute simple ideas, and that constellations of the latter come together resulting in complex ideas. Accordingly, complex ideas are reducible in principle to elementary sensations. Again, we have a corpuscularian theory according to which elementary, invisible entities are fused (by something akin to gravitational forces) to form ever more complex entities. Locke wrote only tangentially about the principle of 'association' as the means by which sensations and simple ideas come to be held together. As we shall see, the fuller treatment of associationism would be given by David Hume. But even in this there is the repetition of a Newtonian theme, for in Book III, Part I of his treatise on *Opticks*, Newton had noted that the most elementary constituents of matter formed by God are 'solid, massy, hard, impenetrable, movable Particles . . . And therefore, that Nature may be lasting, the Changes of corporeal Things are to be placed only in the various Separations and new Associations and motions of these permanent Particles . . .'

Also included here from Locke's *Essay* are passages from Book III, ch. III where Locke draws a sharp distinction between *real* and *nominal essences*. Here he is at one with the medieval *nominalists* (e.g. Ockham), as he must be. For if there were really existing *species*, of which individual corporeal entities were but instances, then any claim to the effect that these species are known and knowable would be in the service of, alas, innate ideas. How else could such be known, as they could not be known by way of experience? However, the corpuscular theory itself is based on the reality of entities that are not subjects of experience. Locke must therefore contrast the non-existent nominal essences with the actual but unperceived real essences. The relevant criterion is satisfied only by the latter: actual corporeal bodies have 'a real, but unknown, constitution of their insensible parts; from which flow those sensible qualities which serve us to distinguish them one from another'. Locke's influence is vividly apparent in the nineteenth century when John Stuart Mill is found defining matter itself as 'the permanent possibility of sensations'.

David Hume's *A Treatise of Human Nature* was published in 1739 but proved to be less than summoning to his contemporaries, though it has since become one of the most cited works in the history of philosophy. It was a *tour de force* begun, Hume would admit, even before the author had completed his college days and finished when the author was a mere 26 years old. Over a course of years Hume would prune and refine the *Treatise*, developing defences against its critics and rendering its arguments more widely accessible in a series of essays. His last written words on the subjects that had been explored in the *Treatise* would appear in the posthumously published *Enquiries* of 1777. It is in the *Enquiry Concerning Human Understanding* that his empiricistic theory of mind is developed and defended. Chosen here are portions of Sections II–IV.

The theory of mind advanced in these sections identifies as the fundamental contents of mental life *ideas* and *impressions*, the latter being the lively and distinct consequence of direct sensory encounters with the world. Ideas, on the other hand, are the less lively and temporally displaced reflections on these very impressions. In a sense, the 'idea' in Hume's theory is doing the work here of Locke's 'reflection'. And as for the allegedly unbounded (transcendental?) nature of thought, Hume is unequivocal in his rejection: the mind's vaunted creative power is no more than 'the faculty of compounding, transposing, augmenting, or diminishing the materials afforded us by the senses and experience'. Closely examined, every idea 'is copied from a similar impression'. The test of whether a term has any meaning is direct: '*from what impression is that supposed idea derived?*' Note the Humean roots of that verificationist slogan of twentieth-century logical positivism: 'The meaning of a proposition is its method of verification'.

Any meaningful idea is, indeed, derived from impressions on Hume's account, but ideas are rendered complex and inexhaustibly varied through the mental processes of compounding, transposing, augmenting, etc. These very processes, however, are reducible to lawful explanations, these being the laws or principles of association. Although such principles are found in

Aristotle and in many writers before Hume, it is in Hume's *Treatise* and *Enquiry* that they are given their fullest and psychologically most explicit treatment. Stated by Hume with commendable efficiency, 'there appear to be only three principles of connexion among ideas, namely *Resemblance*, *Contiguity* in time and place, and *Cause* or *Effect*'.

These are what knit our ideas together. All other factors being equal, the more strongly connected ideas are of objects or events that share some similarity or resemblance; objects or events that have been spatially and temporally contiguous in experience; objects or events which, by virtue of their being *constantly conjoin'd* in experience, stand in the relationship of *cause and effect*.

Against the traditional rationalist objection that the mind is in possession of necessary and certain truths which, by their very nature, could not possibly arise from impressions, Hume insists on a categorical distinction between *relations of ideas* and *matters of fact*. The former are achieved by the 'mere operations of thought', Hume says, and are independent of anything having real existence. But matters of fact are never necessary, never certain, always merely contingent. It is by way of the relations of ideas that abstract mathematical systems are produced. However, there is nothing in the abstract theorems of geometry or algebra that will supply knowledge about matters of fact. The Newtonian achievement is grounded in actual observations which never reach the level of ultimate causes and cannot be brought there by mathematics. Beyond the evidence of immediate perception and of memory, there is only one way we are able to reason about matters of fact, and that is by way of 'the relation of *Cause and Effect*'. Thus, when a man finds a watch on a desert island, he concludes that there had once been others on the island. This knowledge of what is given neither by impressions nor by memory can be based on nothing else but this relation of cause and effect, which is itself the gift of experience and not reason.

One of the most controversial of Hume's philosophical claims is that the concept of causation is the outcome of the *constant conjunction* of objects and events in experience. Hume did not doubt that there were actual causal relations in the material world. Rather, his essentially psychological analysis pertained to the basis on which one ever has the *concept* of such relations. His conclusion is drawn from a larger 'spectator theory' of a Lockian nature and augmented by associationist principles. Apart from the (ontological) question of whether or not there are actual causes operating in the world, Hume offers the (psychological) operations and habits of mind by which we attribute causality to certain perceptual events. Nothing in the external world offers direct evidence of causation. When one billiard ball strikes another and the second has motion imparted to it, Hume can find 'no third term betwixt them', as he says in the *Treatise*. He cannot perceive causes directly. Where, then, is causation to be found, if not in the fixed tendencies of mind itself to treat as causal any pair of events constantly conjoined in experience, one member of the paper faithfully succeeding the other?

Hume's most successful contemporary critic and fellow Scot, Thomas Reid, found in these views an untested theory as old as ancient Greek philosophy and adopted by philosophers who agreed on little else; a theory Reid calls the 'ideal' theory, according to which we never have direct knowledge of the world but only of certain 'ideas' that come about as a result of mediating sensations. Reid regards this as based on mere speculation and thus as unfaithful to the accepted Baconian and Newtonian modes of philosophizing. It is a view also at variance with the common-sense understandings of the non-philosophical world; understandings universally honoured in language and in all of the practical affairs of life. As defined by Reid, a principle of common sense is not merely a widely held prejudice or belief but a precept one is under a veritable obligation to take for granted. That up is not down, that a thing cannot at once be and not be, that the thoughts I have are mine—these are principles on which every mental act must depend. Where the habits and the very language of the human race record acceptance of such precepts, without exception, it is not for philosophers to offer correctives.

There is, argues Reid, no evidence whatever that our knowledge of the external world is actually some sort of inward inspection of our ideas, or that we are somehow confused as to whether what is perceived is actually and objectively external to us or is but a figment of the imagination. If our knowledge were thus hostage to sensations, we could never recognize the same book on two successive occasions. With each alteration in the position of the eyes or of the head, with each change in the distance between the percipient and the object, there are gross changes at the level of sensation. But the known object has what in modern times is called 'object permanence', which survives whole storms of sensory alterations.

Furthermore, Reid finds in the 'ideal' theory no respect for the difference between sensations and perceptions, though ordinary experience is not confused by the two. The sentences, 'I feel a pain' and 'I see a rose' are grammatically the same in that both contain subject, verb, and direct object. But in the former, there is not distinction between the object and the verb, for the feeling just *is* the pain. And so it is with all sensations. There isn't both the sensation and something other than it which is sensed. With perception, however, the distinction between verb and object is not merely grammatical, it is also ontological. To see a rose entails an object of perception. Were ideas to be no more than congeries of sensations there could be no external world at all, for sensations have virtually nothing in common with the external objects that bring them about. The sharp pain induced by the point of the needle has nothing in common with needles.

Perception, however, matches up with the features of the external world that are its objects. Contrary to Hume's belief that the mind's contents are some sort of 'copy' of the impressions made on the sense organs, Reid argues that a veritable welter of sensory alterations may have no effect at all on the objects of perception — as in the case of object-permanence. Reid's realist theory begins with assumption that the external world does, indeed, cause alterations in the sense organs. There is, on this account, a natural, biological relationship between the physical features of the stimulus and the sensory response to it. In Reid's (borrowed) terminology, the sensory response is the *natural sign* of the external object. In modern terms, one might say that the decomposition of photopigment in the retina results in electrical changes in the retinal cells and that these electrical alterations are the 'natural sign' of, for example, the colour of an external object. But the percipient sees neither decomposing photopigments nor graded electrical changes in ganglion cells of the retina, nor neural impulses in their axons as these form the optic nerve. The percipient sees red! In some way that Reid cannot explain—but that the unchallengeable facts of daily life confirm—the mind is able to go from the *natural sign* to the *thing signified*. The objects of experience are the latter, not the former. Thus, the realist's answer to the question, 'How faithfully does experience represent the external world?' is, 'It doesn't *represent* it, it presents it.'

Fully indebted to Hume, John Stuart Mill would find in critiques such as Reid reliance on the same sort of hidden powers or intuitions as were made famous by Kant. Against this, Mill advanced a theory of mind at once empiricistic and associationistic. In selections taken from his *A System of Logic* his definitions of 'body' and of 'mind' leave no room for occult powers or transcendent and innate principles. The 'complex ideas' of Locke are explained in terms of thoughts shaped by various sensations 'amalgamated into one mixed state of consciousness', this process being the only basis on which we can know anything about 'the outward world'. If there is some (Kantian) noumenal existence possessed by the objects of sense it cannot be known by sense, and therefore cannot be known at all, a conclusion, says Mill, that Kant himself reached.

A certain impatience with metaphysical distinctions is also recorded by Mill in the extracts chosen, as for example when he considers the concept of sensible 'qualities' such as the whiteness of snow. The theory he finds suspect here is that of (Lockian) 'secondary qualities' according to which snow is not white *per se* but has in its physical nature something of the power of exciting the sensation of whiteness in the percipient. But Mill is wary of such alleged powers, stripped as they are of the very possibility of direct observation. He is wary, too, of an ontology of 'qualities', as somehow distinct from the sensations themselves. He attributes such forms of speech to 'a certain tendency of the human mind which is the cause of many delusions. I mean, the disposition, whenever we meet with two names which are not precisely synonymous, to suppose that they must be the names of two different things; whereas in reality they may be names of the same things viewed in two different lights'.

This objection, consistent with Reid's own critique of the 'ideal' theory, is developed further by Gilbert Ryle (see below), even as he rejects the sort of phenomenalism espoused by Mill. To propose that snow is perceived as 'white' because it has a power to excite in us the sensation of 'whiteness' is, on Mill's account, cut from the same cloth as Molière's famous physician who explains that opium induces sleep because it possesses a *vis dormativa*. Similarly, dawn and sunrise present themselves to consciousness as a succession of experiences. But there is no need to invoke the (Kantian) 'intuition' of time to account for the succession, for this succession is given in the very fact that there are distinguishable events. To be conscious of the succession is not to be conscious of some third entity (succession) over and against the two entities, dawn and sunrise. In summary, then, the cause of any sensation is just that manifold of phenomena constitutive of the perceived object or event itself.

What, then, of the necessary truths of mathematics which, in virtue of their necessity and certainty, could not be established through experience? Recall that in Hume such truths were taken to be verbal. Mill, on the other hand, asserts boldly that even the axioms of mathematics are to be understood as inductions arising from experience, fortified by the 'extreme generality of the language'. Thus, 'All numbers must be numbers of something; there are no such thing as numbers in the abstract.' (It was this line of argument that led Jean Piaget to declare that the radical empiricist believes the series of positive integers was discovered one at a time!)

With the commitment to eschew unnecessary metaphysical assumptions, a commitment influentially defended by J. S. Mill, comes also the commitment to clear and simplify the ontological terrain that science and philosophy might settle. A bold movement in this direction was made by William James in his *Essays in Radical Empiricism*. That collection included the full text of 'Does Consciousness Exist?', which first appeared as a journal article in 1904. James acknowledges that *thought* exists, but challenges the contention that it exists *in* some other existing entity called 'consciousness'; as if there were some valid ontological distinction between thought and its contents. What James accepts of consciousness is that it is a *function*, not an entity.

The question that arises, then, is whether there are both mental and physical entities to contend with in any developed metaphysics. James is prepared to begin with the most economical of ontologies; that 'there is only one primal stuff or material in the world . . . of which everything is composed'. His answer to the ontological question is the reply of the 'radical empiricist': the one primal stuff is *pure experience*! Rejected is the dualistic supposition that there is both content and consciousness in experience. There is *content*. The metaphor James uses is that of paint in a pot and the same paint spread across a canvas. In a pot it is an item to be sold; put on the canvas in a certain way it may well serve spiritual purposes: 'Just so, I maintain, does a given undivided portion of experience, taken in one context of associates, play the part of knower, of a state of mind, of "consciousness"; while in a different context the same undivided bit of experience plays the part of a thing known, of an objective "content" '. It is the context that determines it to be thought or thing.

We conclude this Section with passages from Gilbert Ryle's *The Concept of Mind*, one of the most influential of twentieth-century wars against transcendentalist or 'Cartesian' or essentialist theories of mind. Opposed and exposed by Ryle is what he calls *the official doctrine* according to which minds and bodies have separate if mysteriously interacting existences, neither of them possessing the defining properties of the other, one public and the other forever private. Mind according to the doctrine is *the ghost in the machine*, and it is Ryle's project to exorcize it once and for all.

Ryle hopes to explode the myth of the ghost in the machine first by revealing the logical howler it instantiates; that of the *category mistake*. The foreign visitor to Oxford or Cambridge illustrates the mistake when, after touring about, visiting colleges, attending lectures and tutorials, etc., he then asks where he must go now to see the 'University'. Akin to this might be the mistake of assuming that in addition to buying a left glove and a right glove one is also buying a pair of gloves. So too with mental ascriptions. The official doctrine supposes incorrectly that, in addition to experiences, feelings, actions, and the like, there is a separate entity—a mind—in which such things inhere or which causally brings them about.

It was in the great age of mechanistic science that Hobbes and Descartes drew inspiration from Galileo's explanatory principles. Hobbes took them in one direction and reached utterly materialistic conclusions. Descartes, as Ryle reads him, moved in the other direction and reached a dualism which seemed to call for the abandonment of all such modes of explanation. Ryle argues that Hobbes and Descartes were both wrong, as have been the traditions that would repeat their errors. The 'mind', as such a term could ever be meaningful, refers to a complex pattern of (typically) observable actions and achievements; an assortment of things known, dispositions, competencies. It is not an inner screen on which the world becomes projected. Phenomenalism presupposes that having a sensation is somehow 'finding something'. Reid was just as concerned about this feature of the received empiricistic theories of mind. They share at the bottom philosophical confusions found not only in Locke and Hume, but in Descartes as well, as Reid observed. The mistake of *phenomenalism* is the assumption that percipients do not look at the world but at (privately held) 'phenomena', these (ironically) introduced in order to rid mental philosophy of occult entities. But phenomenalism still gives us 'the locked door' and the 'still to be discovered key'. This, says Ryle, is all wrong. If 'mind' is to be studied it is to be studied as much by economists as by artists, politicians, historians; by all able to gather observable facts and integrate them into intelligible accounts of activities that clearly have and reach ends. The data will be the same for all, even if the psychologist's handling of them is in some sense scientific.

14 **Posterior Analytics**

Now as for deduction and demonstration, it is evident both what each is and how it comes about—and at the same time this goes for demonstrative understanding too (for that is the same thing). But as for the principles—how they become familiar and what is the state that becomes familiar with them—that will be clear from what follows, when we have first set down the puzzles.

Now, we have said earlier that it is not possible to understand through demonstration if we are not aware of the primitive, immediate, principles. But as to knowledge of the immediates, one might puzzle both whether it is the same or not the same—whether there is understanding of each, or rather understanding of the one and some other kind of thing of the other—and also whether the states are not present in us but come about in us, or whether they are present in us but escape notice.

Well, if we have them, it is absurd; for it results that we have pieces of knowledge more precise than demonstration and yet this escapes notice. But if we get them without having them earlier, how might we become familiar with them and learn them from no pre-existing knowledge? For that is impossible, as we said in the case of demonstration too. It is evidently impossible, then, both for us to have them and for them to come about in us when we are ignorant and have no such state at all. Necessarily, therefore, we have some capacity, but do not have one of a type which will be more valuable than these in respect of precision.

And *this* evidently belongs to all animals; for they have a connate discriminatory capacity, which is called perception. And if perception is present in them, in some animals retention of the percept comes about, but in others it does not comes about. Now for those in which it does not come about, there is no knowledge outside perceiving (either none at all, or none with regard to that of which there is no retention); but for some perceivers, it is possible to grasp it in their minds. And when many such things come about, then a difference comes about, so that some come to have an account from the retention of such things, and others do not.

So from perception there comes memory, as we call it, and from memory (when it occurs often in connection with the same thing), experience; for memories that are many in number from a single experience. And from experience, or from the whole universal that has come to rest in the soul (the one apart from the many, whatever is one and the same in all those things), there comes a principle of skill and of understanding—of skill if it deals with how things come about, of understanding if it deals with what is the case.

Thus the states neither belong in us in a determinate form, nor come about from other states that are more cognitive; but they come about from perception—as in a battle when a rout occurs, if one man makes a stand another does and then another, until a position of strength is reached. And the soul is such as to be capable of undergoing this.

What we have just said but not said clearly, let us say again: when one of the undifferentiated things makes a stand, there is a primitive universal in the mind (for though one perceives the particular, perception is of the universal—e.g. of man but not of Callias the man); again a stand is made in these, until what has no parts and is universal stands—e.g. *such and such* an animal stands, until animal does, and in this a stand is made in the same way. Thus it is clear that it is necessary for us to become familiar with the primitives by induction; for perception too instils the universal in this way.

Since of the intellectual states by which we grasp truth some are always true and some admit falsehood (e.g. opinion and reasoning—whereas understanding and comprehension are always true), and no kind other than comprehension is more precise than understanding, and the principles of demonstrations are more familiar, and all understanding involves an account—there will not be understanding of the principles; and since it is not possible for anything to be truer than understanding, except comprehension, there will be comprehension of the principles—both if we inquire from these facts and because demonstration is not a principle of demonstration so that understanding is not a principle of understanding either—so if we have no other true kind apart from understanding, comprehension will be the principle of understanding. And the principle will be of the principle, and understanding as a whole will be similarly related to the whole object. [. . .]

[From *Posterior Analytics*, Bk. II, ch. 19, in *The Complete Works of Aristotle*, ed. J. Barnes (Princeton: Princeton University Press, 1984), 165–6.]

Actual knowledge is identical with its object: potential knowledge in the individual is in time prior to actual knowledge but absolutely it has no priority even in time; for all things that come into being arise from what actually is. In the case of sense clearly the sensitive faculty already was potentially what the object makes it to be actually; the faculty is not affected or altered. This must therefore be a different kind of movement; for movement is an activity of what is imperfect, activity in the unqualified sense, i.e. that of what has been perfected, is different.

To perceive then is like bare asserting or thinking; but when the object is pleasant or painful, the soul makes a sort of affirmation or negation, and pursues or avoids the object. To feel pleasure or pain is to act with the sensitive mean towards what is good or bad as such. Both avoidance and appetite when actual are identical with this: the faculty of appetite and avoidance are not different, either from one another or from the faculty of sense-perception; but their being is different.

To the thinking soul images serve as if they were contents of perception (and when it asserts or denies them to be good or bad it avoids or pursues them). That is why the soul never thinks without an image. The process is like that in which the air modifies the pupil in this or that way and the pupil transmits the modification to some third thing (and similarly in hearing), while the ultimate point of arrival is one, a single mean, with different manners of being.

With what part of itself the soul discriminates sweet from hot I have explained before and must now describe again as follows: That with which it does so is a sort of unity, but in the way a boundary is; and these things being one by analogy and numerically, are each to each as the qualities discerned are to one another (for what difference does it make whether we raise the problem of discrimination between disparates or between contraries, e.g. white and black?). Let then C be to D as A, white is to B, black: it follows *alternando* that $C: A:: D: B$. If then C and A belong to one subject, the case will be the same with them as with D and B; D and B form a single identity with different modes of being; so too will the former pair. The same reasoning holds if A be sweet and B white.

The faculty of thinking then thinks the forms in the images, and as in the former case what is to be pursued or avoided is marked out for it, so where there is no sensation and it is engaged upon the images it is moved to pursuit or avoidance. E.g. perceiving by sense that the beacon is fire, it recognizes in virtue of the general faculty of sense that it signifies an enemy, because it sees it moving; but sometimes by means of the images or thoughts which are within the soul, just as if it were seeing, it calculates and deliberates what is to come by reference to what is present; and when it makes a pronouncement, as in the case of sensation it pronounces the object to be pleasant or painful, in this case it avoids or pursues; and so generally in cases of action.

That too which involves no action, i.e. that which is true or false, is in the same province with what is good or bad: yet they differ in this, that the one is absolute and the other relative to someone.

The so-called abstract objects the mind thinks just as, in the case of the snub, one might think of it *qua* snub not separately, but if anyone actually thought of it *qua* hollow he would think of it without the flesh in which it is embodied: it is thus that the mind when it is thinking the objects of mathematics thinks of them as separate though they are not separate. In every case the mind which is actively thinking is the objects which it thinks. Whether it is possible for it while not existing separate from spatial conditions to think anything that is separate, or not, we must consider later.

Let us now summarize our results about soul, and repeat that the soul is in a way all existing things; for existing things are either sensible or thinkable, and knowledge is in a way what is knowable, and sensation is in a way what is sensible: in *what* way we must inquire.

Knowledge and sensation are divided to correspond with the realities, potential knowledge and sensation answering to potentialities, actual knowledge and sensation to actualities. Within the soul the faculties of knowledge and sensation are *potentially* these objects, the one what is knowable, the other what is sensible. They must be either the things themselves or their forms. The former alternative is of course impossible: it is not the stone which is present in the soul but its form.

[From *On the Soul*, Bk. III, chs. 7, 8, in *The Complete Works of Aristotle*, ed. J. Barnes (Princeton: Princeton University Press, 1984), 685–6.]

Seventh Article
Whether the intellect can understand actually through the intelligible
species of which it is possessed, without turning to the phantasms?

We proceed thus to the Seventh Article:—

Objection 1. It would seem that the intellect can understand actually through the intelligible species of which it is possessed, without turning to the phantasms. For the intellect is made actual by the intelligible species by which it is informed. But if the intellect is in act, it understands. Therefore the intelligible species suffices for the intellect to understand actually, without turning to the phantasms.

Obj. 2. Further, the imagination is more dependent on the senses than the intellect on the imagination. But the imagination can actually imagine in the absence of the sensible. Therefore much more can the intellect understand without turning to the phantasms.

Obj. 3. There are no phantasms of incorporeal things, for the imagination does not transcend time and space. If, therefore, our intellect cannot understand anything actually without turning to the phantasms, it follows that it cannot understand anything incorporeal. Which is clearly false, for we understand truth, and God, and the angels.

On the contrary, The Philosopher says that *the soul understands nothing without a phantasm.*

I answer that, In the state of the present life, in which the soul is united to a corruptible body, it is impossible for our intellect to understand anything actually, except by turning to phantasms. And of this there are two indications. First of all because the intellect, being a power that does not make use of a corporeal organ, would in no way be hindered in its act through the lesion of a corporeal organ, if there were not required for its act the act of some power that does make use of a corporeal organ. Now sense, imagination and the other powers belonging to the sensitive part make use of a corporeal organ. Therefore it is clear that for the intellect to understand actually, not only when it acquires new knowledge, but also when it uses knowledge already acquired, there is need for the act of the imagination and of the other powers. For when the act of the imagination is hindered by a lesion of the corporeal organ, for instance, in a case of frenzy, or when the act of the memory is hindered, as in the case of lethargy, we see that a man is hindered from understanding actually even those things of which he had a previous knowledge. Secondly, anyone can experience this of himself, that when he tries to understand something, he forms certain phantasms to serve him by way of examples, in which as it were he examines what he is desirous of understanding. For this reason it is that when we wish to help someone to understand something, we lay examples before him, from which he can form phantasms for the purpose of understanding.

Now the reason for this is that the power of knowledge is proportioned to the thing known. Therefore the proper object of the angelic intellect, which is entirely separate from a body, is an intelligible substance separate from a body. Whereas the proper object of the human intellect, which is united to a body, is the quiddity or nature existing in corporeal matter; and it is through these natures of visible things that it rises to a certain knowledge of things invisible. Now it belongs to such a nature to exist in some individual, and this cannot be apart from corporeal matter; for instance, it belongs to the nature of a stone to be in an individual stone, and to the nature of a horse to be in an individual horse, and so forth. Therefore the nature of a stone or any material thing cannot be known completely and truly, except in as much as it is known as existing in the individual. Now we apprehend the individual through the sense and the imagination. And, therefore, for the intellect to understand actually its proper object, it must of necessity turn to the phantasms in order to perceive the universal nature existing in the individual. But if the proper object of our intellect were a separate form, or if, as the Platonists say, the natures of sensible things subsisted apart from the individual, there would be no need for the intellect to turn to the phantasms whenever it understands.

Reply Obj. 1. The species preserved in the possible intellect exist there habitually when it does not understand them actually, as we have said above. Therefore for us to understand actually, the fact that the species are preserved does not suffice; we need further to make use of them in a manner befitting the things of which they are the species, which things are natures existing in individuals.

Reply Obj. 2. Even the phantasm is the likeness of an individual thing; and so the imagination does not need any further likeness of the individual, whereas the intellect does.

Reply Obj. 3. Incorporeal beings, of which there are no phantasms, are known to us by comparison with sensible bodies of which there are phantasms. Thus we understand truth by considering a thing in which we see the truth; and God, as Dionysius says, we know as cause, by way of excess and by way of remotion. Other incorporeal substances we know, in the state of the present life, only by way of remotion or by some comparison to corporeal things. Hence, when we understand something about these beings, we need to turn to the phantasms of bodies, although there are no phantasms of these beings themselves.

Eighth Article
Whether the judgment of the intellect is hindered through suspension of the sensitive powers?

We proceed thus to the Eighth Article:—

Objection 1. It would seem that the judgment of the intellect is not hindered by suspension of the sensitive powers. For the superior does not depend on the inferior. But the judgment of the intellect is higher than the senses. Therefore the judgment of the intellect is not hindered through suspension of the senses.

Obj. 2. Further, to syllogize is an act of the intellect. But during sleep the senses are suspended, as is said in *De Somno et Vigilia*, and yet it sometimes happens to us to syllogize while asleep. Therefore the judgment of the intellect is not hindered through suspension of the senses.

On the contrary, What a man does while asleep, against the moral law, is not imputed to him as a sin, as Augustine says. But this would not be the case if man, while asleep, had free use of his reason and intellect. Therefore the judgment of the intellect is hindered by suspension of the senses.

I answer that, As we have said above, our intellect's proper and proportionate object is the nature of a sensible thing. Now a perfect judgment concerning anything cannot be formed, unless all that pertains to that thing be known; especially if that be ignored which is the term and end of judgment. For the Philosopher says that *as the end of practical science is a work, so the end of the science of nature is that which is perceived principally through the senses*. For the smith does not seek the knowledge of a knife except for the purpose of producing this individual knife; and in like manner the natural philosopher does not seek to know the nature of a stone and of a horse, save for the purpose of knowing the essential properties of those things which he perceives with his senses. Now it is clear that a smith cannot judge perfectly of a knife unless he knows what making this particular knife means; and in like manner the natural philosopher cannot judge perfectly of natural things, unless he knows sensible things. But in the present state of life, whatever we understand we know by comparison with natural sensible things. Consequently it is not possible for our intellect to form a perfect judgment while the senses are suspended, through which sensible things are known to us.

Reply Obj. 1. Although the intellect is superior to the senses, nevertheless in a manner it receives from the senses, and its first and principal objects are founded in sensible things. Hence, suspension of the senses necessarily involves a hindrance to the judgment of the intellect.

Reply Obj. 2. The senses are suspended in the sleeper through certain evaporations and the escape of certain exhalations, as we read in *De Somno et Vigilia.* And, therefore, according to the disposition of such evaporation, the senses are more or less suspended. For when the movement of the vapors is very agitated, not only are the senses suspended, but also the imagination, so that there are no phantasms; as happens especially when a man falls asleep after much eating and drinking. If, however, the movement of the vapors be somewhat less violent, phantasms appear, but distorted and without sequence; as happens in a case of fever. And if the movement be still more attenuated, the phantasms will have a certain sequence; as happens especially towards the end of sleep, and in sober men and those who are gifted with a strong imagination. If the movement be very slight, not only does the imagination retain its freedom, but even the common sense is partly freed; so that sometimes while asleep a man may judge that what he sees is a dream, discerning, as it were, between things and their images. Nevertheless, the common sense remains partly suspended, and therefore, although it discriminates some images from reality, yet it is always deceived in some particular. Therefore, while a man is asleep, according as sense and imagination are free, so is the judgment of his intellect unfettered, though not entirely. Consequently, if a man syllogizes while asleep, when he wakes up he invariably recognizes a flaw in some respect. [. . .]

Question LXXXVIII
How the human soul knows what is above itself (in three articles)

We must now consider how the human soul knows what is above itself, viz., immaterial substances. Under this head there are three points of inquiry: (1) Whether the human soul in the present state of life can understand the immaterial substances, called angels, in themselves? (2) Whether it can arrive at the knowledge thereof by the knowledge of material things? (3) Whether God is the first object of our knowledge?

First Article
Whether the human soul in the present state of life can understand immaterial substances in themselves?

We proceed thus to the First Article:—

   Objection 1. It would seem that the human soul in the present state of life can understand immaterial substances in themselves. For Augustine says: *As the mind itself acquires the knowledge of corporeal things by means of the corporeal senses, so it gains through itself the knowledge of incorporeal things.* But these are the immaterial substances. Therefore the human mind understands immaterial substances.

Obj. 2. Further, like is known by like. But the human mind is more akin to immaterial than to material things; since its own nature is immaterial, as is clear from what we have said above. Since then our mind understands material things, much more is it able to understand immaterial things.

Obj. 3. Further, the fact that objects which are in themselves most eminently sensible are not most perceived by us, comes from the fact that sense is corrupted by their very excellence. But the intellect is not subject to such a corrupting influence from the excellence of its object, as is stated in *De Anima* iii. Therefore things which are in themselves in the highest degree of intelligibility are likewise to us most intelligible. Since material things, however, are intelligible only so far as we make them actually so, by abstracting them from material conditions, it is clear that those substances are more intelligible in themselves whose nature is immaterial. Therefore they are much more known to us than are material things.

Obj. 4. Further, the Commentator says that, *nature would be frustrated in its end* were we unable to understand abstract substances, *because it would have made what in itself is naturally intelligible not to be understood at all.* But in nature nothing is idle or purposeless. Therefore immaterial substances can be understood by us.

Obj. 5. Further, as the sense is to the sensible, so is the intellect to the intelligible. But our sight can see all things corporeal, whether superior and incorruptible, or sublunary and corruptible. Therefore our intellect can understand all intelligible substances, including the superior and immaterial.

On the contrary, It is written (*Wis.* ix. 16): *The things that are in heaven who shall search out?* But these substances are said to be in heaven, according to *Matthew* xviii. 10, *Their angels in heaven,* etc. Therefore immaterial substances cannot be known by human investigation.

I answer that, In the opinion of Plato, immaterial substances are not only understood by us, but are also the objects we understand first of all. For Plato taught that immaterial subsisting Forms, which he called *Ideas,* are the proper objects of our intellect, and are thus first and essentially understood by us. Furthermore, material things are known by the soul inasmuch as imagination and sense are joined to the intellect. Hence the purer the intellect is, so much the more clearly does it perceive the intelligible reality of immaterial things.

But in Aristotle's opinion, which experience corroborates, our intellect in its present state of life has a natural relation to the natures of material things; and therefore it can understand only by turning to the phantasms, as we have said above. Thus it clearly appears that immaterial substances, which do not fall under sense and imagination, cannot be known by us first and essentially, according to the mode of knowledge of which we have experience.

Nevertheless Averroes teaches that in this present life man can in the end arrive at the knowledge of separate substances by being joined or united to some separate substance, which he calls the *agent intellect*, and which, being a separate substance itself, can naturally understand separate substances. Hence, when it is perfectly united to us, so that through it we are able to understand perfectly, we too shall be able to understand separate substances; just as in the present life, through the possible intellect united to us, we can understand material things.

Now he said that the agent intellect is united to us as follows. For since we understand by means of both the agent intellect and intelligible objects (as, for instance, we understand conclusions by principles understood), the agent intellect must be compared to the objects understood, either as the principle agent is to the instrument, or as form to matter. For an action is ascribed to two principles in one of these two ways: to a principal agent and to an instrument, as cutting to the workman and the saw; to a form and its subject, as heating to heat and fire. In both these ways the agent intellect can be compared to the intelligible object as perfection is to the perfectible, and as act is to potentiality. Now a subject is made perfect and receives its perfection at one and the same time, as the reception of what is actually visible synchronizes with the reception of light in the eye. Therefore the possible intellect receives the intelligible object and the agent intellect together. And the more numerous the intelligible objects received, so much the nearer do we come to the point of perfect union between ourselves and the agent intellect; so much so, that when we shall have understood all the intelligible objects, the agent intellect will become perfectly united to us, and through it we shall understand all things material and immaterial. In this he makes the ultimate happiness of man to consist. Nor, as regards the present inquiry, does it matter whether the possible intellect in that state of happiness understands separate substances through the agent intellect, as he himself maintains, or whether (as he imputes to Alexander) the possible intellect can never understand separate substances (because according to him it is corruptible), but man understands separate substances through the agent intellect.

All this, however, is untrue. First, because, supposing the agent intellect to be a separate substance, we could not formally understand through it; for the formal medium of an agent's action is its form and act, since every agent acts according to its actuality, as was said of the possible intellect. Secondly, this opinion is untrue because the agent intellect, supposing it to be a separate substance, would not be joined to us in its substance, but only in its light, as participated in what we understood. But this would not extend to the other acts of the agent intellect so as to enable us to understand immaterial substances; just as when we see colors set off by the sun, we are not united to the substance of the sun so as to act like the sun, but only its light is united to us, that we may see the colors.

Thirdly, this opinion is untrue because, granted that, as was above explained, the agent intellect were united to us in substance, still it is not said that it is wholly united to us on the basis of one intelligible object, or two; but rather on the basis of all intelligible objects. But all such objects together do not equal the power of the agent intellect, as it is a much greater thing to understand separate substances than to understand all material things. Hence it clearly follows that the knowledge of all material things would not make the agent intellect to be so united to us as to enable us to understand separate substances through it.

Fourthly, this opinion is untrue because it is hardly possible for anyone in this world to understand all material things; and thus no one, or very few, would reach perfect felicity. This is against what the Philosopher says, that happiness is a *kind of common good, communicable to all capable of virtue*. Further, it is against reason that only the few of any species attain to the end of the species.

Fifthly, the Philosopher expressly says that happiness is *an operation according to perfect virtue;* and after enumerating many virtues in the tenth book of the *Ethics,* he concludes that ultimate happiness, consisting in the knowledge of the highest things intelligible, is attained through the virtue of *wisdom,* which in the sixth book he had named as *the chief of the speculative sciences*. Hence Aristotle clearly placed the ultimate felicity of man in that knowledge of separate substances which is obtainable by speculative science; and not in any union with the agent intellect, as some have imagined.

Sixthly, as was shown above, the agent intellect is not a separate substance, but a power of the soul, extending itself actively to the same objects to which the possible intellect extends receptively; because, as Aristotle states, the possible intellect is *all things potentially,* and the agent intellect is *all things in act*. Therefore both intellects, according to the present state of life, extend only to material things, which are made actually intelligible by the agent intellect, and are received in the possible intellect. Hence, in the present state of life, we cannot understand separate immaterial substances in themselves, either by the possible or by the agent intellect.

Reply Obj. I. Augustine may be taken to mean that the knowledge of incorporeal things in the mind can be gained through the mind itself. This is so true that philosophers also say that the knowledge concerning the soul is a principle for the knowledge of separate substances. For by knowing itself, the soul attains to some knowledge of incorporeal substances, such as is within its compass; not that the knowledge of itself gives it a perfect and absolute knowledge of them.

Reply Obj. 2. The likeness of nature is not a sufficient principle of knowledge. Otherwise, what Empedocles said would be true—that the soul needs to have the nature of all in order to know all. But knowledge requires that the likeness of the thing known be in the knower, as a kind of form in the knower. Now our possible intellect, in the present state of life, is such that it can be informed with the likeness abstracted from phantasms: and therefore it knows material things rather than immaterial substances.

Reply Obj. 3. There must needs be some proportion between the object and the power of knowledge; such as of the active to the passive, and of perfection to the perfectible. Hence that sensible objects of great excellence are not grasped by the senses is due not merely to the fact that they corrupt the organ, but also to their not being proportionate to the sensitive powers. And it is thus that immaterial substances are not proportionate to our intellect, in our present state of life, so that it cannot understand them.

Reply Obj. 4. This argument of the Commentator fails in several ways. First, because if separate substances are not understood by us, it does not follow that they are not understood by any intellect; for they are understood by themselves, and by one another.

Secondly, to be understood by us is not the end of separate substances and only that is vain and purposeless which fails to attain its end. It does not follow, therefore, that immaterial substances are purposeless, even if they are not at all understood by us.

Reply Obj. 5. Sense knows bodies, whether superior or inferior, in the same way, that is, by the sensible thing acting on the organ. But we do not understand material and immaterial substances in the same way. The former we understand by abstraction, which is impossible in the case of the latter, for there are no phantasms of what is immaterial.

[From *Summa Theologica*, ed. A. C. Pegis (New York: Random House, 1943), i. 808–11, 843–7.]

WILLIAM OF OCKHAM

17   On Universals

Since it is not sufficient merely to assert this without proving it by manifest reasoning, I shall advance a few reasons for what has been said above and I shall confirm by arguments from authority.

That a universal is not a substance existing outside the mind can in the first place be evidently proved as follows: No universal is a substance that is single and numerically one. For if that were supposed, it would follow that Socrates is a universal, since there is no stronger reason for one singular substance to be a universal than for another; therefore no singular substance is a universal, but every substance is numerically one and singular. For everything is either one thing and not many, or it is many things. If it is one and not many, it is numerically one. If, however, a substance is many things, it is either many singular things or many universal things. On the first supposition it follows that a substance would be several singular substances; for the same reason, then, some substance would be several men; and thus, although a universal would be distinguished from one particular thing, it would yet not be distinguished from particular things. If, however, a substance were several universal things, let us take one of these universal things and ask 'Is this one thing and not many, or is it many things?' If the first alternative is granted, then it follows that it is singular; if the second is granted, we have to ask again 'Is it many singular or many universal things?' And thus either this will go on *in infinitum*, or we must take the stand that no substance is universal in such a way that it is not singular. Hence, the only remaining alternative is that no substance is universal.

Furthermore, if a universal were one substance existing in singular things and distinct from them, it would follow that it could exist apart from them; for every thing naturally prior to another thing can exist apart from it by the power of God. But this consequence is absurd.

Furthermore, if that opinion were true, no individual could be created, but something of the individual would pre-exist; for it would not get its entire being from nothing, if the universal in it has existed before in another individual. For the same reason it would follow that God could not annihilate one individual of a substance, if He did not destroy the other individuals. For if He annihilated one individual, He would destroy the whole of the essence of the individual, and consequently he would destroy that universal which is in it and in others; consequently, the other individuals do not remain, since they cannot remain without a part of themselves, such as the universal is held to be.

Furthermore, we could not assume such a universal to be something entirely extrinsic to the essence of an individual; therefore, it would be of the essence of the individual, and consequently the individual would be composed of universals; and thus the individual would not be more singular than universal. [. . .]

From these and many other texts it is clear that a universal is a mental content of such nature as to be predicated of many things. [. . .]

[A universal is a thought-object]

[. . .] I maintain that a universal is not something real that exists in a subject [of inherence], either inside or outside the mind, but that it has being only as a thought-object in the mind. It is a kind of mental picture which as a thought-object has a being similar to that which the thing outside the mind has in its real existence. What I mean is this: The intellect, seeing a thing outside the mind, forms in the mind a picture resembling it, in such a way that if the mind had the power to produce as it has the power to picture, it would produce by this act a real outside thing which would be only numerically distinct from the former real thing. The case would be similar, analogously speaking, to the activity of an artist. For just as the artist who sees a house or building outside the mind first pictures in the mind a similar house and later produces a similar house in reality which is only numerically distinct from the first, so in our case the picture in the mind that we get from seeing something outside would act as a pattern. For just as the imagined house would be a pattern for the architect, if he who imagines it had the power to produce it in reality, so likewise the other picture would be a pattern for him who forms it. And this can be called a universal, because it is a pattern and relates indifferently to all the singular things outside the mind. Because of the similarity between its being as a thought-object and the being of like things outside the mind, it can stand for such things. And in this way a universal is not the result of generation, but of abstraction, which is only a kind of mental picturing.

I shall first show that something exists in the mind whose being is that of an object of thought only, without inhering in the mind as an independent subject.

This is clear from the following: According to the philosophers, existence is primarily divided into existence in the mind and existence outside the mind, the latter being subdivided into the ten categories. If this is admitted, then I ask 'What is understood here by "existence in the mind"?' It means either existence as a thought-object, and then we have our intended thesis, or it means existence as in a subject. The latter, however, is not possible; for, whatever exists truly in the mind as a subject, is contained under existence that is divided into the ten categories, since it falls under quality. For an act of intellect, and indeed in general every accident or form of the mind, is a true quality, like heat or whiteness, and hence does not fall under the division of existence that is set over against existence in the ten categories. [Consequently the main distinction of the philosophers would be futile.]

Furthermore, fictions have being in the mind, but they do not exist independently, because in that case they would be real things and so a chimera and a goat-stag and so on would be real things. So some things exist only as thought-objects.

Likewise, propositions, syllogisms, and other similar objects of logic do not exist independently; therefore they exist only as thought-objects, so that their being consists in being known. Consequently, there are beings which exist only as thought-objects.

Again, works of art do not seem to inhere in the mind of the craftsman as independent subjects any more than the creatures did in the divine mind before creation.

Likewise, conceptual relations are commonly admitted by the [scholastic] doctors. If this is conceded, then I ask 'Do they exist only in a subject?' In that case they will be genuine things and real relations. Or do they exist only as thought-objects? In that case we have our intended thesis.

Again, according to those who think differently, the term 'being' means a univocal concept, and nevertheless does not mean a distinct reality.

Likewise, practically all men distinguish second intentions from first intentions, and they do not call the second intentions real qualities of the mind. Since they are not in reality outside the mind, they can only exist as thought-objects in the mind.

Secondly, I maintain that this mental picture is what is primarily and immediately meant by the concept 'universal', and has the nature of a thought-object, and is that which is the immediate term of an act of intellection having no singular object. This mental picture, in the manner of being that a thought-object has, is just whatever the corresponding singular is, in the manner of being proper to a subject; and so by its very nature it can stand for the singulars of which it is in a way a likeness . . .

I maintain, therefore, that just as a spoken word is universal and is a genus or a species, but only by convention, in the same way the concept thus mentally fashioned and abstracted from singular things previously known is universal by its nature . . .

[From *Philosophical Writings*, trans. P. Boehner (Indianapolis: Bobbs-Merrill, 1964), 38–9, 44–6.]

THOMAS HOBBES
....

18 Of Man

Concerning the Thoughts of man, I will consider them first *Singly*, and afterwards in *Trayne*, or dependance upon one another. *Singly*, they are every one a *Representation* or *Apparence*, of some quality, or other Accident of a body without us; which is commonly called an *Object*. Which Object worketh on the Eyes, eares, and other parts of mans body; and by diversity of working, produceth diversity of apparences.

The Originall of them all, is that which we call SENSE; (For there is no conception in mans mind, which hath not at first, totally, or by parts, been begotten upon the organs of Sense). The rest are derived from that originall. [. . .]

The cause of Sense, is the Externall Body, or Object. [. . .]

There is no other act of mans mind, that I can remember, naturally planted in him, so, as to need no other thing, to the exercise of it, but to be born a man, and live with the use of his five Senses. Those other Faculties [. . .] which seem proper to man onely, are acquired, and encreased by study and industry; and of most men learned by instruction, and discipline; and proceed all from the invention of Words, and Speech. For besides Sense, and Thoughts, and the Trayne of thoughts, the mind of man has no other motion; though by the help of Speech, and Method, the same Facultyes may be improved to such a height, as to distinguish men from all other living Creatures.

[From *Leviathan* (1651), Part I, chs. 1–3, ed. C. B. Macpherson (Harmondsworth: Penguin Books, 1974).]

JOHN LOCKE

19   Of Ideas

1. *Idea is the object of thinking.* Every man being conscious to himself that he thinks; and that which his mind is applied about whilst thinking being the *ideas* that are there, it is past doubt that men have in their minds several ideas,—such as are those expressed by the words *whiteness, hardness, sweetness, thinking, motion, man, elephant, army, drunkenness,* and others: it is in the first place then to be inquired, *How he comes by them?*

I know it is a received doctrine, that men have native ideas, and original characters, stamped upon their minds in their very first being. This opinion I have at large examined already; and, I suppose what I have said in the foregoing Book will be much more easily admitted, when I have shown whence the understanding may get all the ideas it has; and by what ways and degrees they may come into the mind;—for which I shall appeal to every one's own observation and experience.

2. *All ideas come from sensation or reflection.* Let us then suppose the mind to be, as we say, white paper, void of all characters, without any ideas:—How comes it to be furnished? Whence comes it by that vast store which the busy and boundless fancy of man has painted on it with an almost endless variety? Whence has it all the *materials* of reason and knowledge? To this I answer, in one word, from EXPERIENCE. In that all our knowledge is founded; and from that it ultimately derives itself. Our observation employed either, about external sensible objects, or about the internal operations of our minds perceived and reflected on by ourselves, is that which supplies our understandings with all the *materials* of thinking. These two are the fountains of knowledge, from whence all the ideas we have, or can naturally have, do spring.

3. *The objects of sensation one source of ideas.* First, our Senses, conversant about particular sensible objects, do convey into the mind several distinct perceptions of things, according to those various ways wherein those objects do affect them. And thus we come by those *ideas* we have of *yellow, white, heat, cold, soft, hard, bitter, sweet,* and all those which we call sensible qualities; which when I say the senses convey into the mind, I mean, they from external objects convey into the mind what produces there those perceptions. This great source of most of the ideas we have, depending wholly upon our senses, and derived by them to the understanding, I call SENSATION.

4. *The operations of our minds, the other source of them.* Secondly, the other fountain from which experience furnisheth the understanding with ideas is,—the perception of the operations of our own mind within us, as it is employed about the ideas it has got;—which operations, when the soul comes to reflect on and consider, do furnish the understanding with another set of ideas, which could not be had from things without. And such are *perception, thinking, doubting, believing, reasoning, knowing, willing,* and all the different actings of our own minds;—which we being conscious of, and observing in ourselves, do from these receive into our understandings as distinct ideas as we do from bodies affecting our senses. This source of ideas every man has wholly in himself; and though it be not sense, as having nothing to do with external objects, yet it is very like it, and might properly enough be called *internal sense.* But as I call the other SENSATION, so I call this REFLECTION, the ideas it affords being such only as the mind gets by reflecting on its own operations within itself. By reflection then, in the following part of this discourse, I would be understood to mean, that notice which the mind takes of its own operations, and the manner of them, by reason whereof there come to be ideas of these operations in the understanding. These two, I say, viz. external material things, as the objects of SENSATION, and the operations of our own minds within, as the objects of REFLECTION, are to me the only originals from whence all our ideas take their beginnings. The term *operations* here I use in a large sense, as comprehending not barely the actions of the mind about its ideas, but some sort of passions arising sometimes from them, such as is the satisfaction or uneasiness arising from any thought.

5. *All our ideas are of the one or the other of these.* The understanding seems to me not to have the least glimmering of any ideas which it doth not receive from one of these two. *External objects* furnish the mind with the ideas of sensible qualities, which are all those different perceptions they produce in us; and *the mind* furnishes the understanding with ideas of its own operations.

These, when we have taken a full survey of them, and their several modes, combinations, and relations, we shall find to contain all our whole stock of ideas; and that we have nothing in our minds which did not come in one of these two ways. Let any one examine his own thoughts, and thoroughly search into his understanding; and then let him tell me, whether all the original ideas he has there, are any other than of the objects of his senses, or of the operations of his mind, considered as objects of his reflection. And how great a mass of knowledge soever he imagines to be lodged there, he will, upon taking a strict view, see that he has not any idea in his mind but what one of these two have imprinted;—though perhaps, with infinite variety compounded and enlarged by the understanding, as we shall see hereafter.

6. *Observable in children.* He that attentively considers the state of a child, at his first coming into the world, will have little reason to think him stored with plenty of ideas, that are to be the matter of his future knowledge. It is *by degrees* he comes to be furnished with them. And though the ideas of obvious and familiar qualities imprint themselves before the memory begins to keep a register of time or order, yet it is often so late before some unusual qualities come in the way, that there are few men that cannot recollect the beginning of their acquaintance with them. And if it were worth while, no doubt a child might be so ordered as to have but a very few, even of the ordinary ideas, till he were grown up to a man. But all that are born into the world, being surrounded with bodies that perpetually and diversely affect them, variety of ideas, whether care be taken of it or not, are imprinted on the minds of children. Light and colours are busy at hand everywhere, when the eye is but open; sounds and some tangible qualities fail not to solicit their proper senses, and force an entrance to the mind;—but yet, I think, it will be granted easily, that if a child were kept in a place where he never saw any other but black and white till he were a man, he would have no more ideas of scarlet or green, than he that from his childhood never tasted an oyster, or a pine-apple, has of those particular relishes.

7. *Men are differently furnished with these, according to the different objects they converse with.* Men then come to be furnished with fewer or more simple ideas from without, according as the objects they converse with afford greater or less variety; and from the operations of their minds within, according as they more or less reflect on them. For, though he that contemplates the operations of his mind, cannot but have plain and clear ideas of them; yet, unless he turn his thoughts that way, and considers them *attentively*, he will no more have clear and distinct ideas of all the operations of his mind, and all that may be observed therein, than he will have all the particular ideas of any landscape, or of the parts and motions of a clock, who will not turn his eyes to it, and with attention heed all the parts of it. The picture, or clock may be so placed, that they may come in his way every day; but yet he will have but a confused idea of all the parts they are made up of, till he applies himself with attention, to consider them each in particular.

8. *Ideas of reflection later, because they need attention.* And hence we see the reason why it is pretty late before most children get ideas of the operations of

their own minds; and some have not any very clear or perfect ideas of the greatest part of them all their lives. Because, though they pass there continually, yet, like floating visions, they make not deep impressions enough to leave in their mind clear, distinct, lasting ideas, till the understanding turns inward upon itself, reflects on its own operations, and makes them the objects of its own contemplation. Children when they come first into it, are surrounded with a world of new things, which, by a constant solicitation of their senses, draw the mind constantly to them; forward to take notice of new, and apt to be delighted with the variety of changing objects. Thus the first years are usually employed and diverted in looking abroad. Men's business in them is to acquaint themselves with what is to be found without; and so growing up in a constant attention to outward sensations, seldom make any considerable reflection on what passes within them, till they come to be of riper years; and some scarce ever at all.

9. *The soul begins to have ideas when it begins to perceive.* To ask, at what *time* a man has first any ideas, is to ask, when he begins to perceive;—*having ideas*, and *perception*, being the same thing. I know it is an opinion, that the soul always thinks and that it has the actual perception of ideas in itself constantly, as long as it exists; and that actual thinking is as inseparable from the soul as actual extension is from the body; which if true, to inquire after the beginning of a man's ideas is the same as to inquire after the beginning of his soul. For, by this account, soul and its ideas, as body and its extension, will begin to exist both at the same time.

[From *An Essay Concerning Human Understanding*, ed. A. C. Fraser, 2 vols. (New York: Dover Books, 1704; 1st edn. 1690), 121–3.]

JOHN LOCKE

20 Of General Terms

15. But since the essences of things are thought by some (and not without reason) to be wholly unknown, it may not be amiss to consider the several significations of the word *essence*.

First, Essence may be taken for the very being of anything, whereby it is what it is. And thus the real internal, but generally (in substances) unknown constitution of things, whereon their discoverable qualities depend, may be called their essence. This is the proper original signification of the word, as is evident from the formation of it; *essentia*, in its primary notation, signifying properly, being. And in this sense it is still used, when we speak of the essence of *particular* things, without giving them any name.

Secondly, The learning and disputes of the schools having been much busied about *genus* and *species*, the word *essence* has almost lost its primary signification: and, instead of the real constitution of things, has been almost wholly applied to the artificial constitution of *genus* and *species*. It is true, there is ordinarily supposed a real constitution of the sorts of things; and it is past doubt there must be some real constitution, on which any collection of simple ideas co-existing must depend. But, it being evident that things are ranked under names into sorts or species, only as they agree to certain abstract ideas, to which we have annexed those names, the essence of each *genus*, or sort, comes to be nothing but that abstract idea which the general, or sortal (if I may have leave so to call it from sort, as I do general from genus,) name stands for. And this we shall find to be that which the word essence imports in its most familiar use.

These two sorts of essences, I suppose, may not unfitly be termed, the one the *real*, the other *nominal essence*.

16. Between the *nominal essence* and the *name* there is so near a connexion, that the name of any sort of things cannot be attributed to any particular being but what has this essence, whereby it answers that abstract idea whereof that name is the sign.

17. Concerning the *real essences* of corporeal substances (to mention these only) there are, if I mistake not, two opinions. The one is of those who, using the word essence for they know not what, suppose a certain number of those essences, according to which all natural things are made, and wherein they do exactly every one of them partake, and so become of this or that species. The other and more rational opinion is of those who look on all natural things to have a real, but unknown, constitution of their insensible parts; from which flow those sensible qualities which serve us to distinguish them one from another, according as we have occasion to rank them into sorts, under common denominations. The former of these opinions, which supposes these essences as a certain number of forms or moulds, wherein all natural things that exist are cast, and do equally partake, has, I imagine, very much perplexed the knowledge of natural things. The frequent productions of monsters, in all the species of animals, and of changelings, and other strange issues of human birth, carry with them difficulties, not possible to consist with this hypothesis; since it is as impossible that two things partaking exactly of the same real essence should have different properties, as that two figures partaking of the same real essence of a circle should have different properties. But were there no other reason against it, yet the supposition of essences that cannot be known; and the making of them, nevertheless, to be that which distinguishes the species of things, is so wholly useless and unserviceable to any part of our knowledge, that that alone were sufficient to make us lay it by, and content ourselves with such essences of the sorts or species of things as come within the reach of our knowledge: which, when seriously considered, will be found, as I have said,

to be nothing else but, those *abstract* complex ideas to which we have annexed distinct general names.

[From *An Essay Concerning Human Understanding*, ed. A. C. Fraser, 2 vols. (New York: Dover Books, 1704; 1st edn. 1690), ii. 25–8.]

DAVID HUME

21   An Enquiry Concerning Human Understanding

Sect. II. Of the Origin of Ideas

12. [. . .] we may divide all the perceptions of the mind into two classes or species, which are distinguished by their different degrees of force and vivacity. The less forcible and lively are commonly denominated *Thoughts* or *Ideas*. The other species want a name in our language, and in most others; I suppose, because it was not requisite for any, but philosophical purposes, to rank them under a general term or appellation. Let us, therefore, use a little freedom, and call them *Impressions*; employing that word in a sense somewhat different from the usual. By the term *impression*, then, I mean all our more lively perceptions, when we hear, or see, or feel, or love, or hate, or desire, or will. And impressions are distinguished from ideas, which are the less lively perceptions, of which we are conscious, when we reflect on any of those sensations or movements above mentioned.

13. Nothing, at first view, may seem more unbounded than the thought of man, which not only escapes all human power and authority, but is not even restrained within the limits of nature and reality. To form monsters, and join incongruous shapes and appearances, costs the imagination no more trouble than to conceive the most natural and familiar objects. And while the body is confined to one planet, along which it creeps with pain and difficulty; the thought can in an instant transport us into the most distant regions of the universe; or even beyond the universe, into the unbounded chaos, where nature is supposed to lie in total confusion. What never was seen, or heard of, may yet be conceived; nor is any thing beyond the power of thought, except what implies an absolute contradiction.

But though our thought seems to possess this unbounded liberty, we shall find, upon a nearer examination, that it is really confined within very narrow limits, and that all this creative power of the mind amounts to no more than the faculty of compounding, transposing, augmenting, or diminishing the materials afforded us by the senses and experience. When we think of a golden mountain, we only join two consistent ideas, *gold*, and *mountain*, with which we were formerly acquainted. A virtuous horse we can conceive; because, from our own feeling, we can conceive virtue; and this we may unite to the figure and shape of a horse, which is an animal familiar to us. In short, all the materials of thinking are derived either from our outward or inward sentiment: the mixture and composition of these belongs alone to the mind and will. Or, to express myself in philosophical language, all our ideas or more feeble perceptions are copies of our impressions or more lively ones.

14. To prove this, the two following arguments will, I hope, be sufficient. First, when we analyze our thoughts or ideas, however compounded or sublime, we always find that they resolve themselves into such simple ideas as were copied from a precedent feeling or sentiment. Even those ideas, which, at first view, seem the most wide of this origin, are found, upon a nearer scrutiny, to be derived from it. The idea of God, as meaning an infinitely intelligent, wise, and good Being, arises from reflecting on the operations of our own mind, and augmenting, without limit, those qualities of goodness and wisdom. We may prosecute this enquiry to what length we please; where we shall always find, that every idea which we examine is copied from a similar impression. Those who would assert that this position is not universally true nor without exception, have only one, and that an easy method of refuting it; by producing that idea, which, in their opinion, is not derived from this source. It will then be incumbent on us, if we would maintain our doctrine, to produce the impression, or lively perception, which corresponds to it.

15. Secondly. If it happen, from a defect of the organ, that a man is not susceptible of any species of sensation, we always find that he is as little susceptible of the correspondent ideas. A blind man can form no notion of colours; a deaf man of sounds. Restore either of them that sense in which he is deficient; by opening this new inlet for his sensations, you also open an inlet for the ideas; and he finds no difficulty in conceiving these objects. The case is the same, if the object, proper for exciting any sensation, has never been applied to the organ. A Laplander or Negro has no notion of the relish of wine. And though there are few or no instances of a like deficiency in the mind, where a person has never felt or is wholly incapable of a sentiment or passion that belongs to his species; yet we find the same observation to take place in a less degree. A man of mild manners can form no idea of inveterate revenge or cruelty; nor can a selfish heart easily conceive the heights of friendship and generosity. It is readily allowed, that other beings may possess many senses of which we can have no conception; because the ideas of them have never been introduced to us in the only manner by which an idea can have access to the mind, to wit, by the actual feeling and sensation.

16. There is, however, one contradictory phenomenon, which may prove that it is not absolutely impossible for ideas to arise, independent of their correspondent impressions. I believe it will readily be allowed, that the several distinct ideas of colour, which enter by the eye, or those of sound, which are conveyed by the ear, are really different from each other; though,

at the same time, resembling. Now if this be true of different colours, it must be no less so of the different shades of the same colour; and each shade produces a distinct idea, independent of the rest. For if this should be denied, it is possible, by the continual gradation of shades, to run a colour insensibly into what is most remote from it; and if you will not allow any of the means to be different, you cannot, without absurdity, deny the extremes to be the same. Suppose, therefore, a person to have enjoyed his sight for thirty years, and to have become perfectly acquainted with colours of all kinds except one particular shade of blue, for instance, which it never has been his fortune to meet with. Let all the different shades of that colour, except that single one, be placed before him, descending gradually from the deepest to the lightest; it is plain that he will perceive a blank, where that shade is wanting, and will be sensible that there is a greater distance in that place between the contiguous colours than in any other. Now I ask, whether it be possible for him, from his own imagination, to supply this deficiency, and raise up to himself the idea of that particular shade, though it had never been conveyed to him by his senses? I believe there are few but will be of opinion that he can: and this may serve as a proof that the simple ideas are not always, in every instance, derived from the correspondent impressions; though this instance is so singular, that it is scarcely worth our observing, and does not merit that for it alone we should alter our general maxim.

17. Here, therefore, is a proposition, which not only seems, in itself, simple and intelligible; but, if a proper use were made of it, might render every dispute equally intelligible, and banish all that jargon, which has so long taken possession of metaphysical reasonings, and drawn disgrace upon them. All ideas, especially abstract ones, are naturally faint and obscure: the mind has but a slender hold of them: they are apt to be confounded with other resembling ideas; and when we have often employed any term, though without a distinct meaning, we are apt to imagine it has a determinate idea annexed to it. On the contrary, all impressions, that is, all sensations, either outward or inward, are strong and vivid: the limits between them are more exactly determined: nor is it easy to fall into any error or mistake with regard to them. When we entertain, therefore, any suspicion that a philosophical term is employed without any meaning or idea (as is but too frequent), we need but enquire, *from what impression is that supposed idea derived?* And if it be impossible to assign any, this will serve to confirm our suspicion. By bringing ideas into so clear a light we may reasonably hope to remove all dispute, which may arise, concerning their nature and reality.

Sect. III. Of the Association of Ideas

18. It is evident that there is a principle of connexion between the different thoughts or ideas of the mind, and that, in their appearance to the memory or

imagination, they introduce each other with a certain degree of method and regularity. In our more serious thinking or discourse this is so observable that any particular thought, which breaks in upon the regular tract or chain of ideas, is immediately remarked and rejected. And even in our wildest and most wandering reveries, nay in our very dreams, we shall find, if we reflect, that the imagination ran not altogether at adventures, but that there was still a connexion upheld among the different ideas, which succeeded each other. Were the loosest and freest conversation to be transcribed, there would immediately be observed something which connected it in all its transitions. Or where this is wanting, the person who broke the thread of discourse might still inform you, that there had secretly revolved in his mind a succession of thought, which had gradually led him from the subject of conversation. Among different languages, even where we cannot suspect the least connexion or communication, it is found, that the words, expressive of ideas, the most compounded, do yet nearly correspond to each other: a certain proof that the simple ideas, comprehended in the compound ones, were bound together by some universal principle, which had an equal influence on all mankind.

19. Though it be too obvious to escape observation, that different ideas are connected together; I do not find that any philosopher has attempted to enumerate or class all the principles of association; a subject, however, that seems worthy of curiosity. To me, there appear to be only three principles of connexion among ideas, namely, *Resemblance*, *Contiguity* in time or place, and *Cause and Effect*.

That these principles serve to connect ideas will not, I believe, be much doubted. A picture naturally leads our thoughts to the original: the mention of one apartment in a building naturally introduces an enquiry or discourse concerning the others: and if we think of a wound, we can scarcely forbear reflecting on the pain which follows it. But that this enumeration is complete, and that there are no other principles of association except these, may be difficult to prove to the satisfaction. All we can do, in such cases, is to run over several instances, and examine carefully the principle which binds the different thoughts to each other, never stopping till we render the principle as general as possible. The more instances we examine, and the more care we employ, the more assurance shall we acquire, that the enumeration, which we form from the whole, is complete and entire.

Sect. IV. Sceptical Doubts concerning the Operations of the Understanding

20. All the objects of human reason or enquiry may naturally be divided into two kinds, to wit, *Relations of Ideas*, and *Matters of Fact*. Of the first kind are the sciences of Geometry, Algebra, and Arithmetic; and in short, every

affirmation which is either intuitively or demonstratively certain. *That the square of the hypothenuse is equal to the square of the two sides*, is a proposition which expresses a relation between these figures. *That three times five is equal to the half of thirty*, expresses a relation between these numbers. Propositions of this kind are discoverable by the mere operation of thought, without dependence on what is anywhere existent in the universe. Though there never were a circle or triangle in nature, the truths demonstrated by Euclid would for ever retain their certainty and evidence.

21. Matters of fact, which are the second objects of human reason, are not ascertained in the same manner; nor is our evidence of their truth, however great, of a like nature with the foregoing. The contrary of every matter of fact is still possible; because it can never imply a contradiction, and is conceived by the mind with the same facility and distinctness, as if ever so conformable to reality. *That the sun will not rise tomorrow* is no less intelligible a proposition, and implies no more contradiction than the affirmation, *that it will rise*. We should in vain, therefore, attempt to demonstrate its falsehood. Were it demonstratively false, it would imply a contradiction, and could never be distinctly conceived by the mind.

It may, therefore, be a subject worthy of curiosity, to enquire what is the nature of that evidence which assures us of any real existence and matter of fact, beyond the present testimony of our senses, or the records of our memory. This part of philosophy, it is observable, has been little cultivated, either by the ancients or moderns; and therefore our doubts and errors, in the prosecution of so important an enquiry, may be the more excusable; while we march through such difficult paths without any guide or direction. They may even prove useful, by exciting curiosity, and destroying that implicit faith and security, which is the bane of all reasoning and free enquiry. The discovery of defects in the common philosophy, if any such there be, will not, I presume, be a discouragement, but rather an incitement, as is usual, to attempt something more full and satisfactory than has yet been proposed to the public.

22. All reasonings concerning matter of fact seem to be founded on the relation of *Cause and Effect*. By means of that relation alone we can go beyond the evidence of our memory and senses. If you were to ask a man, why he believes any matter of fact, which is absent; for instance, that his friend is in the country, or in France; he would give you a reason; and this reason would be some other fact; as a letter received from him, or the knowledge of his former resolutions and promises. A man finding a watch or any other machine in a desert island, would conclude that there had once been men in that island. All our reasonings concerning fact are of the same nature. And here it is constantly supposed that there is a connexion between the present fact and that which is inferred from it. Were there nothing to bind them together, the inference would be entirely precarious. The hearing of an

articulate voice and rational discourse in the dark assures us of the presence of some person: Why? because these are the effects of the human make and fabric, and closely connected with it. If we anatomize all the other reasonings of this nature, we shall find that they are founded on the relation of cause and effect, and that this relation is either near or remote, direct or collateral. Heat and light are collateral effects of fire, and the one effect may justly be inferred from the other.

23. If we would satisfy ourselves, therefore, concerning the nature of that evidence, which assures us of matters of fact, we must enquire how we arrive at the knowledge of cause and effect.

I shall venture to affirm, as a general proposition, which admits of no exception, that the knowledge of this relation is not, in any instance, attained by reasonings *a priori*; but arises entirely from experience, when we find that any particular objects are constantly conjoined with each other. Let an object be presented to a man of ever so strong natural reason and abilities; if that object be entirely new to him, he will not be able, by the most accurate examination of its sensible qualities, to discover any of its causes or effects. Adam, though his rational faculties be supposed, at the very first, entirely perfect, could not have inferred from the fluidity and transparency of water that it would suffocate him, or from the light and warmth of fire that it would consume him. No object ever discovers, by the qualities which appear to the senses, either the causes which produced it, or the effects which will arise from it; nor can our reason, unassisted by experience, ever draw any inference concerning real existence and matter of fact.

24. This proposition, *that causes and effects are discoverable, not by reason but by experience*, will readily be admitted with regard to such objects, as we remember to have once been altogether unknown to us; since we must be conscious of the utter inability, which we then lay under, of foretelling what would arise from them. Present two smooth pieces of marble to a man who has no tincture of natural philosophy; he will never discover that they will adhere together in such a manner as to require great force to separate them in a direct line, while they make so small a resistance to a lateral pressure. Such events, as bear little analogy to the common course of nature, are also readily confessed to be known only by experience; nor does any man imagine that the explosion of gunpowder, or the attraction of a loadstone, could ever be discovered by arguments *a priori*. In like manner, when an effect is supposed to depend upon an intricate machinery or secret structure of parts, we make no difficulty in attributing all our knowledge of it to experience. Who will assert that he can give the ultimate reason, why milk or bread is proper nourishment for a man, not for a lion or a tiger?

But the same truth may not appear, at first sight, to have the same evidence with regard to events, which have become familiar to us from our first appearance in the world, which bear a close analogy to the whole course of nature, and which are supposed to depend on the simple qualities of objects, without any secret structure of parts. We are apt to imagine that we could discover these effects by the mere operation of our reason, without experience. We fancy, that were we brought on a sudden into this world, we could at first have inferred that one billiard-ball would communicate motion to another upon impulse; and that we needed not to have waited for the event, in order to pronounce with certainty concerning it. Such is the influence of custom, that, where it is strongest, it not only covers our natural ignorance, but even conceals itself, and seems not to take place, merely because it is found in the highest degree.

25. But to convince us that all the laws of nature, and all the operations of bodies without exception, are known only by experience, the following reflections may, perhaps, suffice. Were any object presented to us, and were we required to pronounce concerning the effect, which will result from it, without consulting past observation; after what manner, I beseech you, must the mind proceed in this operation? It must invent or imagine some event, which it ascribes to the object as its effect; and it is plain that this invention must be entirely arbitrary. The mind can never possibly find the effect in the supposed cause, by the most accurate scrutiny and examination. For the effect is totally different from the cause, and consequently can never be discovered in it. Motion in the second billiard-ball is a quite distinct event from motion in the first; nor is there anything in the one to suggest the smallest hint of the other. A stone or piece of metal raised into the air, and left without any support, immediately falls: but to consider the matter *a priori*, is there anything we discover in the situation which can beget the idea of a downward, rather than an upward, or any other motion, in the stone or metal?

And as the first imagination or invention of a particular effect, in all natural operations, is arbitrary, where we consult not experience; so must we also esteem the supposed tie or connexion between the cause and effect, which binds them together, and renders it impossible that any other effect could result from the operation of that cause. When I see, for instance, a billiard-ball moving in a straight line towards another; even suppose motion in the second ball should by accident be suggested to me, as the result of their contact or impulse; may I not conceive, that a hundred different events might as well follow from that cause? May not both these balls remain at absolute rest? May not the first ball return in a straight line, or leap off from the second in any line or direction? All these suppositions are consistent and conceivable. Why then should we give the preference to one, which is no more consistent or conceivable than the rest? All our reasonings *a priori* will never be able to show us any foundation for this preference.

In a word, then, every effect is a distinct event from its cause. It could not, therefore, be discovered in the cause, and the first invention or conception of it, *a priori*, must be entirely arbitrary. And even after it is suggested, the conjunction of it with the cause must appear equally arbitrary; since there are always many other effects, which, to reason, must seem fully as consistent and natural. In vain, therefore, should we pretend to determine any single event, or infer any cause or effect, without the assistance of observation and experience.

26. Hence we may discover the reason why no philosopher, who is rational and modest, has ever pretended to assign the ultimate cause of any natural operation, or to show distinctly the action of that power, which produces any single effect in the universe. It is confessed, that the utmost effort of human reason is to reduce the principles, productive of natural phenomena, to a greater simplicity, and to resolve the many particular effects into a few general causes, by means of reasonings from analogy, experience, and observation. But as to the causes of these general causes, we should in vain attempt their discovery; nor shall we ever be able to satisfy ourselves, by any particular explication of them. These ultimate springs and principles are totally shut up from human curiosity and enquiry. Elasticity, gravity, cohesion of parts, communication of motion by impulse; these are probably the ultimate causes and principles which we shall ever discover in nature; and we may esteem ourselves sufficiently happy, if, by accurate enquiry and reasoning, we can trace up the particular phenomena to, or near to, these general principles. The most perfect philosophy of the natural kind only staves off our ignorance a little longer: as perhaps the most perfect philosophy of the moral or metaphysical kind serves only to discover larger portions of it. Thus the observation of human blindness and weakness is the result of all philosophy, and meets us at every turn, in spite of our endeavours to elude or avoid it.

27. Nor is geometry, when taken into the assistance of natural philosophy, ever able to remedy this defect, or lead us into the knowledge of ultimate causes, by all that accuracy of reasoning for which it is so justly celebrated. Every part of mixed mathematics proceeds upon the supposition that certain laws are established by nature in her operations; and abstract reasonings are employed, either to assist experience in the discovery of these laws, or to determine their influence in particular instances, where it depends upon any precise degree of distance and quantity. Thus, it is a law of motion, discovered by experience, that the moment or force of any body in motion is in the compound ratio or proportion of its solid contents and its velocity; and consequently, that a small force may remove the greatest obstacle or raise the greatest weight, if, by any contrivance or machinery, we can increase the velocity of that force, so as to make it an overmatch for its antagonist. Geometry assists us in the application of this law, by giving us the just dimensions of all the parts and figures which can enter into any species of machine; but still the discovery of the law itself is owing merely to

experience, and all the abstract reasonings in the world could never lead us one step towards the knowledge of it. When we reason *a priori*, and consider merely any object or cause, as it appears to the mind, independent of all observation, it never could suggest to us the notion of any distinct object, such as its effect; much less, show us the inseparable and inviolable connexion between them. A man must be very sagacious who could discover by reasoning that crystal is the effect of heat, and ice of cold, without being previously acquainted with the operation of these qualities.

[From *An Enquiry Concerning Human Understanding*, Part I, sects. ii–iv, ed. L. A. Selby-Bigge (Oxford: Oxford University Press, 1748), 455–60.]

THOMAS REID

22   An Inquiry into the Human Mind

The fabric of the human mind is curious and wonderful, as well as that of the human body. The faculties of the one are with no less wisdom adapted to their several ends, than the organs of the other. Nay, it is reasonable to think, that as the mind is a nobler work, and of a higher order than the body, even more of the wisdom and skill of the Divine Architect hath been employed in its structure. It is therefore a subject highly worthy on account of the extensive influence which the knowledge of it hath over every other branch of science.

In the arts and sciences which have least connection with the mind, its faculties are the engines which we must employ: and the better we understand their nature and use, their defeets and disorders, the more skilfully we shall apply them, and with the greater success. But in the noblest arts, the mind is also the subject upon which we operate. The painter, the poet, the actor, the orator, the moralist, and the statesman attempt to operate upon the mind in different ways, and for different ends; and they succeed, according as they touch properly the strings of the human frame. Nor can their several arts ever stand on a solid foundation, or rise to the dignity of science, until they are built on the principles of the human constitution.

Wise men now agree, or ought to agree in this, that there is but one way to the knowledge of nature's works; the way of observation and experiment. By our constitution, we have a strong propensity to trace particular facts and observations to general rules, and to apply such general rules to account for other effects, or to direct us in the production of them. This procedure of the understanding is familiar to every human creature in the common affairs of life, and it is the only one by which any real discovery in philosophy can be made.

The man who first discovered that cold freezes water, and that heat turns it into vapour, proceeded on the same general principles, and in the same method, by which Newton discovered the law of gravitation, and the properties of light. His *regulæ philosophandi* are maxims of common sense, and are practised every day in common life; and he who philosophizes by other rules, either concerning the material system, or concerning the mind, mistakes his aim.

Conjectures and theories are the creatures of men, and will always be found very unlike the creatures of God. If we would know the works of God, we must consult themselves with attention and humility, without daring to add any thing of ours to what they declare. A just interpretation of nature is the only sound and orthodox philosophy: whatever we add of our own, is apocryphal, and of no authority.

All our curious theories of the formation of the earth, of the generation of animals, of the origin of natural and moral evil, so far as they go beyond a just induction from facts, are vanity and folly, no less than the vortices of Des Cartes, or the Archæus of Paracelsus. Perhaps the philosophy of the mind has been no less adulterated by theories than that of the material system. The theory of ideas is indeed very ancient, and hath been very universally received; but as neither of these titles can give it authenticity, they ought not to screen it from a free and candid examination; especially in this age, when it hath produced a system of skepticism, that seems to triumph over all science, and even over the dictates of common sense.

All that we know of the body, is owing to anatomical dissection and observation, and it must be by anatomy of the mind that we can discover its powers and principles. [. . .]

If there are certain principles, as I think there are, which the constitution of our nature leads us to believe, and which we are under a necessity to take for granted in the common concerns of life, without being able to give a reason for them; these are what we call the principles of common sense; and what is manifestly contrary to them, is what we call absurd.

Indeed, if it is true, and to be received as a principle of philosophy, that sensation and thought may be without a thinking being; it must be acknowledged to be the most wonderful discovery that this or any other age hath produced. The received doctrine of ideas is the principle from which it is deduced, and of which indeed it seems to be a just and natural consequence. And it is probable that it would not have been so late a discovery, but that it is so shocking and repugnant to the common apprehensions of mankind, that it required an uncommon degree of philosophical intrepidity to usher it into the world. It is a fundamental principle of the ideal system, that every object of thought must be an impression, or an idea, that is, a faint copy of some preceding impression. This is a principle so commonly received, that the author above mentioned, although his whole system is built upon it; never offers the least proof of it. It is upon this principle, as a fixed point, that he erects his metaphysical engines, to overturn heaven and earth, body and spirit. And indeed, in my apprehension, it is altogether sufficient for the purpose. For if impressions and ideas are the only objects of thought, then heaven and earth, and body and spirit, and every thing you please, must signify only impressions and ideas, or they must be words without any meaning. It seems, therefore, that this notion, however strange, is closely connected with the received doctrine of ideas, and we must either admit the conclusion, or call in question the premises.

Ideas seem to have something in their nature unfriendly to other existences. They were first introduced into philosophy, in the humble character of images or representatives of things; and in this character they seemed not only to be inoffensive, but to serve admirably well for explaining the operation of the human understanding. But since men began to reason clearly and distinctly about them, they have by degrees supplanted their constituents, and undermined the existence of every thing but themselves. First, they discarded all secondary qualities of bodies; and it was found out by their means, that fire is not hot, nor snow cold, nor honey sweet; and, in a word, that heat and cold, sound, colour, taste, and smell, are nothing but ideas or impressions. Bishop Berkeley advanced them a step higher, and found out, by just reasoning, from the same principles, that extension, solidity, space, figure, and body, are ideas, and that there is nothing in nature but ideas and spirits. But the triumph of ideas was completed by the Treatise of Human Nature, which discards spirits also, and leaves ideas and impressions as the sole existences in the universe. What if at last, having nothing else to contend with, they should fall foul of one another, and leave no existence in nature at all? This would surely bring philosophy into danger; for what should we have left to talk or to dispute about? However, hitherto these philosophers acknowledge the existence of impressions and ideas; they acknowledge certain laws of attraction, or rules of precedence, according to which ideas and impressions range themselves in various forms, and succeed one another: but that they should belong to a mind, as its proper goods and chattels, this they have found to be a vulgar error. These ideas are as free and independent as the birds of the air, or as Epicurus's atoms when they pursued their journey in the vast inane. Shall we conceive them like the films of things in the Epicurean system? [. . .]

There is no phenomenon in nature more unaccountable, than the intercourse that is carried on between the mind and the external world: there is no phenomenon which philosophical spirits have shown greater avidity to pry into and to resolve. It is agreed by all, that this intercourse is carried on by means of the senses; and this satisfies the vulgar curiosity, but not the philosophic. Philosophers must have some system, some hypothesis, that shews the manner in which our senses make us acquainted with external things. All the fertility of human invention seems to have produced only one hypothesis for this purpose, which therefore hath been universally received: and that is, that the mind, like a mirror, receives the images of things from without, by means of the senses: so that their use must be to convey these images into the mind.

Whether to these images of external things in the mind, we give the name of *sensible forms* or *sensible species*, with the Peripatetics, or the name *of ideas of sensation*, with Locke; or whether, with later philosophers, we distinguish *sensations*, which are immediately conveyed by the senses, from *ideas of sensation*, which are faint copies of our sensations retained in the memory and imagination; these are only differences about words. The hypothesis I have mentioned is common to all these different systems.

The necessary and allowed consequence of this hypothesis is, that no material thing, nor any quality of material things, can be conceived by us or made an object of thought, until its image is conveyed to the mind by means of the senses. We shall examine this hypothesis particularly afterward, and at this time only observe, that, in consequence of it, one would naturally expect, that to every quality and attribute of body we know or can conceive, there should be a sensation corresponding, which is the image and resemblance of that quality; and that the sensations which have no similitude or resemblance to body, or to any of its qualities, should give us no conception of a material world, or of any thing belonging to it. These things might be expected as the natural consequences of the hypothesis we have mentioned.

Now we have considered, in this and the preceding chapters, extension, figure, solidity, motion, hardness, roughness, as well as colour, heat and cold, sound, taste, and smell. We have endeavoured to show, that our nature and constitution lead us to conceive these as qualities of body, as all mankind have always conceived them to be. We have likewise examined, with great attention, the various sensations we have by means of the five senses, and are not able to find among them all, one single image of body, or of any of its qualities. From whence then come those images of body and of its qualities into the mind? Let philosophers resolve this question. All I can say is, that they come not by the senses. I am sure that by proper attention and care I may know my sensations, and be able to affirm with certainty what they resemble, and what they do not resemble. I have examined them one by one, and compared them with matter and its qualities; and I cannot find one of them that confesses a resembling feature.

A truth so evident as this, that our sensations are not images of matter, or of any of its qualities, ought not to yield to a hypothesis such as that above mentioned, however ancient, or however universally received by philosophers; nor can there be any amicable union between the two: This will appear by some reflections upon the spirit of the ancient and modern philosophy concerning sensation.

During the reign of the Peripatetic philosophy, our sensations were not minutely or accurately examined. The attention of philosophers, as well as of the vulgar, was turned to the things signified by them: therefore, in consequence of the common hypothesis, it was taken for granted, that all the sensations we have from external things, are the forms or images of these external things. And thus the truth we have mentioned, yielded entirely to the hypothesis, and was altogether suppressed by it.

Des Cartes gave a noble example of turning our attention inward, and scrutinizing our sensations, and this example hath been very worthily followed by modern philosophers, particularly by Malebranche, Locke, Berkeley, and Hume. The effect of this scrutiny hath been a gradual discovery of the truth above mentioned, to wit, the dissimilitude between the sensations of our minds, and the qualities or attributes of an insentient inert substance, such as we conceive matter to be. But this valuable and useful discovery, in its different stages, hath still been unhappily united to the ancient hypothesis; and, from this inauspicious match of opinions, so unfriendly and discordant in their natures, have arisen those monsters of paradox and skepticism with which the modern philosophy is too justly chargeable.

Locke saw clearly, and proved incontestably, that the sensations we have by taste, smell, and hearing, as well as the sensations of colour, heat and cold, are not resemblances of any thing in bodies; and in this he agrees with Des Cartes and Malebranche. Joining this opinion with the hypothesis, it follows necessarily, that three senses of the five are cut off from giving us any intelligence of the material world, as being altogether inept for that office. Smell, and taste, and sound, as well as well as colour and heat, can have no more relation to body, than anger or gratitude; nor ought the former to be called qualities of body, whether primary or secondary, any more than the latter. For it was natural and obvious to argue thus from that hypothesis: if heat, and colour, and sound, are real qualities of body, the sensations, by which we perceive them, must be resemblances of those qualities: but these sensations are not resemblances; therefore those are not real qualities of body.

We see then, that Locke, having found that the ideas of secondary qualities are no resemblances, was compelled, by a hypothesis common to all philosophers, to deny that they are real qualities of body. It is more difficult to assign a reason, why, after this, he should call them *secondary qualities;* for this name, if I mistake not, was of his invention. Surely he did not mean that they were secondary qualities of the mind; and I do not see with what propriety, or even by what tolerable license, he could call them secondary qualities of body, after finding that they were no qualities of body at all. In this, he seems to have sacrificed to common sense, and to have been led by her authority, even in opposition to his hypothesis. The same sovereign mistress of our opinions that led this philosopher to call those things secondary qualities of body, which, according to his principles and reasonings, were no qualities of body at all, hath led, not the vulgar of all ages only, but philosophers also, and even the disciples of Locke, to believe them to be real qualities of body: she hath led them to investigate, by experiments, the nature of colour, and sound, and heat, in bodies. Nor hath this investigation been fruitless, as it must have been, if there had been no such thing in bodies: on the contrary, it hath produced very noble and useful discoveries, which make a very considerable part of natural philosophy. If then natural philosophy be not a dream, there is something in bodies, which we call *colour*, and *heat*, and *sound*. And if this be so, the hypothesis from which the contrary is concluded must be false: for the argument, leading to a false conclusion, recoils against the hypothesis from which it was drawn, and thus directs its force backward. If the qualities of body were known to us only by sensations that resemble them, then colour, and sound, and heat, could be no qualities of body; but these are real qualities of body; and therefore the qualities of body are not known only by means of sensations that resemble them.

But to proceed: what Locke had proved with regard to the sensations we have by smell, taste and hearing, bishop Berkeley proved no less unanswerably with regard to all our other sensations; to wit, that none of them can in the least resemble the qualities of a lifeless and insentient being, such as matter is conceived to be. Mr Hume hath confirmed this by his authority and reasoning. This opinion surely looks with a very malign aspect upon the old hypothesis; yet that hypothesis hath still been retained, and conjoined with it. And what a brood of monsters hath this produced.

The firstborn of this union, and perhaps the most harmless, was, that the secondary qualities of body were mere sensations of the mind. To pass by Malebranche's notion of seeing all things in the ideas of the divine mind, as a foreigner never naturalized in this island; the next was Berkeley's system, that extension, and figure, and hardness and motion; that land, and sea, and houses, and our own bodies, as well as those of our wives, and children, and friends, are nothing but ideas of the mind; and that there is nothing existing in nature, but minds and ideas.

The progeny that followed, is still more frightful; so that it is surprising, that one could be found who had the courage to act the midwife, to rear it up, and to usher it into the world. No causes nor effects; no substances, material or spiritual; no evidence even in mathematical demonstration; no liberty nor active power; nothing existing in nature, but impressions and ideas following each other, without time, place, or subject. Surely no age ever produced such a system of opinions, justly deduced with great acuteness, perspicuity, and elegance, from a principle universally received. The hypothesis we have mentioned, is the father of them all. The dissimilitude of our sensations and feelings to external things, is the innocent mother of most of them.

[From *An Inquiry into the Human Mind* (US edn., Charlestown, 1813), 171–3, 200–2, 274–9.]

JOHN STUART MILL

23   Inductive Logic

A body, according to the received doctrine of modern metaphysicians, may be defined, the external cause to which we ascribe our sensations. When I see and touch a piece of gold, I am conscious of a sensation of yellow colour, and sensations of hardness and weight; and by varying the mode of handling, I may add to these sensations many others completely distinct from them. The sensations are all of which I am directly conscious; but I consider them as produced by something not only existing independently of my will, but external to my bodily organs and to my mind. This external something I call a body.

It may be asked, how come we to ascribe our sensations to any external cause? And is there sufficient ground for so ascribing them? It is known, that there are metaphysicians who have raised a controversy on the point; maintaining that we are not warranted in referring our sensations to a cause such as we understand by the word Body, or to any external cause whatever. Though we have no concern here with this controversy, nor with the metaphysical niceties on which it turns, one of the best ways of showing what is meant by Substance is, to consider what position it is necessary to take up, in order to maintain its existence against opponents.

It is certain, then, that a part of our notion of a body consists of the notion of a number of sensations of our own, or of other sentient beings, habitually occurring simultaneously. My conception of the table at which I am writing is compounded of its visible form and size, which are complex sensations of sight; its tangible form and size, which are complex sensations of our organs of touch and of our muscles; its weight, which is also a sensation of touch and of the muscles: its colour, which is a sensation of sight; its hardness, which is a sensation of the muscles; its composition, which is another word for all the varieties of sensation which we receive under various circumstances from the wood of which it is made, and so forth. All or most of these various sensations frequently are, and, as we learn by experience, always might be, experienced simultaneously, or in many different orders of succession at our own choice: and hence the thought of any one of them makes us think of the others, and the whole becomes mentally amalgamated into one mixed state of consciousness, which, in the language of the school of Locke and Hartley, is termed a Complex Idea.

Now, there are philosophers who have argued as follows. If we conceive an orange to be divested of its natural colour without acquiring any new one; to lose its softness without becoming hard, its roundness without becoming square or pentagonal, or of any other regular or irregular figure whatever; to be deprived of size, of weight, of taste, of smell; to lose all its mechanical and all its chemical properties, and acquire no new ones; to become in short, invisible, intangible, imperceptible not only by all our senses, but by the senses of all other sentient beings, real or possible; nothing, say these thinkers, would remain. For of what nature, they ask, could be the residuum? and by what token could it manifest its presence? To the unreflecting its existence seems to rest on the evidence of the senses. But to the senses nothing is apparent except the sensations. We know, indeed, that these sensations are bound together by some law; they do not come together at random, but according to a systematic order, which is part of the order established in the universe. When we experience one of these sensations, we usually experience the others also, or know that we have it in our power to experience them. But a fixed law of connection, making the sensations occur together, does not, say these philosophers, necessarily require what is called a substratum to support them. The conception of a substratum is but one of many possible forms in which that connection presents itself to our imagination; a mode of, as it were, realizing the idea. If there be such a substratum, suppose it at this instant miraculously annihilated, and let the sensations continue to occur in the same order, and how would the substratum be missed? By what signs should we be able to discover that its existence had terminated? Should we not have as much reason to believe that it still existed as we now have? And if we should not then be warranted in believing it, how can we be so now? A body, therefore, according, to these metaphysicians, is not anything intrinsically different from the sensations which the body is said to produce in us; it is, in short, a set of sensations, or rather, of possibilities of sensation, joined together according to a fixed law.

The controversies to which these speculations have given rise, and the doctrines which have been developed in the attempt to find a conclusive answer to them, have been fruitful of important consequences to the Science of Mind. The sensations (it was answered) which we are conscious of, and which we receive, not at random, but joined together in a certain uniform manner, imply not only a law or laws of connection, but a cause external to our mind, which cause, by its own laws, determines the laws according to which the sensations are connected and experienced. The schoolmen used to call this external cause by the name we have already employed, a *substratum*; and its attributes (as they expressed themselves) *inherent*, literally *stuck* in it. To this substratum the name Matter is usually given in philosophical discussions. It was soon, however, acknowledged by all who reflected on the subject, that the existence of matter cannot be proved by extrinsic evidence. The answer, therefore, now usually made to Berkeley and his followers, is, that the belief is intuitive; that mankind, in all ages, have felt themselves compelled, by a necessity of their nature, to refer their sensations to an external cause: that even those who deny it in theory, yield to the necessity in practice, and both in speech, thought, and feeling, do, equally with the vulgar, acknowledge their sensations to be the effects of something external to them: this knowledge, therefore, it is affirmed, is as evidently intuitive as our knowledge of our sensations themselves is intuitive. And here the question merges in the fundamental problem of metaphysics properly so called: to which science we leave it.

But although the extreme doctrine of the Idealist metaphysicians, that objects are nothing but our sensations and the laws which connect them, has not been generally adopted by subsequent thinkers; the point of most real importance is one on which those metaphysicians are now very generally considered to have made out their case: viz, that *all we know* of objects, is the sensations which they give us, and the order of the occurrence of those sensations. Kant himself, on this point, is as explicit as Berkeley or Locke. However firmly convinced that there exists an universe of 'Things in themselves,' totally distinct from the universe of phenomena, or of things as they appear to our senses; and even when bringing into use a technical expression (*Noumenon*) to denote what the thing is in itself, as contrasted with the *representation* of it in our minds; he allows that this representation (the matter of which, he says, consists of our sensations, though the form is given by the laws of the mind itself) is all we know of the object: and that the real nature of the Thing is, and by the constitution of our faculties ever must remain, at least in the present state of existence, an impenetrable mystery to us. 'Of things absolutely or in themselves,' says Sir William Hamilton, 'be they external, be they internal, we know nothing, or know them only as incognisable; and become aware of their incomprehensible existence, only as this is indirectly and accidentally revealed to us, through certain qualities related to our faculties of knowledge, and which qualities, again, we cannot think as unconditioned, irrelative, existent in and of themselves. All that we know is therefore phænomenal,—phænomenal of the unknown.' The same doctrine is laid down in the clearest and strongest terms by M. Cousin, whose observations on the subject are the more worthy of attention, as, in consequence of the ultra-German and ontological character of his philosophy in other respects, they may be regarded as the admissions of an opponent.

There is not the slightest reason for believing that what we call the sensible qualities of the object are a type of anything inherent in itself, or bear any affinity to its own nature. A cause does not, as such, resemble its effects; an east wind is not like the feeling of cold, nor heat like the steam of boiling water. Why then should matter resemble our sensations? Why should the inmost nature of fire and water resemble the impressions made by those objects upon our senses? Or on what principle are we authorized to deduce from the effects, anything concerning the cause, except that it is a cause adequate to produce those effects? It may, therefore, safely be laid down as a truth both obvious in itself, and admitted by all whom it is at present necessary to take into consideration, that, of the outward world, we know and can know absolutely nothing, except the sensations which we experience from it.

Body having now been defined the external cause, and (according to the more reasonable opinion) the unknown external cause, to which we refer our sensations; it remains to frame a definition of Mind. Nor, after the preceding observations, will this be difficult. For, as our conception of a body is that of an unknown exciting cause of sensations, so our conception of a mind is that of an unknown recipient, or percipient, of them; and not of them alone, but of all our other feelings. As body is understood to be the mysterious something which excites the mind to feel, so mind is the mysterious something which feels and thinks. It is unnecessary to give in the case of mind, as we gave in the case of matter, a particular statement of the sceptical system by which its existence as a Thing in itself, distinct from the series of what are denominated its states, is called in question. But it is necessary to remark, that on the inmost nature (whatever be meant by inmost nature) of the thinking principle, as well as on the inmost nature of matter, we are, and with our faculties must always remain, entirely in the dark. All which we are aware of, even in our own minds, is (in the words of James Mill) a certain 'thread of consciousness;' a series of feelings, that is, of sensations, thoughts, emotions, and volitions, more or less numerous and complicated. There is something I call Myself, or, by another form of expression, my mind, which I consider as distinct from these sensations, thoughts, &c.; a something which I conceive to be not the thoughts, but the being that has the thoughts, and which I can conceive as existing for ever in a state of quiescence, without any thoughts at all. But what this being is, though it is myself, I have no knowledge, other than the series of its states of consciousness. As bodies manifest themselves to me only through the sensations of which I regard them as the causes, so the thinking principle, or mind, in my own nature, makes itself known to me only by the feelings of which it is conscious. I know nothing about myself, save my capacities of feeling or being conscious (including, of course, thinking and willing): and were I to learn anything new concerning my own nature, I cannot with my present faculties conceive this new information to be anything else, than that I have some additional capacities, as yet unknown to me, of feeling, thinking, or willing.

Thus, then, as body is the unsentient cause to which we are naturally prompted to refer a certain portion of our feelings, so mind may be described as the sentient *subject* (in the scholastic sense of the term) of all feelings; that which has or feels them. But of the nature of either body or mind, further than the feelings which the former excites, and which the latter experiences, we do not, according to the best existing doctrine, know anything; and if anything, logic has nothing to do with it, or with the manner in which the knowledge is acquired. With this result we may conclude this portion of our subject, and pass to the third and only remaining class or division of Nameable Things. [. . .]

From what has already been said of Substance, what is to be said of Attribute is easily deducible. For if we know not, and cannot know, anything of bodies but the sensations which they excite in us or in others, those sensations must be all that we can, at bottom, mean by their attributes; and the distinction which we verbally make between the properties of things and the sensations we receive from them, must originate in the convenience of discourse rather than in the nature of what is signified by the terms.

Attributes are usually distributed under the three heads of Quality, Quantity, and Relation. We shall come to the two latter presently: in the first place we shall confine ourselves to the former.

Let us take, then, as our example, one of what are termed the sensible qualities of objects, and let that example be whiteness. When we ascribe whiteness to any substance, as, for instance, snow; when we say that snow has the quality whiteness, what do we really assert? Simply, that when snow is present to our organs, we have a particular sensation, which we are accustomed to call the sensation of white. But how do I know that snow is present? Obviously by the sensations which I derive from it, and not otherwise. I infer that the object is present, because it gives me a certain assemblage or series of sensations. And when I ascribe to it the attribute whiteness, my meaning is only, that, of the sensations composing this group or series, that which I call the sensation of white colour is one.

This is one view which may be taken of the subject. But there is also another and a different view. It may be said, that it is true we *know* nothing of sensible objects, except the sensations they excite in us; that the fact of our receiving from snow the particular sensation which is called a sensation of white, is the *ground* on which we ascribe to that substance the quality whiteness; the sole proof of its possessing that quality. But because one thing may be the sole evidence of the existence of another thing, it does not follow that the two are one and the same. The attribute whiteness (it may be said) is not the fact of receiving the sensation, but something in the object itself; a *power* inherent in it; something in *virtue* of which the object produces the sensation. And when we affirm that snow possesses the attribute whiteness, we do not merely assert that the presence of snow produces in us that sensation, but that it does so through, and by reason of, that power or quality.

For the purposes of logic it is not of material importance which of these opinions we adopt. The full discussion of the subject belongs to the other department of scientific enquiry, so often alluded to under the name of metaphysics; but it may be said here, that for the doctrine of the existence of a peculiar species of entities called qualities, I can see no foundation except in a tendency of the human mind which is the cause of many delusions. I mean, the disposition, wherever we meet with two names which are not precisely synonymous, to suppose that they must be the names of two different things; whereas in reality they may be names of the same thing viewed in two different lights, or under different suppositions as to surrounding circumstances. Because *quality* and *sensation* cannot be put indiscriminately one for the other, it is supposed that they cannot both signify the same thing, namely, the impression or feeling with which we are affected through our senses by the presence of an object; though there is at least no absurdity in supposing that this identical impression or feeling may be called a sensation when considered merely in itself, and a quality when looked at in relation to any one of the numerous objects, the presence of which to our organs excites in our minds that among various other sensations or feelings. And if this be admissible as a supposition, it rests with those who contend for an entity *per se* called a quality, to show that their opinion is preferable, or is anything in fact but a lingering remnant of the old doctrine of occult causes: the very absurdity which Molière so happily ridiculed when he made one of his pedantic physicians account for the fact that opium produces sleep by the maxim, Because it has a soporific virtue.

It is evident that when the physician stated that opium has a soporific virtue, he did not account for, but merely asserted over again, the fact that it produces sleep. In like manner, when we say that snow is white because it has the quality of whiteness, we are only re-asserting in more technical language the fact that it excites in us the sensation of white. If it be said that the sensation must have some cause, I answer, its cause is the presence of the assemblage of phenomena which is termed the object. When we have asserted that as often as the object is present, and our organs in their normal state, the sensation takes place, we have stated all that we know about the matter. There is no need, after assigning a certain and intelligible cause, to suppose an occult cause besides, for the purpose of enabling the real cause to produce its effect. If I am asked, why does the presence of the object cause this sensation in me, I cannot tell: I can only say that such is my nature, and the nature of the object; that the fact forms a part of the constitution of things. And to this we must at last come, even after interpolating the imaginary entity. Whatever number of links the chain of causes and effects may consist of, how any one link produces the one which is next to it, remains equally inexplicable to us. It is as easy to comprehend that the object should produce the sensation directly and at once, as that it should produce the same sensation by the aid of something else called the *power* of producing it.

But, as the difficulties which may be felt in adopting this view of the subject cannot be removed without discussions transcending the bounds of our science, I content myself with a passing indication, and shall, for the purposes of logic, adopt a language compatible with either view of the nature of qualities. I shall say,—what at least admits of no dispute,—that the quality of whiteness ascribed to the object snow, is *grounded* on its exciting in us the sensation of white; and adopting the language already used by the school logicians in the case of the kind of attributes called Relations, I shall term the sensation of white the *foundation* of the quality whiteness. For logical purposes the sensation is the only essential part of what is meant by the word; the only part which we ever can be concerned in proving. When that is proved, the quality is proved; if an object excites a sensation, it has, of course, the power of exciting it. [. . .]

From these consideration it would appear that Deductive or Demonstrative Sciences are all, without exception, Inductive Sciences; that their evidence is that of experience; but that they are also, in virtue of the peculiar character of one indispensable portion of the general formulæ according to which their inductions are made, Hypothetical Sciences. Their conclusions are only true on certain suppositions, which are, or ought to be, approximations to the truth, but are seldom, if ever, exactly true; and to this hypothetical character is to be ascribed the peculiar certainty which is supposed to be inherent in demonstration.

What we have now asserted, however, cannot be received as universally true of Deductive or Demonstrative Sciences, until verified by being applied to the most remarkable of all those sciences, that of Numbers; the theory of the Calculus; Arithmetic and Algebra. It is harder to believe of the doctrines of this science than of any other, either that they are not truths *à priori*, but experimental truths, or that their peculiar certainty is owing to their being not absolute, but only conditional truths. This, therefore, is a case which merits examination apart; and the more so, because on this subject we have a double set of doctrines to contend with; that of the *à priori* philosophers on one side; and on the other, a theory the most opposite to theirs, which was at one time very generally received, and is still far from being altogether exploded among metaphysicians.

This theory attempts to solve the difficulty apparently inherent in the case, by representing the propositions of the science of numbers as merely verbal, and its processes as simple transformations of language, substitutions of one expression for another. The proposition, Two and one is equal to three, according to these writers, is not a truth, is not the assertion of a really existing fact, but a definition of the word three; a statement that mankind have agreed to use the name three as a sign exactly equivalent to two and one; to call by the former name whatever is called by the other more clumsy phrase. According to this doctrine the longest process in algebra is but a succession of changes in terminology, by which equivalent expressions are substituted one for another; a series of translations of the same fact, from one into another language; though how, after such a series of translations, the fact itself comes out changed, (as when we demonstrate a new geometrical theorem by algebra,) they have not explained; and it is a difficulty which is fatal to their theory.

It must be acknowledged that there are peculiarities in the processes of arithmetic and algebra which render the theory in question very plausible, and have not unnaturally made those sciences the stronghold of Nominalism. The doctrine that we can discover facts, detect the hidden processes of nature, by an artful manipulation of language, is so contrary to common sense, that a person must have made some advances in philosophy to believe it; men fly to so paradoxical a belief to avoid, as they think, some even greater difficulty, which the vulgar do not see. What has led many to believe that reasoning is a mere verbal process is, that no other theory seemed reconcilable with the nature of the Science of Numbers. For we do not carry any ideas along with us when we use the symbols of arithmetic or of algebra. In a geometrical demonstration we have a mental diagram, if not one on paper; AB, AC, are present to our imagination as lines, intersecting other lines, forming an angle with one another, and the like; but not so a and b. These may represent lines or any other magnitudes, but those magnitudes are never thought of; nothing is realised in our imagination but a and b. The ideas which, on the particular occasion, they happen to represent, are banished from the mind during every intermediate part of the process, between the beginning, when the premises are translated from things into signs, and the end, when the conclusion is translated back from signs into things. Nothing, then, being in the reasoner's mind but the symbols, what can seem more inadmissible than to contend that the reasoning process has to do with anything more! We seem to have come to one of Bacon's Prerogative Instances; an *experimentum crucis* on the nature of reasoning itself.
[. . .]

The Science of Numbers is thus no exception to the conclusion we previously arrived at, that the processes even of deductive sciences are altogether inductive, and that their first principles are generalisations from experience. It remains to be examined whether this science resembles geometry in the further circumstance that some of its inductions are not exactly true; and that the peculiar certainty ascribed to it, on account of which its propositions are called necessary truths, is fictitious and hypothetical, being true in no other sense than that those propositions legitimately follow from the hypothesis of the truth of premises which are avowedly mere approximations to truth.

[From *A System of Logic Ratiocinative and Inductive* (London: Longmans, Green, 1900), 36–42, 166–9.]

WILLIAM JAMES

24 Does 'Consciousness' Exist?

'Thoughts' and 'things' are names for two sorts of object, which common sense will always find contrasted and will always practically oppose to each other. Philosophy, reflecting on the contrast, has varied in the past in her explanations of it, and may be expected to vary in the future. At first, 'spirit and matter,' 'soul and body,' stood for a pair of equipollent substances quite on a par in weight and interest. But one day Kant undermined the soul and brought in the transcendental ego, and ever since then the bipolar relation has been very much off its balance. The transcendental ego seems nowadays in rationalist quarters to stand for everything, in empiricist quarters for almost nothing. In the hands of such writers as Schuppe, Rehmke, Natorp, Münsterberg—at any rate in his earlier writings, Schubert-Soldern and others, the spiritual principle attenuates itself to a thoroughly ghostly condition, being only a name for the fact that the 'content' of experience *is known*. It loses personal form and activity—these passing over to the content—and becomes a bare *Bewusstheit* or *Bewusstsein überhaupt*, of which in its own right absolutely nothing can be said.

I believe that 'consciousness,' when once it has evaporated to this estate of pure diaphaneity, is on the point of disappearing altogether. It is the name of a nonentity, and has no right to a place among first principles. Those who still cling to it are clinging to a mere echo, the faint rumor left behind by the disappearing 'soul' upon the air of philosophy. During the past year, I have read a number of articles whose authors seemed just on the point of abandoning the notion of consciousness,[1] and substituting for it that of an absolute experience not due to two factors. But they were not quite radical enough, not quite daring enough in their negations. For twenty years past I have mistrusted 'consciousness' as an entity; for seven or eight years past I have suggested its non-existence to my students, and tried to give them its pragmatic equivalent in realities of experience. It seems to me that the hour is ripe for it to be openly and universally discarded.

To deny plumply that 'consciousness' exists seems so absurd on the face of it—for undeniably 'thoughts' do exist—that I fear some readers will follow me no farther. Let me then immediately explain that I mean only to deny that the word stands for an entity, but to insist most emphatically that it does stand for a function. There is, I mean, no aboriginal stuff or quality of being, contrasted with that of which material objects are made, out of which our thoughts of them are made; but there is a function in experience which thoughts perform, and for the performance of which this quality of being is invoked. That function is *knowing*. 'Consciousness' is supposed necessary to explain the fact that things not only are, but get reported, are known. Whoever blots out the notion of consciousness from his list of first principles must still provide in some way for that function's being carried on.

I

My thesis is that if we start with the supposition that there is only one primal stuff or material in the world, a stuff of which everything is composed, and if we call that stuff 'pure experience,' then knowing can easily be explained as a particular sort of relation towards one another into which portions of pure experience may enter. The relation itself is a part of pure experience; one of its 'terms' becomes the subject or bearer of the knowledge, the knower, the other becomes the object known. This will need much explanation before it can be understood. The best way to get it understood is to contrast it with the alternative view; and for that we may take the recentest alternative, that in which the evaporation of the definite soul-substance has proceeded as far as it can go without being yet complete. If neo-Kantism has expelled earlier forms of dualism, we shall have expelled all forms if we are able to expel neo-Kantism in its turn.

For the thinkers I call neo-Kantian, the word consciousness today does no more than signalize the fact that experience is indefeasibly dualistic in structure. It means that not subject, not object, but object-plus-subject is the minimum that can actually be. The subject-object distinction meanwhile is entirely different from that between mind and matter, from that between body and soul. Souls were detachable, had separate destinies; things could happen to them. To consciousness as such nothing can happen, for, timeless itself, it is only a witness of happenings in time, in which it plays no part. It is, in a word, but the logical correlative of 'content' in an Experience of which the peculiarity is that *fact comes to light* in it, that *awareness of content* takes place. Consciousness as such is entirely impersonal—'self' and its activities belong to the content. To say that I am self-conscious, or conscious of putting forth volition, means only that certain contents, for which 'self' and 'effort of will' are the names, are not without witness as they occur.

Thus, for these belated drinkers at the Kantian spring, we should have to admit consciousness as an 'epistemological' necessity, even if we had no direct evidence of its being there.

But in addition to this, we are supposed by almost every one to have an immediate consciousness of consciousness itself. When the world of outer fact ceases to be materially present, and we merely recall it in memory, or fancy it, the consciousness is believed to stand out and to be felt as a kind of impalpable inner flowing, which, once known in this sort of experience, may equally be detected in presentations of the outer world. 'The moment we try to fix our attention upon consciousness and to see *what*, distinctly, it is,' says a recent writer, 'it seems to vanish. It seems as if we had before us a mere emptiness. When we try to introspect the sensation of blue, all we can see is the blue; the other element is as if it were diaphanous. Yet it *can* be distinguished, if we look attentively enough, and know that there is something to look for.' 'Consciousness' (Bewusstheit), says another philosopher, 'is inexplicable and hardly describable, yet all conscious experiences have this in common that what we call their content has this peculiar reference to a centre for which "self" is the name, in virtue of which reference alone the content is subjectively given, or appears . . . While in this way consciousness, or reference to a self, is the only thing which distinguishes a conscious content from any sort of being that might be there with no one conscious of it, yet this only ground of the distinction defies all closer explanations. The existence of consciousness, although it is the fundamental fact of psychology, can indeed be laid down as certain, can be brought out by analysis, but can neither be defined nor deduced from anything but itself.'

'Can be brought out by analysis,' this author says. This supposes that the consciousness is one element, moment, factor—call it what you like—of an experience of essentially dualistic inner constitution, from which, if you abstract the content, the consciousness will remain revealed to its own eye. Experience, at this rate, would be much like a paint of which the world pictures were made. Paint has a dual constitution, involving, as it does, a menstruum (oil, size or what not) and a mass of content in the form of pigment suspended therein. We can get the pure menstruum by letting the pigment settle, and the pure pigment by pouring off the size or oil. We operate here by physical subtraction; and the usual view is, that by mental subtraction we can separate the two factors of experience in an analogous way—not isolating them entirely, but distinguishing them enough to know that they are two.

II

Now my contention is exactly the reverse of this. *Experience, I believe, has no such inner duplicity; and the separation of it into consciousness and content comes, not by way of subtraction, but by way of addition*—the addition, to a given concrete piece of it, of other sets of experiences, in connection with which severally its use or function may be of two different kinds. The paint will also serve here as an illustration. In a pot in a paint-shop, along with other paints, it serves in its entirety as so much saleable matter. Spread on a canvas, with other paints around it, it represents, on the contrary, a feature in a picture and performs a spiritual function. Just so, I maintain, does a given undivided portion of experience, taken in one context of associates, play the part of a knower, of a state of mind, of 'consciousness'; while in a different context the same undivided bit of experience plays the part of a thing known, of an objective 'content.' In a word, in one group it figures as a thought, in another group as a thing. And, since it can figure in both groups simultaneously we have every right to speak of it as subjective and objective both at once. The dualism connoted by such double-barrelled terms as 'experience,' 'phenomenon,' 'datum,' 'Vorfindung'—terms which, in philosophy at any rate, tend more and more to replace the single-barrelled terms of 'thought' and 'thing'—that dualism, I say, is still preserved in this account, but reinterpreted, so that, instead of being mysterious and elusive, it becomes verifiable and concrete. It is an affair of relations, it falls outside, not inside, the single experience considered, and can always be particularized and defined.

The entering wedge for this more concrete way of understanding the dualism was fashioned by Locke when he made the word 'idea' stand indifferently for thing and thought, and by Berkeley when he said that what common sense means by realities is exactly what the philosopher means by ideas. Neither Locke nor Berkeley thought his truth out into perfect clearness, but it seems to me that the conception I am defending does little more than consistently carry out the 'pragmatic' method which they were the first to use.

If the reader will take his own experiences, he will see what I mean. Let him begin with a perceptual experience, the 'presentation,' so called, of a physical object, his actual field of vision, the room he sits in, with the book he is reading as its centre; and let him for the present treat this complex object in the common-sense way as being 'really' what it seems to be, namely, a collection of physical things cut out from an environing world of other physical things with which these physical things have actual or potential relations. Now at the same time it is just *those self-same things* which his mind, as we say, perceives; and the whole philosophy of perception from Democritus's time downwards has been just one long wrangle over the paradox that what is evidently one reality should be in two places at once, both in outer space and in a person's mind. 'Representative' theories of perception avoid the logical paradox, but on the other hand they violate the reader's sense of life, which knows no intervening mental image but seems to see the room and the book immediately just as they physically exist.

The puzzle of how the one identical room can be in two places is at bottom just the puzzle of how one identical point can be on two lines. It can, if it be situated at their intersection; and similarly, if the 'pure experience' of the room were a place of intersection of two processes, which connected it with different groups of associates respectively, it could be counted twice over, as belonging to either group, and spoken of loosely as existing in two places, although it would remain all the time a numerically single thing.

Well, the experience is a member of diverse processes that can be followed away from it along entirely different lines. The one self-identical thing has so many relations to the rest of experience that you can take it in disparate systems of association, and treat it as belonging with opposite contexts. In one of these contexts it is your 'field of consciousness'; in another it is 'the room in which you sit,' and it enters both contexts in its wholeness, giving no pretext for being said to attach itself to consciousness by one of its parts or aspects, and to outer reality by another. What are the two processes, now, into which the room-experience simultaneously enters in this way?

One of them is the reader's personal biography, the other is the history of the house of which the room is part. The presentation, the experience, the *that* in short (for until we have decided *what* it is it must be a mere *that*) is the last term of a train of sensations, emotions, decisions, movements, classifications, expectations, etc., ending in the present, and the first term of a series of similar 'inner' operations extending into the future, on the reader's part. On the other hand, the very same *that* is the *terminus ad quem* of a lot of previous physical operations, carpentering, papering, furnishing, warming, etc., and the *terminus a quo* of a lot of future ones, in which it will be concerned when undergoing the destiny of a physical room. The physical and the mental operations form curiously incompatible groups. As a room, the experience has occupied that spot and had that environment for thirty years. As your field of consciousness it may never have existed until now. As a room, attention will go on to discover endless new details in it. As your mental state merely, few new ones will emerge under attention's eye. As a room, it will take an earthquake, or a gang of men, and in any case a certain amount of time, to destroy it. As your subjective state, the closing of your eyes, or any instantaneous play of your fancy will suffice. In the real world, fire will consume it. In your mind, you can let fire play over it without effect. As an outer object, you must pay so much a month to inhabit it. As an inner content, you may occupy it for any length of time rent-free. If, in short, you follow it in the mental direction, taking it along with events of personal biography solely, all sorts of things are true of it which are false, and false of it which are true if you treat it as a real thing experienced, follow it in the physical direction, and relate it to associates in the outer world.

[From *Does Consciousness Exist?* (1904), in *The Writings of William James*, ed. J. McDermott (Chicago: University of Chicago Press, 1967), 169–74 (repr. from *Journal of Philosophy, Psychology and Scientific Methods*, 1904).]

The Official Doctrine

There is a doctrine about the nature and place of minds which is so prevalent among theorists and even among laymen that it deserves to be described as the official theory. Most philosophers, psychologists and religious teachers subscribe, with minor reservations, to its main articles and, although they admit certain theoretical difficulties in it, they tend to assume that these can be overcome without serious modifications being made to the architecture of the theory. It will be argued here that the central principles of the doctrine are unsound and conflict with the whole body of what we know about minds when we are not speculating about them.

The official doctrine, which hails chiefly from Descartes, is something like this. With the doubtful exceptions of idiots and infants in arms every human being has both a body and a mind. Some would prefer to say that every human being is both a body and a mind. His body and his mind are ordinarily harnessed together, but after the death of the body his mind may continue to exist and function.

Human bodies are in space and are subject to the mechanical laws which govern all other bodies in space. Bodily processes and states can be inspected by external observers. So a man's bodily life is as much a public affair as are the lives of animals and reptiles and even as the careers of trees, crystals and planets.

But minds are not in space, nor are their operations subject to mechanical laws. The workings of one mind are not witnessable by other observers; its career is private. Only I can take direct cognisance of the states and processes of my own mind. A person therefore lives through two collateral histories, one consisting of what happens in and to his body, the other consisting of what happens in and to his mind. The first is public, the second private. The events in the first history are events in the physical world, those in the second are events in the mental world.

It has been disputed whether a person does or can directly monitor all or only some of the episodes of his own private history; but, according to the official doctrine, of at least some of these episodes he has direct and unchallengeable cognisance. In consciousness, self-consciousness and intro-spection he is directly and authentically apprised of the present states and operations of his mind. He may have great or small uncertainties about concurrent and adjacent episodes in the physical world, but he can have none about at least part of what is momentarily occupying his mind.

It is customary to express this bifurcation of his two lives and of his two worlds by saying that the things and events which belong to the physical world, including his own body, are external, while the workings of his own mind are internal. This antithesis of outer and inner is of course meant to be construed as a metaphor, since minds, not being in space, could not be described as being spatially inside anything else, or as having things going on spatially inside themselves. But relapses from this good intention are common and theorists are found speculating how stimuli, the physical sources of which are yards or miles outside a person's skin, can generate mental responses inside his skull, or how decisions framed inside his cranium can set going movements of his extremities.

Even when 'inner' and 'outer' are construed as metaphors, the problem how a person's mind and body influence one another is notoriously charged with theoretical difficulties. What the mind wills, the legs, arms and the tongue execute; what affects the ear and the eye has something to do with what the mind perceives; grimaces and smiles betray the mind's moods and bodily castigations lead, it is hoped, to moral improvement. But the actual transactions between the episodes of the private history and those of the public history remain mysterious, since by definition they can belong to neither series. They could not be reported among the happenings described in a person's autobiography of his inner life, but nor could they be reported among those described in some one else's biography of that person's overt career. They can be inspected neither by introspection nor by laboratory experiment. They are theoretical shuttlecocks which are forever being bandied from the physiologist back to the psychologist and from the psychologist back to the physiologist

Underlying this partly metaphorical representation of the bifurcation of a person's two lives there is a seemingly more profound and philosophical assumption. It is assumed that there are two different kinds of existence or status. What exists or happens may have the status of physical existence, or it may have the status of mental existence. Somewhat as the faces of coins are either heads or tails, or somewhat as living creatures are either male or female, so, it is supposed, some existing is physical existing, other existing is mental existing. It is a necessary feature of what has physical existence that it is in space and time, it is a necessary feature of what has mental existence that it is in time but not in space. What has physical existence is composed of matter, or else is a function of matter; what has mental existence consists of consciousness, or else is a function of consciousness.

There is thus a polar opposition between mind and matter, an opposition which is often brought out as follows. Material objects are situated in a common field, known as 'space', and what happens to one body in one part of space is mechanically connected with what happens to other bodies in other parts of space. But mental happenings occur in insulated fields, known as 'minds', and there is, apart maybe from telepathy, no direct causal connection between what happens in one mind and what happens in another. Only through the medium of the public physical world can the mind of one person make a difference to the mind of another. The mind is its own place and in his inner life each of us lives the life of a ghostly Robinson Crusoe. People can see, hear and jolt one another's bodies, but they are irremediably blind and deaf to the workings of one another's minds and inoperative upon them. [. . .]

As a necessary corollary of this general scheme there is implicitly prescribed a special way of construing our ordinary concepts of mental powers and operations. The verbs, nouns and adjectives, with which in ordinary life we describe the wits, characters and higher-grade performances of the people with whom we have do, are required to be construed as signifying special episodes in their secret histories, or else as signifying tendencies for such episodes to occur. When someone is described as knowing, believing or guessing something, as hoping, dreading, intending or shirking something, as designing this or being amused at that, these verbs are supposed to denote the occurrence of specific modifications in his (to us) occult stream of consciousness. Only his own privileged access to this stream in direct awareness and introspection could provide authentic testimony that these mental-conduct verbs were correctly or incorrectly applied. The onlooker, be he teacher, critic, biographer or friend, can never assure himself that his comments have any vestige of truth. Yet it was just because we do in fact all know how to make such comments, make them with general correctness and correct them when they turn out to be confused or mistaken, that philosophers found it necessary to construct their theories of the nature and place of minds. Finding mental-conduct concepts being regularly and effectively used, they properly sought to fix their logical geography. But the logical geography officially recommended would entail that there could be no regular or effective use of these mental-conduct concepts in our descriptions of, and prescriptions for, other people's minds.

The Absurdity of the Official Doctrine

Such in outline is the official theory. I shall often speak of it, with deliberate abusiveness, as 'the dogma of the Ghost in the Machine'. I hope to prove that it is entirely false, and false not in detail but in principle. It is not merely an assemblage of particular mistakes. It is one big mistake and a mistake of a special kind. It is, namely, a category-mistake. It represents the facts of mental life as if they belonged to one logical type or category (or range of types or categories), when they actually belong to another. The dogma is therefore a philosopher's myth. In attempting to explode the myth I shall probably be taken to be denying well-known facts about the mental life of human beings, and my plea that I aim at doing nothing more than rectify the logic of mental-conduct concepts will probably be disallowed as mere subterfuge.

I must first indicate what is meant by the phrase 'Category-mistake'. This I do in a series of illustrations.

A foreigner visiting Oxford or Cambridge for the first time is shown a number of colleges, libraries, playing fields, museums, scientific departments and administrative offices. He then asks 'But where is the University? I have seen where the members of the Colleges live, where the Registrar works, where the scientists experiment and the rest. But I have not yet seen the University in which reside and work the members of your University.' It has then to be explained to him that the University is not another collateral institution, some ulterior counterpart to the colleges, laboratories and offices which he has seen. The University is just the way in which all that he has already seen is organized. When they are seen and when their co-ordination is understood, the University has been seen. His mistake lay in his innocent assumption that it was correct to speak of Christ Church, the Bodleian Library, the Ashmolean Museum *and* the University, to speak, that is, as if 'the University' stood for an extra member of the class of which these other units are members. He was mistakenly allocating the University to the same category as that to which the other institutions belong. [. . .]

The theoretically interesting category-mistakes are those made by people who are perfectly competent to apply concepts, at least in the situations with which they are familiar, but are still liable in their abstract thinking to allocate those concepts to logical types to which they do not belong. An instance of a mistake of this sort would be the following story. A student of politics has learned the main differences between the British, the French and the American Constitutions, and has learned also the differences and connections between the Cabinet, Parliament, the various Ministries, the Judicature and the Church of England. But he still becomes embarrassed when asked questions about the connections between the Church of England, the Home Office and the British Constitution. For while the Church and the Home Office are institutions, the British Constitution is not another institution in the same sense of that noun. So inter-institutional relations which can be asserted or denied to hold between the Church and the Home Office cannot be asserted or denied to hold between either of them and the British Constitution. 'The British Constitution' is not a term of the same logical type as 'the Home Office' and 'the Church of England'. [. . .]

It is pertinent to our main subject to notice that, so long as the student of politics continues to think of the British Constitution as a counterpart to the other institutions, he will tend to describe it as a mysteriously occult institution [. . .].

The Origin of the Category-mistake

One of the chief intellectual origins of what I have yet to prove to be the Cartesian category-mistake seems to be this. When Galileo showed that his methods of scientific discovery were competent to provide a mechanical theory which should cover every occupant of space, Descartes found in himself two conflicting motives. As a man of scientific genius he could not but endorse the claims of mechanics, yet as a religious and moral man he could not accept, as Hobbes accepted, the discouraging rider to those claims, namely that human nature differs only in degree of complexity from clockwork. The mental could not be just a variety of the mechanical.

He and subsequent philosophers naturally but erroneously availed themselves of the following escape-route. Since mental-conduct words are not to be construed as signifying the occurrence of mechanical processes, they must be construed as signifying the occurrence of non-mechanical processes; since mechanical laws explain movements in space as the effects of other movements in space, other laws must explain some of the non-spatial workings of minds as the effects of other non-spatial workings of minds. The difference between the human behaviours which we describe as intelligent and those which we describe as unintelligent must be a difference in their causation; so, while some movements of human tongues and limbs are the effects of mechanical causes, others must be the effects of non-mechanical causes, i.e. some issue from movements of particles of matter, others from workings of the mind.

The differences between the physical and the mental were thus represented as differences inside the common framework of the categories of 'thing', 'stuff', 'attribute', 'state', 'process', 'change', 'cause' and 'effect'. Minds are things, but different sorts of things from bodies; mental processes are causes and effects, but different sorts of causes and effects from bodily movements. And so on. Somewhat as the foreigner expected the University to be an extra edifice, rather like a college but also considerably different, so the repudiators of mechanism represented minds as extra centres of causal processes, rather like machines but also considerably different from them. Their theory was a para-mechanical hypothesis.

That this assumption was at the heart of the doctrine is shown by the fact that there was from the beginning felt to be a major theoretical difficulty in explaining how minds can influence and be influenced by bodies. How can a mental process, such as willing, cause spatial movements like the movements of the tongue? How can a physical change in the optic nerve have among its effects a mind's perception of a flash of light? This notorious crux by itself shows the logical mould into which Descartes pressed his theory of the mind.
[. . .]

As thus represented, minds are not merely ghosts harnessed to machines, they are themselves just spectral machines. Though the human body is an engine, it is not quite an ordinary engine, since some of its workings are governed by another engine inside it—this interior governor-engine being one of a very special sort. It is invisible, inaudible and it has no size or weight. It cannot be taken to bits and the laws it obeys are not those known to ordinary engineers. Nothing is known of how it governs the bodily engine. [. . .]

[Descartes] had mistaken the logic of his problem. Instead of asking by what criteria intelligent behaviour is actually distinguished from non-intelligent behaviour, he asked 'Given that the principle of mechanical causation does not tell us the difference, what other causal principle will tell it us?' He realised that the problem was not one of mechanics and assumed that it must therefore be one of some counterpart to mechanics. Not unnaturally psychology is often cast for just this role.

When two terms belong to the same category, it is proper to construct conjunctive propositions embodying them. Thus a purchaser may say that he bought a left-hand glove and a right-hand glove, but not that he bought a left-hand glove, a right-hand glove and a pair of gloves. 'She came home in a flood of tears and a sedan-chair' is a well-known joke based on the absurdity of conjoining terms of different types. It would have been equally ridiculous to construct the disjunction 'She came home either in a flood of tears or else in a sedan-chair'. Now the dogma of the Ghost in the Machine does just this. It maintains that there exist both bodies and minds; that there occur physical processes and mental processes; that there are mechanical causes of corporeal movements and mental causes of corporeal movements. I shall argue that these and other analogous conjunctions are absurd; but, it must be noticed, the argument will not show that either of the illegitimately conjoined propositions is absurd in itself. I am not, for example, denying that there occur mental processes. Doing long division is a mental process and so is making a joke. But I am saying that the phrase 'there occur mental processes' does not mean the same sort of thing as 'there occur physical processes', and, therefore, that it makes no sense to conjoin or disjoin the two.

If my argument is successful, there will follow some interesting consequences. First, the hallowed contrast between Mind and Matter will be dissipated, but dissipated not by either of the equally hallowed absorptions of Mind by Matter or of Matter by Mind, but in quite a different way. For the seeming contrast of the two will be shown to be as illegitimate as would be the contrast of 'she came home in a flood of tears' and 'she came home in a sedan-chair'. The belief that there is a polar opposition between Mind and Matter is the belief that they are terms of the same logical type.

It will also follow that both Idealism and Materialism are answers to an improper question. The 'reduction' of the material world to mental states and processes, as well as the 'reduction' of mental states and processes to physical states and processes, presuppose the legitimacy of the disjunction 'Either there exist minds or there exist bodies (but not both)'. It would be like saying, 'Either she bought a left-hand and a right-hand glove or she bought a pair of gloves (but not both)'.

It is perfectly proper to say, in one logical tone of voice, that there exist minds and to say, in another logical tone of voice, that there exist bodies. But these expressions do not indicate two different species of existence, for 'existence' is not a generic word like 'coloured' or 'sexed'. They indicate two different senses of 'exist', somewhat as 'rising' has different senses in 'the tide is rising', 'hopes are rising', and 'the average age of death is rising'. A man would be thought to be making a poor joke who said that three things are now rising, namely the tide, hopes and the average age of death. It would be just as good or bad a joke to say that there exist prime numbers and Wednesdays and public opinions and navies; or that there exist both minds and bodies.

[From *The Concept of Mind* (New York: Harper & Row, 1949), 11–13, 15–16, 17–23.]

....

Mind, Brain, and Modules

....

INTRODUCTION

The era of pre-Socratic Greek thought hosted philosophical views of a radically materialistic cast. Democritus of Abdera advanced the influential thesis of *atomism*. An atom—*a-tomos*, or that which is *uncut*—is what he took to be the indivisible unit of reality. All existence, he taught, is but 'atoms and a void'. By the conclusion of the fourth century BC such thinking had ripened into a developed naturalistic perspective on both the inanimate and the animate. Aristotle's scientific writings were immensely important to these developments, as were the philosophical teachings of the major Stoics beginning at about 300 BC. It is within this tradition of thought—though more centrally within its own tradition of professional practice—that ancient Greek physicians developed objective, observational approaches to the diagnosis, treatment, and explanation of diseases. Great and even spectacular advances have been made in the 'brain sciences' in the most recent decades. But the daring thesis that mental life is entirely dependent on the states and condition of the brain can be directly traced to these physicians and, more particularly, to those dubbed 'Hippocratic'. Selected for this Section are passages from the Hippocratic works that illustrate both the naturalistic perspective and the specific theory that the brain is the very organ of consciousness.

There is still no settled scholarly position on the debt of the entire Hippocratic *corpus* owed to that famous if modest physician from Cos. But the term 'Coan medicine' does honour what was clearly Hippocrates' approach to health and disease; an approach that was observational and largely detached from and to some extent hostile to merely philosophical modes of enquiry. In the works that have come down over the centuries the emphasis is on what nowadays is called 'holistic' medicine, due regard paid to diet, exercise, mental fitness, and, when needed, medical and surgical interventions. Opposed at every turn is quackery and witchcraft of old, including that practised by seers and priests whose concocted stories and treatments 'secured their own position'.

The extract from *Ancient Medicine* leaves no doubt but that the author expects knowledge of human nature to advance chiefly by way of progress in medicine. Then, in *The Sacred Disease*, the reader learns at the very outset that no disease is any more 'sacred' than any other, and that all talk to the contrary is ignorance, pure and simple. The cause of epilepsy, 'as of the more serious diseases generally, is the brain'. Dissections have made clear to the author that human and animal brains are similar, symmetrical and with apparently divided functions. Clinical experience and, yes, autopsies supply sufficient information to permit the conclusion that 'from the brain, and from the brain only, arise our pleasures, joys, laughter and jests, as well as our sorrows, pains, griefs and tears'. Similarly, it is through the proper functioning of the brain that cognitive, moral and aesthetic powers, not to mention sanity itself, arise. Thus is the brain the very 'interpreter of consciousness'.

With Galen we move from vague if confident theories to an early master of experimental science in physiology. There were no doubt vivisectors before Galen, but his is the earliest record of systematic studies, making use of several species, including primates, and employing surgical methods by which to establish structure-function relationships. His studies, as well as observations of those 'stricken with apoplexy', lead him to the conclusion (clearly enunciated in the first excerpt) that, even when the sense organs are healthy and properly constituted, their operation can come to nothing in the absence of the encephalon.

In the brief passage taken from his *The Soul's Dependence on the Body* Galen advances three general points worthy of reflection. First, he takes it as an obvious fact of common experience that young children differ from each other and then, at a later age, differ in important psychological respects from their former selves. This establishes that there are different capacities in place from the earliest years, and also that the expression of these faculties undergoes significant change over the course of time. All this points to the individuation of psychic powers and thus, at least indirectly, to biological individuality. The experiences of a lifetime change the psychic powers and expressions, and these must be reflecting changes in something on which experience itself can work; viz. the body.

The second general point is that the very concept of a 'faculty' can be misleading. Anticipating Ryle's 'category mistake', Galen insists that there is no psychic power or faculty over and against the actual *actions* (behaviour, emotion, perception) displayed. To say, then, that the 'rational soul' has the faculties of perception, memory, and judgement is no more than to say that beings of a given constitution are able to perceive, remember, and judge, with these very functions served by the brain. There is the hint of a 'modularity' theory in this, as well as a warning against the reification of 'faculties' as something apart from the actual operations and performances of the system.

Finally, Galen is no radical materialist, nor is he at war against the transcendentalist foundations of Christian (or, for that matter, Platonic) teaching. But he is a scientist first, committed to scientific explanations where these are vindicated in the arena of actual clinical observations. A theory that supposes the soul to be independent of the body (and specifically the brain) is, therefore, one that must account for the clear loss of psychic power when body and brain are disturbed by toxins, disease, excessive heat and cold, etc. Galen wishes that Plato were alive to clarify all this, especially in light of the utter failure of his disciples to make the theory conform to the facts. There is no doubt but that Galen is a dualist in that he is not at all doubtful about the reality of the mental. There is much in his work that is itself transcendentalist and expressly Platonic. But he retains his commitment to *efficient* causality even as he grants at the metaphysical level the validity of (Aristotelian) *final causes*.

Descartes, of course, is the textbook dualist, committed to the now widely discredited 'Cartesian' theory of the unembodied mind. In light of the current wave of criticism within the brain sciences and philosophy of mind that routinely flows over the name of Descartes, it is easy to forget that he is perhaps the most important philosophical source of these very sciences. True, he removed the abstract cognitive and linguistic achievements of human beings from the causal-biological nexus in which all non-human animal functions are determined. But he never denied the coextensive nature of psychological and physiological processes. Indeed, for his time, Descartes was as materialistic in his theoretical psychology as one could be without being patently radical. La Mettrie, in the selection included in this Section, goes so far as to speculate that the spiritistic elements in Descartes's theory of mind were put there by him to assuage the thought-police of the Church. This is doubtful in the extreme, but it does establish the ease with which one can locate a consistent materialism in Descartes's psychological treatises. Nowhere is this clearer than in his posthumously published *Principles of Philosophy*, where it is claimed that 'the human soul . . . has its principal seat in the brain; it is here alone that the soul not only understands and imagines but also has sensory awareness'.

Note the subtle distinction Descartes makes between the physiological antecedents of emotion and the emotion itself. To imagine oneself enjoying something, it is not imagination that experiences joy; rather, the imagination results in the movement of 'spirits' (the ultra-fine aetherous matter that flows in the tubules of the nerves) from brain to heart. The heart expands, thus exciting its own tiny nerves, and the result is the sensation of joy. Such experiences, indeed *all* sensory awareness, can come about only by way of activity induced in the brain. Descartes's discussion of *phantom limb* illustrates that the girl who continues to feel pain in an amputated arm is not feeling something in the arm—which is gone—but in the brain.

When Descartes's *Meditations* were completed he asked Marsenne to obtain critical appraisals of the arguments in the work. Marsenne himself composed a detailed criticism and secured the same from several others, including Thomas Hobbes and Pierre Gassendi. Playfully, Gassendi addresses Descartes as, 'O Mind', owing to Descartes's insistence that essentially he is a *thinking thing* who may otherwise be deceived about everything in the sensible world, including his own body. As we see in the pages reproduced here Gassendi is prepared to accept the separation between the essential Descartes and Descartes's body. What he is not prepared to accept, however, is a distinct Descartes that is in no sense body of any kind whatever. Gassendi, who had done so much to revive interest in the naturalistic philosophy and materialistic psychology of Epicurus is found defending the possibility that the essential Descartes is but 'a rarefied body infused into this solid one or occupying some part of it'. Nor does Gassendi agree that Descartes could have so much as an idea of extended things unless he were such a thing. Extended things are projected on the organs of sense—which are extended—and their extensive attributes must be similarly registered. If mind itself is lacking in shape, 'how will it represent a thing that has a shape?' asks Gassendi. Descartes seems to have granted that in some sense the brain is the repository of all influences on the essential Descartes, leaving ample room for the conclusion that this ineffable Descartes is but the activity within the brain itself.

In *Man: A Machine* La Mettrie laid down the gauntlet in a manner so strident and uncompromising as to force him to seek asylum in Prussia. All of the soul's powers, insists La Mettrie, depend on the proper organization of the body and more especially of the brain. Accordingly, *the soul is an enlightened machine*. Science need no longer defer to religious superstition and speculation. The evidence as La Mettrie reads it leads to one and only one conclusion, which is the one reached by Epicurus centuries earlier. A dualism of mind and body is a vestige of mystical thought. 'Man is a machine, and . . . in the whole universe there is but a single substance differently modified.' Moreover, the differences between and among the animals of creation express differences in their physical organization. 'Man's pre-eminent advantage is his organism'. Differences between human beings and non-human animals, as with differences between human beings themselves, reflect nothing more than this organization, 'a truth which the dissection of Descartes's and of Newton's brains would have proved; you will be persuaded that the imbecile and the fool are animals with human faces, as the intelligent ape is a little man in another shape'.

At about the same time as La Mettrie's book resulted in self-exile, David Hartley's *Observations on Man* presented a detailed, systematic, and coherent physiological psychology based on and expressly indebted to Newtonian science. Hartley adopted and developed Newton's theoretical notions of a century earlier regarding the manner in which external stimuli become represented within the nervous system. The mechanism is that of *small vibrations* of the ultra-fine particles found in the medullary substance of nerves and brain (Proposition 4). Information is moved to and from the brain in the form of vibrational propagation in the nervous system.

By Hartley's time advances in clinical medicine and gross anatomy had progressed to the point at which speculation was either confirmed or challenged by mounting and reliable evidence. The severing or compressing of nerves have now been shown to result in loss of function, loss of sensation, paralysis. Compressing or sectioning of the spine leads to paralysis of the body below the locus of injury. Post mortem examination of patients known to have 'Apoplexies, Palsies, Epilepsies, and other Distempers' typically reveal brain tumours, vascular lesions, pus, etc. either in the brain itself or in its ventricles. The *Observations*, in the reprinted pages, is replete with such general findings used by Hartley to explain insanity as well as normal cognitive and perceptual functioning. Madness is accepted as both bodily and mental in its aetiology, but Hartley's 'dualism' here is not at the expense of an essentially mechanistic, Newtonian explanatory framework. As in normal thought, pathological thought arises from the formation of associations, these strengthened by repetition and similarity. When thought turns to a familiar theme, the strength of the vibrations is enhanced. Opportunity for 'coalescences with each other' arises, giving rise to new trains of thought leading often to unexpected conclusions. The system is able to correct itself before truly bizarre conclusions are reached 'unless the whole nervous System be deranged'. In the latter instance, memory too is disordered such that its normal correctives are no longer available. Again, the post mortem studies of the insane suggest that 'violent Vibrations took place in the internal Parts of the Brain, the peculiar Residence of Ideas and Passions'. But more research is needed!

Pierre Cabanis, who might have become a poet if Voltaire had assessed his efforts more favourably, was associated with leading lights of the French Enlightenment and formed acquaintances with Benjamin Franklin and Thomas Jefferson as well. With Destutt Tracy he developed a version of empiricism dubbed *idéologie* according to which all political and moral terms are meaningful only insofar as they refer to objects and events accessible to experience. Because of Cabanis's opposition to certain of his measures, Napoleon referred pejoratively to those '*idéologues*'. The term has retained this meaning ever since. However, the pristine sense of *idéologie* is preserved in the passages included here.

In his Preface to *The Relationship between the Physical and the Moral* Cabanis links Hippocratic and Enlightenment thought otherwise separated by two millennia. As with the first of the Hippocratic selections in this Section, Cabanis rejects any firm distinction between the aims of the physician and those of one who would understand human nature. The moralist and the scientist are engaged in the same undertaking. Both seek to establish the lawful relationships obtaining between human nature and human needs. No artificial dualism can be profitably adopted by either: 'those who, in order to explain various functions, have thought it necessary to suppose of man two provinces of a different nature have, likewise, recognized that it is impossible to remove the intellectual and moral operations from the domain of science'.

Such arbitrary separation of the moral and the physical long yielded only vague metaphysical hypotheses by which contact with the actual moral dimensions of life—with life as lived—had proved to be impossible. This, says Cabanis, was the state of things before Locke, though even greater geniuses (Democritus and, in his way, Aristotle) could have been profitably consulted. In these references Cabanis wishes only to make clear what the turning point was: progress of a measurable sort became possible when, thanks chiefly to Locke, we came to grips with the fact *that all ideas come to be through the senses, or are the product of sensations.* And even before this Lockian insight Democritus and Epicurus had reduced reality to a common material composition. From these advances it was for Cabanis but a short step to recognizing the ineliminable connection between the physical and the moral sides of human life.

Cabanis completed his *Memoirs* just after the turn of the century, at about the same time that the 'science' of phrenology was presented in the pioneering volumes of Franz Joseph Gall. Reduced to the absurd by Gall's critics, phrenology was dismissed as no more than (in William James's words) 'bumpology', as if it claimed that the bumps on the surface of the cranium were sufficient to establish the intellectual and moral contents of the given mind. But Gall was a relentless researcher, a well-trained physician, and a defender of scientific approaches to matters long relegated to those in armchairs or pulpits. He had studied and sketched the nervous systems of foetuses aborted spontaneously during different gestational stages, thereby doing much to promote the field of developmental neuroanatomy, as his studies of non-human nervous systems advanced the field of comparative neuroanatomy. It is fair to say that, of those writing on the mind/body problem from the middle to the end of the eighteenth century (e.g. La Mettrie, Hartley, Holbach, Cabanis), Gall was clearly the most accomplished as a trained and practising scientist. What they all had in common was that Enlightenment conviction that the scientific method, so incredibly fertile in yielding solutions to problems in the physical world, was to be comparably successful in revealing the causal laws of biology as well. Voltaire had chided those who believed that, although all the stars and planets obeyed fixed and eternal laws, there was nonetheless, 'a little creature, five feet high, who acts solely according to his own caprice'. The mood of the age was against such exceptions. One by one, ambitious general theories of mind were propounded, each claiming support from direct clinical or experimental or anecdotal findings. Lombroso in Italy is found advancing a general theory of the 'criminal type'; the Swiss naturalist, Joseph Lavater, defends his science of physiognomy by which studies of the face are to establish the nature of the underlying personality; and Gall sets down the principles of phrenology according to which all the mental, moral, and social powers and penchants of the individual are related to the unique organization and development of specific parts of the brain.

How seriously these proposals were taken is a question settled not only by the numerous societies and publications organized around the works of such men but also by the generally favourable commentaries that would be written many years after it became clear that the promises were not to be fulfilled. On both of these accounts, Gall and phrenology still deserve serious respectful attention. It is worth noting that Captain FitzRoy of the *Beagle* was a 'Lavaterian' of sorts. Darwin recalls that, when interviewed for the position of naturalist on the *Beagle* he found the Captain's eyes returning to Darwin's nose. Later, sharing FitzRoy's quarters and establishing a friendship with him, Darwin was to discover that he had nearly been rejected by the Captain, owing to the fact that Darwin did not have 'the nose of a naturalist'! The same playful dismissals of phrenology could be heard by the middle of the nineteenth century but there were also sober and very positive appraisals published by such distinguished writers as Alexander Bain. His estimation of the science kept a proper distance from Gall's notions about cranial bumps, but Bain was quick to recognize that the overall phrenological perspective had already been vindicated in scores of experiments and in hundreds of clinical reports. To wit: specific mental functions, including those of a perceptual, memorial, cognitive, emotional, and motivational nature, vary in their expression as a function of the activity or state of health of specific regions of the brain. The theory of phrenology, then, was the first developed *modularity* theory of mind of which there are now abundant contemporary versions. At base, such theories all defend the proposition that complex mental operations are reducible to more elementary operations performed by specific areas in the brain. In Gall's hands, the theory established *localization of function* as the central problem in the brain sciences. It is the problem that has guided research from Gall's time to the present.

As early as the Hippocratic treatises the brain was identified as the organ of thought and sensation, but it was largely in response to the specific findings and theories of Gall and his disciples that a systematic programme of research was initiated to explore ever more exactly the relationship between psychological processes and specific structures within the brain. Gall was not the first to suggest specific structure–function relationships within the brain, for such relationships had long been observed in the history of medicine. Rather, phrenology focused on the functions of the mind, partitioned these into distinct 'faculties', and then set out to determine how each faculty depended for its expression and degree on a specific 'organ' in the brain. The utter abandonment of phrenology by the scientific community has left this 'modularity theory' largely untouched. Moreover, the criticisms of this theory advanced by Gall's contemporaries find an echo in today's critiques of present-day theories of the same type.

Writing in the 1830s Spurzheim presented the main arguments and conclusions of phrenology with confidence, not at all chastened by merely metaphysical theories about the incommensurability of the mental and the bodily. In chapters III–VI (reproduced here) of his *Outlines of Phrenology* Spurzheim simply refers to the clinical record, to well-known gender differences, to the familial incidence of mental defects, and to the coextensive development of mental and cerebral growth in children. The phrenological conclusion—that *the brain is the organ of the mind*—needs no further defence, and is vindicated each time the proper method for addressing such issues is adopted.

In the patrimony of Gall, even as he seeks to refine and correct features of Gall's system, Spurzheim notes the incompleteness of anatomy itself for a science of the mind. What is needed is *functional* anatomy; anatomy tied at once to physiology and to systematic observations of the behaving, striving organism. Only through the intercorrelation of the three—the actual anatomical details of the given brain, the general physiological laws governing these structures, and the specific performance of various persons and animals—is it possible to develop a science of the mind. The crucial test of the main phrenological thesis is one that reveals no major differences between the brains of animals whose mental powers differ. The test, that is, is an *experimental* test, not a metaphysical argument.

Perhaps the most interesting passages in Spurzheim's *Outline* are those in which he expresses grave doubts about the method of ablation; i.e. the surgical removal of a given region of the brain. This would come to be the dominant method in the brain sciences by the early decades of the nineteenth century and is still one of the principal research tools. It was the theory of phrenology itself that gave impetus to this method. In *Phrenology Examined* Pierre Flourens, one of the pioneers in the brain sciences, would criticize Gall on the basis of Flourens's own studies employing ablations of brain tissue. Before considering his criticism it is worth attending to Spurzheim's doubts about this very method. He declares that the method 'will remain useless', owing to the fact that it is not only violent but based on a mistaken line or reasoning. Various mental faculties 'might be retained without being manifested', notes Spurzheim. Moreover, the relationship between the detailed structure and function of the brain and the powers of the animal (or person) is unique to the given individual. What matters is not how large a given region of the brain is, but how large a fraction of the total brain mass is contributed by the specific region. Each species will reflect a species-defining relationship such that comparisons across species are hazardous even when the same 'organ' of the brain is under scrutiny. Nonetheless, the general principles that a science seeks to discover will be illustrated in the individual case.

Pierre Flourens was one of the earliest and most influential critics of phrenology, and one of the pioneers in the field of experimental neurosurgery. His research was guided by the specific claims of the phrenologists. Flourens set out to determine whether, in fact, specific mental and moral 'faculties' could be eliminated selectively by destruction of (phrenologically identified) specific regions of the animal brain. His numerous—and, many would say, ghoulish—surgical assaults on the brains of unanaesthetized animals made clear that very little of the total mass of the brain participated in genuinely intellectual or mental phenomena; rather such phenomena depend uniquely on the functioning of the cerebral hemispheres.

Interestingly, Flourens rather confirms the chief tenets of phrenology even as his research challenges the details of the theory. Functions Gall assigned to the entire brain Flourens reserves to the hemispheres. Against Gall's claim that the brain contains a number of distinct 'organs', each providing the necessary condition for a specific mental faculty, Flourens presents disconfirming evidence. Not only are intellectual powers vested in the hemispheres alone but one can remove 'a very considerable slice of the hemisphere of the brain, without destroying the intelligence'. Flourens had shown that the post-operative animal, now with a significant fraction of the cerebral hemispheres surgically removed, was capable of adaptive and purposive behaviour. Flourens's conclusion—that 'quite a restricted portion of the hemispheres may suffice for the purposes of intellection' is one that Gall's disciples easily could have incorporated into a general theory of phrenology. Flourens also reported a result that would be confirmed frequently over the succeeding century and in support of the same general conclusion. He found that the degree of intellectual loss occasioned by ablations depended less on the region than on the amount of cortical tissue removed. He is led to conclude that in these respects the cerebral hemispheres function as a unit which, in human beings, subserves the unity of the *self*.

The issue of the unity or multiplicity of 'self' will be considered in a later section. It is instructive to pause here, however, to examine further the relationship between cognitive deficits and cortical ablations. One of the best-known essays on this relationship is Karl Lashley's 'In Search of the Engram', published in 1960 and after Lashley had completed decades of research employing the ablation technique. Lashley would train preoperative animals on mazes of varying degrees of complexity and would then surgically remove regions of the cerebral cortex separately, in combination, successively, simultaneously. No matter what the combination, the results that reliably unfolded made clear that (*a*) even profound post-operative deficits could be overcome by retraining, (*b*) there was no specific region of the brain which selectively removed the memory 'engrams' of a learned task, and (c) the degree of deficit depended chiefly on the *mass* of tissue removed rather than on its location.

It was with intended irony that Lashley offered the playful conclusion, based on scores of studies conducted over thirty years, 'that learning just is not possible'! After all, if there is no place within the brain in which the memory 'engram' or physiologically coded record of experience is stored, and if all learned adaptive behaviour depends on the functions of the brain, then there can be no learning.

All this led Lashley to two general principles regarding brain function and cognitive ability; first, the *principle of mass action*, according to which (in keeping with Flourens's critique of Gall) the cerebral cortex functions *as an integrated whole*, rather than piecemeal; second, the *principle of equipotentiality*, according to which nearly any region of the cerebral cortex can come to serve a given function, just in case some more primary area has been destroyed. It is this latter principle that underscores the well-established *plasticity* of the central nervous system.

A century earlier, Alexander Bain's *The Senses and the Intellect* addressed this same set of issues, providing at once an assured reflection on the half-century of research following Gall's writings and a bridge to the conclusions and perspectives reached by Lashley and his contemporaries. Chosen for this Section are passages from that work that record the untroubled conclusion of the scientific world of 1855, viz. 'That the brain is the principal organ of the mind'; and still other passages offering a prescient critique of 'place' theories of mental functions. Bain's insistence that we 'must discard for ever the notion of the *sensorium commune*, the cerebral closet, as a central seat of the mind' awaits only Gilbert Ryle's 1949 book-length defence.

When Bain concludes his argument with, 'no currents, no mind', he completes the exorcism. The functions of the nervous system are not brought to the attention of some internal, all-viewing 'mind' seated somewhere inside the cerebral closet. Rather 'mind' and physiological functions are two sides of the same reality, not two distinct and separate realities. Bain, then, advances what is sometimes called the 'double aspect' solution to the mind/body problem; a solution predicated on the assumption that mental and physical ascriptions are ascriptions about the same singular reality, but viewed from different aspects. Aristotle offered a comparable thesis, noting that the philosopher (*dialektikos*) and the natural scientist (*phusikos*), who might be the same person, explain anger differently. The former accounts for it on the basis of one judging oneself to have been wrongly slighted, the latter in terms of changes in the temperature of the blood. These are accounts of the same event, rendered in different terms depending on just which aspect of the event is the object of enquiry.

This line of reasoning proved worrisome to moralists and theologians who found in it not only an essential materialism of the old stripe but a deterministic psychology judged to be incompatible with that very autonomy presupposed by all moral theories. If the contents of the mind are supplied entirely through the operation of the senses in commerce with the external world, and if the 'mind' is but the complex activity of a brain thus informed, then the course of action taken by anyone is the nearly mechanical inevitability immanent in the processes.

Thomas Henry Huxley, Darwin's 'bulldog', addressed such concerns in various lectures and publications, one of the most celebrated being excerpted in this Section. Not included are the opening pages in which Huxley lavishes praise on Descartes who, for all his dualistic temporizing, placed the psychological dimensions of human life squarely in the court of the biological sciences. Huxley correctly understands Descartes's theory of non-human psychology to be mechanistic and reflex-based such that the behaving organism is properly regarded as a *conscious automaton*. On this point, Huxley says, he fears 'no risk of either Papal or Presbyterian condemnation'. But then he takes what he judges to be that inductive leap sanctioned by evolutionary theory itself and concludes that, 'the argumentation which applies to brutes holds equally good of men; and therefore, that all states of consciousness in us, as in them, are immediately caused by molecular changes of the brain-substance'. Does this not turn morality on its head, and are not the logical consequences of such a thesis repugnant? For Huxley, 'logical consequences are the scarecrows of fools and the beacons of wise men'. The only question that counts is whether the thesis is true or false.

However, Huxley rejects both fatalism and materialism; the former as a species of logical but not *physical* necessity, and the latter because he is 'utterly incapable of conceiving the existence of matter if there is no mind in which to picture that existence'. This gracious nod to Berkeley is just Huxley's devotion to common sense rather than to the productions of metaphysics, but nothing on which he is prepared to dilate. Instead, he wishes his readers to consider that pious Christian scholars—Leibniz, Hartley, and Jonathan Edwards, to cite but three—embraced one or another version of the 'conscious automaton' thesis, so Huxley is on orthodox turf. His lengthy quote from Bonnet is retained here, for it makes Huxley's own position even clearer. That position is one that regards consciousness as but an *epiphenomenon* arising out of the brain's own complex operations and states. In what must be the most famous one-sentence statement of epiphenomenalism, Huxley declares, 'The soul stands related to the body as the bell of a clock to the works, and consciousness answers to the sound which the bell gives out when it is struck.' Conscious mental life is not something with an independent life of its own. It is but one manifestation of the brain's ceaseless and various activity.

The implications of this general orientation were not lost on the legal profession. It is within the juridical context that concepts of responsibility, autonomy, and blameworthiness have their most practical and dire application. Two works have been included here to illustrate the influence of the emerging 'brain sciences' on legal thinking. The first is taken from the transcript of the trial of James Hadfield (1800), who had been charged with making an attempt on the life of George III. In his defence of Hadfield, Thomas Erskine did much to overturn the traditional understanding of the degree of mental infirmity that is exculpatory. Seventy-five years later Henry Maudsley's textbook-treatise leaves no doubt but that issues of this sort are medical issues, and that their moral side awaits scientific elucidation.

The insanity defence, in one or another form, is virtually coextensive with Western jurisprudence. As early as the *Iliad* we find Agamemnon claiming to have been possessed and impelled by the gods on the day he and Achilles nearly came to blows. The earliest homicide laws promulgated in the archonship of Draco distinguish between intentional and unintended offences, and Rome's Twelve Tables provide for the management of the estate of those *furiosi* whose profligacy threatens to bankrupt them. The settled law from ancient times until the trial of Hadfield had required of those pleading insanity a degree of mental deficiency that included either profound retardation (*ideotus*) or such patent madness as to render one indistinguishable from 'an infant, a brute or a wild beast'. What Erskine successfully attempted in *Hadfield* was the overturning of this 'wild beast' standard and its replacement with the criterion of *delusion*. In the passages reprinted here from the trial transcript the testimony of the medical experts looms large in importance, as does evidence of traumatic injury to the brain. Little doubt is left but that Hadfield's pathetic and failing attempts against the king were impelled by a disordered brain. The Dr Creighton giving testimony is actually Dr Alexander Crichton who, two years earlier, published the pioneering *An Inquiry into the Nature and Origins of Mental Derangement, Comprehending a Concise System of Physiology and Pathology of the Human Mind, and History of the Passions and Their Effects*. It was a work that acquainted English and French physicians with advances in German medicine in fields that would soon merge to form the speciality of psychiatry. 'Creighton' (*sic*) makes clear that Hadfield's conduct is not at all uncommon among those whose brains have been comparably injured, especially in hot weather!

By the time Maudsley addresses the matter the progress of research and theory is evident. 'Insanity is, in fact, disorder of brain producing disorder of mind', he writes, adding as a footnote a definition of mind: 'Mind may be defined physiologically as a general term denoting the sum total of those functions of the brain which are known as thought, feeling, and will. By disorder of mind is meant disorder of those functions.' Maudsley accepts so-called 'moral causes', but only insofar as habitual practices and modes of stimulation can produce diseases in the organs thus exercised. The brain is no exception. But he then reminds readers that the symptoms assumed to arise from moral causes can be readily achieved by experimental manipulations of the brain or more generally of the overall physiology. What is beyond dispute, what is in fact 'an incontestable axiom', is that only the physiological method of study will unearth the causes and establish the remedies of the disordered mind.

The culmination of the arc of thought from Epicurus to Bain and Huxley, from Hippocrates to Crichton and Maudsley, is the point at which all talk of the 'mental' *as such* becomes first dubious and then gratuitous. Granting that, viewed in one *aspect*, events take on a mental or psychological character, it no longer follows that this aspect is divorced from or ontologically distinct from the actual physical events occurring in the body and specifically in the brain. So, the culmination of the broad materialistic perspective on mind/brain relations is the elimination of mind entirely; it is *eliminative materialism*. Two confident defences of this position are offered here; first the classic article by J. J. C. Smart, defending what is called the 'identity thesis'; and then Paul Churchland's summary of *eliminativism* and his defence of it against typical criticisms.

The 'identity thesis' sets out to solve two problems; the traditional problem of dualism which would have utterly immaterial, spaceless, massless 'mental' entities nonetheless bringing about all sorts of physical happenings, such as arms being raised and ships being launched; and the problem of *reference* when persons report 'mental' occurrences such as sensations. In adopting an identity theory of the mind/body relationship, Smart insists that there are not two sorts of things having some kind of influence on each other, but only one sort of thing, and that is a *brain process*. The problem of causality is eliminated, for nothing 'mental' is being caused. And the problem of reference is solved, too. For when Smith claims to see a blue light the answer to the question, 'To what is Smith referring?' is, *A process in his brain*. That is, if Smith's sensation-statement is referring to anything having actual ontological standing, then it is referring to a brain-state.

The identity thesis is economical but judged by some to be fatally flawed, or at least fatally incoherent. It is not clear, for example, just what sort of 'identity' is asserted. It cannot be a *logical* identity for, in that case, it would be totally necessary that sensations are brain processes, and the denial of this would be an out-and-out logical contradiction. Surely, even if it were the case that sensations are, in fact, brain processes, there is no logical requirement that this be the case. Logically there could be sensations without there being brains and vice versa.

Smart has argued for what he calls a *contingent identity*: true, it is not a logical requirement that sensations just are brain processes but, given the manner in which the physical universe is constituted, it happens that *sensations are brain processes*. Thus, 'morning star' and 'evening star' suggest two stars, but there is in fact (contingently) only one. So, too, 'toothache' and 'brain process-Q' suggest two ontologically distinct entities, but in fact there is only one. It remains contestable, however, whether the notion of a 'contingent' identity is coherent, at least to the extent that the proposition, 'A and B are identical' even *could* admit of exceptions; i.e. *could* be contingent. The 'relationship' between Morning Star and Evening Star on this account is chimerical, for nothing is 'related' to itself. Relations entail multiples. One might think that there are two things when, in fact, there is only one. One might think, while living at the north pole, that a new sun is created at six-month intervals. But if it is, in fact, the same sun, reappearing at six-month intervals, it is surely not *contingently* the same sun, for in that case it could have been something other than what it is, which is incoherent. Smith may never have been, but Smith could not have been Jones.

The now customary criticism of the identity thesis (and by extension of *eliminativism*, too) is based on the authority one has in the matter of one's own sensations (aches, pains, and after-images), contrasted with the fallibility of all statements one might make about brains and brain-states. On this view what Smith says about his toothache is *incorrigible*; it is not subject to correction by any source other than Smith himself. But what Smith (or anyone else) says about brains is always subject to correction. Accordingly, first-person sensation-reports have an epistemic property not possessed by any other empirical claim.

At one level, this criticism seeks to vindicate what is often dubbed 'folk psychology', the specific target of Paul Churchland's excerpted article. Unlike the identity theorist, who would preserve the vocabulary and explanations of folk psychology, joining them by identity-relations to the actual brain states to which they refer, Churchland seeks to eliminate them entirely. His reasons include scientific parsimony and fidelity to fact, but also the conviction that folk psychology as a theory is hopelessly flawed and fundamentally false. It has failed utterly in attempts to understand and explain mental illness, imagination and creativity, differences between individuals, learning itself. Moreover, it is outside the mainstream developments in all the sciences germane to the human condition; biology, chemistry, neuroscience. It has none of the resources necessary to become integrated within these rapidly developing fields.

If folk psychology has any credible support external to itself it has come from the school of thought known as *functionalism*, to be considered again in the next Section. The functionalist argues that the right theory of mind is one able to account for the actual functions served, *whatever the hardware*. A computer that achieves solutions to problems which presuppose rationality is 'rational', though it lacks a genotype, neurons, cortical cells, etc. The functionalist accepts that human performance is made possible by a given configuration of hardware, further shaped and directed by that software that just is the history of learning and experience. But there is no reason in principle to reserve such outcomes to one and only one sort of material system. The functions that count (in the matter of 'mind') are and must be expressed in the idiom of problem-solving, recognition, memory, judgement—the idiom of folk psychology. Thus, folk psychology on this account could not be replaced 'by any descriptive theory of neural mechanisms'.

This is all 'appealing', says Churchland, but, 'It needs to be revealed for the short-sighted and reactionary position it is.' As Churchland reads it, functionalism is not unlike the alchemy of old, imputing occult powers to the elements, and refusing to accept that it was not the 'spirits' in the matter that resulted in the desired effects, it was the matter itself. The functionalist position, relocated in history, would have made peace with the alchemical explanations; with the abstract vocabulary and, alas, the *functional state* that comes about when something is 'ensouled by mercury'! It is time to abandon all this, Churchland counsels, and to accept the monistic ontology on which all science and all progressive thought within science has so profitably depended. Only matter matters.

The strong inclination toward parsimony is at the bottom of most reductive and eliminativist proposals, but some find in this inclination the corresponding tendency to deny what is manifest in mental life. There are, to be sure, any number of similarities between physical and psychological functions, so the temptation to analogize is great. There are, however, places at which the analogies either clearly break down or are strained to the point of incredulity, and at these places admissions of ignorance are the better part of valour. Such wise counsel is illustrated in two selections separated by two centuries; the chapter 'Of Analogy' from Thomas Reid's *Essay on the Intellectual Powers of Man* and excerpts from Galen Strawson's *Mental Reality*.

Reid is often credited with putting 'faculty psychology' on the map, for his major treatises did, indeed, partition mental life into a number of roughly distinct perceptual, intellectual, emotional, and moral powers. The delineation of these powers gave the early phrenologists the mental entities of which there must be corresponding 'organs' in the brain. Reid, then, is justly placed in the 'modularity of mind' tradition, though it would be misleading to leave it at that. For Reid was also famously—even notoriously—ill-disposed toward theorizing. A tireless defender of the science of Bacon and of Newton, he criticized all who would replace systematic observation and experiment with little more than metaphysical enthusiasm. In the chapter preceding the one excerpted in this Section Reid declares how absurd it would be 'to say, that my memory, another man's imagination, and a third man's reason, may make one individual intelligent being'. Over and against such distinct powers or faculties the mind may be assumed to have, there is the undivided *person* whose powers these are. Accordingly, Reidian modularity is to be understood as a set of descriptions of the sorts of things possible for entities endowed with a mental life, and not as a set of separate and replaceable functional units. The latter conception arises from precisely that tendency to analogize from body to mind which Reid censures, finding it at once insufficiently defended and insensitive to the manifest differences between the terms of the analogy.

To Galen Strawson, too, who is willing to declare himself an 'agnostic materialist', the claims of eliminative materialism are all too simple and evasive. In *Mental Reality*, excerpted here, he reduces the problem of materialism to a single term: materialism faces only a single problem; not the problem of rationality or problem solving or pattern recognition or chess playing, for actual and readily imaginable physical systems can already claim such powers. Rather, 'the existence of experience is the only hard part of the mind–body problem', but Strawson takes this problem seriously. Functionalism fails to address it, and eliminative materialists refuse to own up to total ignorance of it. The sensible interim position for Strawson is akin to the 'neutral monism' of old; there is, indeed, only one sort of 'stuff' constitutive of reality, but what sort it is we do not know. It is not the complexity or peculiarity of consciousness that imposes ignorance here, according to Strawson, but 'our current conception of the physical [which] is fundamentally incomplete on its own terms'. As for eliminativism, 'The trouble with this view is that it is obviously false.' It would summon us to ignore 'one of the most dramatic and puzzling aspects of reality that there is'.

Still another and spirited defence of folk psychology (FP) is offered by John Searle in *The Rediscovery of the Mind*. With Strawson, Searle insists that our beliefs and desires (intentional states) are not 'postulated' in a way that might be disconfirmed by a behavioural or brain scientist; rather 'We simply experience conscious beliefs and desires', and these need not lead to observable behaviour at all. Moreover, eliminativism can find no sanctuary in the alleged fact that mental events will not be smoothly 'reduced' to neurobiology and, therefore, must be eliminated instead. Searle insists that 'real entities, from split-level ranch houses to cocktail parties . . . do not undergo smooth reduction . . . Why should they?' We don't eliminate the entity 'ranch house' because it is not readily reduced to bricks, insulation, and a two-car garage. Simply put, eliminativism rejects what is patent to every normal percipient, and said percipient is under no obligation to abandon the manifest facts of experience for the mixed pleasures of adopting a counter-intuitive theory. Searle is confident that the brain is at the bottom of all this, but that there is no 'simple or single path to the rediscovery of the mind'.

Excerpted portions of a chapter from Wilder Penfield's *The Mystery of the Mind* record the findings of one of the great neurosurgeons of the twentieth century; a surgeon who pioneered the technique of local anaesthesia during brain surgery, allowing surgeon and patient to converse. What he discovered was that 'the highest brain-mechanism is the mind's executive. Somehow, the executive accepts direction from the mind . . .'. After decades of observations, involving thousands of patients and the application of stimuli to various regions of the exposed human brain, Penfield found himself to be an unreconstructed dualist. He could accept no alternative to the view that there is in fact a conscious, striving, judging mind; served by the brain and, indeed, often tragically in its thrall, but not reducible to its sheer materiality.

The penultimate selection is taken from C. G. Jung's 'Basic Postulates of Analytical Philosophy'. It presents Jung's (characteristically) interpretive gloss on the historical movement from the transcendentalism of 'the Gothic Age' to the gritty materialism of the age of science and commerce. 'Consciousness ceased to grow upward', he writes. But with all the research and supporting rhetoric, the speculative intellect is still free, says Jung, to regard the mind as 'a mere play of electrons' or, for that matter, to regard the electrons' own unpredictability 'as the sign of mental life even in them'. The modern world of scientific progress is impatient with claims not grounded in visible facts. It is, however, the impatience of what Jung takes to be the simple mind.

The last selection is taken from Alan Turing's classic essay in *Mind* in which he did much to found the entire field of artificial intelligence (AI). In this essay Turing not only advances the strong AI thesis—to the effect that human cognitive powers can in principle be achieved by a universal digital computer properly programmed—but replies to a range of objections not unlike those still arrayed against the thesis. He remains undaunted in the face of Gödel's incompleteness theorem, Lady Lovelace's and Descartes's assurances that devices of such a sort would never achieve *creative* solutions to problems, etc. It is, indeed, the *classic* statement and has not been significantly improved in the intervening half-century.

HIPPOCRATES

26 **Ancient Medicine**

Certain physicians and philosophers assert that nobody can know medicine who is ignorant what a man is; he who would treat patients properly must, they say, learn this. But the question they raise is one for philosophy; it is the province of those who, like Empedocles, have written on natural science, what man is from the beginning, how he came into being at the first, and from what elements he was originally constructed. But my view is, first, that all that philosophers or physicians have said or written on natural science no more pertains to medicine than to painting. I also hold that clear knowledge about natural science can be acquired from medicine and from no other source, and that one can attain this knowledge when medicine itself has been properly comprehended, but till then it is quite impossible—I mean to possess this information, what man is, by what causes he is made, and similar points accurately.

[From *Ancient Medicine*, trans. W. H. Jones, Loeb edn. vol. i (Cambridge, Mass.: Harvard University Press, 1972), 53.]

HIPPOCRATES

27   The Sacred Disease

I am about to discuss the disease called 'sacred'. It is not, in my opinion, any more divine or more sacred than other diseases, but has a natural cause, and its supposed divine origin is due to men's inexperience, and to their wonder at its peculiar character. Now while men continue to believe in its divine origin because they are at a loss to understand it, they really disprove its divinity by the facile method of healing which they adopt, consisting as it does of purifications and incantations. But if it is to be considered divine just because it is wonderful, there will be not one sacred disease but many, for I will show that other diseases are no less wonderful and portentous, and yet nobody considers them sacred. For instance, quotidian fevers, tertians and quartans seem to me to be no less sacred and god-sent than this disease, but nobody wonders at them. Then again one can see men who are mad and delirious from no obvious cause, and committing many strange acts; while in their sleep, to my knowledge, many groan and shriek, others choke, others dart up and rush out of doors, being delirious until they wake, when they become as healthy and rational as they were before, though pale and weak; and this happens not once but many times. Many other instances, of various kinds, could be given, but time does not permit us to speak of each separately.

My own view is that those who first attributed a sacred character to this malady were like the magicians, purifiers, charlatans and quacks of our own day, men who claim great piety and superior knowledge. Being at a loss, and having no treatment which would help, they concealed and sheltered themselves behind superstition, and called this illness sacred, in order that their utter ignorance might not be manifest. They added a plausible story, and established a method of treatment that secured their own position. [. . .]

The fact is that the cause of this affection, as of the more serious diseases generally, is the brain. The manner and the cause I will now set forth clearly. The brain of man, like that of all animals, is double, being parted down its centre by a thin membrane. For this reason pain is not always felt in the same part of the head, but sometimes on one side, sometimes on the other, and occasionally all over. [. . .]

Men ought to know that from the brain, and from the brain only, arise our pleasures, joys, laughter and jests, as well as our sorrows, pains, griefs and tears. Through it, in particular, we think, see, hear, and distinguish the ugly from the beautiful, the bad from the good, the pleasant from the unpleasant, in some cases using custom as a test, in others perceiving them from their utility. It is the same thing which makes us mad or delirious, inspires us with dread and fear, whether by night or by day, brings sleeplessness, inopportune mistakes, aimless anxieties, absent-mindedness, and acts that are contrary to habit. These things that we suffer all come from the brain, when it is not healthy, but becomes abnormally hot, cold, moist, or dry, or suffers any other unnatural affection to which it was not accustomed. Madness comes from its moistness. When the brain is abnormally moist, of necessity it moves, and when it moves neither sight nor hearing are still, but we see or hear now one thing and now another, and the tongue speaks in accordance with the things seen and heard on any occasion. But all the time the brain is still a man is intelligent.

XVIII. The corruption of the brain is caused not only by phlegm but by bile. You may distinguish them thus. Those who are mad through phlegm are quiet, and neither shout nor make a disturbance; those maddened through bile are noisy, evil-doers and restless, always doing something inopportune. These are the causes of continued madness. But if terrors and fears attack, they are due to a change in the brain. Now it changes when it is heated, and it is heated by bile which rushes to the brain from the rest of the body by way of the blood-veins. The fear besets the patient until the bile re-enters the veins and the body. Then it is allayed. [. . .]

XIX. In these ways I hold that the brain is the most powerful organ of the human body, for when it is healthy it is an interpreter to us of the phenomena caused by the air, as it is the air that gives it intelligence. Eyes, ears, tongue, hands and feet act in accordance with the discernment of the brain; in fact the whole body participates in intelligence in proportion to its participation in air. To consciousness the brain is the messenger. For when a man draws breath into himself, the air first reaches the brain, and so is dispersed through the rest of the body, though it leaves in the brain its quintessence, and all that it has of intelligence and sense. If it reached the body first and the brain afterwards, it would leave discernment in the flesh and the veins, and reach the brain hot, and not pure but mixed with the humour from flesh and blood, so as to have lost its perfect nature.

Wherefore I assert that the brain is the interpreter of consciousness.

[From *The Sacred Disease*, trans. W. H. Jones, Loeb edn. vol. ii (Cambridge, Mass.: Harvard University Press, 1952), 139–41, 153, 175–9.]

There are four sense instruments in the head, namely, the eyes, ears, nose, and tongue, all of which take the source of their sensation from the encephalon, and although in this respect at least they seem to be similar, they differ specifically in the sensitive faculties themselves and in the bodies [nerves] through which the faculties reach them. For these faculties are able severally to distinguish odors, flavors, sounds, and colors. [. . .]

It is absolutely necessary for each of the latter to be altered if sensation is to occur. They are not, however, all altered by every perceptible thing; rather, the bright, luminous sense instrument is altered by colors, the airlike instrument by sounds, the vaporous instrument by odors, and in a word, like is perceptible by like. The airlike sense instrument can never be altered by colors, for if an instrument is to undergo alteration by colors easily and simply, it must be radiant, pure, and bright, as I have shown in my book *On Vision*. [. . .] Hence none of the sense instruments except the instrument of vision will be altered by colors; for vision alone has a sense instrument that is radiant, pure, and glistening, namely, the crystalline humour [the lens], as I have also demonstrated in my book *On Vision*. But it would be of no use for this alteration to take place unless it was recognized by the ruling principle which forms images, remembers, and reasons. Accordingly, the encephalon extends a part [*n. opticus*] of itself to the crystalline humor in order to know how it is being affected, and this outgrowth is properly the only one to have a perceptible channel, because it alone contains a very large amount of the psychic pneuma. [. . .]

Unless the alteration in each sense instrument comes from the encephalon and returns to it, the animal will still remain without sense perception. You could learn this by observing persons stricken with apoplexy, whose sense instruments are all uninjured, but who, for all that, receive no benefit from them in distinguishing sensations. [. . .]

It was entirely necessary for offshoots [*nn. vestibulocochleares*] of the encephalon to descend to the ears too in order to receive the external impressions falling upon them. Since, however, these impressions were noises or sounds caused by the air striking against something or being struck (it makes no difference which, so long as we agree on this one thing, namely, that the motion resulting from the stroke must proceed like a wave and ascend to the encephalon).

[From *On the Usefulness of the Parts of the Body*, trans. M. T. May (Ithaca, NY: Cornell University Press, 1968), 400–3.]

29 The Soul's Dependence on the Body

The faculties of the soul depend on the mixtures of the body. The truth of this proposition is something I have confirmed on more than one occasion; nor does it rest purely on my own experience, however substantial [. . .] The starting point for this whole enquiry is an understanding of the differences of behaviour and affection of the soul in small children; for these differences give clear evidence of the various faculties of the soul . . . On this point many of the philosophers appear to be in some confusion, lacking a clearly articulated notion of 'faculty'. They seem to conceive of faculties as things which inhabit 'substances' in much the same way as we inhabit our houses, and not to realize that the effective cause of every event is conceived of in relational terms; there is a way of talking of this cause as of a specific object, but the faculty arises *in relation to* the event caused. We therefore attribute as many faculties to a substance as activities. For example, aloe has a cleansing and toning faculty in relation to the throat, and a faculty of binding bleeding wounds, of scarring over grazes, and of drying the moisture in the eyes. But there is no other object apart from the aloe which is performing all these actions. The aloe is what is active, and it is because of its ability to perform these actions that it is said to have these faculties—as many faculties, in fact, as the actions in question. [. . .] In the same way, if we say: 'the rational soul, seated in the brain, is able to perceive through the organs of perception, through the objects of that perception to remember, and by itself to discern the conflict and consistency between facts, and to analyse and collate them,' this statement means exactly the same as: 'the rational soul has several faculties: perception, memory, and understanding, as well as all the others.' [. . .]

If, then, the reasoning faculty is a form of the soul, it must be mortal: for it too will be a mixture, namely a mixture within the brain. If, on the other hand, it is immortal, as Plato believes, there is a problem as to why it should depart when the brain undergoes excessive cooling, heating, drying, or moistening [. . .] But why does a great loss of blood, or the drinking of hemlock, or a raging fever cause such separation? If Plato were alive, I would most gladly receive instruction from him on that point. But he is dead, and none of the present-day Platonists has ever shown me the cause for the soul leaving the body in the circumstances I have mentioned.

[From *Galen, Selected Works*, trans. P. N. Singer (Oxford: Oxford University Press, 1997), 150–3.]

What sensation is and how it operates

It must be realized that the human soul, while informing the entire body, nevertheless has its principal seat in the brain; it is here alone that the soul not only understands and imagines but also has sensory awareness. Sensory awareness comes about by means of nerves, which stretch like threads from the brain to all the limbs, and are joined together in such a way that hardly any part of the human body can be touched without producing movement in several of the nerve-ends that are scattered around in that area. This movement is then transmitted to the other ends of the nerves which are all grouped together in the brain around the seat of the soul [. . .] The result of these movements being set up in the brain by the nerves is that the soul or mind that is closely joined to the brain is affected in various ways, corresponding to the various different sorts of movements. And the various different states of mind, or thoughts, which are the immediate result of these movements are called sensory perceptions, or in ordinary speech, sensations.

Various kinds of sensation. First, internal sensations, i.e. emotional states of the mind and natural appetites

The wide variety in sensations is a result, firstly, of differences in the nerves themselves, and secondly of differences in the sorts of motion which occur in particular nerves. It is not that each individual nerve produces a particular kind of sensation; indeed, there are only seven principal groups of nerves, of which two have to do with internal sensations and five with external sensations. The nerves which go to the stomach, oesophagus, throat, and other internal parts whose function is to keep our natural wants supplied, produce one kind of internal sensation, which is called 'natural appetite' e.g. hunger and thirst. The nerves which go to the heart and the surrounding area including the diaphragm, despite their very small size, produce another kind of internal sensation which comprises all the disturbances or passions and emotions of the mind such as joy, sorrow, love, hate and so on. For example, when the blood has the right consistency so that it expands in the heart more readily than usual, it relaxes the nerves scattered around the openings, and sets up a movement which leads to a subsequent movement in the brain producing a natural feeling of joy in the mind; and other causes produce the same sort of movement in these tiny nerves, thereby giving the same feeling of joy. Thus, if we imagine ourselves enjoying some good, the act of imagination does not itself contain the feeling of joy, but it causes the spirits to travel from the brain to the muscles in which these nerves are embedded. This causes the openings of the heart to expand, and this in turn produces the movement in the tiny nerves of the heart which must result in the feeling of joy. In the same way, when we hear good news, it is first of all the mind which makes a judgement about it and rejoices with that intellectual joy which occurs without any bodily disturbance and which, for that reason, the Stoics allowed that the man of wisdom could experience (although they required him to be free of all passion). But later on, when the good news is pictured in the imagination, the spirits flow from the brain to the muscles around the heart and move the tiny nerves there, thereby causing a movement in the brain which produces in the mind a feeling of animal joy. [. . .] Other movements in these tiny nerves produce different emotions such as love, hatred, fear, anger and so on; I am here thinking of these simply as emotions or passions of the soul, that is, as confused thoughts, which the mind does not derive from itself alone but experiences as a result of something happening to the body with which it is closely conjoined. These emotions are quite different in kind from the distinct thoughts which we have concerning what is to be embraced or desired or shunned. The same applies to the natural appetites such as hunger and thirst which depend on the nerves of the stomach, throat and so forth: they are completely different from the volition to eat, drink and so on. But, because they are frequently accompanied by such volition or appetition, they are called appetites. [. . .]

The soul has sensory awareness only in so far as it is in the brain

There is clear proof that the soul's sensory awareness, via the nerves, of what happens to the individual limbs of the body does not come about in virtue of the soul's presence in the individual limbs, but simply in virtue of its presence in the brain or because the nerves by their motions transmit to it the actions of external objects which touch the parts of the body where the nerves are embedded. Firstly, there are various diseases which affect only the brain but remove or interfere with all sensation. Again, sleep occurs only in the brain, yet every day it deprives us of a great part of our sensory faculties, though these are afterwards restored on waking. Next, when the brain is undamaged, if there is an obstruction in the paths by which the nerves reach the brain from the external limbs, this alone is enough to destroy sensation in those limbs. Lastly, we sometimes feel pain in certain limbs even though there is nothing to cause pain in the limbs themselves; the cause of the pain lies in the other areas through which the nerves travel in their journey from the limbs to the brain. This last point can be proved by countless observations, but it will suffice to mention one here. A girl with a seriously infected hand used to have her eyes bandaged whenever the surgeon visited her, to prevent her being upset by the surgical instruments. After a few days her arm was amputated at the elbow because of a creeping gangrene, and wads of bandages were put in its place so that she was quite unaware that she had lost her arm: However she continued to complain of pains, now in one then in another finger of the amputated hand. The only possible reason for this is that the nerves which used to go from the brain down to the hand now terminated in the arm near the elbow, and were being agitated by the same sorts of motion as must previously have been set up in the hand, so as to produce in the soul, residing in the brain, the sensation of pain in this or that finger. And this shows clearly that pain in the hand is felt by the soul not because it is present in the hand but because it is present in the brain.

The nature of the mind is such that various sensations can be produced in it simply by motions in the body

It can also be proved that the nature of our mind is such that the mere occurrence of certain motions in the body can stimulate it to have all manner of thoughts which have no likeness to the movements in question. This is especially true of the confused thoughts we call sensations or feelings. For we see that spoken or written words excite all sorts of thoughts and emotions in our minds. With the same paper, pen and ink, if the tip of the pen is pushed across the paper in a certain way it will form letters which excite in the mind of the reader thoughts of battles, storms and violence, and emotions of indignation and sorrow; but if the movements of the pen are just slightly different they will produce quite different thoughts of tranquillity, peace and pleasure, and quite opposite emotions of love and joy. It may be objected that speech or writing does not immediately excite in the mind any emotions, or images of things apart from the words themselves; it merely occasions various acts of understanding which afterwards result in the soul's constructing within itself the images of various things. But what then will be said of the sensations of pain and pleasure? A sword strikes our body and cuts it; but the ensuing pain is completely different from the local motion of the sword or of the body that is cut—as different as colour or sound or smell or taste. We clearly see, then, that the sensation of pain is excited in us merely by the local motion of some parts of our body in contact with another body; so we may conclude that the nature of our mind is such that it can be subject to all the other sensations merely as a result of other local motions.

[From *Principles of Philosophy*, in *The Philosophical Writings of Descartes*, ed. and trans. J. Cottingham, R. Stoothoff, and D. Murdoch (Cambridge: Cambridge University Press, 1984), i. 279–84.]

I shall consider you instead (and you will be quite happy with this) as a specific sort of intellect exercising control in the body.

Now the difficulty, to repeat, is not about whether or not you are separable from this body (and this is why I suggested above that you had no need to have recourse to God's power in order to establish that things which you understand apart from each other are separate). Rather, the difficulty concerns the body which you yourself are—for you may be a rarefied body infused into this solid one or occupying some part of it. At all events you have not yet convinced us that you are something wholly incorporeal. And although in the Second Meditation you declared that you are not a wind, fire, air or breath, I did warn you that you had asserted this without any proof.

You said there that you were not arguing about these things at that stage; but you never went on to discuss them, and you never gave any sort of proof that you are not a body of this sort. I had hoped that you would now offer one; but what discussion and proof you do offer simply establishes that you are not this solid body, and, as I have just said, there is no difficulty about this.

4. 'But', you say, 'on the one hand I have a clear and distinct idea of myself, in so far as I am simply a thinking, non-extended thing; and on the other hand I have a distinct idea of body, in so far as it is simply an extended, non-thinking thing.' Now as far as the idea of body is concerned, it does not seem that it ought to cause us too much trouble. If you are talking of the idea of body in the general sense, then we must repeat our objection that you still have to prove that being capable of thought is inconsistent with the nature of body. For you would be begging the question, if you set up the inquiry as to whether you are a rarefied body in such a way as to presuppose that thought and body are incompatible.

But your claim undoubtedly concerns merely this solid body from which you maintain you are distinct and separable. And thus I do not so much dispute that you have an idea of this body as insist that you could not have such an idea if you were really an unextended thing. For how, may I ask, do you think that you, an unextended subject, could receive the semblance or idea of a body that is extended? If such a semblance comes from a body then it is undoubtedly corporeal, and has a number of parts or layers, and so is extended. If it is imprinted in you from some other source, since it must still represent an extended body, it must still have parts and hence be extended. For if it lacks parts, how will it manage to represent parts? If it lacks extension, how will it represent an extended thing? If it lacks shape, how will it represent a thing that has a shape? If it has no position, how will it represent a thing which has upper and lower parts, parts on the right and parts on the left, and parts in the middle? If it lacks all variation, how will it represent various colours and so on? It seems, then, that the idea does not wholly lack extension. Yet if it is extended, how can you, if you are unextended, have become its subject? How will you adapt it to yourself or make use of it? And how will you gradually experience its fading and disappearing?

As far as your idea of yourself is concerned, there is nothing to add to what I have already said, especially regarding the Second Meditation. For what emerges there is that, far from having a clear and distinct idea of yourself you have no idea of yourself at all. This is because although you recognize that you are thinking, you still do not know what kind of thing you, who are thinking, are. And since it is only this operation that you are aware of, the most important element is still hidden from you, namely the substance which performs this operation. [. . .]

But I will not press this point, but ask you this instead. You say you are a thing which is not extended; but are you not diffused throughout the body? I have no idea what reply you will give, for although from the start I gathered that you were in the brain, this was something I arrived at by conjecture rather than by simply following your views. The source of my conjecture was a later passage, where you say that you are 'not affected by all parts of the body but only by the brain, or only by one small part of it'. But I was not at all certain whether this meant that you were in fact present only in the brain (or a part of it); for you might be present throughout the body but affected only in one part of it—just as we commonly say that the soul is diffused throughout the whole body but sees only in the eye.

[From *Objections* to Descartes's *Meditations*, in *The Philosophical Writings of Descartes*, ed. and trans. J. Cottingham, R. Stoothoff, and D. Murdoch (Cambridge: Cambridge University Press, 1984), ii. 233–5.]

JULIEN OFFRAY DE LA METTRIE

32   Man a Machine

As a violin string or a harpsichord key vibrates and gives forth sound, so the cerebral fibres, struck by waves of sound, are stimulated to render or repeat the words that strike them. And as the structure of the brain is such that when eyes well formed for seeing, have once perceived the image of objects, the brain can not help seeing their images and their differences, so when the signs of these differences have been traced or imprinted in the brain, the soul necessarily examines their relations—an examination that would have been impossible without the discovery of signs or the invention of language. At the time when the universe was almost dumb, the soul's attitude toward all objects was that of a man without any idea of proportion toward a picture or a piece of sculpture, in which he could distinguish nothing; or the soul was like a little child (for the soul was then in its infancy) who, holding in his hand small bits of straw or wood, sees them in a vague and superficial way without being able to count or distinguish them. But let some one attach a kind of banner, or standard, to this bit of wood (which perhaps is called a mast), and another banner to another similar object; let the first be known by the symbol 1, and the second by the symbol or number 2, then the child will be able to count the objects, and in this way he will learn all of arithmetic. As soon as one figure seems equal to another in its numerical sign, he will decide without difficulty that they are two different bodies, that $1 + 1$ make 2, and $2 + 2$ make 4,[1] etc.

This real or apparent likeness of figures is the fundamental basis of all truths and of all we know. Among these sciences, evidently those whose signs are less simple and less sensible are harder to understand than the others, because more talent is required to comprehend and combine the immense number of words by which such sciences express the truths in their province. On the other hand, the sciences that are expressed by numbers or by other small signs, are easily learned; and without doubt this facility rather than its demonstrability is what has made the fortune of algebra.

All this knowledge, with which vanity fills the balloon-like brains of our proud pedants, is therefore but a huge mass of words and figures, which form in the brain all the marks by which we distinguish and recall objects. All our ideas are awakened after the fashion in which the gardener who knows plants recalls all stages of their growth at sight of them. These words and the objects designated by them are so connected in the brain that it is comparatively rare to imagine a thing without the name or sign that is attached to it.

I always use the word 'imagine,' because I think that everything is the work of imagination, and that all the faculties of the soul can be correctly reduced to pure imagination in which they all consist. Thus judgment, reason, and memory are not absolute parts of the soul, but merely modifications of this kind of medullary screen upon which images of the objects painted in the eye are projected as by a magic lantern.

But if such is the marvelous and incomprehensible result of the structure of the brain, if everything is perceived and explained by imagination, why should we divide the sensitive principle which thinks in man? Is not this a clear inconsistency in the partisans of the simplicity of the mind? For a thing that is divided can no longer without absurdity be regarded as indivisible. See to what one is brought by the abuse of language and by those fine words (spirituality, immateriality, etc.) used haphazard and not understood even by the most brilliant. [. . .]

Man's preeminent advantage is his organism. In vain all writers of books on morals fail to regard as praiseworthy those qualities that come by nature, esteeming only the talents gained by dint of reflection and industry. For whence come, I ask, skill, learning, and virtue, if not from a disposition that makes us fit to become skilful, wise and virtuous? And whence again, comes this disposition, if not from nature? Only through nature do we have any good qualities; to her we owe all that we are. [. . .]

If one's organism is an advantage, and the preeminent advantage, and the source of all others, education is the second. The best made brain would be a total loss without it, just as the best constituted man would be but a common peasant, without knowledge of the ways of the world. But, on the other hand, what would be the use of the most excellent school, without a matrix perfectly open to the entrance and conception of ideas? It is . . . impossible to impart a single idea to a man deprived of all his senses. [. . .]

Let us observe the ape, the beaver, the elephant, etc., in their operations. If it is clear that these activities can not be performed without intelligence, why refuse intelligence to these animals? And if you grant them a soul, you are lost, you fanatics! You will in vain say that you assert nothing about the nature of the animal soul and that you deny its immortality. Who does not see that this is a gratuitous assertion; who does not see that the soul of an animal must be either mortal or immortal, whichever ours [is], and that it must therefore undergo the same fate as ours, whatever that may be, and that thus [in admitting that animals have souls], you fall into Scylla in the effort to avoid Charybdis?

Break the chain of your prejudices, arm yourselves with the torch of experience, and you will render to nature the honor she deserves, instead of inferring anything to her disadvantage, from the ignorance in which she has left you. Only open wide your eyes, only disregard what you can not understand, and you will see that the ploughman whose intelligence and ideas extend no further than the bounds of his furrow, does not differ essentially from the greatest genius,—a truth which the dissection of Descartes's and of Newton's brains would have proved; you will be persuaded that the imbecile and the fool are animals with human faces, as the intelligent ape is a little man in another shape; in short, you will learn that since everything depends absolutely on difference of organization, a well constructed animal which has studied astronomy, can predict an eclipse, as it can predict recovery or death when it has used its genius and its clearness of vision, for a time, in the school of Hippocrates and at the bedside of the sick. By this line of observations and truths, we come to connect the admirable power of thought with matter, without being able to see the links, because the subject of this attribute is essentially unknown to us. [. . .]

Let us then conclude boldly that man is a machine, and that in the whole universe there is but a single substance differently modified. This is no hypothesis set forth by dint of a number of postulates and assumptions; it is not the work of prejudice, nor even of my reason alone; I should have disdained a guide which I think to be so untrustworthy, had not my senses, bearing a torch, so to speak, induced me to follow reason by lighting the way themselves. Experience has thus spoken to me in behalf of reason; and in this way I have combined the two.

But it must have been noticed that I have not allowed myself even the most vigorous and immediately deduced reasoning, except as a result of a multitude of observations which no scholar will contest; and furthermore, I recognize only scholars as judges of the conclusions which I draw from the observations; and I hereby challenge every prejudiced man who is neither anatomist, nor acquainted with the only philosophy which can here be considered, that of the human body. Against so strong and solid an oak, what could the weak reeds of theology, of metaphysics, and of the schools, avail,—childish arms, like our parlor foils, that may well afford the pleasure of fencing, but can never wound an adversary. Need I say that I refer to the empty and trivial notions, to the pitiable and trite arguments that will be urged (as long as the shadow of prejudice or of superstition remains on earth) for the supposed incompatibility of two substances which meet and move each other unceasingly? Such is my system, or rather the truth, unless I am much deceived. It is short and simple. Dispute it now who will.

[From *Man a Machine*, trans. M. W. Calkins (La Salle, Ill.: Open Court, 1912), 105–11, 146–9.]

DAVID HARTLEY

33   Observations on Man

Of the Doctrine of Vibrations, and its Use for explaining the Sensations

PROP. I.
The white medullary Substance of the Brain, Spinal Marrow, and the Nerves proceeding from them, is the immediate Instrument of Sensation and Motion

Under the Word *Brain*, in these *Observations*, I comprehend all that lies within the Cavity of the Skull, *i.e.* the *Cerebrum*, or *Brain* properly so called, the *Cerebellum*, and the *Medulla oblongata*.

This Proposition seems to be sufficiently proved in the Writings of Physicians and Anatomists; from the Structure and Functions of the several Organs of the Human Body; from Experiments on living Animals; from the Symptoms of Diseases, and from Dissections of morbid Bodies. Sensibility, and the Power of Motion, seem to be conveyed to all the Parts, in their natural State, from the Brain and Spinal Marrow, along the Nerves. These arise from the medullary, not the cortical Part, every-where, and are themselves of a white medullary Substance. When the Nerves of any Part are cut, tied, or compressed in any considerable Degree, the Functions of that Part are either intirely destroyed, or much impaired. When the Spinal Marrow is compressed by a Dislocation of the *Vertebræ* of the Back, all the Parts, whose Nerves arise below the Place of Dislocation, become paralytic. When any considerable Injury is done to the medullary Substance of the Brain, Sensation, voluntary Motion, Memory and Intellect, are either intirely lost, or much impaired; and if the Injury be very great, this extends immediately to the vital Motions also, *viz.* to those of the Heart, and Organs of Respiration, so as to occasion Death. But this does not hold equally in respect of the cortical Substance of the Brain; perhaps not at all, unless as far as Injuries done to it extend themselves to the medullary Substance. In Dissections after Apoplexies, Palsies, Epilepsies, and other Distempers affecting the Sensations and Motions, it is usual to find some great Disorder in the Brain, from preternatural Tumors, from Blood, Matter, or Serum, lying upon the Brain, or in its Ventricles, &c. This may suffice as general Evidence for the present. The particular Reasons of some of these Phænomena, with more definite Evidences, will offer themselves in the Course of these *Observations*.

PROP. 2.

The white medullary Substance of the Brain is also the immediate Instrument, by which Ideas are presented to the Mind: Or, in other Words, whatever Changes are made in this Substance, corresponding Changes are made in our Ideas; and vice versa

The Evidence for this Proposition is also to be taken from the Writings of Physicians and Anatomists; but especially from those Parts of these Writings, which treat of the Faculties of Memory, Attention, Imagination, &c. and of mental Disorders. It is sufficiently manifest from hence, that the Perfection of our mental Faculties depends upon the Perfection of this Substance; that all Injuries done to it, affect the Trains of Ideas proportionably; and that these cannot be restored to their natural Course, till such Injuries be repaired. Poisons, Spirituous Liquors, Opiates, Fevers, Blows upon the Head, &c. all plainly affect the Mind, by first disordering the medullary Substance. And Evacuations, Rest, Medicines, Time, &c. as plainly restore the Mind to its former State, by reversing the foregoing Steps. But there will be more and more definite Evidence offered in the Course of these *Observations*. [. . .]

PROP. 4.

External Objects impressed upon the Senses occasion, first in the Nerves on which they are impressed, and then in the Brain, Vibrations of the finall, and, as one may say, infinitesimal, medullary Particles

These Vibrations are Motions backwards and forwards of the small Particles; of the same kind with the Oscillations of Pendulums, and the Tremblings of the Particles of sounding Bodies. They must be conceived to be exceedingly short and small, so as not to have the least Efficacy to disturb or move the whole Bodies of the Nerves or Brain. [. . .]

OF MADNESS

The Causes of Madness are of two Kinds, bodily and mental. That which arises from bodily Causes is nearly related to Drunkenness, and to the Deliriums attending Distempers. That from mental Causes is of the same Kind with temporary Alienations of the Mind during violent Passions, and with the Prejudices and Opinionativeness, which much Application to one Set of Ideas only occasions.

We may thus distinguish the Causes for the more easy Conception and Analysis of the Subject; but, in fact, they are both united for the most part. The bodily Cause lays hold of that Passion or Affection, which is most disproportionate; and the mental Cause, when that is primary, generally waits till some bodily Distemper gives it full Scope to exert itself. Agreeably to this, the Prevention and Cure of all Kinds of Madness require an Attention both to the Body and Mind; which coincides in a particular manner with the general Doctrine of these Papers.

It is observed, that mad Persons often speak rationally and consistently upon the Subjects that occur, provided that single one which most affects them, be kept out of View. And the Reason of this may be, that whether they first become mad, because a particular, original, mental Uneasiness falls in with an accidental, bodily Disorder; or because an original, bodily Disorder falls in with an accidental mental one; it must follow, that a particular Set of Ideas shall be extremely magnified, and, consequently, an unnatural Association of Sameness or Repugnancy between them generated, all other Ideas and Associations remaining nearly the same. Thus, suppose a Person, whose nervous System is disordered, to turn his Thoughts accidentally to some barely possible Good or Evil. If the nervous Disorder falls in with this, it increases the Vibrations belonging to its Idea so much, as to give it a Reality, a Connexion with *Self.* For we distinguish the Recollection and Anticipation of things relating to ourselves, from those of things relating to other Persons, chiefly by the Difference of Strength in the Vibrations, and in their Coalescences with each other. When one false Position of this Kind is admitted, it begets more of course, the same bodily and mental Causes also continuing; but then this Process stops after a certain Number of false Positions are adopted from their mutual Inconsistency (unless the whole nervous System be deranged); and it is often confined to a certain Kind, as the irascible, the terrifying, &c.

The Memory is often much impaired in Madness, which is both a Sign of the Greatness of the bodily Disorder, and a Hindrance to mental Rectification; and therefore a bad Prognostic. If an opposite State of Body and Mind can be introduced early, before the unnatural Associations are too much cemented, the Madness is cured; if otherwise, it will remain, tho' both the bodily and mental Cause should be at last removed.

Inquiries after the Philosophers Stone, the Longitude, &c. to which Men are prompted by strong ambitious, or covetous Desires, are often both Cause and Effect, in respect of Madness. Excessive Fits of Anger and Fear are also found often to hurry Persons into Madness.

In Dissections after Madness the Brain is often found dry, and the Blood-vessels much distended; which are Arguments, that violent Vibrations took place in the internal Parts of the Brain, the peculiar Residence of Ideas and Passions; and that it was much compressed, so as to obstruct the natural Course of Association.

As in mad Persons the Vibrations in the internal Parts of the Brain are preternaturally increased, so they are defective in the external Organs, in the Glands, &c. Hence, Maniacs eat little, are costive, make little Water, and take scarce any notice of external Impressions. The Violence of the Ideas and Passions may give them great muscular Strength upon particular Occasions, when the violent Vibrations descend from the internal Parts of the Brain into the Muscles, according to former Associations of these with the voluntary Motions (the same Increase of Vibrations in the internal Parts of the Brain, which hinders the ascending Vibrations of Sensation, augmenting the descending ones of Motion). But Maniacs are often very sluggish, as well as insensible, from the great Prevalence of the ideal Vibrations; just as Persons in a State of deep Attention are. An accurate History of the several Kinds of Madness from those Physicians, who are much conversant with this Distemper, is greatly wanted, and it would probably receive considerable Light from this Theory.

[From *Observations on Man* (1749), facsimile edn. sect. I (Gainesville, Fla.: Scholars' Facsimiles of Reprints, 1966), 7–11, 401–3.]

34 The Relationship between the Moral and the Physical

The study of man's physical constitution holds the same concern for the physician and the moral philosopher, and is, almost to the same extent, indispensable to both.

In observing natural phenomena and in striving to uncover the secrets of physical organization, the physician seeks to discover just what constitutes the state of perfect health, what conditions are capable of disturbing the equilibrium, and what can be done to preserve or restore it.

The moral philosopher endeavors to attain an understanding of the most concealed physiological processes which form the functions of the intellect and the resolutions of the will. He searches these processes for the rules which must guide life, and the avenues which lead to happiness.

Man has certain needs: he possesses faculties in order to satisfy these needs; and both needs and faculties are directly dependent on his physical constitution.

Is it possible to ascertain when thoughts are born and when intentions are formed from the effect produced by particular movements on certain organs of the body? And is it possible to determine whether these organs are subject to the same laws as these functions?

When man is among his fellows, do all the relationships that might become established between them and him result directly from their mutual needs, or from the exercise of the faculties which their needs activate? And do these same relationships, which are for the moral philosopher what they are for the physician—the phenomena of physical life—offer various corresponding states to those of sickness and health? Is one able to recognize, through observation, the conditions which give rise to, and maintain, these same states? And, in turn, are these states able to furnish us, through reasoning and experience, with those methods of hygiene or of cure which must be employed in behalf of moral man?

Such are the questions which the moral philosopher aims to resolve by proceeding back in his search to the study of physical organization and biological phenomena.

Writers who have possessed some penetration with respect to the analysis of ideas, of language, or of the other signs which are representative of them, and of public or private morality, have nearly all recognized the need to proceed in their investigations toward an understanding of the physical nature of man. How, in effect, is it possible to describe with accuracy, to limit and estimate without error, the movements of a machine and the consequences of its actions, if one does not know in advance its structure and its properties? At all times, one has endeavored to grant to this subject several incontestable points, or as such regarded. Each philosopher has rendered his theory of man: those who, in order to explain various functions, have thought it necessary to suppose of man two provinces of a different nature have, likewise, recognized that it is impossible to remove the intellectual and moral operations from the domain of science. And within the strict relationship that philosophers admit of between these two driving forces, the form and the character of the movements remain always subordinate to the laws of natural organization.

But if knowledge of the structure and properties of the human body is necessary to give direction to the study of life's diverse phenomena, then conversely, when these phenomena, which become visible to us in action, are comprehended as a whole and considered from every point of view, they throw a great light on these same properties. These phenomena establish the nature of these properties and circumscribe their force. Above all, they reveal more clearly by what connections these properties are bound up with the structure of living bodies and continue to be subject to the same laws which preside at the inception of life, regulate its development, and tend to preserve it.

Here, the moral philosopher and the physician still proceed along the same path. The latter acquires complete understanding of *physical man* only by considering him in every state which allows motion to be imparted to external bodies and which allows modifications of his appropriate sensory faculty. The former presents ideas which are much wider in scope and are more applicable to *moral man*, having followed him carefully in all circumstances in which the fortunes of life, the affairs of society, the variety of governments and laws, and the totality of errors—or of truths—have surrounded him.

Thus, the moral philosopher and the physician have two direct methods of inquiry—uniquely cultivated by each—to offer to speculation in the different branches of science; methods which, in all certainty, are accessible to the other natural sciences and which cannot be reduced to a mathematical formula. By these methods the moral philosopher and the physician are in a position to bring their conclusions to that high degree of probability which constitutes 'certainty' in those professions [devoted to natural phenomena].

But ever since it was judged appropriate to separate the study of physical man from that of moral man, the principles relevant to the latter were necessarily found to be obscured by the vagueness of the metaphysical hypotheses. Indeed, after the introduction of these hypotheses to the study of the moral sciences, there no longer remained a solid foundation nor fixed point to which one could connect the results of observation and experiment. At this moment, adrift in the capriciousness of the most fanciful ideas, these hypotheses are, to some extent, returning to the domain of the imagination.

Some good minds have been able to reduce to the strictest bounds of empiricism the precepts of which these hypotheses are composed.

Such was the state of the moral sciences before Locke; such is the objection to them which, at one time, could have been made with some foundation—before a more confident philosophy had recognized, in the same laws or in the same properties which determine biological actions, the primary source of all the marvels of the moral and intellectual world.

Still, some men, endowed with more genius, perhaps, than even this revered philosopher [*i.e.*, Locke], foresaw the fundamental verities, as we see in their writings. One finds traces of these truths in Aristotle's philosophy, and in that of Democritus, whose philosophy was revived by Epicurus. The immortal Bacon had discovered or anticipated nearly all that would call for the total remodeling, not only of science but, following his expression, of the *human understanding*, itself. Hobbes, especially, through nothing less than the singular precision of his language, was driven, without digression, to the veritable origin of our understanding. He carefully traces the paths to it; he establishes, with certainty, its boundaries. But it was not at all from Hobbes, but from Locke, his successor, that philosophy's greatest and most beneficial revolution would receive its first impetus. Because of Locke it became necessary for the first time to state clearly and confirm through his direct proofs that fundamental axiom: *that all ideas come to be through the senses, or are the product of sensations.*

[From the Preface to *On the Relationship between the Moral and the Physical*, trans. F. Robinson (Paris: Presses Universitaires de France, 1956), 1–4.]

GEORGE SPURZHEIM

35   Outlines of Phrenology

Chap. III
The brain is the organ of the mind

The proofs in support of this position are as follows:
1. Without brain there is no manifestation of feelings or of intellectual functions.

2. If the cerebral organization be defective, the manifestations of the mind are also defective; as happens in many idiots from birth.

3. If in the healthy state the development of the brain be very considerable, the manifestations of the affective and intellectual powers are very energetic.

4. The manifestations of the mind follow the ordinary or extraordinary growth of the brain. This organ is pulpy in young children, and the mental

powers are scarcely perceptible; but in proportion as it becomes perfect, the mental faculties appear; in its state of maturity, the mental powers arrive at the greatest energy, and in proportion as it grows old and weak, the energy of the mental faculties diminishes also.

5. Certain faculties are more active in women, others in men; the cerebral organization of both sexes, presents differences that coincide with those varied manifestations.

6. The feelings and intellectual faculties are hereditary in the same proportion, as the cerebral organization is propagated from parents to children.

7. The manifestations of the mind are deranged, if the respective organs in the brain be injured.

OBJECTIONS

There are, however, several objections, more or less plausible, against the first principle of Phrenology. Metaphysicians, for instance, say, that the manifestations of the mind cannot depend on bodily conditions, since the mind is not conscious of its organs. It must be answered, that the mind does not know the instruments, by which it manifests its feelings and intellectual powers, precisely as it is inscious of the muscles by means of which it executes voluntary motions, or of the nerves on which sight, hearing, tasting and smelling depend.

There are also many cases that record injuries of the brain, and losses of portions of its substance, whilst the mental faculties continued to be manifested.

Another objection has been founded on the disease called hydrocephalus, in which the brain was said to be wanting, or disorganized, or dissolved by water, at the same time that the mental functions continued unimpaired.

It has also been asserted, that ossification of the brain has not hindered the mind from manifesting its powers.

These objections are answered, to full extent, in my work on Phrenology, and are beyond the reach of this elementary work. I think that the first principle of Phrenology, *the brain is the organ of the affective and intellectual functions*, stands unshaken.

Chap. IV
Of the absolute or proportionate size of the brain

A great number of natural philosophers, convinced that the brain is the organ of understanding, have concluded that its functions must be proportionate to its absolute size. More exact observations however, show this conclusion to be erroneous. The ox has more brain than the dog, and the elephant more than man, &c. It is indeed impossible, in animals of different species, and even in various individuals of the same species, to estimate innate mental dispositions by the absolute size of the brain in general, or of its parts in particular; because the size of the cerebral organs is not the only condition to the greater or less energy of their functions.

Others, therefore, endeavored to show that the powers of the mind are indicated by the proportionate volume of the brain to the size of the body.

Experience, however, proves that this mode of measurement is also inexact. Small singing birds have larger brains, in proportion to their bodies, than man and the elephant. According to the manner of judging stated, the elephant would be a very stupid animal; but this is far from the fact. In mankind, it may be well to add, that middle-sized persons have commonly the largest brains.

From the preceding considerations it results, that something else must be done in order to establish a doctrine of the mind, in relation to the body.

Chap. V
Plurality of mental powers and of cerebral organs

The *second* principle of Phrenology is, that the mind manifests a plurality of faculties, each individually by means of a peculiar organic apparatus. Phrenologists name *faculty*, each species of feeling and thinking; and they give the name *organs* to the apparatuses by means of which the faculties of the mind are manifested.

The doctrine of the plurality of mental faculties and the necessity of special organs is very ancient. As soon as philosophers studied the human mind and its manifestations, they found it indispensable to admit several powers. Phrenology, it is true, establishes a greater number of primitive faculties of the mind than any school of philosophy has yet done, and many faculties demonstrated by Phrenology are different from those hitherto admitted. It also proves every proposition by positive facts.

Chap. VI
Means of determining the functions of the brain and its parts

Anatomy shows that the brain is composed of two halves, and that each half is an aggregation of parts developed in different degrees; but anatomy does not reveal the functions of any organ whatever, consequently it can neither show the functions of the brain generally, nor of its parts in particular; just as it is impossible to infer from the structure of the muscles that they are contractile; or from the texture of the optic nerve, that it is destined to propagate impressions of light. Yet physiology without anatomy is imperfect, and Phrenology is greatly supported by anatomy, since its anatomical and physiological branches are found to harmonize. Were it possible to prove the absence of differences in the brains of animals whose powers differ;—or to show that all parts of the brain increase simultaneously;—or that large hydrocephalic heads, exhibiting intellectual faculties, are without brain, &c., Phrenology would be completely undermined. But as the anatomical discoveries made in the brain are in harmony with the phrenological ideas of its functions, that science stands on more solid ground.

Several natural philosophers have endeavored by mutilations, viz. by cutting away various parts of the brain, to discover their functions. These means have been pursued without fruit and will remain useless. They are too violent, and several faculties might be retained without being manifested; at all events they cannot teach more than may be ascertained in the healthy state.

The best method of determining the nature of the cerebral functions, is that employed by Phrenologists: it is to observe the size of the cerebral parts in relation to particular mental manifestation, and it is the third principle of phrenology, that in *the same individual*, larger organs show greater, and smaller organs less energy. It is, however, important to remark that, though the size of the organs is sufficient to discover the nature of their functions, it does not alone produce their different degrees of activity. Their internal constitution, their exercise and mutual influence also contribute to this; for which reason Phrenologists cannot compare the same organ in different species of animals, nor even in different individuals of the same species; but must judge of each animal or man individually; but then they run no risk of erring, for in the same individual larger organs always show more activity than those that are smaller.

Gall, to whom is due the great merit of having laid the foundation of this doctrine, compared particular cerebral parts with determinate characters and particular talents, and according to these gave names to the organs he discovered: thus he spoke of the organs of haughtiness, of ambition, of cunning, of benevolence, of religion, of theft, of murder, of the mechanical arts, of music, of painting, of poetry, of mathematics, of metaphysics, &c.

It became necessary, however, to modify this manner of considering Phrenology, as it appeared that actions, talents, and determinate characters result from the mutual influence of the primitive faculties. I therefore undertook to specify the nature or elements of the fundamental powers, and to name them independently of any action or outward application. I also discovered several new organs, established a new division of the mental powers according to their inherent natures and modes of action, and separated that which belongs to each power itself from what depends on its combinations with other faculties.

The nomenclature, introduced by Gall, was not only incorrect, inasmuch as it indicated determinate actions, or results of combination among the powers,—but it was further objectionable as several organs were even named from abuses of their primitive functions. Disorders, however, are the effect of predominance of powers, on account of the disproportionately large size or over excitement of their organs, but are not to be confounded with the regular operations of the faculties. Gall, it is true, was right in stating that, in *inveterate* thieves and murderers certain portions of the brain are large, but he erred in speaking of an organ of theft and of another of murder, because the primitive faculties which lead to such criminal actions are not given for that commission; though they may be abused like every other primitive power. The aim and the disorders of every faculty and the influence of its inactivity on the functions of the other active powers, must be distinguished from each other and specified.

[From *Outlines of Phrenology* (Boston: Marsh, Capen and Lyon, 1832), 6–14.]

PIERRE FLOURENS

36 Phrenology Examined

When the phrenologists promiscuously place the intellectual and moral faculties in the brain, considered en masse, they deceive themselves. Neither the cerebellum, the quadrigeminal tubercles, nor the medulla oblongata can be regarded as seats of these faculties. All these faculties dwell solely in the brain, properly so called, or the hemispheres.

The question as to the precise seat of the intelligence, has undergone a great change since the time of Gall. Gall believed that the intelligence was seated indifferently in the whole encephalon, and it has been proved that it resides only in the hemispheres.

Further, it is not the encephalon taken en masse that is developed in the ratio of the intelligence of the creature, but the hemispheres. The mammifera are the animals most highly endowed with intelligence; they have, other things being equal, the most voluminous hemispheres. Birds are the animals most highly endowed with power of motion; their cerebellum is, other things being equal, the largest. Reptiles are the most torpid and apathetic of animals; they have the smallest brain, &c.

Every thing concurs then to prove, that the encephalon, in mass, is a multiple organ with multiple functions, consisting of different parts, of which some are destined to subserve the locomotive motions, others the motions of the respiration, &c., while one single one, the brain proper, is designed for the purposes of the intellection.

This being conceded, it is evident that the entire brain cannot be divided, as the phrenologists divide it, into a number of small organs, each of which is the seat of a distinct intellectual faculty; for the entire brain does not serve the purposes of what is called the intelligence. The hemispheres alone are the seats of the intellectual power; and consequently, the question as to whether the organ, the seat of the intelligence may be divided into several distinct organs, is a question relative solely to the uses and powers of the hemispheres.

Gall avers, and this is the second fundamental proposition of his doctrine, that the brain is divided into several organs, each one of which lodges a particular faculty of the soul. By the word *brain*, he understood the *whole brain*, and he thus deceived himself. Let us reduce the application of his proposition to the hemispheres alone, and we shall see that he has deceived himself again.

It has been shown by my late experiments, that we may cut away, either in front, or behind, or above, or on one side, a very considerable slice of the hemisphere of the brain, without destroying the intelligence. Hence it appears, that quite a restricted portion of the hemispheres may suffice for the purposes of intellection in an animal.[1]

On the other hand, in proportion as these reductions by slicing away the hemispheres are continued, the intelligence becomes enfeebled, and grows gradually less; and certain limits being passed, is wholly extinguished. Hence it appears, that the cerebral hemispheres concur, by their whole mass, in the full and entire exercise of the intelligence.[2]

In fine, as soon as one sensation is lost, all sensation is lost; when one faculty disappears, all the faculties disappear. There are not, therefore, different seats for the different faculties, nor for the different sensations. The faculty of feeling, of judging, of willing any thing, resides in the same place as the faculty of feeling, judging, or willing any other thing, and consequently this faculty, essentially a unit, resides essentially in a single organ.[3]

The understanding is, therefore, a unit.

According to Gall, there are as many particular kinds of intellect as there are distinct faculties of the mind. According to him, each faculty has its perception, its memory, its judgment, will, &c., that is to say, all the attributes of the understanding, properly so called.[4]

'All the intellectual faculties,' says he, 'are endowed with the perceptive faculty, with attention, recollection, memory, judgment, and imagination.'[5]

Thus each faculty perceives, remembers, judges, imagines, compares, creates; but these are trifles—for each faculty *reasons*. 'Whenever,' says Gall, 'a faculty compares and judges of the relations of analogous or different ideas, there is an act of comparison, there is an act of judgment; a sequence of comparisons and judgments constitutes reasoning,' &c.[6]

Therefore, each and every faculty is an understanding by itself, and Gall says so expressly. 'There are,' says he, 'as many different kinds of intellect or understanding as there are distinct faculties.'[7] 'Each distinct faculty,' says he, further, 'is intellect or understanding—each *individual intelligence* (the words are precise) has its proper organ.'[8]

But, admitting all these *kinds of intellects*, all these *individual understandings*, where are we to seek for the General Intelligence, the understanding, properly so called? It must, as you may please, be either an *attribute* of each faculty,[9] or the *collective expression* of all the faculties, or even the mere simple *result* of their common and simultaneous action;[10] in one word, it cannot be that positive and single faculty which we understand, conceive of, and feel in ourselves, when we pronounce the word *soul* or *understanding*.

Now here is the sum and the substance of Gall's psycology. For the understanding, essentially a unit faculty, he substitutes a multitude of little understandings or faculties, distinct and isolate. And, as these faculties, which perform just as he wills them to do—which he multiplies according to his pleasure, seem in his eyes to explain certain phenomena which are not well explained by the lights of ordinary philosophy, he triumphs!

[From *Phrenology Examined*, trans. C. Meigs (Philadelphia: Hogan & Thompson, 1846), 31–8.]

KARL LASHLEY

37 In Search of the Engram

When the mind wills to recall something, this volition causes the little [pineal] gland, by inclining successively to different sides, to impel the animal spirits toward different parts of the brain, until they come upon that part where the traces are left of the thing which it wishes to remember; for these traces are nothing else than the circumstance that the pores of the brain through which the spirits have already taken their course on presentation of the object, have thereby acquired a greater facility than the rest to be opened again the same way by the spirits which come to them; so that these spirits coming upon the pores enter therein more readily than into the others.

So wrote Descartes just three hundred years ago in perhaps the earliest attempt to explain memory in terms of the action of the brain. In the intervening centuries much has been learned concerning the nature of the impulses transmitted by nerves. Innumerable studies have defined conditions under which learning is facilitated or retarded, but, in spite of such progress, we seem little nearer to an understanding of the nature of the memory trace than was Descartes. His theory has in fact a remarkably modern sound. Substitute nerve impulse for animal spirits, synapse for pore and the result is the doctrine of learning as change in resistance of synapses. There is even a theory of scanning which is at least more definite as to the scanning agent and the source of the scanning beam than is its modern counterpart.

As interest developed in the functions of the brain the doctrine of the separate localization of mental functions gradually took form, even while the ventricles of the brain were still regarded as the active part. From Prochaska and Gall through the nineteenth century, students of clinical neurology sought the localization of specific memories. Flechsig defined the association areas as distinct from the sensory and motor. Aphasia, agnosia, and apraxia were interpreted as the result of the loss of memory images, either of objects or of kinesthetic sensations of movements to be made. The theory that memory traces are stored in association areas adjacent to the corresponding primary sensory areas seemed reasonable and was supported by some clinical evidence. The extreme position was that of Henschen, who speculated concerning the location of single ideas or memories in single cells. In spite of the fact that more critical analytic studies of clinical symptoms, such as those of Henry Head and of Kurt Goldstein, have shown that aphasia and agnosia are primarily defects in the organization of ideas rather than the result of amnesia, the conception of the localized storing of memories is still widely prevalent [. . .]

In experiments extending over the past 30 years I have been trying to trace conditioned reflex paths through the brain or to find the locus of specific memory traces. The results for different types of learning have been inconsistent and often mutually contradictory, in spite of confirmation by repeated tests. I shall summarize today a number of experimental findings. Perhaps they obscure rather than illuminate the nature of the engram, but they may serve at least to illustrate the complexity of the problem and to reveal the superficial nature of many of the physiological theories of memory that have been proposed. [. . .]

The animals studied have been rats and monkeys with, recently, a few chimpanzees. Two lines of approach to the problem have been followed. One is purely behavioural and consists in the analysis of the sensory excitations which are actually associated with reactions in learning and which are effective in eliciting the learned reactions. The associated reactions are similarly analysed. These studies define the patterns of nervous activity at receptor and effector levels and specify certain characteristics which the memory trace must have. The second approach is by surgical destruction of parts of the brain. Animals are trained in various tasks ranging from direct sensory-motor associations to the solution of difficult problems. Before or after training, associative tracts are cut or portions of the brain removed and effects of these operations on initial learning or postoperative retention are measured. At the termination of the experiments the brains are sectioned and the extent of damage reconstructed from serial sections. [. . .] After such animals, lacking the visual cortex, have learned the brightness reaction, any other part of the cerebral cortex may be destroyed without disturbing the habit. [. . .]

The evidence thus indicates that in sensory-motor habits of the conditioned reflex type no part of the cerebral cortex is essential except the primary sensory area. There is no transcortical conduction from the sensory areas to the motor cortex, and the major subcortical nuclear masses, thalamus, striatum, colliculi and cerebellum, do not play a part in the recognition of sensory stimuli or in the habit patterning of motor reactions.

The Engram within Sensory Areas (Equipotential Regions)

The experiments reported indicate that performance of habits of the conditioned reflex type is dependent upon the sensory areas and upon no other part of the cerebral cortex. What of localization within the sensory areas? Direct data upon this question are limited, but point to the conclusion that so long as some part of the sensory field remains intact and there is not a total loss of primary sensitivity, the habit mechanism can still function. Thus, in a series of experiments attempting to locate accurately the visual cortex of the rat, parts of the occipital lobes were destroyed in a variety of combinations. In these experiments it appeared that, so long as some part of the anterolateral surface of the striate cortex (the projection field of the temporal retina corresponding to the macula of primates) remained intact, there was no loss of habit. Any small part of the region was capable of maintaining the habits based on discrimination of intensities of light [. . .]

In a later experiment an attempt was made to determine the smallest amount of visual cortex which is capable of mediating habits based upon detail vision. The extent of visual cortex remaining after operation was determined by counting undegenerated cells in the lateral geniculate nucleus. Discrimination of visual figures could be learned when only one-sixtieth of the visual cortex remained. No comparable data are available on post-operative retention, but from incidental observations in other experiments I am confident that retention would be possible with the same amount of tissue.

In an early study by Franz the lateral surfaces of the occipital lobes of the monkey were destroyed after the animals had been trained in pattern and colour discrimination. These operations involved the greater part of what is now known to be the projection field of the macula. There was no loss of the habits. I have destroyed the cortex of the retrocalcarine fissure (the perimacular field) without destroying visual memories. The results with monkeys thus support the more ample data for the rat; the visual memory traces survive any cortical lesion, provided some portion of the field of acute vision remains intact. [. . .]

Summary

This series of experiments has yielded a good bit of information about what and where the memory trace is not. It has discovered nothing directly of the real nature of the engram. I sometimes feel, in reviewing the evidence on the localization of the memory trace, that the necessary conclusion is that learning just is not possible. It is difficult to conceive of a mechanism which can satisfy the conditions set for it. Nevertheless, in spite of such evidence against it, learning does sometimes occur. Although the negative data do not provide a clear picture of the nature of the engram, they do establish limits within which concepts of its nature must be confined, and thus indirectly define somewhat more clearly the nature of the nervous mechanisms which must be responsible for learning and retention. Some general conclusions are, I believe, justified by the evidence.

1. It seems certain that the theory of well-defined conditioned reflex paths from sense organ via association areas to the motor cortex is false. The motor areas are not necessary for the retention of sensory-motor habits or even of skilled manipulative patterns.

2. It is not possible to demonstrate the isolated localization of a memory trace anywhere within the nervous system. Limited regions may be essential for learning or retention of a particular activity, but within such regions the parts are functionally equivalent. The engram is represented throughout the region.

3. The so-called associative areas are not storehouses for specific memories. They seem to be concerned with modes of organization and with general facilitation or maintenance of the level of vigilance. The defects which occur after their destruction are not amnesias but difficulties in the performance of tasks which involve abstraction and generalization, or conflict of purposes. It is not possible as yet to describe these defects in the present psychological terminology. Goldstein has expressed them in part as a shift from the abstract to the concrete attitude, but this characterization is too vague and general to give a picture of the functional disturbance. For our present purpose the important point is that the defects are not fundamentally those of memory.

4. The trace of any activity is not an isolated connexion between sensory and motor elements. It is tied in with the whole complex of spatial and temporal axes of nervous activity which forms a constant substratum of behaviour. Each association is oriented with respect to space and time. Only by long practice under varying conditions does it become generalized or dissociated from these specific coordinates.

[From *In Search of the Engram*, repr. from *Society of Experimental Biology Symposium No. 4* (Cambridge University Press), in *The Neuropsychology of Lashley: Selected Papers* (New York: McGraw-Hill, 1960). 478–9, 490–1, 500–1.]

The connexion of the mental processes with certain of the bodily organs is now understood to be of the most intimate kind. A knowledge of the structure of those organs may therefore be expected to aid us in the study of mind. The contribution at present obtained from this source is something considerable; which makes it not improper to introduce a small portion of the Anatomy and Physiology of the human body into the present work. The parts of the human frame that chiefly concern the student of mental science are the Nerves and Nerve Centres (principally collected in the Brain), the Organs of Sense, and the Muscular System. The organs of sense and movement will fall to be described in Book First; a brief description of the Nerves and Nerve Centres will occupy this preliminary chapter, in which we shall confine ourselves as far as possible to the facts bearing directly upon Mind, introducing only such further explanations as may be needed to make those facts clear and evident.

That the Brain is the principal organ of Mind is proved by such observations as the following:—

1. From the local feelings that we experience during mental excitement. In most cases of bodily irritation we can assign the place or seat of the disturbance. We localise indigestion in the stomach, irritation of the lungs in the chest, toothache in the gums or jaws, and when the mental workings give rise to pain we point to the head. In ordinary circumstances the action of the brain is unconscious, but in a time of great mental agitation, or after any unusual exertion of thought, the aching or oppression within the skull tells where the seat of action is, precisely as aching limbs prove what muscles have been exercised during a long day's march. The observation can occasionally be carried much farther; for it is found that a series of intense mental emotions, or an excessive action of the powers of thinking, will end in a diseased alteration of the substance of the brain.

2. Injury or disease of the brain impairs in some way or other the powers of the mind. A blow on the head will destroy consciousness for the time; a severe hurt will cause a loss of memory. The various disorders of the brain, as for example, softening, &c., are known to affect the mental energies. Insanity is often accompanied by palpable disease of the cerebral substance, as shown by outward symptoms during life and by dissection after death.

3. The products of nervous waste are increased when the mind is more than ordinarily exerted. It is ascertained that the kidneys are mainly concerned

in removing from the blood the saline and other matters arising from the waste of nervous substance; and it is well known that the secretions from the kidneys are greatly increased in times of mental excitement. Chemical analysis proves that the products on such occasions are derived from the nervous tissue.

4. There is an indisputable connexion between size of brain and the mental energy displayed by the individual man or animal. It cannot be maintained that size is the only circumstance that determines the amount of mental force; *quality* is as important as quantity, whether in nerve, muscle, or any other portion of the animal structure. But just as largeness of muscle gives greater strength of body as a general rule, so largeness of brain gives greater vigour of mental impulse. The facts proving the large size and great weight of the heads of remarkable men have often been quoted. 'All other circumstances being alike,' says Dr Sharpey, 'the size of the brain appears to bear a general relation to the mental power of the individual,—although instances occur in which this rule is not applicable. The brain of Cuvier weighed upwards of 64 oz., and that of the late Dr Abercrombie about 63 oz. avoirdupois. On the other hand, the brain in idiots is remarkably small. In three idiots, whose ages were sixteen, forty, and fifty years, Tiedemann found the weight of their respective brains to be $19\frac{3}{4}$ oz., $25\frac{3}{4}$ oz., and $22\frac{1}{2}$ oz.; and Dr Sims records the case of a female idiot twelve years old, whose brain weighed 27 oz. The weight of the human brain is taken at about 3 lbs. (48 oz.).'—Quain's *Anatomy*, 5th edition, p. 671.

5. The specific experiments on the nerve cords and nerve centres, to be afterwards quoted, have proved the immediate dependence of sensation, intelligence, and volition on those parts.

No fact in our constitution can be considered more certain than this, that the brain is the chief organ of mind, and has mind for its principal function. As we descend in the animal scale, through Quadrupeds, Birds, Reptiles, Fishes, &c., the nervous system dwindles according to the decreasing measure of mental endowment. [. . .] What is called vitality is not so much a peculiar force as a collocation of the forces of inorganic matter for the purpose of keeping up a living structure. If our means of observation and measurement were more perfect, we might render account of all the nutriment consumed in any animal or human being; we might calculate the entire amount of energy evolved in the changes that constitute this consumption, and allow one portion for animal heat, another for the processes of secretion, a third for the action of the heart, lungs, and intestines, a fourth for the muscular exertion made within the period, a fifth for the activity of the brain, and so on till we had a strict balancing of receipt and expenditure. The nerve force that is derived from the waste of a given amount of food, is capable of being transmuted into any other force of animal life. Poured into the muscles during violent conscious effort, it increases their activity; passing to the alimentary canal, it aids in the force of digestion; in moments of excitement the power is converted into sensible heat; the same power is found capable of yielding true electrical currents. The evidence that establishes the common basis of mechanical and chemical force, heat, and electricity, namely, their mutual convertibility and common origin, establishes the nerve force as a member of the same group.

The current character of the nerve force leads to a considerable departure from the common mode of viewing the position of the brain as the organ of mind. We have seen that the cerebrum is a mixed mass of grey and white matter,—the matter of centres and the matter of conduction. Both are required in any act of the brain known to us. The smallest cerebral operation includes the transmission of an influence from one centre to another centre, from a centre to an extremity, or the reverse. Hence we cannot separate the centres from their communicating branches; and if so, we cannot separate the centres from the other organs of the body that originate or receive nerve stimulus. The organ of mind is not the brain by itself; it is the brain, nerves, muscles, and organs of sense. When the brain is in action, there is some transmission of nerve power, and the organ that receives or that originated the power is an essential part of the mechanism. A brain bereft of the spinal cord and spinal nerves is dead though the blood continues to flow to it; and these nerves, if plucked out of the limbs and other parts where they terminate, would probably not suffice to sustain the currents associated with mental life.

It is, therefore, in the present state of our knowledge, an entire misconception to talk of a *sensorium* within the brain, a *sanctum sanctorum*, or inner chamber, where impressions are poured in and stored up to be reproduced in a future day. There is no such chamber, no such mode of reception of outward influence. A stimulus or sensation acting on the brain exhausts itself in the production of a number of transmitted currents or influences; while the stimulus is alive, these continue, and when these have ceased the impression is exhausted. The revival of the impression is the setting on of the currents anew; such currents show themselves in actuating the bodily members,—the voice, the eyes, the features—in productive action, or in mere expression and gesture. The currents may have all degrees of intensity, from the fury of a death struggle to the languor of a half-sleeping reverie, or the fitful flashes of a dream, but their nature is still the same.

We must thus discard for ever the notion of the *sensorium commune*, the cerebral closet, as a central seat of mind, or receptacle of sensation and imagery. We may be very far from comprehending the full and exact character of nerve force, but the knowledge we have gained is sufficient to destroy the hypothesis that has until lately prevailed as to the material processes of perception. Though we have not attained a final understanding of this obscure and complicated machinery, we can at least substitute a more exact view for a less; and such is the substitution now demanded of current action for the crude conception of a central receptacle of stored up impressions. Our present insight enables us to say with great probability, no current, no mind.

[From *The Senses and the Intellect* (London: John W. Parker & Son, 1855), 10–12, 60–2.]

THOMAS HENRY HUXLEY

39   On the Hypothesis that Animals are Automata

Much ingenious argument has, at various times, been bestowed upon the question: How is it possible to imagine that volition, which is a state of consciousness, and, as such, has not the slightest community of nature with matter in motion, can act upon the moving matter of which the body is composed, as it is assumed to do in voluntary acts? But if, as is here suggested, the voluntary acts of brutes—or, in other words, the acts which they desire to perform—are as purely mechanical as the rest of their actions, and are simply accompanied by the state of consciousness called volition, the inquiry, so far as they are concerned, becomes superfluous. Their volitions do not enter into the chain of causation of their actions at all.

The hypothesis that brutes are conscious automata is perfectly consistent with any view that may be held respecting the often discussed and curious question whether they have souls or not; and, if they have souls, whether those souls are immortal or not. It is obviously harmonious with the most literal adherence to the text of Scripture concerning 'the beast that perisheth;' but it is not inconsistent with the amiable conviction ascribed by Pope to his 'untutored savage,' that when he passes to the happy hunting-grounds in the sky, 'his faithful dog shall bear him company.' If the brutes have consciousness and no souls, then it is clear that, in them, consciousness is a direct function of material changes; while, if they possess immaterial subjects of consciousness, or souls, then, as consciousness is brought into existence only as the consequence of molecular motion of the brain, it follows that it is an indirect product of material changes. The soul stands related to the body as the bell of a clock to the works, and consciousness answers to the sound which the bell gives out when it is struck.

Thus far I have strictly confined myself to the problem with which I proposed to deal at starting—the automatism of brutes. The question is, I believe, a perfectly open one, and I feel happy in running no risk of either Papal or Presbyterian condemnation for the views which I have ventured to put forward. And there are so very few interesting questions which one is, at present, allowed to think out scientifically—to go as far as reason leads, and stop where evidence comes to an end—without speedily being deafened by the tattoo of 'the drum ecclesiastic'—that I have luxuriated in my rare freedom, and would now willingly bring this disquisition to an end if I could hope that other people would go no further. Unfortunately, past experience debars me from entertaining any such hope, even if

> ' . . . that drum's discordant sound
> Parading round and round and round,'

were not, at present, as audible to me, as it was to the mild poet who ventured to express his hatred of drums in general, in that well-known couplet.

It will be said, that I mean that the conclusions deduced from the study of the brutes are applicable to man, and that the logical consequences of such application are fatalism, materialism, and atheism—whereupon the drums will beat the *pas de charge*.

One does not do battle with drummers; but I venture to offer a few remarks for the calm consideration of thoughtful persons, untrammelled by foregone conclusions, unpledged to shore-up tottering dogmas, and anxious only to know the true bearings of the case.

It is quite true that, to the best of my judgment, the argumentation which applies to brutes holds equally good of men; and, therefore, that all states of consciousness in us, as in them, are immediately caused by molecular changes of the brain-substance. It seems to me that in men, as in brutes, there is no proof that any state of consciousness is the cause of change in the motion of the matter of the organism. If these positions are well based, it follows that our mental conditions are simply the symbols in consciousness of the changes which take place automatically in the organism; and that, to take an extreme illustration, the feeling we call volition is not the cause of a voluntary act, but the symbol of that state of the brain which is the immediate cause of that act. We are conscious automata, endowed with free will in the only intelligible sense of that much-abused term—inasmuch as in many respects we are able to do as we like—but none the less parts of the great series of causes and effects which, in unbroken continuity, composes that which is, and has been, and shall be—the sum of existence.

As to the logical consequences of this conviction of mine, I may be permitted to remark that logical consequences are the scarecrows of fools and the beacons of wise men. The only question which any wise man can ask himself, and which any honest man will ask himself, is whether a doctrine is true or false. Consequences will take care of themselves; at most their importance can only justify us in testing with extra care the reasoning process from which they result.

So that if the view I have taken did really and logically lead to fatalism, materialism, and atheism. I should profess myself a fatalist, materialist, and atheist; and I should look upon those who, while they believed in my honesty of purpose and intellectual competency, should raise a hue and cry against me, as people who by their own admission preferred lying to truth, and whose opinions therefore were unworthy of the smallest attention.

But, as I have endeavoured to explain on other occasions, I really have no claim to rank myself among fatalistic, materialistic, or atheistic philosophers. Not among fatalists, for I take the conception of necessity to have a logical, and not a physical foundation; not among materialists, for I am utterly incapable of conceiving the existence of matter if there is no mind in which to picture that existence; not among atheists, for the problem of the ultimate cause of existence is one which seems to me to be hopelessly out of reach of my poor powers. Of all the senseless babble I have ever had occasion to read, the demonstrations of those philosophers who undertake to tell us all about the nature of God would be the worst, if they were not surpassed by the still greater absurdities of the philosophers who try to prove that there is no God.

And if this personal disclaimer should not be enough, let me further point out that a great many persons whose acuteness and learning will not be contested, and whose Christian piety, and, in some cases, strict orthodoxy, is above suspicion, have held more or less definitely the view that man is a conscious automaton.

It is held, for example, in substance, by the whole school of predestinarian theologians, typified by St Augustine, Calvin, and Jonathan Edwards—the great work of the latter on the will showing in this, as in other cases, that the growth of physical science has introduced no new difficulties of principle into theological problems, but has merely given visible body, as it were, to those which already existed.

Among philosophers, the pious Geulinex and the whole school of occasionalist Cartesians held this view; the orthodox Leibnitz invented the term 'automate spirituel,' and applied it to man; the fervent Christian, Hartley, was one of the chief advocates and best expositors of the doctrine; while another zealous apologist of Christianity in a sceptical age, and a contemporary of Hartley, Charles Bonnet, the Genevese naturalist, has embodied the doctrine in language of such precision and simplicity, that I will quote the little-known passage of his 'Essai de Psychologie' at length:—

Another Hypothesis concerning the Mechanism of Ideas[1]

'Philosophers accustomed to judge of things by that which they are in themselves, and not by their relation to received ideas, would not be shocked if they met with the proposition that the soul is a mere spectator of the movements of its body: that the latter performs of itself all that series of actions which constitutes life: that it moves of itself: that it is the body alone which reproduces ideas, compares and arranges them; which forms reasonings, imagines and executes plans of all kinds, &c. This hypothesis, though perhaps of an excessive boldness, nevertheless deserves some consideration.

It is not to be denied that Supreme Power could create an automaton which should exactly imitate all the external and internal actions of man.

I understand by external actions, all those movements which pass under our eyes; I term internal actions, all the motions which in the natural state cannot be observed because they take place in the interior of the body—such as the movements of digestion, circulation, sensation, &c. Moreover, I include in this category the movements which give rise to ideas, whatever be their nature.

In the automaton which we are considering everything would be precisely determined. Everything would occur according to the rules of the most admirable mechanism: one state would succeed another state, one operation would lead to another operation, according to invariable laws; motion would become alternately cause and effect, effect and cause; reaction would answer to action, and reproduction to production.

Constructed with definite relations to the activity of the beings which compose the world, the automaton would receive impressions from it, and, in faithful correspondence thereto, it would execute a corresponding series of motions.

Indifferent towards any determination, it would yield equally to all, if the first impressions did not, so to speak, wind up the machine and decide its operations and its course.

The series of movements which this automaton could execute would distinguish it from all others formed on the same model, but which not having been placed in similar circumstances would not have experienced the same impressions, or would not have experienced them in the same order.

The senses of the automaton, set in motion by the objects presented to it, would communicate their motion to the brain, the chief motor apparatus of the machine. This would put in action the muscles of the hands and feet, in virtue of their secret connection with the senses. These muscles, alternately contracted and dilated, would approximate or remove the automaton from the objects, in the relation which they would bear to the conservation or the destruction of the machine.

The motions of perception and sensation which the objects would have impressed on the brain, would be preserved in it by the energy of its mechanism. They would become more vivid according to the actual condition of the automaton, considered in itself and relatively to the objects.

Words being only the motions impressed on the organ of hearing and that of voice, the diversity of these movements, their combination, the order in which they would succeed one another, would represent judgments, reasoning, and all the operations of the mind.

A close correspondence between the organs of the senses, either by the opening into one another of their nervous ramifications, or by interposed springs (*ressorts*), would establish such a connection in their working, that, on the occasion of the movements impressed on one of these organs, other movements would be excited, or would become more vivid in some of the other senses.

Give the automaton a soul which contemplates its movements, which believes itself to be the author of them, which has different volitions on the occasion of the different movements, and you will on this hypothesis construct a man.

But would this man be free? Can the feeling of our liberty, this feeling which is so clear and so distinct and so vivid as to persuade us that we are the authors of our actions, be conciliated with this hypothesis? If it removes the difficulty which attends the conception of the action of the soul on the body, on the other hand it leaves untouched that which meets us in endeavouring to conceive the action of the body on the soul.'

But if Leibnitz, Jonathan Edwards, and Hartley—men who rank among the giants of the world of thought—could see no antagonism between the doctrine under discussion and Christian orthodoxy, is it not just possible that smaller folk may be wrong in making such a coil about 'logical consequences'? And, seeing how large a share of this clamour is raised by the clergy of one denomination or another, may I say, in conclusion, that it really would be well if ecclesiastical persons would reflect that ordination, whatever deep-seated graces it may confer, has never been observed to be followed by any visible increase in the learning or the logic of its subject. Making a man a Bishop, or entrusting him with the office of ministering to even the largest of Presbyterian congregations, or setting him up to lecture to a Church congress, really does not in the smallest degree augment such title to respect as his opinions may intrinsically possess. And when such a man presumes on an authority which was conferred upon him for other purposes, to sit in judgment upon matters his incompetence to deal with which is patent, it is permissible to ignore his sacerdotal pretensions, and to tell him, as one would tell a mere common, unconsecrated, layman: that it is not necessary for any man to occupy himself with problems of this kind unless he so choose. Life is filled full enough by the performance of its ordinary and obvious duties. But that, if a man elect to become a judge of these grave questions; still more, if he assume the responsibility of attaching praise or blame to his fellow-men for the conclusions at which they arrive touching them, he will commit a sin more grievous than most breaches of the Decalogue, unless he avoid a lazy reliance upon the information that is gathered by prejudice and filtered through passion, unless he go back to the prime sources of knowledge—the facts of nature, and the thoughts of those wise men who for generations past have been her best interpreters.

[From 'On the Hypothesis that Animals are Automata', *Fortnightly Review* (1874), 576–80.]

40 The Trial of Hadfield

Gentlemen, the facts of this melancholy case lie within a narrow compass.

The unfortunate person before you was a soldier. He became so, I believe in the year 1793—and is now about twenty-nine years of age. He served in Flanders under the duke of York, as appears by his Royal Highness's evidence; and being a most approved soldier, he was one of those singled out as an orderly man to attend upon the person of the commander in chief. You have been witnesses, gentlemen, to the calmness with which the prisoner has sitten in his place during the trial.—There was but one exception to it.—You saw the emotion which overpowered him when the illustrious person now in court, took his seat upon the bench. Can you then believe, from the evidence, for I do not ask you to judge as physiognomists, or to give the rein to compassionate fancy: but can there be any doubt that it was the generous emotion of the mind, on seeing the prince, under whom he had served with so much bravery and honour? Every man certainly must judge for himself:—I am counsel, not a witness, in the cause; but it is a most striking circumstance, when you find from the crown's evidence, that when he was dragged through the orchestra under the stage, and charged with an act for which he considered his life as forfeited, he addressed the duke of York with the same enthusiasm which has marked the demeanor I am adverting to:—Mr Richardson, who showed no disposition in his evidence to help the prisoner, but who spoke with the calmness and circumspection of truth, and who had no idea that the person he was examining was a lunatic, has given you the account of the burst of affection on his first seeing the duke of York, against whose father and sovereign he was supposed to have had the consciousness of treason. The king himself whom he was supposed to have so malignantly attacked, never had a more gallant, loyal, or suffering soldier. His gallantry and loyalty will be proved; his sufferings speak for themselves.

About five miles from Lisle, upon the attack made on the British army, this unfortunate soldier was in the fifteenth light dragoons, in the thickest of the ranks, exposing his life for his prince, whom he is supposed to-day to have sought to murder:—the first wound he received is most materially connected with the subject we are considering; you may see the effect of it now.[1] The point of a sword was impelled against him with all the force of a man urging his horse in battle. When the Court put the prisoner under my protection, I thought it my duty to bring Mr Cline to inspect him in Newgate; and it will appear by the evidence of that excellent and conscientious person, who is known to be one of the first anatomists in the world, that from this wound one of two things must have happened: either, that by the immediate operation of surgery the displaced part of the skull must have been taken away, or been forced inward on the brain. The second stroke, also speaks for itself: you may now see its effects.—[*Here Mr Erskine touched the head of the prisoner.*] He was cut across all the nerves which give sensibility and animation to the body, and his head hung down almost dissevered, until by the act of surgery it was placed in the position in which you now see it; but thus, almost destroyed, he still recollected his duty, and continued to maintain the glory of his country, when a sword divided the membrane of his neck where it terminates in the head; yet he still kept his place though his helmet had been thrown off by the blow which I secondly described, when by another sword he was cut into the very brain—you may now see its membrane uncovered. Mr Cline will tell you that he examined these wounds, and he can better describe them; I have myself seen them, but am no surgeon: from his evidence you will have to consider their consequences. It may be said that many soldiers receive grievous wounds without their producing insanity. So they may undoubtedly; but we are here upon *the fact*. There was a discussion the other day, on whether a man, who had been seemingly hurt by a fall beyond remedy, could get up and walk: the people around said it was impossible; but he did get up and walk, and so there was an end to the impossibility. The effects of the prisoner's wounds were known by the *immediate* event of insanity, and Mr Cline will tell you, that it would have been strange indeed if any other event had followed. We are not here upon a case of insanity arising from the spiritual part of man, as it may be affected by hereditary taint—by intemperance, or by violent passions, the operations of which are various and uncertain; but we have to deal with a species of insanity more resembling what has been described as idiocy, proceeding from original mal-organization. *There* the disease is, from its very nature, *incurable*; and so where a man (*like the prisoner*) has become insane from *violence to the brain, which permanently affects its structure*, however such a man may appear occasionally to others, his disease is *immovable*; and if the prisoner, therefore, were to live a thousand years, he *never* could recover from the consequence of that day. [. . .]

He was afterwards carried to an hospital, where he was known by his tongue to one of his countrymen, who will be examined as a witness, who found him, not merely as a wounded soldier deprived of the powers of his body, but bereft of his senses for ever. [. . .]

Henry Cline, esq. sworn.—Examined by Mr Erskine

I need not ask you what you are; you are very well known to the Court and jury. Have you had an opportunity of examining the wounds of the prisoner at the bar?—I examined them yesterday, which was the first time that I saw the prisoner.

Did you examine this wound upon his temple?—I did.

What remarks did you make upon that wound in his temple?—The wound on his temple is very considerable, but it is not probable that that should have at all injured the brain; it is a considerable wound, but the direction which it appears to have taken was not of a nature to injure the brain.

Did you observe whether there was any thing displaced in that part of the skull?—There is a wound immediately above the eyebrow, which appears to have penetrated the skull; and in all probability the brain was injured in consequence of that wound.

Did you examine a wound the prisoner has in the back of his head?—I did; there are likewise two other wounds situated near the upper part of his head, which appear also to have penetrated the skull, and probably injured the brain likewise in those parts.

Taking that person to have been subject to no insanity before those wounds that you observed, and immediately afterwards to have been affected with insanity, should you consider, from your knowledge of the human body and the anatomy of it, that the injury to the brain was likely to be the cause of those symptoms?—It frequently happens, that after injury of the brain, there is some derangement of the understanding; the mental faculties are variously affected; sometimes by loss of memory, at other times of some particular sense, and very frequently that derangement taking place which is commonly called insanity.

If insanity does arise from an injury to the brain by violent wounds, is it an insanity likely to go off or likely to continue from time to time?—That depends very much on the duration; if it has existed for some length of time after the accident has happened, there is great probability of its permanency.

If it has lasted four, five, or six years, with paroxysms of strong insanity commencing at the time of the wounds, is it likely to continue?—I should conceive it would be permanent.

Lord *Kenyon.*—Without any intermission?—No; there are certain existing causes; that are occasionally taking place, that will even increase those effects, and sometimes under favourable circumstances there may be no apparent derangement at the time.

Mr *Erskine.*—Have you frequently observed persons that were lunatics, whether from hereditary taint, wounds on the brain, or other circumstances that are invisible, have you frequently seen such persons, though under paroxysms of lunacy, capable of conversing and appearing rational?—In every respect rational.

From your experience, have you not known persons who were lunatic, whether from an original hereditary taint or wounds in the brain, or from any other invisible cause, and in the paroxysms of madness as high as it can operate, capable of conversing, reasoning, and speaking, as if they were sane?—Yes; it very frequently occurs that they will appear rational in every answer that they will give to the questions commonly put to them, and rational in their conduct.

Though at that time in a paroxysm of their peculiar madness?—I do not mean just during the time of paroxysms.

I am supposing a person to have a morbid imagination which constitutes the lunacy, and subject to that morbid imagination, may that person within your own experience converse upon common subjects, as if he were not visited by or subject to the dominion of that disease?—I mean they would talk perfectly rationally for one instant of time, and then immediately after, perhaps, they will show symptoms of insanity; and as we can only judge of the paroxysm by the effect, therefore I conceive it cannot be said a paroxysm is upon the patient, till he shows it by some irregularity in his conduct or his conversation.

Doctor Creighton, sworn.—Examined by Mr Sergeant Best

You are a physician I believe?—Yes.

Have you applied particular attention to the disease of madness?—Yes, I have.

I believe you have seen the prisoner at the bar?—I have.

From the examination you have had of him, is it your opinion that he is now a person of sane mind or otherwise?—I have not the smallest doubt that he is insane. I believe him to be insane. He is not a maniac, but he labours under mental derangement of a very common but a particular kind.

I believe you have examined his wounds?—I have.

Are the wounds which he appears to have received, likely to have been the occasion of that madness?—I think that they are very probable causes of the disposition to that madness: there are many instances of this kind of madness having been occasioned by such injuries done to the brain.

Supposing this to be the cause of his madness, is it likely that that madness should continue?—I believe him to have laboured under this kind of madness constantly from its first attack. When any question concerning a common matter is made to him, he answers very correctly; but when any question is put to him which relates to the subject of his lunacy, he answers irrationally.

Is that a common thing with all madmen?—With all madmen of this description.

Then, although you said you believe that this madness has continued from the first cause of it, is it probable that he might at times have conducted himself rationally?—Most undoubtedly; for it requires that the thoughts which have relation to his madness should be awakened in his mind, in order to make him act unreasonably.

Are there any particular seasons of the year when a person labouring under these infirmities would be more likely to be affected than another?—Yes; there are instances where it has occurred periodically, but it depends much more upon certain variations in the state of his health.

Would the approach of hot weather affect his health?—It is a very common cause of the augmentation of the disorder.

[From *A Complete Collection of State Trials*, comp. T. B. Howell, vol. xxvii (London, 1800), 1319–21, 1332–4.]

HENRY MAUDSLEY

41 Responsibility in Mental Disease

If a madman be supposed to know he is doing wrong, or doing that which is contrary to law, when he does some act of violence, he is held to be not less responsible than a sane person. The conclusions reached by the observations of self-consciousness in a sane mind are strictly applied to the phenomena of diseased mind; not otherwise than as if it were solemnly enacted that the disorder and violence of convulsions should be measured by the order and method of voluntary movements, and that whosoever, being seized with convulsions, and knowing that he was convulsed, transgressed that measure, should be punished as a criminal. The unfortunate sufferer, or others on his behalf, might, it is true, innocently argue that the very nature of convulsions excluded the idea of full voluntary control; but the metaphysical intuitionist would rejoin that it was certain from experience that man has a power of control over his movements; that the convulsive movements were a clear proof to all the world that he had not exercised that power; and that his convulsions, therefore, were justly punishable as crime. This pathological comparison is scientifically just, and its justness has oftentimes received terribly striking illustration in the effects of the legal criterion of responsibility; for it is certain that in conformity with it many persons unquestionably insane, who have done homicide, not because they *would* not, but because they *could* not, exercise efficient control, have been, and still from time to time are, executed as simple criminals. Harsh and exaggerated as this statement might seem, there is not, I believe, in this or any other civilized country a physician, practically acquainted with the insane, who would not unhesitatingly endorse it.

No one now-a-days who is engaged in the treatment of mental disease doubts that he has to do with the disordered function of a bodily organ—of the brain. Whatever opinion may be held concerning the essential nature of mind, and its independence of matter, it is admitted on all sides that its manifestations take place through the nervous system, and are affected by the condition of the nervous system, and are affected by the condition of the nervous parts which minister to them. If these are healthy, they are sound; if these are diseased, they are unsound. Insanity is, in fact, disorder of brain producing disorder of mind; or, to define its nature in greater detail, it is a disorder of the supreme nerve-centres of the brain—the special organs of mind—producing derangement of thought, feeling, and action, together or separately, of such degree or kind as to incapacitate the individual for the relations of life.[1]

The opinion that insanity is a disease of the so-called immaterial part of our nature we may look upon as exploded even in its last retreat. The arguments that have been adduced in favour of it—first, that madness is produced sometimes by moral causes, and, secondly, that it is cured sometimes by moral means—are entirely consistent with the theory of material disease, while the arguments in favour of the materialistic theory are quite inconsistent with the spiritualistic hypothesis, which has the further disadvantage of not being within the range of rational human conception.

To the argument that madness is produced sometimes by moral causes, which must be admitted, it is sufficient to reply, first, that long-continued or excessive stimulation of any organ does notably induce physical disease of it, and that in this respect, therefore, the brain only obeys a general law of the organism; and, secondly, that it is possible to produce experimentally, by entirely physical causes, mental derangement exactly similar to that which is produced by moral causes. There are many facts which would justify us in laying it down as a generalization of inductive mental science, that a state of consciousness may be changed experimentally by agents which produce changes in the molecular constitution of those parts of the nervous system which minister to the manifestations of consciousness. Take, for example, the way in which, by the administration of opium or haschisch, we modify in a remarkable manner a person's conceptions of space and time and of other relations. To the second argument in favour of the immaterial nature of unsound mind, which is founded on the distinctly curative influence of moral treatment, the easy reply is, that moral means are beneficial in insanity by yielding repose to parts much needing repose, and by stimulating to activity parts much needing to be active; by yielding repose to morbid thought and feeling, and by rousing into action healthy thought, feeling, and will.

The aim of the physician in the treatment of insanity is to bring the means at his command to bear, directly or indirectly, on the disordered nerve-element. But, in striving to do this, he soon learns with how many bodily organs and functions he has really to do. To call mind a function of the brain may lead to much misapprehension, if it be thereby supposed that the brain is the only organ which is concerned in the function of mind. There is not an organ in the body which is not in intimate relation with the brain by means of its paths of nervous communication, which has not, so to speak, a special correspondence with it through internuncial fibres, and which does not, therefore, affect more or less plainly and specially its function as an organ of mind. It is not merely that a palpitating heart may cause anxiety and apprehension, or a disordered liver gloomy feelings, but there are good reasons to believe that each organ has its specific influence on the constitution and function of mind; an influence not yet to be set forth scientifically, because it is exerted on that unconscious mental life which is the basis of all that we consciously feel and think. Were the heart of one man to be placed in the body of another it would probably make no difference in the circulation of the blood, but it might make a real difference in the temper of his mind. So close is the physiological sympathy of parts in the commonwealth of the body, that it is necessary in the physiological study of mind to regard it as a function of the whole organism, as comprehending the whole bodily life.

It has been one of the results of the study of morbid mental action to make clear the importance of recognizing the influence of particular organs upon the constitution and function of mind. Pathological instances of perturbation of function have yielded intimations which we should have failed to obtain by observation only of the smooth and regular action of the organism in health; and we can now say with the utmost confidence that although the mind may be studied by the psychological method of observing self-consciousness, it cannot be investigated fully by that method alone. As it was in time past, so in time to come error, confusion, and contradiction must flow from so exclusive and insufficient a method. In consequence of the theological and metaphysical views of mind, and of the way in which it was kept isolated from all other subjects of human inquiry, the phenomena of disordered mental action were, until quite recently, as much neglected by mental philosophers as the insane patients who exhibited them were neglected by those who had the care of them. It seems never to have occurred to metaphysicians that these phenomena could have any bearing on a philosophy of mind; certainly, had it done so, their exclusive method of inquiry would have proved singularly unfit for the observation of them; and it is only recently, since the nature of insanity has been recognized, and the insane have been treated as sufferers from disease, that attempts have been systematically made to use the valuable material which they furnish for the building up of an inductive mental science. Now, however, it may be laid down as an incontestable axiom, that the physiological method of study is essential to a scientific knowledge of mind, to a real acquaintance with its disorders, and to a successful treatment of them.

[From *Responsibility in Mental Disease* (New York: D. Appleton & Co., 1876), 14–19.]

J. J. C. SMART

42   Sensations and Brain Processes

This paper[1] takes its departure from arguments to be found in U. T. Place's 'Is Consciousness a Brain Process?'[2] I have had the benefit of discussing Place's thesis in a good many universities in the United States and Australia, and I hope that the present paper answers objections to his thesis which Place has not considered and that it presents his thesis in a more nearly unobjectionable form. This paper is meant also to supplement the paper 'The "Mental" and the "Physical,"' by H. Feigl,[3] which in part argues for a similar thesis to Place's.

Suppose that I report that I have at this moment a roundish, blurry-edged after-image which is yellowish towards its edge and is orange towards its center. What is it that I am reporting? One answer to this question might be that I am not reporting anything, that when I say that it looks to me as though there is a roundish yellowy-orange patch of light on the wall I am expressing some sort of *temptation*, the temptation to say that there *is* a roundish yellowy-orange patch on the wall (though I may know that there is not such a patch on the wall). This is perhaps Wittgenstein's view in the *Philosophical Investigations* (see §§ 367, 370). Similarly, when I 'report' a pain, I am not really reporting anything (or, if you like, I am reporting in a queer sense of 'reporting'), but am doing a sophisticated sort of wince. (See § 244: 'The verbal expression of pain replaces crying and does not describe it.' Nor does it describe anything else?)[4] I prefer most of the time to discuss an after-image rather than a pain, because the word pain brings in something which is irrelevant to my purpose: the notion of 'distress.' I think that 'he is in pain' entails 'he is in distress,' that is, that he is in a certain agitation-condition.[5] Similarly, to say 'I am in pain' may be to do more than 'replace pain behavior': it may be partly to report something, though this something is quite nonmysterious, being an agitation-condition, and so susceptible of behavioristic analysis. The suggestion I wish if possible to avoid is a different one, namely that 'I am in pain' is a genuine report, and that what it reports is an irreducibly psychical something. And similarly the suggestion I wish to resist is also that to say 'I have a yellowish-orange after-image' is to report something irreducibly psychical.

Why do I wish to resist this suggestion? Mainly because of Occam's razor. It seems to me that science is increasingly giving us a viewpoint whereby organisms are able to be seen as physicochemical mechanisms:[6] it seems that even the behavior of man himself will one day be explicable in mechanistic terms. There does seem to be, so far as science is concerned, nothing in the world but increasingly complex arrangements of physical constituents. All except for one place: in consciousness. That is, for a full description of what is going on in a man you would have to mention not only the physical processes in his tissues, glands, nervous system, and so forth, but also his states of consciousness: his visual, auditory, and tactual sensations, his aches and pains. That these should be *correlated* with brain processes does not help, for to say that they are *correlated* is to say that they are something 'over and above.' You cannot correlate something with itself. You correlate footprints with burglars, but not Bill Sikes the burglar with Bill Sikes the burglar. So sensations, states of consciousness, do seem to be the one sort of thing left outside the physicalist picture, and for various reasons I just cannot believe that this can be so. That everything should be explicable in terms of physics (together of course with descriptions of the ways in which the parts are put together—roughly, biology is to physics as radio-engineering is to electro-magnetism) except the occurrence of sensations seems to me to be frankly unbelievable. Such sensations would be 'nomological danglers,' to use Feigl's expression.[7] It is not often realized how odd would be the laws whereby these nomological danglers would dangle. It is sometimes asked, 'Why can't there be psychophysical laws which are of a novel sort, just as the laws of electricity and magnetism were novelties from the standpoint of Newtonian mechanics?' Certainly we are pretty sure in the future to come across new ultimate laws of a novel type, but I expect them to relate simple constituents: for example, whatever ultimate particles are then in vogue. I cannot believe that ultimate laws of nature could relate simple constituents to configurations consisting of perhaps billions of neurons (and goodness knows how many billion billions of ultimate particles) all put together for all the world as though their main purpose in life was to be a negative feedback mechanism of a complicated sort. Such ultimate laws would be like nothing so far known in science. They have a queer 'smell' to them. I am just unable to believe in the nomological danglers themselves, or in the laws whereby they would dangle. If any philosophical arguments seemed to compel us to believe in such things, I would suspect a catch in the argument. In any case it is the object of this paper to show that there are no philosophical arguments which compel us to be dualists.

The above is largely a confession of faith, but it explains why I find Wittgenstein's position (as I construe it) so congenial. For on this view there are, in a sense, no sensations. A man is a vast arrangement of physical particles, but there are not, over and above this, sensations or states of consciousness. There are just behavioral facts about this vast mechanism, such as that it expresses a temptation (behavior disposition) to say 'there is a yellowish-red patch on the wall' or that it goes through a sophisticated sort of wince, that is, says 'I am in pain.' Admittedly Wittgenstein says that though the sensation 'is not a something,' it is nevertheless 'not a nothing either' (§ 304), but this need only mean that the word 'ache' has a use. An ache is a thing, but only in the innocuous sense in which the plain man, in the first paragraph of Frege's *Foundations of Arithmetic*, answers the question 'What is the number one?' by 'a thing.' It should be noted that when I assert that to say 'I have a yellowish-orange after-image' is to express a temptation to assert the physical-object statement 'There is a yellowish-orange patch on the wall,' I mean that saying 'I have a yellowish-orange after-image' is (partly) the exercise of the disposition[8] which is the temptation. It is not to *report* that I have the temptation, any more than is 'I love you' normally a report that I love someone. Saying 'I love you' is just part of the behavior which is the exercise of the disposition of loving someone.

Though for the reasons given above, I am very receptive to the above 'expressive' account of sensation statements, I do not feel that it will quite do the trick. Maybe this is because I have not thought it out sufficiently, but it does seem to me as though, when a person says 'I have an after-image,' he *is* making a genuine report, and that when he says 'I have a pain,' he *is* doing more than 'replace pain-behavior,' and that 'this more' is not just to say that he is in distress. I am not so sure, however, that to admit this is to admit that there are nonphysical correlates of brain processes. Why should not sensations just be brain processes of a certain sort? There are, of course, well-known (as well as lesser-known) philosophical objections to the view that reports of sensations are reports of brain-processes, but I shall try to argue that these arguments are by no means as cogent as is commonly thought to be the case.

Let me first try to state more accurately the thesis that sensations are brain-processes. It is not the thesis that, for example, 'after-image' or 'ache' means the same as 'brain process of sort X' (where 'X' is replaced by a description of a certain sort of brain process). It is that, in so far as 'after-image' or 'ache' is a report of a process, it is a report of a process that *happens to be* a brain process. It follows that the thesis does not claim that sensation statements can be *translated* into statements about brain processes.[9] Nor does it claim that the logic of a sensation statement is the same as that of a brain-process statement. All it claims is that in so far as a sensation statement is a report of something, that something is in fact a brain process. Sensations are nothing over and above brain processes. Nations are nothing 'over and above' citizens, but this does not prevent the logic of nation statements being very different from the logic of citizen statements, nor does it insure the translatability of nation statements into citizen statements. (I do not, however, wish to assert that the relation of sensation statements to brain-process statements is very like that of nation statements to citizen statements. Nations do not just *happen to be* nothing over and above citizens, for example. I bring in the 'nations' example merely to make a negative point: that the fact that the logic of A-statements is different from that of B-statements does not insure that A's are anything over and above B's.)

Remarks on Identity

When I say that a sensation is a brain process or that lightning is an electric discharge, I am using 'is' in the sense of strict identity. (Just as in the—in this case necessary—proposition '7 is identical with the smallest prime number greater than 5.') When I say that a sensation is a brain process or that lightning is an electric discharge I do not mean just that the sensation is somehow spatially or temporally continuous with the brain process or that the lightning is just spatially or temporally continuous with the discharge. When on the other hand I say that the successful general is the same person as the small boy who stole the apples I mean only that the successful general I see before me is a time slice[10] of the same four-dimensional object of which the small boy stealing apples is an earlier time slice. However, the four-dimensional object which has the general-I-see-before-me for its late time slice is identical in the strict sense with the four-dimensional object which has the small-boy-stealing-apples for an early time slice. I distinguish these two senses of 'is identical with' because I wish to make it clear that the brain-process doctrine asserts identity in the *strict* sense.

I shall now discuss various possible objections to the view that the processes reported in sensation statements are in fact processes in the brain. Most of us have met some of these objections in our first year as philosophy students. All the more reason to take a good look at them. Others of the objections will be more recondite and subtle.

Objection 1. Any illiterate peasant can talk perfectly well about his after-images, or how things look or feel to him, or about his aches and pains, and yet he may know nothing whatever about neurophysiology. A man may, like Aristotle, believe that the brain is an organ for cooling the body without any impairment of his ability to make true statements about his sensations. Hence the things we are talking about when we describe our sensations cannot be processes in the brain.

Reply. You might as well say that a nation of slugabeds, who never saw the Morning Star or knew of its existence, or who had never thought of the expression 'the Morning Star,' but who used the expression 'the Evening Star' perfectly well, could not use this expression to refer to the same entity as we refer to (and describe as) 'the Morning Star.'[11]

You may object that the Morning Star is in a sense not the very same thing as the Evening Star, but only something spatiotemporally continuous with it. That is, you may say that the Morning Star is not the Evening Star in the strict sense of 'identity' that I distinguished earlier.

There is, however, a more plausible example. Consider lightning.[12] Modern physical science tells us that lightning is a certain kind of electrical discharge due to ionization of clouds of water vapor in the atmosphere. This, it is now believed, is what the true nature of lightning is. Note that there are not two things: a flash of lightning and an electrical discharge. There is one thing, a flash of lightning, which is described scientifically as an electrical discharge to the earth from a cloud of ionized water molecules. The case is not at all like that of explaining a footprint by reference to a burglar. We say that what lightning really is, what its true nature as revealed by science is, is an electrical discharge. (It is not the true nature of a footprint to be a burglar.)

To forestall irrelevant objections, I should like to make it clear that by 'lightning' I mean the publicly observable physical object, lightning, not a visual sense-datum of lightning. I say that the publicly observable physical object lightning is in fact the electrical discharge, not just a correlate of it. The sense-datum, or rather the having of the sense-datum, the 'look' of lightning, may well in my view be a correlate of the electrical discharge. For in my view it is a brain state *caused* by the lightning. But we should no more confuse sensations of lightning with lightning than we confuse sensations of a table with the table.

In short, the reply to Objection 1 is that there can be contingent statements of the form 'A is identical with B,' and a person may well know that something is an A without knowing that it is a B. An illiterate peasant might well be able to talk about his sensations without knowing about his brain processes, just as he can talk about lightning though he knows nothing of electricity.

Objection 2. It is only a contingent fact (if it is a fact) that when we have a certain kind of sensation there is a certain kind of process in our brain. Indeed it is possible, though perhaps in the highest degree unlikely, that our present physiological theories will be as out of date as the ancient theory connecting mental processes with goings on in the heart. It follows that when we report a sensation we are not reporting a brain-process.

Reply. The objection certainly proves that when we say 'I have an after-image' we cannot *mean* something of the form 'I have such and such a brain-process.' But this does not show that what we report (having an after-image) is not *in fact* a brain process. 'I see lightning' does not *mean* 'I see an electrical discharge.' Indeed, it is logically possible (though highly unlikely) that the electrical discharge account of lightning might one day be given up. Again, 'I see the Evening Star' does not *mean* the same as 'I see the Morning Star,' and yet 'The Evening Star and the Morning Star are one and the same thing' is a contingent proposition. Possibly Objection 2 derives some of its apparent strength from a 'Fido'—Fido theory of meaning. If the meaning of an expression were what the expression named, then of course it *would* follow from the fact that 'sensation' and 'brain-process' have different meanings that they cannot name one and the same thing.

Objection 3.[13] Even if Objections 1 and 2 do not prove that sensations are something over and above brain-processes, they do prove that the qualities of sensations are something over and above the qualities of brain-processes. That is, it may be possible to get out of asserting the existence of irreducibly psychic processes, but not out of asserting the existence of irreducibly psychic *properties*. For suppose we identify the Morning Star with the Evening Star. Then there must be some properties which logically imply that of being the Morning Star, and quite distinct properties which entail that of being the Evening Star. Again, there must be some properties (for example, that of being a yellow flash) which are logically distinct from those in the physicalist story.

Indeed, it might be thought that the objection succeeds at one jump. For consider the property of 'being a yellow flash.' It might seem that this property lies inevitably outside the physicalist framework within which I am trying to work (either by 'yellow' being an objective emergent property of physical objects, or else by being a power to produce yellow sense-data, where 'yellow,' in this second instantiation of the word, refers to a purely phenomenal or introspectible quality). I must therefore digress for a moment and indicate how I deal with secondary qualities. I shall concentrate on color.

First of all, let me introduce the concept of a normal percipient. One person is more a normal percipient than another if he can make color discriminations that the other cannot. For example, if A can pick a lettuce leaf out of a heap of cabbage leaves, whereas B cannot though he can pick a lettuce leaf out of a heap of beetroot leaves, then A is more normal than B. (I am assuming that A and B are not given time to distinguish the leaves by their slight difference in shape, and so forth.) From the concept of 'more normal than' it is easy to see how we can introduce the concept of 'normal.' Of course, Eskimos may make the finest discriminations at the blue end of the spectrum, Hottentots at the red end. In this case the concept of a normal percipient is a slightly idealized one, rather like that of 'the mean sun' in astronomical chronology. There is no need to go into such subtleties now. I say that 'This is red' means something roughly like 'A normal percipient would not easily pick this out of a clump of geranium petals though he would pick it out of a clump of lettuce leaves.' Of course it does not exactly mean this: a person might know the meaning of 'red' without knowing anything about geraniums, or even about normal percipients. But the point is that a person can be *trained* to say 'This is red' of objects which would not easily be picked out of geranium petals by a normal percipient, and so on. (Note that even a color-blind person can reasonably assert that something is red, though of course he needs to use another human being, not just himself, at his 'color meter.') This account of secondary qualities explains their unimportance in physics. For obviously the discriminations and lack of discriminations made by a very complex neurophysiological mechanism are hardly likely to correspond to simple and nonarbitrary distinctions in nature.

I therefore elucidate colors as powers, in Locke's sense, to evoke certain sorts of discriminatory responses in human beings. They are also, of course, powers to cause sensations in human beings (an account still nearer Locke's). But these sensations, I am arguing, are identifiable with brain processes.

Now how do I get over the objection that a sensation can be identified with a brain process only if it has some phenomenal property, not possessed by brain processes, whereby one-half of the identification may be, so to speak, pinned down?

Reply. My suggestion is as follows. When a person says, 'I see a yellowish-orange after-image,' he is saying something like this: '*There is something going on which is like what is going on when* I have my eyes open, am awake, and there is an orange <u>illuminated in good light in front of me, that is, when I really see an orange.</u>' (And there is no reason why a person should not say the same thing when he is having a veridical sense-datum, so long as we construe 'like' in the last sentence in such a sense that something can be like itself.) Notice that the italicized words, namely 'there is something going on which is like what is going on when,' are all quasilogical or topic-neutral words. This explains why the ancient Greek peasant's reports about his sensations can be neutral between dualistic metaphysics or my materialistic metaphysics. It explains how sensations can be brain-processes and yet how a man who reports them need know nothing about brain-processes. For he reports them only very abstractly as 'something going on which is like what is going on when . . .' Similarly, a person may say 'someone is in the room,' thus reporting truly that the doctor is in the room, even though he has never heard of doctors. (There are not two people in the room: 'someone' *and* the doctor.) This account of sensation statements also explains the singular elusiveness of 'raw feels'—why no one seems to be able to pin any properties on them.[14] Raw feels, in my view, are colorless for the very same reason that *something* is colorless. This does not mean that sensations do not have plenty of properties, for if they are brain-processes they certainly have lots of neurological properties. It only means that in speaking of them as being like or unlike one another we need not know or mention these properties.

[From 'Sensations and Brain Processes', in V. C. Chappell (ed.), *The Philosophy of Mind* (Englewood Cliffs, NJ: Prentice-Hall, 1962), 160–7.]

43 Eliminative Materialism and the Propositional Attitudes

Eliminative materialism is the thesis that our common-sense conception of psychological phenomena constitutes a radically false theory, a theory so fundamentally defective that both the principles and the ontology of that theory will eventually be displaced, rather than smoothly reduced, by completed neuroscience. Our mutual understanding and even our introspection may then be reconstituted within the conceptual framework of completed neuroscience, a theory we may expect to be more powerful by far than the common-sense psychology it displaces, and more substantially integrated within physical science generally. My purpose in this paper is to explore these projections, especially as they bear on (1) the principal elements of common-sense psychology: the propositional attitudes (beliefs, desires, etc.), and (2) the conception of rationality in which these elements figure.

This focus represents a change in the fortunes of materialism. Twenty years ago, emotions, qualia, and 'raw feels' were held to be the principal stumbling blocks for the materialist program. With these barriers dissolving, the locus of opposition has shifted. Now it is the realm of the intentional, the realm of the propositional attitude, that is most commonly held up as being both irreducible to and ineliminable in favor of anything from within a materialist framework. Whether and why this is so, we must examine.

Such an examination will make little sense, however, unless it is first appreciated that the relevant network of common-sense concepts does indeed constitute an empirical theory, with all the functions, virtues, *and perils* entailed by that status. I shall therefore begin with a brief sketch of this view and a summary rehearsal of its rationale. The resistance it encounters still surprises me. After all, common sense has yielded up many theories. Recall the view that space has a preferred direction in which all things fall; that weight is an intrinsic feature of a body; that a force-free moving object will promptly return to rest; that the sphere of the heavens turns daily; and so on. These examples are clear, perhaps, but people seem willing to concede a theoretical component within common sense only if (1) the theory and the common sense involved are safely located in antiquity, and (2) the relevant theory is now so clearly false that its speculative nature is inescapable. Theories are indeed easier to discern under these circumstances. But the vision of hindsight is always 20/20. Let us aspire to some foresight for a change.

I Why folk psychology is a theory

Seeing our common-sense conceptual framework for mental phenomena as a theory brings a simple and unifying organization to most of the major topics in the philosophy of mind, including the explanation and prediction of behavior, the semantics of mental predicates, action theory, the other-minds problem, the intentionality of mental states, the nature of introspection, and the mind–body problem. Any view that can pull this lot together deserves careful consideration.

Let us begin with the explanation of human (and animal) behavior. The fact is that the average person is able to explain, and even predict, the behavior of other persons with a facility and success that is remarkable. Such explanations and predictions standardly make reference to the desires, beliefs, fears, intentions, perceptions, and so forth, to which the agents are presumed subject. But explanations presuppose laws—rough and ready ones, at least—that connect the explanatory conditions with the behavior explained. The same is true for the making of predictions, and for the justification of subjunctive and counterfactual conditionals concerning behavior. Reassuringly, a rich network of common-sense laws can indeed be reconstructed from this quotidean commerce of explanation and anticipation; its principles are familiar homilies; and their sundry functions are transparent. Each of us understands others, as well as we do, because we share a tacit command of an integrated body of lore concerning the lawlike relations holding among external circumstances, internal states, and overt behavior. Given its nature and functions, this body of lore may quite aptly be called 'folk psychology.'

This approach entails that the semantics of the terms in our familiar mentalistic vocabulary is to be understood in the same manner as the semantics of theoretical terms generally: the meaning of any theoretical term is fixed or constituted by the network of laws in which it figures. (This position is quite distinct from logical behaviorism. We deny that the relevant laws are analytic, and it is the lawlike connections generally that carry the semantic weight, not just the connections with overt behavior. But this view does account for what little plausibility logical behaviorism did enjoy.)

More importantly, the recognition that folk psychology is a theory provides a simple and decisive solution to an old skeptical problem, the problem of other minds. The problematic conviction that another individual is the subject of certain mental states is not inferred deductively from his behavior, nor is it inferred by inductive analogy from the perilously isolated instance of one's own case. Rather, that conviction is a singular *explanatory hypothesis* of a perfectly straightforward kind. Its function, in conjunction with the background laws of folk psychology, is to provide explanations/predictions/understanding of the individual's continuing behavior, and it is credible to the degree that it is successful in this regard over competing hypotheses. In the main, such hypotheses are successful, and so the belief that others enjoy the internal states comprehended by folk psychology is a reasonable belief.

Knowledge of other minds thus has no essential dependence on knowledge of one's own mind. Applying the principles of our folk psychology to our behavior, a Martian could justly ascribe to us the familiar run of mental states, even though his own psychology were very different from ours. He would not, therefore, be 'generalizing from his own case.'

As well, introspective judgments about one's own case turn out not to have any special status or integrity anyway. On the present view, an introspective judgment is just an instance of an acquired habit of conceptual response to one's internal states, and the integrity of any particular response is always contingent on the integrity of the acquired conceptual framework (theory) in which the response is framed. Accordingly, one's *introspective* certainty that one's mind is the seat of beliefs and desires may be as badly misplaced as was the classical man's *visual* certainty that the star-flecked sphere of the heavens turns daily.

Another conundrum is the intentionality of mental states. The 'propositional attitudes,' as Russell called them, form the systematic core of folk psychology; and their uniqueness and anomalous logical properties have inspired some to see here a fundamental contrast with anything that mere physical phenomena might conceivably display. The key to this matter lies again in the theoretical nature of folk psychology. The intentionality of mental states here emerges not as a mystery of nature, but as a structural feature of the concepts of folk psychology. Ironically, those same structural features reveal the very close affinity that folk psychology bears to theories in the physical sciences. Let me try to explain.

Consider the large variety of what might be called 'numerical attitudes' appearing in the conceptual framework of physical science: ' . . . has a mass$_{kg}$ of n', ' . . . has a velocity of n', ' . . . has a temperature$_k$ of n', and so forth. These expressions are predicate-forming expressions: when one substitutes a singular term for a number into the place held by 'n', a determinate predicate results. More interestingly, the relations between the various 'numerical attitudes' that result are precisely the relations between the numbers 'contained' in those attitudes. More interesting still, the argument place that takes the singular terms for numbers is open to quantification. All this permits the expression of generalizations concerning the lawlike relations that hold between the various numerical attitudes in nature. Such laws involve quantification over numbers, and they exploit the mathematical relations holding in that domain. [. . .]

Not only is folk psychology a theory, it is so *obviously* a theory that it must be held a major mystery why it has taken until the last half of the twentieth century for philosophers to realize it. The structural features of folk psychology parallel perfectly those of mathematical physics; the only difference lies in the respective domain of abstract entities they exploit—numbers in the case of physics, and propositions in the case of psychology.

Finally, the realization that folk psychology is a theory puts a new light on the mind–body problem. The issue becomes a matter of how the ontology of one theory (folk psychology) is, or is not, going to be related to the ontology of another theory (completed neuroscience); and the major philosophical positions on the mind–body problem emerge as so many different anticipations of what future research will reveal about the intertheoretic status and integrity of folk psychology.

The identity theorist optimistically expects that folk psychology will be smoothly *reduced* by completed neuroscience, and its ontology preserved by dint of transtheoretic identities. The dualist expects that it will prove *ir*reducible to completed neuroscience, by dint of being a nonredundant description of an autonomous, nonphysical domain of natural phenomena. The functionalist also expects that it will prove irreducible, but on the quite different grounds that the internal economy characterized by folk psychology is not, in the last analysis, a law-governed economy of natural states, but an abstract organization of functional states, an organization instantiable in a variety of quite different material substrates. It is therefore irreducible to the principles peculiar to any of them.

Finally, the eliminative materialist is also pessimistic about the prospects for reduction, but his reason is that folk psychology is a radically inadequate account of our internal activities, too confused and too defective to win survival through intertheoretic reduction. On his view it will simply be displaced by a better theory of those activities.

Which of these fates is the real destiny of folk psychology, we shall attempt to divine presently. For now, the point to keep in mind is that we shall be exploring the fate of a theory, a systematic, corrigible, speculative *theory*.

II Why folk psychology might (really) be false

Given that folk psychology is an empirical theory, it is at least an abstract possibility that its principles are radically false and that its ontology is an illusion. With the exception of eliminative materialism, however, none of the major positions takes this possibility seriously. None of them doubts the basic integrity or truth of folk psychology (hereafter, 'FP'), and all of them anticipate a future in which its laws and categories are conserved. This conservatism is not without some foundation. After all, FP does enjoy a substantial amount of explanatory and predictive success. And what better grounds than this for confidence in the integrity of its categories?

What better grounds indeed? Even so, the presumption in FP's favor is spurious, born of innocence and tunnel vision. A more searching examination reveals a different picture. First, we must reckon not only with FP's successes, but with its explanatory failures, and with their extent and seriousness. Second, we must consider the long-term history of FP, its growth, fertility, and current promise of future development. And third, we must consider what sorts of theories are *likely* to be true of the etiology of our behavior, given what else we have learned about ourselves in recent history. That is, we must evaluate FP with regard to its coherence and continuity with fertile and well-established theories in adjacent and overlapping domains—with evolutionary theory, biology, and neuroscience, for example—because active coherence with the rest of what we presume to know is perhaps the final measure of any hypothesis.

A serious inventory of this sort reveals a very troubled situation, one which would evoke open skepticism in the case of any theory less familiar and dear to us. Let me sketch some relevant detail. When one centers one's attention not on what FP can explain, but on what it cannot explain or fails even to address, one discovers that there is a very great deal. As examples of central and important mental phenomena that remain largely or wholly mysterious within the framework of FP, consider the nature and dynamics of mental illness, the faculty of creative imagination, or the ground of intelligence differences between individuals. Consider our utter ignorance of the nature and psychological functions of sleep, that curious state in which a third of one's life is spent. Reflect on the common ability to catch an outfield fly ball on the run, or hit a moving car with a snowball. Consider the internal construction of a 3-D visual image from subtle differences in the 2-D array of stimulations in our respective retinas. Consider the rich variety of perceptual illusions, visual and otherwise. Or consider the miracle of memory, with its lightning capacity for relevant retrieval. On these and many other mental phenomena, FP sheds negligible light.

One particularly outstanding mystery is the nature of the learning process itself, especially where it involves large-scale conceptual change, and especially as it appears in its pre-linguistic or entirely nonlinguistic form (as in infants and animals), which is by far the most common form in nature. FP is faced with special difficulties here, since its conception of learning as the manipulation and storage of propositional attitudes founders on the fact that how to formulate, manipulate, and store a rich fabric of propositional attitudes is itself something that is learned, and is only one among many acquired cognitive skills. FP would thus appear constitutionally incapable of even addressing this most basic of mysteries.

Failures on such a large scale do not (yet) show that FP is a false theory, but they do move that prospect well into the range of real possibility, and they do show decisively that FP is *at best* a highly superficial theory, a partial and unpenetrating gloss on a deeper and more complex reality. Having reached this opinion, we may be forgiven for exploring the possibility that FP provides a positively misleading sketch of our internal kinematics and dynamics, one whose success is owed more to selective application and forced interpretation on our part than to genuine theoretical insight on FP's part. [. . .]

Explanatory success to date is of course not the only dimension in which a theory can display virtue or promise. A troubled or stagnant theory may merit patience and solicitude on other grounds; for example, on grounds that it is the only theory or theoretical approach that fits well with other theories about adjacent subject matters, or the only one that promises to reduce to or be explained by some established background theory whose domain encompasses the domain of the theory at issue. In sum, it may rate credence because it holds promise of theoretical integration. How does FP rate in this dimension?

It is just here, perhaps, that FP fares poorest of all. If we approach *Homo sapiens* from the perspective of natural history and the physical sciences, we can tell a coherent story of his constitution, development, and behavioral capacities which encompasses particle physics, atomic and molecular theory, organic chemistry, evolutionary theory, biology, physiology, and materialistic neuroscience. That story, though still radically incomplete, is already extremely powerful, outperforming FP at many points even in its own domain. And it is deliberately and self-consciously coherent with the rest of our developing world picture. In short, the greatest theoretical synthesis in the history of the human race is currently in our hands, and parts of it already provide searching descriptions and explanations of human sensory input, neural activity, and motor control.

But FP is no part of this growing synthesis. [. . .]

III Arguments against elimination

[. . .] An antipathy toward eliminative materialism arises from two distinct threads running through contemporary functionalism. The first thread concerns the *normative* character of FP, or at least of that central core of FP which treats of the propositional attitudes. FP, some will say, is a characterization of an ideal, or at least praiseworthy mode of internal activity. It outlines not only what it is to have and process beliefs and desires, but also (and inevitably) what it is to be rational in their administration. The ideal laid down by FP may be imperfectly achieved by empirical humans, but this does not impugn FP as a normative characterization. Nor need such failures seriously impugn FP even as a descriptive characterization, for it remains true that our activities can be both usefully and accurately understood as rational *except for* the occasional lapse due to noise, interference, or other breakdown, which defects empirical research may eventually unravel. Accordingly, though neuroscience may usefully augment it, FP has no pressing need to be displaced, even as a descriptive theory; nor could it be replaced, *qua* normative characterization, by any descriptive theory of neural mechanisms, since rationality is defined over propositional attitudes like beliefs and desires. FP, therefore, is here to stay. [. . .]

The second thread concerns the *abstract* nature of FP. The central claim of functionalism is that the principles of FP characterize our internal states in a fashion that makes no reference to their intrinsic nature or physical constitution. Rather, they are characterized in terms of the network of causal relations they bear to one another, and to sensory circumstances and overt behavior. Given its abstract specification, that internal economy may therefore be realized in a nomically heterogeneous variety of physical systems. All of them may differ, even radically, in their physical constitution, and yet at another level, they will all share the same nature. [. . .]

All of this is appealing. But almost none of it, I think, is right. Functionalism has too long enjoyed its reputation as a daring and *avant garde* position. It needs to be revealed for the short-sighted and reactionary position it is.

IV The conservative nature of functionalism

A valuable perspective on functionalism can be gained from the following story. To begin with, recall the alchemists' theory of inanimate matter. We have here a long and variegated tradition, of course, not a single theory, but our purposes will be served by a gloss.

The alchemists conceived the 'inanimate' as entirely continuous with animated matter, in that the sensible and behavioral properties of the various substances are owed to the ensoulment of baser matter by various spirits or essences. These nonmaterial aspects were held to undergo development, just as we find growth and development in the various souls of plants, animals, and humans. The alchemist's peculiar skill lay in knowing how to seed, nourish, and bring to maturity the desired spirits enmattered in the appropriate combinations.

On one orthodoxy, the four fundamental spirits (for 'inanimate' matter) were named 'mercury,' 'sulphur,' 'yellow arsenic,' and 'sal ammoniac.' Each of these spirits was held responsible for a rough but characteristic syndrome of sensible, combinatorial, and causal properties. The spirit mercury, for example, was held responsible for certain features typical of metallic substances—their shininess, liquefiability, and so forth. Sulphur was held responsible for certain residual features typical of metals, and for those displayed by the ores from which running metal could be distilled. Any given metallic substance was a critical orchestration principally of these two spirits. A similar story held for the other two spirits, and among the four of them a certain domain of physical features and transformations was rendered intelligible and controllable.

The degree of control was always limited, of course. Or better, such prediction and control as the alchemists possessed was owed more to the manipulative lore acquired as an apprentice to a master, than to any genuine insight specified by the theory. The theory followed, more than it dictated, practice. But the theory did supply some rhyme to the practice, and in the absence of a developed alternative it was sufficiently compelling to sustain a long and stubborn tradition.

The tradition had become faded and fragmented by the time the elemental chemistry of Lavoisier and Dalton arose to replace it for good. But let us suppose that it had hung on a little longer—perhaps because the four-spirit orthodoxy had become a thumb-worn part of everyman's common sense—and let us examine the nature of the conflict between the two theories and some possible avenues of resolution.

No doubt the simplest line of resolution, and the one which historically took place, is outright displacement. The dualistic interpretation of the four essences—as immaterial spirits—will appear both feckless and unnecessary given the power of the corpuscularian taxonomy of atomic chemistry. And a reduction of the old taxonomy to the new will appear impossible, given the extent to which the comparatively toothless old theory cross-classifies things relative to the new. Elimination would thus appear the only alternative—*unless* some cunning and determined defender of the alchemical vision has the wit to suggest the following defense.

Being 'ensouled by mercury,' or 'sulphur,' or either of the other two so-called spirits, is actually a *functional* state. The first, for example, is defined by the disposition to reflect light, to liquefy under heat, to unite with other matter in the same state, and so forth. And each of these four states is related to the others, in that the syndrome for each varies as a function of which of the other three states is also instantiated in the same substrate. Thus, the level of description comprehended by the alchemical vocabulary is abstract: various material substances, suitably 'ensouled,' can display the features of a metal, for example, or even of gold specifically. For it is the total syndrome of occurrent and causal properties which matters, not the corpuscularian details of the substrate. Alchemy, it is concluded, comprehends a level of organization in reality distinct from and irreducible to the organization found at the level of corpuscularian chemistry.

This view might have had considerable appeal. After all, it spares alchemists the burden of defending immaterial souls that come and go; it frees them from having to meet the very strong demands of a naturalistic reduction; and it spares them the shock and confusion of outright elimination. Alchemical theory emerges as basically all right! Nor need they appear too obviously stubborn or dogmatic in this. Alchemy as it stands, they concede, may need substantial tidying up, and experience must be our guide. But we need not fear its naturalistic displacement, they remind us, since it is the particular orchestration of the syndromes of occurrent and causal properties which makes a piece of matter gold, not the idiosyncratic details of its corpuscularian substrate. A further circumstance would have made this claim even more plausible. For the fact is, the alchemists *did* know how to make gold, in this relevantly weakened sense of 'gold', and they could do so in a variety of ways. Their 'gold' was never as perfect, alas, as the 'gold' nurtured in nature's womb, but what mortal can expect to match the skills of nature herself? [. . .]

Research into the neural structures that fund the organization and processing of perceptual information reveals that they are capable of administering a great variety of complex tasks, some of them showing a complexity far in excess of that shown by natural language. Natural languages, it turns out, exploit only a very elementary portion of the available machinery, the bulk of which serves far more complex activities beyond the ken of the propositional conceptions of FP. The detailed unraveling of what that machinery is and of the capacities it has makes it plain that a form of language far more sophisticated than 'natural' language, though decidedly 'alien' in its syntactic and semantic structures, could also be learned and used by our innate systems. Such a novel system of communication, it is quickly realized, could raise the efficiency of information exchange between brains by an order of magnitude, and would enhance epistemic evaluation by a comparable amount, since it would reflect the underlying structure of our cognitive activities in greater detail than does natural language.

Guided by our new understanding of those internal structures, we manage to construct a new system of verbal communication entirely distinct from natural language, with a new and more powerful combinatorial grammar over novel elements forming novel combinations with exotic properties. The compounded strings of this alternative system—call them 'übersätze'—are not evaluated as true or false, nor are the relations between them remotely analogous to the relations of entailment, etc., that hold between sentences. They display a different organization and manifest different virtues.

Once constructed, this 'language' proves to be learnable; it has the power projected; and in two generations it has swept the planet. Everyone uses the new system. The syntactic forms and semantic categories of so-called 'natural' language disappear entirely. And with them disappear the propositional attitudes of FP, displaced by a more revealing scheme in which (of course) 'übersatzenal attitudes' play the leading role. FP again suffers elimination.

This second story, note, illustrates a theme with endless variations. There are possible as many different 'folk psychologies' as there are possible differently structured communication systems to serve as models for them.

A third and even stranger possibility can be outlined as follows. We know that there is considerable lateralization of function between the two cerebral hemispheres, and that the two hemispheres make use of the information they get from each other by way of the great cerebral commissure—the corpus callosum—a giant cable of neurons connecting them. Patients whose commissure has been surgically severed display a variety of behavioral deficits that indicate a loss of access by one hemisphere to information it used to get from the other. However, in people with callosal agenesis (a congenital defect in which the connecting cable is simply absent), there is little or no behavioral deficit, suggesting that the two hemispheres have learned to exploit the information carried in other less direct pathways connecting them through the subcortical regions. This suggests that, even in the normal case, a developing hemisphere *learns* to make use of the information the cerebral commissure deposits at its doorstep. What we have then, in the case of a normal human, is two physically distinct cognitive systems (both capable of independent function) responding in a systematic and learned fashion to exchanged information. And what is especially interesting about this case is the sheer amount of information exchanged. The cable of the commissure consists of $\approx$ 200 million neurons, and even if we assume that each of these fibres is capable of one of only two possible states each second (a most conservative estimate), we are looking at a channel whose information capacity is $< 2 \times 10^8$ binary bits/second. Compare this to the > 500 bits/ second capacity of spoken English.

Now, if two distinct hemispheres can learn to communicate on so impressive a scale, why shouldn't two distinct brains learn to do it also? This would require an artificial 'commissure' of some kind, but let us suppose that we can fashion a workable transducer for implantation at some site in the brain that research reveals to be suitable, a transducer to convert a symphony of neural activity into (say) microwaves radiated from an aerial in the forehead, and to perform the reverse function of converting received microwaves back into neural activation. Connecting it up need not be an insuperable problem. We simply trick the normal processes of dendritic arborization into growing their own myriad connections with the active microsurface of the transducer.

Once the channel is opened between two or more people, they can learn (*learn*) to exchange information and coordinate their behavior with the same intimacy and virtuosity displayed by your own cerebral hemispheres. Think what this might do for hockey teams, and ballet companies, and research teams! If the entire population were thus fitted out, spoken language of any kind might well disappear completely, a victim of the 'why crawl when you can fly?' principle. Libraries become filled not with books, but with long recordings of exemplary bouts of neural activity. These constitute a growing cultural heritage, an evolving 'Third World,' to use Karl Popper's terms. But they do not consist of sentences or arguments. [. . .]

These speculations, I hope, will evoke the required sense of untapped possibilities, and I shall in any case bring them to a close here. Their function is to make some inroads into the aura of inconceivability that commonly surrounds the idea that we might reject FP.

[From 'Eliminative Materialism and the Propositional Attitudes', in W. Lycan (ed.), *Mind and Cognition* (Oxford: Basil Blackwell, 1990), 206–21.]

THOMAS REID

44   Of Analogy

It is natural to men to judge of things less known by some similitude they observe, or think they observe, between them and things more familiar or better known. In many cases, we have no better way of judging. And where the things compared have really a great similitude in their nature, when there is reason to think that they are subject to the same laws, there may be a considerable degree of probability in conclusions drawn from analogy.

Thus, we may observe a very great similitude between this earth which we inhabit, and the other planets, Saturn, Jupiter, Mars, Venus, and Mercury. They all revolve round the sun, as the earth does, although at different distances, and in different periods. They borrow all their light from the sun, as the earth does. Several of them are known to revolve round their axis like the earth, and, by that means, must have a like succession of day and night. Some of them have moons, that serve to give them light in the absence of the sun, as our moon does to us. They are all, in their motions, subject to the same law of gravitation, as the earth is. From all this similitude, it is not unreasonable to think, that those planets may, like our earth, be the habitation of various orders of living creatures. There is some probability in this conclusion from analogy.

In medicine, physicians must, for the most part, be directed in their prescriptions by analogy. The constitution of one human body is so like to that of another, that it is reasonable to think, that what is the cause of health or sickness to one, may have the same effect upon another. And this generally is found true, though not without some exceptions.

In politics, we reason, for the most part, from analogy. The constitution of human nature is so similar in different societies or commonwealths, that the causes of peace and war, of tranquility and sedition, of riches and poverty, of improvement and degeneracy, are much the same in all.

Analogical reasoning, therefore, is not, in all cases, to be rejected. It may afford a greater or a less degree of probability, according as the things compared are more or less similar in that nature. But it ought to be observed, that, as this kind of reasoning can afford only probable evidence at best, so, unless great caution be used, we are apt to be led into error by it. For men are naturally disposed to conceive a greater similitude in things than there really is.

To give an instance of this: anatomists, in ancient ages, seldom dissected human bodies; but very often the bodies of those quadrupeds, whose internal structure was thought to approach nearest to that of the human body. Modern anatomists have discovered many mistakes the ancients were led into, by their conceiving a greater similitude between the structure of men and of some beasts than there is in reality. By this, and many other instances that might be given, it appears, that conclusions built on analogy stand on a slippery foundation; and that we ought never to rest upon evidence of this kind, when we can have more direct evidence.

I know no author who has made a more just and a more happy use of this mode of reasoning, than bishop Butler, in his Analogy of Religion, Natural and Revealed, to the Constitution and Course of Nature. In that excellent work, the author does not ground any of the truths of religion upon analogy, as their proper evidence. He only makes use of analogy to answer objections against them. When objections are made against the truths of religion, which may be made with equal strength against what we know to be true in the course of nature, such objections can have no weight.

Analogical reasoning, therefore, may be of excellent use in answering objections against truths which have other evidence. It may likewise give a greater or a less degree of probability in cases where we can find no other evidence. But all arguments, drawn from analogy, are still the weaker, the greater disparity there is between the things compared; and therefore must be weakest of all when we compare body with mind, because there are no two things in nature more unlike.

There is no subject in which men have always been so prone to form their notions by analogies of this kind, as in what relates to the mind. We form an early acquaintance with material things by means of our senses, and are bred up in a constant familiarity with them. Hence we are apt to measure all things by them; and to ascribe to things most remote from matter, the qualities that belong to material things. It is for this reason, that mankind have, in all ages, been so prone to conceive the mind itself to be some subtile kind of matter: that they have been disposed to ascribe human figure, and human organs, not only to angels, but even to the Deity. Though we are conscious of the operations of our own minds when they are exerted, and are capable of attending to them, so as to form a distinct notion of them; this is so difficult a work to men, whose attention is constantly solicited by external objects, that we give them names from things that are familiar, and which are conceived to have some similitude to them; and the notions we form of them are no less analogical than the names we give them. Almost all the words, by which we express the operations of the mind, are borrowed from material objects. To *understand*, to *conceive*, to *imagine*, to *comprehend*, to *deliberate*, to *infer*, and many others, are words of this kind; so that the very language of mankind, with regard to the operation of our minds, is analogical. Because bodies are effected only by contact and pressure, we are apt to conceive, that what is an immediate object of thought, and affects the mind, must be in contact with it, and make some impression upon it. When we imagine any thing, the very word leads us to think, that there must be some image in the mind, of the thing conceived. It is evident, that these notions are drawn from some similitude conceived between body and mind, and between the properties of body and the operations of mind.

To illustrate more fully that analogical reasoning from a supposed similitude of mind to body, which I conceive to be the most fruitful source of error with regard to the operations of our minds, I shall give an instance of it.

When a man is urged by contrary motives, those on one hand inciting him to do some action, those on the other to forbear it; he deliberates about it, and at last resolves to do it, or not to do it. The contrary motives are here compared to the weights in the opposite scales of a balance; and there is not perhaps any instance that can be named of a more striking analogy between body and mind. Hence the phrases of weighing motives, of deliberating upon actions, are common to all languages.

From this analogy, some philosophers draw very important conclusions. They say, that, as the balance cannot incline to one side more than the other, when the opposite weights are equal; so a man cannot possibly determine himself, if the motives on both hands are equal: and, as the balance must necessarily turn to that side which has most weight; so the man must necessarily be determined to that hand where the motive is strongest. And on this foundation, some of the schoolmen maintained, that, if a hungry ass were placed between two bundles of hay equally inviting, the beast must stand still and starve to death, being unable to turn to either, because there are equal motives to both. This is an instance of that analogical reasoning, which I conceive ought never to be trusted: for, the analogy between a balance and a man deliberating, though one of the strongest that can be found between matter and mind, is too weak to support any argument. A piece of dead inactive matter, and an active intelligent being, are things very unlike; and because the one would remain at rest in a certain case, it does not follow that the other would be inactive in a case somewhat similar. The argument is no better than this, that, because a dead animal moves only as it is pushed, and if pushed with equal force in contrary directions, must remain at rest; therefore the same thing must happen to a living animal; for surely the similitude between a dead animal and a living, is as great as that between a balance and a man.

The conclusion I would draw from all that has been said on analogy, is, that, in our inquiries concerning the mind, and its operations, we ought never to trust to reasonings, drawn from some supposed similitude of body to mind; and that we ought to be very much upon our guard, that we be not imposed upon by those analogical terms and phrases, by which the operations of the mind are expressed in all languages.

[From *Essays on the Intellectual Powers of Man* (Cambridge, Mass.: MIT Press, 1969), Essay I, ch. 4.]

GALEN STRAWSON

45 Agnostic Materialism

[. . .] The existence of experience is the only hard part of the mind–body problem for materialists. [. . .]

Many actual and possible beings do not, we assume, have any experience, although they can behave just as if they were both intelligent and capable of sensation. That is, they can behave just as if they had certain properties and abilities of a sort that we naturally think of as mental properties and abilities, when we think of them as possessed by ourselves and other animals. The present claim is that none of these apparently mental abilities and properties pose any problem, so far as the mind–body problem is concerned. [. . .]

Now consider the apparently sensory abilities. Suppose that the very existence of physical beings that can detect and discriminate differences in their environment is said to pose a special problem within the philosophy of mind. The reply is that their existence is no more problematic, within materialist philosophy of mind, than the existence of experienceless machines that can detect differences of shape or temperature, or differences that we register as color or sound differences. And this is again to say that it is not problematic at all. We can give detailed physical-science explanations of how such discriminatory abilities are or can be realized in or by physical entities that we assume to be experienceless. We can have a full understanding, on the terms of our current conception of the physical, of how it is possible for these abilities to be physically realized. We can build machines that possess them. But we can do nothing like this for experience. [. . .]

One might put the point by saying that even if we could make a machine that had experience, and even if we could know (per impossibile) that we had done so, we still would not be able to give any explanation, in physics terms, of how it was possible that it had experience—so long as we were operating within the confines of our current physics-based conception of the physical. Nor does current physics seem to have any obvious promising gaps or valences, where conceptual extensions could possibly bring in radically new predicates of a sort that might help us begin to see how the physical as described by physics could be the basis of, or involve, or be, experience.

Quantum enthusiasts may doubt this, but the strangenesses of quantum mechanics have no obvious affinity with, or potential for explaining, the existence of experience. [. . .]

These, then, are my reasons for taking the mind–body problem to be nothing but the experience–matter problem or, more accurately, and speaking within the materialist framework, to be nothing but the problem of the relation between the experiential physical and the nonexperiential physical. The things we think of as higher intellectual achievements are just not a philosophical problem, except insofar as they involve a capacity for experience. [. . .]

I have suggested that materialists must confess their ignorance and their faith. I will now consider the suggestion that they might do better to describe themselves not as materialists but rather as *neutral monists* or *agnostic monists*.

'Neutral monism' is a name that carries a number of historical associations. I take it to be the view that although the universe is indeed composed of one fundamental kind of stuff, this stuff is neither mental nor physical. Or rather, it is neither mental nor physical as we currently understand these terms. [. . .]

Should anyone ask why philosophers should be attracted to neutral monism, the answer seems clear. It provides a complete if merely promissory solution to the mind–body problem. According to neutral monism, there is no problem about the relation between experiential and nonexperiential phenomena, for they are mere appearances of a single and single-natured substance whose nature we do not know. [. . .]

Insofar as I am any sort of materialist, then, I am an agnostic materialist: our current conception of the physical is fundamentally incomplete on its own terms. Quite independently of the mind–body problem, it is a commonplace that there is a sense in which our ordinary concepts of space, time, and matter are profoundly inadequate and partial representations of the nature of the reality to which they are a response. [. . .]

I have suggested that materialism ought to be explicitly agnostic. But many materialists may now object that I have not given any good reason to suppose that all the blame for the intractability of the mind–body problem should be laid on the inadequacy of our current conception of those phenomena that are traditionally called 'physical'. They may say that at least part of the reason why the mind–body problem appears intractable lies in the inadequacy of our current conception of those phenomena that are traditionally called 'mental' (although they are just as physical as those that are traditionally called 'physical', according to materialism). [. . .]

Obviously, my inclination is the other way. For the mental includes the experiential; and whatever faults there may be in our conception of the experiential, our acquaintance with the experiential simply doesn't leave room for us to make a mistake about its basic nature of such a fundamental kind that exposing the mistake could entirely dissolve the mind–body problem without there being any change in the descriptive scheme of current physics. [. . .]

The current dominant view is still that mental notions will give way. Somehow they will be entirely subsumed under nonmental notions, or entirely reductively characterized in terms of nonmental notions, or entirely *eliminated* in favor of nonmental notions. Somehow or other we will be able to give, at least in principle, a full and satisfactory account of the general nature of reality using only those notions that we already deploy in 'contemporary physical science' [. . .]. But when one reflects on the point just made—[a] that mental phenomena include experiential or what-it's-like-ness phenomena, [b] that there is a crucial sense in which current physics lacks the resources for either describing or explaining experiential or what-it's-like-ness phenomena, [c] that (b) is still true even after everything that we have discovered about the structure and function of the brain (and the atom)—this view seems astonishing. It is a very great act of faith. [. . .]

Perhaps there is a way of formulating the doctrine of eliminativism that makes it sound much more reasonable, according to which it does not claim that there is really nothing that we are talking about when we talk about pains, feelings of joy, tastes, beliefs, desires, and so on. It allows that these terms refer to something real but insists [a] that we fundamentally misconceptualize the reality in question, and [b] that a correct and fully adequate conceptualization of the nature of this reality will not need to make use of anything more than neuroscience and computational science, both of which are ultimately reducible [. . .] to physics.

The trouble with this view is that it is obviously false. It is false, given current neuroscience, computational science, and physics, and it will continue to be false until there is a revolution in all three. This revolution will be needed to make (b) true. But in making (b) true, it will, I believe, have to cast doubt on (a). For consider (once again) your experience now, and what it's like, and the silence of physics on the subject. Consider its reality and the reality of all the other streams of experience on the planet. As a materialist, one may assume that experiences have, in addition to an experiential description, a nonexperiential description in the terms of physics (although one is not obliged to assume this by materialism). The old point remains: when we have given this description (with or without further, higher-level nonexperiential descriptions in neurophysiological or computational-science terms), we have still said nothing about the experiences considered specifically in respect of their experiential character.

Some may think that this does not matter very much. They may have made a conscious decision not to say anything about experiential phenomena, because they are pursuing the project of eliminating experience-describing terminology from their account of the world. But then they are simply deciding to leave part of reality out of their scientific account of reality. They are just giving up on the great philosophical-scientific project of giving a unified account of the whole of reality, so far as we are acquainted with it and so far as we are able. For if one thing is clear, it is that experience is as real as rabbits and rocks. Indeed, its reality is still, in this post-post-Cartesian age, the thing we can be most certain of. So 'eliminativism', on this last understanding of the term, has now become the name of the doctrine that we can and indeed should, as scientifically inspired philosophers, ignore one of the most dramatic and puzzling aspects of reality that there is. [. . .]

Why do I call myself a materialist, rather than a '?-ist'? My faith, like that of many other materialists, consists in a bundle of connected and unverifiable beliefs. I believe that experience is not all there is to reality. I believe that there is a physical world that involves the existence of space and of space-occupying entities that have nonexperiential properties. [. . .] I believe that however experiential properties are described, there is no good reason to think that they are emergent, relative to other physical properties, in such a way that they can correctly be said to be nonphysical properties. [. . .] I believe that one could in principle create a normally experiencing human being out of a piano. All one would have to do would be to arrange a sufficient number of the piano's constituent electrons, protons, and neutrons in the way in which they are ordinarily arranged in a normal living human being. Experience is as much a physical phenomenon as electric charge.

[From *Mental Reality* (Cambridge, Mass.: MIT Press, 1994), 93–105.]

JOHN R. SEARLE
....

46 **The Rediscovery of the Mind**

Thesis: FP is an empirical thesis like any other, and as such it is subject to empirical confirmation and disconfirmation.

Answer: The actual capacities that people have for coping with themselves and others are for the most part not in propositional form. They are, in my sense, Background capacities. For example, how we respond to facial expressions, what we find natural in behavior, and even how we understand utterances are in large part matters of know-how, not theories. You distort these capacities if you think of them as theories. See chapter 8 for more about this.

Thesis: All the same, you could state theoretical correlates or principles underlying these capacities. This would constitute a folk psychology and will in all likelihood be false, since in general folk theories are false.

Answer: You can, with some distortion, state a theoretical analogue to a practical skill. But it would be miraculous if these were in general false. Where it really matters, where something is at stake, folk theories have to be in general true or we would not have survived. Folk physics can be wrong about peripheral issues, such as the movement of the celestial spheres and the origin of the earth, because it doesn't much matter. But when it comes to which way your body moves if you jump off a cliff or what happens if a huge rock falls on you, folk theories had better be right or we would not have survived.

Thesis: It now becomes a specific matter for cognitive science (CS) to decide which theses of FP are true and which of its ontological commitments are warranted. For example, FP postulates beliefs and desires to account for behavior, but if it turns out that the CS account of behavior is inconsistent with this, then beliefs and desires do not exist.

Answer: Just about everything is wrong with this claim. First, we do not *postulate* beliefs and desires to account for anything. We simply experience conscious beliefs and desires. Think about real-life examples. It is a hot day and you are driving a pickup truck in the desert outside of Phoenix. No air conditioning. You can't remember when you were so thirsty, and you want a cold beer so bad you could scream. Now where is the 'postulation' of a desire? Conscious desires are experienced. They are no more postulated than conscious pains.

Second, beliefs and desires sometimes cause actions, but there is no essential connection. Most beliefs and desires never issue in actions. For example, I believe that the sun is 94 million miles away, and I would like to be a billionaire. Which of my actions do this belief and this desire explain? That if I want to buy a ticket to the sun I will be sure to get a 94-million-mile ticket? That the next time somebody gives me a billion, I won't refuse?

Thesis: All the same, postulated or not, there is unlikely to be a smooth reduction of the entities of FP to the more basic science of neurobiology, so it seems that elimination is the only alternative.

Answer: I have already said what a bad argument this is. Most types of real entities, from split-level ranch houses to cocktail parties, from interest rates to football games, do not undergo a smooth reduction to the entities of some fundamental theory. Why should they? I guess I have a 'theory' of cocktail parties—at least as much as I have a theory of 'folk psychology'—and cocktail parties certainly consist of molecule movements; but my theory of cocktail parties is nowhere near as good a theory as my theory of molecular physics, and there is no type reduction of cocktail parties to the taxonomy of physics. But all the same, cocktail parties really do exist. The question of the reducibility of such entities is irrelevant to the question of their existence.

Why would anyone make such an egregious mistake? That is, why would anyone suppose that the 'smooth reduction' of beliefs and desires to neurobiology is even relevant to the existence of beliefs and desires? The answer is that they are drawing a false analogy with the history of certain parts of physics. Churchland thinks that 'belief' and 'desire' have the same status in the theory of folk psychology that 'phlogiston' and 'caloric fluid' had in physics. But the analogy breaks down in all sorts of ways: Beliefs and desires, unlike phlogiston and caloric fluid, were not postulated as part of some special theory, they are actually experienced as part of our mental life. Their existence is no more theory-relative than is the existence of ranch houses, cocktail parties, football games, interest rates, or tables and chairs. One can always describe one's commonsense beliefs about such things as a 'theory,' but the existence of the phenomena is prior to the theory. Again, always think about actual cases. My theory of cocktail parties would include such things as that big cocktail parties are likely to be noisier than small ones, and my theory of ranch houses would include the claim that they tend to spread out more than most other types of houses. Such 'theories' are no doubt hopelessly inadequate, and the entities do not undergo smooth reduction to physics, where I have a much better theories for describing the same phenomena. But what has all that got to do with the existence of split-level ranch houses? Nothing. Similarly the inadequacy of commonsense psychology and the failure of commonsense taxonomy to match the taxonomy of brain science (this is what is meant by the failure of 'smooth reduction') have nothing to do with the existence of beliefs and desires. In a word, beliefs and split-level ranch houses are totally unlike phlogiston because their ontology is not dependent on the truth of a special theory, and their irreducibility to a more fundamental science is irrelevant to their existence.

Thesis: Yes, but what you are saying begs the question. You are just saying that beliefs and desires, like cocktail parties and split-level ranch houses, are not theoretical entities—their evidentiary base is not derived from some theory. But isn't that precisely one of the points at issue?

Answer: I think is is obvious that beliefs and desires are experienced as such, and they are certainly not 'postulated' to explain behavior, because they are not postulated at all. However even 'theoretical entities' do not in general get their legitimacy from reducibility. Consider economics. Interest rates, effective demand, marginal propensity to consume—are all referred to in mathematical economics. But none of the types of entities in question undergoes a smooth reduction to physics or neurobiology, for example. Again, why should they?

Reducibility is a weird requirement for ontology anyway, because classically one way to show that an entity did *not* really exist has been to reduce it to something else. Thus sunsets are reducible to planetary movements in the solar system, which showed that, as traditionally conceived, sunsets do not exist. The appearance of the sun setting is caused by something else, that is, the rotation of the earth relative to the sun.

Thesis: Still, it is possible to list a lot of folk psychological claims and see that many of them are doubtful.

Answer: If you look at the actual lists given, there is something fishy going on. If I were going to list some propositions of FP, I would list such things as:

1. In general, beliefs can be either true or false.
2. Sometimes people get hungry, and when they are hungry they often want to eat something.
3. Pains are often unpleasant. For this reason people often try to avoid them.

It is hard to imagine what kind of empirical evidence could refute these propositions. The reason is that on a natural construal they are not empirical hypotheses, or not *just* empirical hypotheses. They are more like constitutive principles of the phenomena in question. Proposition 1, for example, is more like the 'hypothesis' that a touchdown in American football counts six points. If you are told that a scientific study has shown that touchdowns actually count only 5.999999999 points, you know that somebody is seriously confused. It is part of the current definition of a touchdown that it counts six points. We can change the definition but not discover a different fact. Similarly, it is part of the definition of 'belief' that beliefs are candidates for truth or falsity. We could not 'discover' that beliefs are not susceptible to being true or false. [. . .]

A candidate for a constitutive principle is Churchland's example that anyone who fears *p* wants it to be the case that not *p*. How would you look for empirical evidence that this is false? It is part of the definition of 'fear.' So the deeper mistake is not just to suppose that FP is a theory, but that all the propositions of the theory are empirical hypotheses.

Since they are constitutive, not empirical, the only way to show them false would be to show that they have no range of application. For example, the 'constitutive principles' of witchcraft don't apply to anything because there aren't any witches. But you could not show that conscious desires and pains do not exist in the way that you can show that witches do not exist, because these are conscious experiences, and you cannot make the usual appearance reality distinction for conscious experiences [. . .].

Lots of commonsense psychological beliefs have been shown to be false, and no doubt more will be. Consider a spectacular example: Common sense tells us that our pains are located in physical space within our bodies, that for example, a pain in the foot is literally inside the area of the foot. But we now know that is false. The brain forms a body image, and pains, like all bodily sensations, are parts of the body image. The pain-in-the-foot is literally in the physical space of the brain.

So common sense was wildly wrong about some aspects of the location of pains in physical space. But even such an extreme falsehood does not show—and could not show—that pains do not exist. [. . .]

In spite of our modern arrogance about how much we know, in spite of the assurance and universality of our science, where the mind is concerned we are characteristically confused and in disagreement. Like the proverbial blind men and the elephant, we grasp onto some alleged feature and pronounce it the essence of the mental. 'There are invisible sentences in there!' (the language of thought). 'There is a computer program in there!' (cognitivism). 'There are only causal relations in there!' (functionalism). 'There is nothing in there!' (eliminativism). And so, depressingly, on.

Just as bad, we let our research methods dictate the subject matter, rather than the converse. Like the drunk who loses his car keys in the dark bushes but looks for them under the streetlight, 'because the light is better here,' we try to find out how humans might resemble our computational models rather than trying to figure out how the conscious human mind actually works. I am frequently asked, 'But how could you study consciousness *scientifically*? How could there be a *theory*?'

I do not believe there is any simple or single path to the rediscovery of the mind. Some rough guidelines are:

First, we ought to stop saying things that are obviously false. The serious acceptance of this maxim might revolutionize the study of the mind.

Second, we ought to keep reminding ourselves of what we know for sure. For example, we know for sure that inside our skulls there is a brain, sometimes it is conscious, and brain processes cause consciousness in all its forms.

Third, we ought to keep asking ourselves what actual facts in the world are supposed to correspond to the claims we make about the mind. It does not matter whether 'true' means corresponds to the facts, because 'corresponds to the facts' does mean corresponds to the facts, and any discipline that aims to describe how the world is aims for this correspondence. If you keep asking yourself this question in the light of the knowledge that the brain is the only thing in there, and the brain causes consciousness, I believe you will come up with the results I have reached in this chapter, and indeed many of the results I have come up with in this book.

But that is only to take a first step on the road back to the mind. A fourth and final guideline is that we need to rediscover the social character of the mind.

[From *The Rediscovery of the Mind* (Cambridge, Mass.: MIT Press, 1992), 58–63, 247–8.]

47 The Mystery of the Mind

A century of scientific progress has passed since Hughlings Jackson suggested that there were high levels of functional organization in the brain. He seemed to consider the highest as most closely related to the mind. Since his time, various partially independent mechanisms have been identified and mapped in the cerebral cortex and the higher brain-stem. None of them can explain the mind. The mind remains a mystery.

I have told the story here of the progress of one pilgrim as he stumbled, sometimes blindly but always hopefully, toward a clearer understanding of what seemed to be the physical basis of the mind. It is almost forty years now since he happened upon the fact that a gentle electric current applied to the interpretive cortex of the temporal lobe could summon a flashback, thus activating the stream of consciousness from the past. Gradually, over the years, he has made critical reports of the nature of these experiential responses. These and the other results of electrical stimulation are reliable data, not opinions. The effects of epileptic discharge are clues to understanding. Valid evidence has been presented that the integrative neuronal action, which makes consciousness possible, is localized in the higher brain-stem rather than in the cerebral cortex.

Now, I have suggested in this essay that there is a special form of energy that activates the mind during waking hours and that it must be derived somehow from neuronal energy. Hippocrates foretold the discovery of the highest brain-mechanism when he said, 'to consciousness the brain is messenger.' The highest brain-mechanism is the messenger between the mind and the other brain-mechanisms. Or, to express it another way, the highest brain-mechanism is the mind's executive. Somehow, the executive accepts direction from the mind and passes it on to various mechanisms of the brain. Thus, it passes on the short-term purposes of the mind to the automatic sensory-motor mechanism, which, in turn, carries a man through much of his apparently conscious behavior in life. These two, the highest mechanism and the sensory-motor mechanism, coordinate sensory-input and motor-output in accordance with the purpose and the direction-of-attention of the mind. They manage the employment of the various skills, including that of speech. Together they carry out the central integrative activity of the brain.

The foregoing statements are, of course, hypotheses in regard to the physical basis of the mind. They will serve to point the way ahead while one waits for an understanding of how messages are sent along neuronal circuits. That such mechanisms do exist, and such messages are carried, is proved by the evidence of epileptic patterns of discharge. It is proved also by electrical stimulation and by the many proofs of clinical experience.

Other, younger men will have to reconsider critically the localization of the gray matter that is activated in experiential responses [. . .] and fill in the detail. [. . .] They must proceed with the elaboration of hypotheses to explain the 'how' of neuronal action during the focusing of attention. Finally, fresh explorers must discover how it is that the movement of potentials becomes awareness, and how purpose is translated into a patterned neuronal message. Neurophysiologists will need the help of chemists and physicists in all this, no doubt.

There are many men of differing disciplines who can use of these data, whether they find it reasonable to attempt to fit them into the hypothesis that the brain explains the mind, or whether they conclude, as I have done, that the mind is a separate but related element. One of these two 'improbabilities' must be chosen.

Taken either way, the nature of the mind presents the fundamental problem, perhaps the most difficult and most important of all problems. For myself, after a professional lifetime spent in trying to discover how the brain accounts for the mind, it comes as a surprise now to discover, during this final examination of the evidence, that the dualist hypothesis seems the more reasonable of the two possible explanations.

Since every man must adopt for himself, without the help of science, his way of life and his personal religion, I have long had my own private beliefs. What a thrill it is, then, to discover that the scientist, too, can legitimately believe in the existence of the spirit! [. . .]

Possibly the scientist and the physician could add something by stepping outside the laboratory and the consulting room to reconsider these strangely gifted human beings about us. Where did the mind—call it the spirit if you like—come from? Who can say? It exists. The mind is attached to the action of a certain mechanism within the brain. A mind has been thus attached in the case of every human being for many thousands of generations, and there seems to be significant evidence of heredity in the mind's character from one generation to the next and the next. But at present, one can only say simply and without explanation, 'the mind is born.'

Physicians, whose task it is to deal with the whole man, take a unique view of him. They have long been aware of the unexplained dichotomy (the functional split) between mind and body. Indeed, they have learned, as the saying goes, to 'treat the mind as well as the body.' They are well aware that body, brain, and mind make up the child. They develop together and yet they seem to remain apart as the years pass. These three, in a sort of ontogenetic symbiosis, go through life together. Each is useless without the other two. Mind takes the initiative in exploring the environment.

Mind decides what is to be learned and recorded. The child grows and the mind comes to depend more and more on the memory and the automatic patterns of action stored away in the brain's computer. The mind conditions the brain. It programs the computer so that it can carry out an increasing number of routine performances. And so, as years pass, the mind has more and more free time to explore the world of the intellect, its own and that of others.

If one were to draw curves to show the excellence of human performance, those of the body and the brain would rise, each to its zenith, in the twenties or the thirties. In the forties, the curves would level off and begin to fall, for there are pathological processes, some peculiar to the body and some to the brain, that inevitably slow them down as though with weights of lead. Thus the curves of excellent physical performance slope downward toward inevitable zero. The Psalmist saw all this 3,000 years ago when he wrote: 'The days of our years are threescore years and ten' or, 'by reason of strength . . . fourscore years.' Man's span of life is predetermined. The legs grow weak. The memory-record, so readily available in early years, opens its 'file' more slowly and reluctantly as the years pass. In the end, the brain may even fail, at times, to make any record at all of current events. Senescence is a symptom of failing performance by the body and the brain. Thus it enters one's life in various forms.

In contrast to the other two, the mind seems to have no peculiar or inevitable pathology. Late in life, it moves to its own fulfillment. As the mind arrives at clearer understanding and better balanced judgment, the other two are beginning to fail in strength and speed.

Here, as I approach the end of this study, is a further suggestion from the physician's point of view. It is an observation relevant to any inquiry into the nature of man's being, and in conformity with the proposition that the mind has a separate existence. It might even be taken as an argument for the feasibility and the possibility of immortality! [. . .]

General conclusion

To suppose that consciousness or the mind has localization is a failure to understand neurophysiology. The great mathematician and philosopher, René Descartes (1596–1650), made a mistake when he placed it in the pineal gland. The amusing aspect is that he came so close to that part of the brain in which the essential circuits of the highest brain-mechanism must be active to make consciousness possible.

[From *The Mystery of the Mind* (Princeton: Princeton University Press, 1972), 83–7, 109.]

It was universally believed in the Middle Ages as well as in the Greco-Roman world that the soul is a substance. Indeed, mankind as a whole has held this belief from its earliest beginnings, and it was left for the second half of the nineteenth century to develop a 'psychology without the soul.' Under the influence of scientific materialism, everything that could not be seen with the eyes or touched with the hands was held in doubt; such things were even laughed at because of their supposed affinity with metaphysics. Nothing was considered 'scientific' or admitted to be true unless it could be perceived by the senses or traced back to physical causes. This radical change of view did not begin with philosophical materialism, for the way was being prepared long before. When the spiritual catastrophe of the Reformation put an end to the Gothic Age, with its impetuous yearning for the heights, its geographical confinement, and its restricted view of the world, the vertical outlook of the European mind was henceforth cut across by the horizontal outlook of modern times. Consciousness ceased to grow upward, and grew instead in breadth of view, geographically as well as philosophically. This was the age of the great voyages, of the widening of man's mental horizon by empirical discoveries. Belief in the substantiality of things spiritual yielded more and more to the obtrusive conviction that material things alone have substance, till at last, after nearly four hundred years, the leading European thinkers and investigators came to regard the mind as wholly dependent on matter and material causation. [. . .] There were always a fair number of intelligent philosophers and scientists who had enough insight and depth of thought to accept this irrational reversal of standpoint only under protest; a few even resisted it, but they had no following and were powerless against the wave of unreasoning, not to say excitable, surrender to the all-importance of the physical world. Let no one suppose that so radical a change in man's outlook could be brought about by reasoned reflection, for no chain of reasoning can prove or disprove the existence of either mind or matter. Both these concepts, as every intelligent person today can ascertain for himself, are mere symbols that stand for something unknown and unexplored, and this something is postulated or denied according to the temperament of the individual or as the spirit of the age dictates. There is nothing to prevent the speculative intellect from treating the mind as a complicated biochemical phenomenon and at bottom a mere play of electrons, or on the other hand from regarding the unpredictable behaviour of electrons as the sign of mental life even in them.

The fact that a metaphysics of the mind was supplanted in the nineteenth century by a metaphysics of matter is, intellectually considered, a mere trick, but from the psychological point of view it is an unexampled revolution in man's outlook. Otherworldliness is converted into matter-of-factness: empirical boundaries are set to every discussion of man's motivations, to his aims and purposes, and even to the assignment of 'meaning.' The whole invisible inner world seems to have become the visible outer world, and no value exists unless founded on a so-called fact. At least, this is how it appears to the simple mind.

[From *Basic Postulates of Analytical Psychology*, trans. R. Hull, in *The Structure and Dynamics of the Psyche* (Princeton: Princeton University Press, 1989), 338–9.]

A. M. TURING

49   Computing Machinery and Intelligence

I propose to consider the question, 'Can machines think?' This should begin with definitions of the meaning of the terms 'machine' and 'think'. The definitions might be framed so as to reflect so far as possible the normal use of the words, but this attitude is dangerous. If the meaning of the words 'machine' and 'think' are to be found by examining how they are commonly used it is difficult to escape the conclusion that the meaning and the answer to the question, 'Can machines think?' is to be sought in a statistical survey such as a Gallup poll. But this is absurd. Instead of attempting such a definition I shall replace the question by another, which is closely related to it and is expressed in relatively unambiguous words.

The new form of the problem can be described in terms of a game which we call the 'imitation game'. It is played with three people, a man (A), a woman (B), and an interrogator (C) who may be of either sex. The interrogator stays in a room apart from the other two. The object of the game for the interrogator is to determine which of the other two is the man and which is the woman. He knows them by labels X and Y, and at the end of the game he says either 'X is A and Y is B' or 'X is B and Y is A'. The interrogator is allowed to put questions to A and B thus:

C: Will X please tell me the length of his or her hair?

Now suppose X is actually A, then A must answer. It is A's object in the game to try and cause C to make the wrong identification. His answer might therefore be

'My hair is shingled, and the longest strands are about nine inches long.'

In order that tones of voice may not help the interrogator the answers should be written, or better still, typewritten. The ideal arrangement is to have a teleprinter communicating between the two rooms. Alternatively the question and answers can be repeated by an intermediary. The object of the game for the third player (B) is to help the interrogator. The best strategy for her is probably to give truthful answers. She can add such things as 'I am the woman, don't listen to him!' to her answers, but it will avail nothing as the man can make similar remarks.

We now ask the question, 'What will happen when a machine takes the part of A in this game?' Will the interrogator decide wrongly as often when the game is played like this as he does when the game is played between a man and a woman? These questions replace our original, 'Can machines think?'

As well as asking, 'What is the answer to this new form of the question', one may ask, 'Is this new question a worthy one to investigate?' This latter question we investigate without further ado, thereby cutting short an infinite regress.

The new problem has the advantage of drawing a fairly sharp line between the physical and the intellectual capacities of a man. No engineer or chemist claims to be able to produce a material which is indistinguishable from the human skin. It is possible that at some time this might be done, but even supposing this invention available we should feel there was little point in trying to make a 'thinking machine' more human by dressing it up in such artificial flesh. The form in which we have set the problem reflects this fact in the condition which prevents the interrogator from seeing or touching the other competitors, or hearing their voices. Some other advantages of the proposed criterion may be shown up by specimen questions and answers. Thus:

Q. Please write me a sonnet on the subject of the Forth Bridge.
A. Count me out on this one. I never could write poetry.
Q. Add 34957 to 70764.
A. (Pause about 30 seconds and then give as answer) 105621.
Q. Do you play chess?
A. Yes.
Q. I have K at my K1, and no other pieces. You have only K at K6 and R at R1. It is your move. What do you play?
A. (After a pause of 15 seconds) R–R8 mate.

The question and answer method seems to be suitable for introducing almost any one of the fields of human endeavour that we wish to include. We do not wish to penalise the machine for its inability to shine in beauty competitions, nor to penalise a man for losing in a race against an aeroplane. The conditions of our game make these disabilities irrelevant. The 'witnesses' can brag, if they consider it advisable, as much as they please about their charms, strength or heroism, but the interrogator cannot demand practical demonstrations.

The game may perhaps be criticised on the ground that the odds are weighted too heavily against the machine. If the man were to try and pretend to be the machine he would clearly make a very poor showing. He would be given away at once by slowness and inaccuracy in arithmetic. May not machines carry out something which ought to be described as thinking but which is very different from what a man does? This objection is a very strong one, but at least we can say that if, nevertheless, a machine can be constructed to play the imitation game satisfactorily, we need not be troubled by this objection.

It might be urged that when playing the 'imitation game' the best strategy for the machine may possibly be something other than imitation of the behaviour of a man. This may be, but I think it is unlikely that there is any great effect of this kind. In any case there is no intention to investigate here the theory of the game, and it will be assumed that the best strategy is to try to provide answers that would naturally be given by a man. [. . .]

A few years ago, when very little had been heard of digital computers, it was possible to elicit much incredulity concerning them, if one mentioned their properties without describing their construction. That was presumably due to a similar application of the principle of scientific induction. These applications of the principle are of course largely unconscious. When a burnt child fears the fire and shows that he fears it by avoiding it, I should say that he was applying scientific induction. (I could of course also describe his behaviour in many other ways.) The works and customs of mankind do not seem to be very suitable material to which to apply scientific induction. A very large part of space-time must be investigated, if reliable results are to be obtained. Otherwise we may (as most English children do) decide that everybody speaks English, and that it is silly to learn French.

There are, however, special remarks to be made about many of the disabilities [. . .]. The inability to enjoy strawberries and cream may have struck the reader as frivolous. Possibly a machine might be made to enjoy this delicious dish, but any attempt to make one do so would be idiotic. What is important about this disability is that it contributes to some of the other disabilities, *e.g.* to the difficulty of the same kind of friendliness occurring between man and machine as between white man and white man, or between black man and black man.

The claim that 'machines cannot make mistakes' seems a curious one. One is tempted to retort, 'Are they any the worse for that?' But let us adopt a more sympathetic attitude, and try to see what is really meant. I think this criticism can be explained in terms of the imitation game. It is claimed that the interrogator could distinguish the machine from the man simply by setting them a number of problems in arithmetic. The machine would be unmasked because of its deadly accuracy. The reply to this is simple. The machine (programmed for playing the game) would not attempt to give the *right* answers to the arithmetic problems. It would deliberately introduce mistakes in a manner calculated to confuse the interrogator. A mechanical fault would probably show itself through an unsuitable decision as to what sort of a mistake to make in the arithmetic. Even this interpretation of the criticism is not sufficiently sympathetic. But we cannot afford the space to go into it much further. It seems to me that this criticism depends on a confusion between two kinds of mistake. We may call them 'errors of functioning' and 'errors of conclusion'. Errors of functioning are due to some mechanical or electrical fault which causes the machine to behave otherwise than it was designed to do. In philosophical discussions one likes to ignore the possibility of such errors; one is therefore discussing 'abstract machines'. These abstract machines are mathematical fictions rather than physical objects. By definition they are incapable of errors of functioning. In this sense we can truly say that 'machines can never make mistakes'. Errors of conclusion can only arise when some meaning is attached to the output signals from the machine. The machine might, for instance, type out mathematical equations, or sentences in English. When a false proposition is typed we say that the machine has committed an error of conclusion. There is clearly no reason at all for saying that a machine cannot make this kind of mistake. It might do nothing but type out repeatedly 'o = 1'. To take a less perverse example, it might have some method for drawing conclusions by scientific induction. We must expect such a method to lead occasionally to erroneous results.

The claim that a machine cannot be the subject of its own thought can of course only be answered if it can be shown that the machine has *some* thought with *some* subject matter. Nevertheless, 'the subject matter of a machine's operations' does seem to mean something, at least to the people who deal with it. If, for instance, the machine was trying to find a solution of the equation $x^2 - 40x - 11 = 0$ one would be tempted to describe this equation as part of the machine's subject matter at that moment. In this sort of sense a machine undoubtedly can be its own subject matter. It may be used to help in making up its own programmes, or to predict the effect of alterations in its own structure. By observing the results of its own behaviour it can modify its own programmes so as to achieve some purpose more effectively. These are possibilities of the near future, rather than Utopian dreams.

The criticism that a machine cannot have much diversity of behaviour is just a way of saying that it cannot have much storage capacity. Until fairly recently a storage capacity of even a thousand digits was very rare. [. . .]

Lady Lovelace's Objection. Our most detailed information of Babbage's Analytical Engine comes from a memoir by *Lady Lovelace*. In it she states, 'The Analytical Engine has no pretensions to *originate* anything. It can do *whatever we know how to order it* to perform' (her italics). This statement is quoted by *Hartree* (p. 70) who adds: 'This does not imply that it may not be possible to construct electronic equipment which will "think for itself", or in which, in biological terms, one could set up a conditioned reflex, which would serve as a basis for "learning". Whether this is possible in principle or not is a stimulating and exciting question, suggested by some of these recent developments. But it did not seem that the machines constructed or projected at the time had this property.'

I am in thorough agreement with Hartree over this. It will be noticed that he does not assert that the machines in question had not got the property, but rather that the evidence available to Lady Lovelace did not encourage her to believe that they had it. It is quite possible that the machines in question had in a sense got this property. For suppose that some discrete-state machine has the property. The Analytical Engine was a universal digital computer, so that, if its storage capacity and speed were adequate, it could by suitable programming be made to mimic the machine in question. Probably this argument did not occur to the Countess or to Babbage. In any case there was no obligation on them to claim all that could be claimed.

This whole question will be considered again under the heading of learning machines.

A variant of Lady Lovelace's objection states that a machine can 'never do anything really new'. This may be parried for a moment with the saw, 'There is nothing new under the sun'. Who can be certain that 'original work' that he has done was not simply the growth of the seed planted in him by teaching, or the effect of following well-known general principles. A better variant of the objection says that a machine can never 'take us by surprise'. This statement is a more direct challenge and can be met directly. Machines take me by surprise with great frequency. This is largely because I do not do sufficient calculation to decide what to expect them to do, or rather because, although I do a calculation, I do it in a hurried, slipshod fashion, taking risks. Perhaps I say to myself, 'I suppose the voltage here ought to be the same as there: anyway let's assume it is'. [. . .]

The reader will have anticipated that I have no very convincing arguments of a positive nature to support my views. If I had I should not have taken such pains to point out the fallacies in contrary views. Such evidence as I have I shall now give.

Let us return for a moment to Lady Lovelace's objection, which stated that the machine can only do what we tell it to do. One could say that a man can 'inject' an idea into the machine, and that it will respond to a certain extent and then drop into quiescence, like a piano string struck by a hammer. Another simile would be an atomic pile of less than critical size: an injected idea is to correspond to a neutron entering the pile from without. Each such neutron will cause a certain disturbance which eventually dies away. If, however, the size of the pile is sufficiently increased, the disturbance caused by such an incoming neutron will very likely go on and on increasing until the whole pile is destroyed. Is there a corresponding phenomenon for minds, and is there one for machines? There does seem to be one for the human mind. The majority of them seem to be 'sub-critical', *i.e.* to correspond in this analogy to piles of sub-critical size. An idea presented to such a mind will on average give rise to less than one idea in reply. A smallish proportion are super-critical. An idea presented to such a mind may give rise to a whole 'theory' consisting of secondary, tertiary and more remote ideas. Animal minds seem to be very definitely sub-critical. Adhering to this analogy we ask, 'Can a machine be made to be super-critical?'

The 'skin of an onion' analogy is also helpful. In considering the functions of the mind or the brain we find certain operations which we can explain in purely mechanical terms. This we say does not correspond to the real mind: it is a sort of skin which we must strip off if we are to find the real mind. But then in what remains we find a further skin to be stripped off, and so on. Proceeding in this way do we ever come to the 'real' mind, or do we eventually come to the skin which has nothing in it? In the latter case the whole mind is mechanical. (It would not be a discrete-state machine however. We have discussed this.)

These last two paragraphs do not claim to be convincing arguments. They should rather be described as 'recitations tending to produce belief'.

The only really satisfactory support that can be given for the view expressed [. . .] will be that provided by waiting for the end of the century and then doing the experiment described. [. . .]

We may hope that machines will eventually compete with men in all purely intellectual fields. But which are the best ones to start with? Even this is a difficult decision. Many people think that a very abstract activity, like the playing of chess, would be best. It can also be maintained that it is best to provide the machine with the best sense organs that money can buy, and then teach it to understand and speak English. This process could follow the normal teaching of a child. Things would be pointed out and named, etc. Again I do not know what the right answer is, but I think both approaches should be tried.

We can only see a short distance ahead, but we can see plenty there that needs to be done.

[From 'Computing Machinery and Intelligence', *Mind*, 59 (1950), 433–5, 448–50, 454–5, 460.]

Section 4

The Evolution of Mind

INTRODUCTION

The Darwinian revolution transformed not only the biological sciences but psychology and the social sciences as well, even as it now begins to influence cosmology. Evolutionary theory explained how there might be design without a designer, how order might arise from chaos, and how even the most defining features of humanity could be observed in non-human animals, some of whom share an alarmingly proximate pedigree.

As Darwin was ever eager to point out, the notion of evolution—even evolution through conflict—was an old one, elements of which can be found in such pre-Socratic philosophers as Empedocles. That dominant *idea of progress* that took hold in the Renaissance and became a veritable gospel of progress in the nineteenth century contained within it fledgling theories about the creative power of unrestrained nature. Long before Richard Dawkins's *The Selfish Gene* Hobbes was able to design an ordered and enduring political community based on self-interest and the instinct to self-defence, just as later Bernard Mandeville's *The Fable of the Bees* would show how public benefits are derived from private vice. Though Mandeville's poem and essays on this theme would cause a scandal, his work influenced Adam Smith and was praised by David Hume.

In the patrimony of Bacon, Newton, Galileo, and Descartes, the Enlightenment of the eighteenth century was won over to the scientific world-view and committed to an unreserved adoption of naturalistic explanations. The rich tradition of British 'sentimentalists' is but another expression of Enlightenment naturalism, now as applied to the once privileged domains of law and morality. What thinkers such as Hutcheson, Smith, Butler, Shaftesbury, Hume, and Reid have in common is the conviction that nature instils in the animal creation just those impulses, sentiments, needs, and emotions by which the survival and flourishing of a species become possible. Human beings, too, are the beneficiary of a defining constitution; an assortment of basic sentiments inclining them strongly toward a given course of action. Locke's good friend Shaftesbury, in *An Inquiry Concerning Virtue*, which was first printed in 1699, takes it for granted that, 'every Creature has a private Good and Interest of his own; which Nature has compel'd him to seek, by all the Advantages afforded him, within the compass of his Make' (Book I, Part II, Sect. 1).

The 'free market' economic theories associated with such Enlightenment figures as Adam Smith in Scotland and Turgot's *physiocrats* in France were advanced at about the same time that still other philosophers were discovering progress through conflict. Note, too, how the Hegelian 'dialectic', borrowing from Fichte's now famous triad of 'thesis-antithesis-synthesis', has creativity dependent on struggle and negation. The dialectical materialism of Karl Marx—whose plan to dedicate his work to Darwin was politely rebuffed— would extend to the social world of classes and to history itself the operation of evolutionary forces arising from patterns of production and exploitation.

None of this, of course, anticipated Darwin's specific theoretical contributions, let alone the factual foundations adduced in support of the theory. Still, there were anticipations even of this, and these certainly helped to pave the way for Darwin. Darwin's own grandfather, Erasmus Darwin, had published his two-volume *Zoonomia* in 1794 and 1796, carefully noting the powerful influence of environmental forces on organisms. In the first volume, where, when discussing competition for mating partners, he would write, 'The final cause of this contest amongst the males seems to be, that the strongest and most active animal should propagate the species, which should thence become improved' (i. 205). Many other passages also match up with Darwinian evolutionary theory, and we know that as a young student Charles Darwin was thoroughly familiar with the writings of his prolific grandfather.

Then there was the greatly influential *Philosophie zoologique* of Jean-Baptiste Lamarck, published in Paris in 1809. Lamarck stated unequivocally that new forms of life arise as a result of evolution, basing his conclusions partly on fossil records. As with Erasmus Darwin, he speculated that adaptive changes acquired as a result of environmental pressures are then transmitted to succeeding generations. Darwin himself would have an on-again, off-again affair with several aspects of the Lamarckian theory (including the presumed inheritance of acquired characteristics), but would nonetheless find comfort in Lamarck's defence of evolution against the supporters of the theory of special creation.

The geologists, too, had already begun to erode confidence in the literal truth of scripture. Charles Lyell in his path-breaking *Principles of Geology*, the first volume appearing in 1830, cautiously corrected the scriptural chronology of creation and, in the process, urged readers to abandon that 'physico-theology' that had for so long required the evidence of science to conform itself to religious orthodoxy. Though he spoke loosely of the earth's age as being greater than 20,000 years, the serious reader had no difficulty recognizing that Lyell's time-frame must be measured in millions, not in thousands of years. Lyell would come to be an outspoken critic of pre-Darwinian versions of evolutionary theory. He would, however, later become Darwin's close friend and adviser; a teacher and elder statesman on whom Darwin would depend often and with profit.

In 1844 *The Vestiges of the Natural History of Creation* was published anonymously, its author later identified as the journalist and encyclopedist, Robert Chambers. It was a work of somewhat scattered thought, punctuated with religious zeal, pointing to the God who never abandons the affairs of the natural world. The religious elements set aside, Chambers's text presented convincing arguments for an evolutionary process able to produce new forms of life continuously, with older forms perishing. *Vestiges* also endorsed a continuity theory of attributes, according to which even human intelligence falls along the same continuum that includes the mental powers of all other species.

Then, too, there was the mysterious Mr Edward Blyth, resurrected in Loren Eiseley's engaging and informative *Darwin and the Mysterious Mr X* (1979). Between 1835 and 1837 Blyth published several provocative articles in the *Magazine of Natural History*, setting down not only the general terms of evolutionary theory but the process of natural selection as its engine. Darwin recorded his high estimation of Blyth, citing his 'large and varied stores of knowledge' in *The Origin of Species*. There is, however, no acknowledgement of Blyth as the source of Darwin's specific theoretical conclusions, though these, too, can be found in the pages of Blyth's articles.

This is not the place to evaluate claims of priority. In any case, no single work or combination of works before *Origin of Species* can be assembled in a fashion that would require Darwin to share the laurel. Rather, the contributions should be seen as setting the stage for Darwin; for tuning the already prepared scientific minds of the age to hear what Darwin had to say. Granting all the peevish resentment and absurd recriminations recorded within some Victorian chapels and drawing rooms, *Origin of Species* appealed at a fundamental level to an age already prepared to treat it with respect and weigh its plausibility. Published reviews predictably would include official condemnations of Darwin's 'horrid genealogy' (as Mivart dubbed it in the *Dublin Review*), but the overall reaction was sober, eager, and not especially surprised.

Nevertheless, there were criticisms of *Origin of Species* mounted by respected and fully informed scientists who found core precepts of the theory problematical. To cite one example, the theory called for the creation of new species through the selection of favoured characteristics over the aeons. But the history of animal breeding offered what seemed to be tellingly disconfirming evidence. Selective breeding did, indeed, modify various characteristics but had never resulted in the appearance of a new species. Moreover, the fossil record—which Darwin found lamentably incomplete— was by some lights *too complete*, and failed to show the orderly succession and utterly gradual modification of types over time. Absent a developed science of genetics, Darwin's theory of evolution could derive no benefit from what is now known about discrete genes making additive contributions to a given characteristic and subject to mutations which might result in quite dramatic alterations in the successor generation. In time, thanks to able defences by Huxley, Alfred Russel Wallace, and others, criticisms of this sort were successfully answered. What remained in the wake of it all was less threats to the theory than sensible requests for even greater detail. In the decade following its publication, *Origin of Species* elevated its author to a position of supremacy in the science of biology, and the theory of evolution to nothing less than the very framework for that science.

A decade later, however, Darwin published two books radically different in tone and content from the systematic and even tedious ethology of *Origin of Species*. In *Descent of Man* and in *The Expression of the Emotions in Man and Animals* the ratio of fact to assumption has shrunk precipitously. The lines of evidence are now often anecdotal and strained, the author's defensiveness sometimes excessive. The theoretical focus has shifted to *sexual* selection, defended with the same vigour that a now demoted *natural* selection had received a decade earlier. The 'horrid genealogy' has been daringly extended from skeletal and general physiological characteristics to human intelligence, feeling, sociality, morality. Even in this Darwin could point to contemporaries who had reached the same conclusions. Herbert Spencer, who had coined the phrase 'survival of the fittest', had long since reached the conclusion that psychology and the social sciences are concerned with phenomena best understood in evolutionary and hereditary terms. It would take another century before E. O. Wilson would name it *sociobiology*, but the evidence and the lines of argument were now in place: what we take to be the unique, defining, unanticipated qualities of human mental and moral life are, alas, richly anticipated and actually expressed characteristics, though in a quantitatively diminished fashion, present throughout much of the animal kingdom. The ball was in play!

The selections included in this Section begin with Aristotle but then jump to the nineteenth century and conclude with very recent works. It is proper to begin with some passages from Aristotle who, though not an evolutionary theorist, was the greatest natural scientist of antiquity and one who undertook detailed examinations of the relationship between structure and function in the plant and animal kingdoms. The son of a physician, he was far more practical and observational in his scientific work than any of the members of Plato's famous Academy.

The first selection is a mere paragraph taken from his *Parts of the Animals*, which is a treatise of extraordinary exactitude in its examination of the gross anatomy of a wide range of species. In the passage chosen, Aristotle exhorts his students never to 'recoil with childish aversion' to studies of comparative anatomy, for every animal 'will reveal to us something natural and something beautiful'. Next, from his truly pioneering ethological treatise on the *History of Animals*, attention turns from the physical features of animals to those traces of 'psychical qualities which are more differentiated in the case of human beings'. It is in this same selection that Aristotle remarks on the progressive modification of types produced by nature. It 'proceeds little by little', he says, 'from things lifeless to animal life'.

Of particular interest is Aristotle's explanation of facts captured by the cliché 'Always something fresh in Libya'. It had long been observed that species found in many places were widely various when found in Libya. Aristotle accounts for this by noting the opportunities afforded there for 'outbreeding'. Owing to the rainless climate of Libya, there are unusually large congregations of animals at the limited number of watering places. Those that might otherwise rebuff potential mates are rendered more docile by thirst itself. Thus, conditions now favour matings that would be unusual or even impossible in other climates. What is clear from passages such as this, quite apart from the question of whether he entertained a version of evolutionary theory, is that Aristotle traced the diversity of animal forms to natural forces interacting with inherited characteristics. His writings are the starting point for that uneven arc of thought that would become so pronounced in eighteenth- and nineteenth-century natural science.

In Herbert Spencer we reach a writer uncommonly influential in his own time. His promotion of evolutionary theory and thinking was relentless and unconstrained. Note his insistence that, 'Alike during the evolution of the Solar System, of a planet, of an organism, of a nation, there is progressive aggregation of the entire mass'; and that what evolution is fundamentally is 'a change from a less coherent form to a more coherent form', a process that describes the development even of personal experience. What we find in Spencer is a theory of evolution-as-information; that is to say, evolution as an essentially *anti-entropic* process by which the purely physical forces that otherwise lead to disintegration are overcome by biogenetic forces of integration and progressive differentiation. Where such forces fail, extinction is inevitable; but where they succeed, extinction, too, results, for the earlier and less organized and differentiated entity is now replaced by a worthier successor. 'Social Darwinism' would have been more aptly dubbed 'Spencerism'; the road to success is paved with—heads!

Consciousness is understood by Spencer as but the subjective face of what objectively are 'nervous excitations and discharges'. These latter must become integrated and differentiated, too, if the mind of the child is ever to evolve into a mature, functional system. Spencer illustrates the process with a brief disquisition on the development of linguistic proficiency, but then assures readers that it is equally applicable to the development of emotion, of species, of societies.

One cannot leave these passages without commenting on Spencer's quintessentially 'Victorian' attitude toward those he denominates 'savages'. To say it is a 'Victorian' attitude needs to be qualified, for the view that alien cultures and societies are 'primitive' and require guidance toward a more mature form is, of course, ancient. Aristotle famously (infamously) declared that it was only 'fitting' that 'Hellenes shall rule barbarians', though any thoughtful study of the larger context of this statement within his *Politics* should spare him the libels that would be heaped upon him. One need not consider the formal productions of philosophy or intellectual history here, however, for it is a veritable fixture in the human imagination to regard human and social development as progressive; as destined for a state or stage by which earlier ones become merely transitional. This is found as readily in Buddhistic and Islamic thought as in Hellenism or Judeo-Christian eschatologies. With Spencer and his age, however, there is the admixture of an expansionist and imperialist political economy of massive proportions; one on which the sun never fully sets. Thus there is the combination of evolutionary science, muscular Christianity, and 'the white man's burden'. In its way, Spencer's version of the theory is a justification, a kind of moral gloss on the policies and practices of the developed nations in their dealings with those who had no choice but to cooperate.

Turning next to passages from *The Descent of Man*, the application of theory to the evolution of the human mind and its moral productions, Darwin is cautious but still courageous. He accepts the great difference in *degree* between human and non-human animals, but not a difference in kind. Morality itself can be traced to 'social instincts' and the evolution of morality should not be ruled out a priori, 'for daily we see these faculties developing in every infant; and we may trace a perfect gradation from the mind of an utter idiot, lower than that of an animal low in the scale, to the mind of a Newton'.

In this passage, as in Spencer before and a legion of writers after Darwin, we see how central the study of child development is within the overall framework of evolutionary theory. Darwin had published in the journal *Mind* an unsigned essay on his systematic observations of his own son during infancy. The method he used was, as he said, the 'natural history' method, which was precisely the method of investigation any naturalist would apply to studies of the animal economy.

When Darwin moves from a consideration of individual intellectual and moral powers to the evolution of 'Civilized Nations', he wrestles with the daunting question of bravery, self-sacrifice, and altruism. As we shall see in the reservations expressed by Alfred Russel Wallace, these phenomena are not easily absorbed with the survivalistic framework of evolutionism. What Darwin attempts to show, in the pages included in this section, is that the survival of the collective depends on such individual sacrifices and that the collective, through institutionalized forms of praise and blame, cultivates just that degree of selflessness that rises to the level of moral duty. With an optimism that seems more hopeful than convincing, he concludes that this is so essential to the survival of communities that 'the standard of morality and the number of well-endowed men will thus everywhere tend to rise and increase'.

It is not only by measures of intelligence and social organization that the human mind comes to be regarded as distinct and separate. To the ordinary observer the human emotions might appear to be even more defining for, unlike cognitive and intellectual achievements which can be matched or exceeded by computers, only we love, laugh, and suffer *humanly*. Moreover, for all the honour we tend to confer on rationality and abstract cogitations, we are impelled by emotion. It is not sufficient to know the right course of action; one must *feel* committed to it. In all, then, an evolutionary theory of mind must include a coherent and credible account of emotionality, and it is to this that Darwin turned in *The Expression of the Emotions in Man and Animals*. The pages included in this Section are illustrative of the general thesis and the facts adduced in its favour. Emotional expression is shaped by the anatomical and physiological nuances of the body. These are shaped by selection pressures favouring certain modes of behaviour over others. There is nothing peculiarly 'human' in human emotionality, except to the extent of these physiological nuances. For, 'if the structure of our organs . . . had differed in only a slight degree . . . most of our expressions would have been wonderfully different'.

This is all so obvious to Ernst Haeckel that in the next selection he is found declaring 'The common descent of man and all the other Mammals from one stem-form [to be] beyond question'. Haeckel was an important defender and promulgator of evolutionary theory. A student of the great Virchow, he was an important contributor to embryology and the source of that suggestive maxim, 'Ontogeny recapitulates phylogeny': the embryonic and foetal development of the organism passes through the successive stages of phyletic evolution that culminated in the organism's own species. Haeckel would argue that the same evolutionary processes that work at the level of the species work at the level of the foetus, the tribe, the nation. Resistance to this scientifically established principle is 'due in most men to feeling rather than to reason'. Confident that such feelings have been cultivated by the sophistries of religion, Haeckel is quite willing to take on the follies and vanities of the faithful, declaring himself to be far more interested in *ascent* than *descent*.

Noting that many had been converted to evolutionary accounts of physical variations in nature, Haeckel turns to those critics who would draw the line at the human mind (or soul); those whose numbers would include even the great naturalist and co-discoverer of the theory, Alfred Wallace. These are all dualists, tied to the old theory of spirits, souls and 'divine sparks'. Haeckel will have none of it, insisting that all manifestations of mind arise from the functions of the brain; that brains evolve from simpler forms of neural organization; that the progressive evolution of the nervous system tracks the progressive evolution of mental power. Human development, including mental development, 'is directed by the same "eternal, iron laws" as the development of any other body'.

Moving from polemic reinforced by science to a modest but earnest application of evolutionary theory to mind, we consult pages from George Romanes's *Animal Intelligence*. This work was inspired by Darwin's writings and was among the foundational works in *Comparative Psychology*. The excerpts include Romanes's criterion of the mental: he regards behaviour as offering evidence of mental operations when that behaviour constitutes a novel adjustment based on experience, rather than a reflex-adjustment mechanically elicited by specific stimuli. The criterion is a flexible one, however, for there may well be mental correlates even of seemingly mechanical adjustments. What Romanes wants to defend against sceptical challenges is the proposition that non-human animals have a mental life. The grounds of such dubiety, he says, will just as well support doubts about the minds of other human beings, for no one has any direct knowledge of minds other than one's own. As he says, here in something of a prelude to a behaviouristic approach to psychology, 'the only evidence we can have of objective mind is that which is furnished by objective activities'.

Later in this Section are portions of Thomas Nagel's 'What is it Like to be a Bat?', in which Nagel draws attention to the manifest disanalogies between human and bat neurophysiology, anatomy, and form of life. Romanes is sensitive to the problems associated with analogical reasoning on such matters. He acknowledges the immense differences between human beings and insects, including the preponderance of reason over instinct exhibited by the former. Nonetheless, the basis on which psychological states are imputed to fellow human beings is just an inference from analogies in behaviour. Romanes, 'having full regard to the progressive weakening of the analogy from human to brute psychology as we recede through the animal kingdom downwards from man, still, as it is the only analogy available . . . shall follow it throughout the animal series'. Doing so, he has ample evidence of a developed mental life in all the vertebrates, and unquestionably in apes and monkeys. The evidence for tool-use, social cooperation, altruism, the education of the young, is abundant and unequivocal.

Yes, but . . .

The problem of *anthropomorphism* has plagued comparative psychology from the start. It even predates the subject, for it is drawn from the larger problem of *other minds*. If all that can be known with any confidence is that which gains representation in one's own experience, then on what basis is it ever warrantable to claim that some other entity possesses a mind? A well-constructed robot might perform 'intelligently', just as modern computers do, yet most (but not all) persons would be reserved about imputing minds to either. Thus, when such is imputed, the justification is by way of inferences drawn from comparable or analogous cases: when Jones is very sad tears form in his eyes. Smith has just learned of the death of a loved one and tears have formed in Smith's eyes. Smith, as viewed by Jones, is assumed to be sad, though Jones has no direct knowledge of Smith's emotions, or even if Smith has them. This, however, is an inference drawn from a still more fundamental inference; namely, that Smith is relevantly 'like' Jones; that Smith is also a human being, the member of the human family, etc. If ever there is to be a valid inference, it will be grounded in the warranted belief that Smith, too, is 'human', and that the tears signify what they customarily signify in human experience.

When tears form in the eyes of an ape is the ape sad? In species incapable of lachrymation, is sadness possible? Is the dog's wagging tail a sign of joy? To attribute human mental states to non-human animals, based on actions or features of the latter that are in some way comparable in form to human actions or features, is to anthropomorphize. Darwin was unabashed in the practice. Romanes was rather more defensive, but still fortified by the very common sense of it all. C. Lloyd Morgan was rather more diffident and disciplined. In the chapter devoted to 'Other Minds than Ours' in his *Introduction to Comparative Psychology*, he anticipates Nagel's concerns: 'The anatomy or the physiology of insects . . . differs tolerably widely from that of man; why then should [one] suppose that their *psychical* endowments are more closely similar?' Morgan does not ask what it is like to be a bat; rather, he gives a chronometer intelligence and reason, and then sets it the task of examining other timepieces. When it observes the movements of hands around the face of the clock, it draws inferences to its own nature, for this is all that it knows directly. 'With no other works would it have any acquaintance'. Just in case it came across a pendulum clock which, unlike itself, had no mainspring, its explanations of that clock's behaviour would make no mention of heavy weights connected to chains, for these are not present in the observing chronometer.

Morgan's caution is not against analogical or anthropomorphic inferences absolutely; only those inferences aloof to significant differences in the functional organization and anatomy of the nervous systems. Satisfied that human mental processes are causally connected to functions of the cerebral cortex, Morgan is prepared to accept inferences from human to non-human behaviour when the non-human organism also has the benefit of the corticalization of the brain. Not included here is Morgan's famous 'canon', a version of Ockham's razor: 'In no case may we interpret an action as the outcome of the exercise of a higher psychical faculty, if it can be interpreted as the outcome of the exercise of one which stands lower in the psychological scale.'

This, too, would inspire the anti-mentalistic orientation of early behaviourists such as John B. Watson, and continues to influence psychologists eager to maintain some sort of largely unexamined 'objectivity'. As a kind of prudence-maxim, Morgan's canon urges students of behaviour to be sure-footed in their inductive leaps. As a binding rule, however, it can have numbing effects. The movement of the pawn to Queen-3 is, among other considerations, the result of the exercise of that 'psychical faculty' that gets one to move one's arm, and thus the movement of the pawn can be thus interpreted. But it happens to be the case that Smith has made this move because his adversary is unaware of a new 'opening', of which this is but the first step. Smith's explanation of why he made the move will appeal to some 'psychical faculties' much 'higher' in the 'scale' than the mere desire to move something. And Smith's explanation is the right one, but not for reasons that could ever be extracted using no more than Morgan's canon.

The problem of inference and of 'other minds' is no less attenuated when study turns to the nature of mental life in infancy and early childhood. As noted, Darwin himself published observations he made of his infant son. In the wake of evolutionary theory there was an ever more concerted enquiry into infant and child psychology. James Sully was a leader in this field and his *Studies of Childhood* retained its influence for nearly a half-century. Pages included here are from his Introduction to the work, where he recounts the debts to Darwin and makes clear that the field itself is properly occupied by those who are evolutionists, whatever their special area of enquiry.

Sully is comfortable with the Lamarckian theory of the inheritance of acquired characteristics. But this is only part of his understanding of the influence of culture on child development and the development of mental and moral powers. Owing to our 'kinship to the lower sentient world', the infant's mind is of further importance in that it is a link, a veritable 'brief *résumé*', as Sully calls it, of the 'slow upward progress of the species'. However, the power of language creates mental possibilities different from anything found lower in phylogeny. One of the most salient marks of the mind is not simply consciousness but *self-consciousness*; that reflexive activity mind by which the 'I-Thou' dyad comes into being. Sully explains the achievement of self-consciousness 'by the appropriation and use of the difficult forms of language, "I", "me", "mine"'. Sully is prescient here in understanding the 'self' as a grammatically grounded concept, inextricably bound up with language and its social origins.

To say 'simply consciousness' is to play fast and loose with the *quaestio vexata* of the ages. Nor is the question made any less vexing by assuming a process of continuous evolution from the simplest forms of animal life to adult human life. In his *Principles of Psychology*, the redoubtable William James paused long enough to consider what he graphically dubbed 'the mind-stuff theory' and to challenge evolutionists either to defend or abandon it. The target of criticism is every version of *emergentism* according to which consciousness and other mental states and events somehow emerge from or are supervenient on or arise from epiphenomena or some other kind of 'stuff'. Casting Spencer among 'the vaguest of evolutionary enthusiasts', James observes that defenders of the mind-stuff theory openly acknowledge the absence of anything that consciousness might have in common with 'a nervous shock'.

Not included in these excerpts is James's equating the mind-stuff theorist with the servant in *Midshipman Easy*. Her out-of-wedlock pregnancy has caused her employer grave embarrassment and concern. She defends herself by assuring him, however, that it was 'such a small baby'. So, too, the mind-stuff evolutionist argues that human consciousness is shared in diminished degrees by other advanced species, the diminution continuing in proportion to the rung on the evolutionary ladder occupied by an organism. Some threshold must be crossed at some point, however, where non-consciousness gives rise to consciousness. At this point, it matters not a whit how 'small' a consciousness this might be, for with its dawning, 'an entirely new nature to seems to slip in'.

Not only does a new nature or kind of thing slip in, but something that transforms the notion of 'survival of the fittest' from a theoretical maxim adopted by an onlooker to 'an imperative decree: "Survival *shall* occur, and therefore organs *must* so work!" Real ends appear for the first time now upon the world's stage.' As a *'fighter for ends'*, as James calls it, consciousness is the ensemble of mental processes capable of ordering the functions of the brain, marshalling its resources, making more probable those of its operations that are consistent with these ends. Unless consciousness is granted this 'teleological function', it is simply meaningless.

As James was not persuaded by the argument from continuity in the matter of consciousness, so too was Alfred Russel Wallace doubtful about its application to three features of human mental life that seem to be divorced from the forces of natural selection: abstract rationality, as expressed in mathematics; aesthetic feelings, as these come to be expressed in music and art; and those moral faculties that ground systems of justice and the power of conscience. Granting the evolution of human physical attributes does not require adoption of a theory of natural selection to account for the appearance of human mental attributes. Different proofs would be needed here and, says Wallace, they have not been produced. Counter-evidence is ready to hand. To wit: where natural selection has operated over great stretches of time, it has produced increasingly homogeneous characteristics, since the same attributes are needed by each member of the species if that member is to survive. Accordingly, both the most civilized and the most 'savage' members of the human race have patently similar physiological mechanisms, behavioural capacities, emotional dispositions. But within the civilized communities are found bona fide *geniuses* contributing to a degree of deviation inexplicable in terms of natural selection; and the same is true in the aesthetic domain. The genius is so rare as to fall outside the boundaries that selection pressures would be expected to draw. Furthermore, the form that genius takes—in areas such as abstract mathematics and art—may make such negligible contact with requirements for survival as to have nothing to do with it at all. Finally, in the moral sphere, the capacity for genuinely altruistic, self-denying, and self-sacrificing conduct, grounded in abstract moral principles as well as in rationally comprehended terms of duty, must be found beyond the sphere of evolutionary and purely biological processes.

Wallace was not just the great naturalist who also advanced a theory of evolution by natural selection. True, redactions of his and of Darwin's theories were presented at the same meeting of the Linnaean Society in order to honour their shared priority. But Wallace was also a man whose integrity and moral purposes were greatly admired by Darwin. The thought of their disagreeing, Darwin would write, gave him sleepless nights. Wallace was also a man of deep religious faith and even mystical attachments. It is easy to dismiss his criticisms and reservations on these grounds. Yet, his *Darwinism* remains one of the most able defences of the theory and nothing less than a monument to the genius of Darwin. 'The facts now set forth', Wallace says here, 'prove the existence of a number of mental faculties which either do not exist at all or exist in a very rudimentary condition in savages, but appear almost suddenly and in perfect development in the higher civilized races'. More Victorian pomposity? Not at all, and especially not with Wallace. Rather, as natural selection alone accounts for the manifest similarities between and among all the races of mankind—this accountable in terms of natural selection—and as instances of intellectual, aesthetic, and moral genius occur ever so rarely even in the most developed civilizations—there seem to be unaccountable exceptions to the law. Thus, the law has its limits.

Well, not for Daniel Dennett, writing a century after Wallace and having the full benefit of modern genetics, computer science, and engineering to support his position. Dennett acknowledges the 'huge difference' between human and non-human minds. It is a difference attributable not only to six million years of evolutionary pressure, but to the resulting capacity for 'cultural transmission'. Language alters not the process of evolution but its speed, for the brain is not merely the product of past pressures, it is also the product of its own inventions. With each new level of competence reached, a new launching pad—a new floor in Dennett's 'Tower of Generate-and-Test' is laid down. This 'impowers the organisms at that level to find better and better moves, and find them more efficiently'.

The 'Skinnerian creatures' of behaviourism are limited (at least within the confines of a Skinner box) to behaviour that taps a hard-wired system unable to try out alternative courses of action. There is only one that works, viz. bar-pressing, and that's the end of the story. (Needless to say, the rat liberated from the cage and dropped off in the nearest field will accomplish ends that go well beyond the bar-press!) But evolution has favoured the appearance of what Dennett calls *Popperian creatures*, in honour of Sir Karl Popper who once credited human rationality with powers that 'permit our hypotheses to die in our stead'. In the Popperian creature nature has designed an organism that has had all the dumber moves eliminated. To be fitted out for the world properly is to be equipped internally with a number of dispositions and capacities already informed as to features of the external world. This is not a return to the theory of innate ideas. Rather, the infant monkey whose auditory cortex responds uniquely to the distress cries of its own species is a monkey more likely to survive than one without such pre-wiring.

There is even great pre-adaptational power built in what Dennett calls *Gregorian creatures*, after Richard Gregory, who minted the term 'Kinetic Intelligence'. We not only learn by doing, we are changed by doing. The pair of scissors invented by the human imagination comes to empower its user in ways that enlarge the realm of the possible and thus enlarge intelligence itself. Of all the enlarging tools, language is supreme, extending the tower 'with no fixed or discernible limit'.

Turning to Thomas Nagel's 'What is it like to be a bat?', the problem cited by James and duly noted in the preceding section by Galen Strawson returns with a vengeance. The central problem of mind is consciousness. Reductionism has not reduced it, and evolutionary theory seems unable to give it a birth date. Worse, even to tie it to earlier adaptive modifications calls for anthropomorphic commitments that become strained even at the level of the bat. Nagel has no doubt but that consciousness is widely diffused in the animal kingdom. Wherever it is found, however, it is its *subjective* character that needs to be explained. Studies of bodies and brains inattentive to this leave unanswered the question of just 'what is required of a physicalist theory'. However, it is simply not possible for us to enter into the subjective life of a creature radically different from ourselves in physical make-up, habitat and habits, sensory apparatus, modes of intraspecific interaction. *We* can't become bats, and if we become *bats* we can't be. We cannot know, therefore, what it is like to be a bat; or, more generally, what it is like to be anything but the sort of creatures we are. The implication Nagel draws from this is disarming: 'If the facts of experience—facts about what is like *for* the experiencing organism—are accessible only from one point of view, then it is a mystery how the true character of experiences could be revealed in the physical operation of that organism.'

It would, then, be a mystery how or even if the evolutionary development and transformation of the human nervous system carried with it the particular point of view expressed in our conscious life.

Yet another reservation concerning the evolutionary story concludes this Section. It appears in Roger Penrose's *The Emperor's New Mind*, though Penrose is by no means an anti-evolutionist. He is, as he says, 'a strong believer in the power of natural selection'. Unlike Dennett, however, Penrose finds that we have not merely complicated algorithms—Dennett's 'Smart Moves'—but still another species of algorithm able to make 'conscious judgements of the *validity* of other algorithms that we seem to have'. Penrose notes that even the slightest mutation in an algorithm renders it useless. The record of human problem-solving isn't of this sort. We don't have instances of gradual improvements to what were hopelessly ineffectual algorithms. It could not have been the case, for example, that human beings spent millennia employing mistaken rules of addition and subtraction, only gradually working toward the correct ones under the influence of natural selection! Penrose requires instead that there be '*ideas* to underlie the algorithms. But ideas are things that, as far as we know, need conscious minds for their manifestation', and so we travel full circle, ending with the very mystery that launched the excursion.

ARISTOTLE

50 Parts of Animals

Having already treated of the celestial world, as far as our conjectures could reach, we proceed to treat of animals, without omitting, to the best of our ability, any member of the kingdom, however ignoble. For if some have no graces to charm the sense, yet nature, which fashioned them, gives amazing pleasure in their study to all who can trace links of causation, and are inclined to philosophy. Indeed, it would be strange if mimic representations of them were attractive, because they disclose the mimetic skill of the painter or sculptor, and the original realities themselves were not more interesting, to all at any rate who have eyes to discern the causes. We therefore must not recoil with childish aversion from the examination of the humbler animals. Every realm of nature is marvellous: and as Heraclitus, when the strangers who came to visit him found him warming himself at the furnace in the kitchen and hesitated to go in, is reported to have bidden them not to be afraid to enter, as even in that kitchen divinities were present, so we should venture on the study of every kind of animal without distaste; for each and all will reveal to us something natural and something beautiful. Absence of haphazard and conduciveness of everything to an end are to be found in nature's works in the highest degree, and the end for which those works are put together and produced is a form of the beautiful. [. . .]

[From *Parts of Animals*, in *The Complete Works of Aristotle*, ed. J. Barnes, vol. i (Princeton: Princeton University Press, 1984), 1004.]

51 **History of Animals**

In the great majority of animals there are traces of psychical qualities which are more markedly differentiated in the case of human beings. For just as we pointed out resemblances in the physical organs, so in a number of animals we observe gentleness or fierceness, mildness or cross temper, courage or timidity, fear or confidence, high spirit or low cunning, and, with regard to intelligence, something equivalent to sagacity. Some of these qualities in man, as compared with the corresponding qualities in animals, differ only quantitatively: that is to say, a man has more of this quality, and an animal has more of some other; other qualities in man are represented by analogous qualities: for instance, just as in man we find knowledge, wisdom, and sagacity, so in certain animals there exists some other natural capacity akin to these. The truth of this statement will be the more clearly apprehended if we have regard to the phenomena of childhood; for in children may be observed the traces and seeds of what will one day be settled habits, though psychologically a child hardly differs for the time being from an animal; so that one is quite justified in saying that, as regards man and animals, certain psychical qualities are identical with one another, whilst others resemble, and others are analogous to, each other.

Nature proceeds little by little from things lifeless to animal life in such a way that it is impossible to determine the exact line of demarcation, nor on which side thereof an intermediate form should lie. Thus, next after lifeless things comes the plant, and of plants one will differ from another as to its amount of apparent vitality; and, in a word, the whole genus of plants, whilst it is devoid of life as compared with an animal, is endowed with life as compared with other corporeal entities. Indeed, as we just remarked, there is observed in plants a continuous scale of ascent towards the animal. So, in the sea, there are certain objects concerning which one would be at a loss to determine whether they be animal or vegetable. [. . .]

As a general rule, wild animals are at their wildest in Asia, at their boldest in Europe, and most diverse in form in Libya; in fact, there is an old saying, 'Always something fresh in Libya.'

It would appear that in that country animals of diverse species meet, on account of the rainless climate, at the watering-places, and there pair together; and that such pairs will breed if they be nearly of the same size and have periods of gestation of the same length. For they are tamed down in their behaviour towards each other by extremity of thirst. And, by the way, unlike animals elsewhere, they require to drink more in winter-time than in summer; for they acquire the habit of not drinking in summer, owing to the circumstance that there is usually no water then; and the mice, if they drink, die.

[From *History of Animals*, Book VIII, in *The Complete Works of Aristotle*, ed. J. Barnes, vol. i (Princeton: Princeton University Press, 1984), 921–3, 946.]

HERBERT SPENCER

52   First Principles

Evolution then, under its primary aspect, is a change from a less coherent form to a more coherent form, consequent on the dissipation of motion and integration of matter. This is the universal process through which sensible existences, individually and as a whole, pass during the ascending halves of their histories. This proves to be a character displayed equally in those earliest changes which the universe at large is supposed to have undergone, and in those latest changes which we trace in society and the products of social life. And throughout, the unification proceeds in several ways simultaneously.

Alike during the evolution of the Solar System, of a planet, of an organism, of a nation, there is progressive aggregation of the entire mass. [. . .]

That, in course of time, species have become more sharply marked off from other species, general from genera, and orders from orders, is a conclusion not admitting of a more positive establishment than the foregoing; and must, indeed, stand or fall with it. If, however, species and genera and orders have arisen by 'natural selection,' then, as Mr Darwin shows, there must have been a tendency to divergence, causing the contrasts between groups to become greater. Disappearance of intermediate forms, less fitted for special spheres of existence than the extreme forms they connected, must have made the differences between the extreme forms decided; and so, from indistinct and unstable varieties, must slowly have been produced distinct and stable species—an inference which is in harmony with what we know respecting races of men and races of domestic animals.

The successive phases through which societies pass, very obviously display the progress from indeterminate arrangement to determinate arrangement. A wandering tribe of savages, being fixed neither in its locality nor in its internal distribution, is far less definite in the relative positions of its parts than a nation. In such a tribe the social relations are similarly confused and unsettled. Political authority is neither well established nor precise. Distinctions of rank are neither clearly marked nor impassable. And save in the different occupations of men and women, there are no complete industrial divisions. Only in tribes of considerable size, which have enslaved other tribes, is the economical differentiation decided.

Any one of these primitive societies, however, that evolves, becomes step by step more specific. Increasing in size, consequently ceasing to be so nomadic, and restricted in its range by neighboring societies, it acquires, after prolonged border warfare, a settled territorial boundary. The distinction between the royal race and the people, eventually amounts in the popular apprehension to a difference of nature. [. . .] A parallel contrast, less extreme but sufficiently decided, is seen when we pass from the lower types of creatures with limbs to the higher types of creatures with limbs. The legs of a Centiped have motions that are numerous, small, and homogeneous; and are so little integrated that when the creature is divided and subdivided, the legs belonging to each part propel that part independently. But in one of the higher *Annulosa*, as a Crab, the relatively few limbs have motions that are comparatively large in their amounts, that are considerably unlike one another, and that are integrated into compound motions of tolerable definiteness.

The last illustrations are introductory to illustrations of the kind we class as psychical. They are the physiological aspects of the simpler among those functions which, under a more special and complex aspect, we distinguish as psychological. The phenomena subjectively known as changes in consciousness, are objectively known as nervous excitations and discharges, which science now interprets into modes of motion. Hence, in following up organic evolution, the advance of retained motion in integration, in heterogeneity, and in definiteness, may be expected to show itself alike in the visible nervomuscular actions and in the correlative mental changes. We may conveniently look at the facts as exhibited during individual evolution, before looking at them as exhibited in general evolution.

The progress of a child in speech, very completely exhibits the transformation. Infantine noises are comparatively homogeneous; alike as being severally long-drawn and nearly uniform from end to end, and as being constantly repeated with but little variation of quality between narrow limits. They are quite uncoördinated—there is no integration of them into compound sounds. They are inarticulate, or without those definite beginnings and endings characterizing the sounds we call words. Progress shows itself first in the multiplication of the inarticulate sounds: the extreme vowels are added to the medium vowels, and the compound to the simple. Presently the movements which form the simpler consonants are achieved, and some of the sounds become sharply cut; but this definiteness is partial, for only initial consonants being used, the sounds end vaguely. While an approach to distinctness thus results, there also results, by combination of different consonants with the same vowels, an increase of heterogeneity; and along with the complete distinctness which terminal consonants give, arises a further great addition to the number of unlike sounds produced. The more difficult consonants and the compound consonants, imperfectly articulated at first, are by and by articulated with precision; and there comes yet another multitude of different and definite words—words that imply many kinds of vocal movements, severally performed with exactness, as well as perfectly integrated into complex groups. The subsequent advance to dissyllables and polysyllables, and to involved combinations of words, shows the still higher degree of integration and heterogeneity eventually reached by these organic motions. The acts of consciousness correlated with these nervo-muscular acts, of course go through parallel phases; and the advance from childhood to maturity yields daily proof that the changes which, on their physical side are nervous processes, and on their mental side are processes of thought, become more various, more defined, more coherent. At first the intellectual functions are very much alike in kind—recognitions and classifications of simple impressions alone go on; but in course of time these functions become multiform. Reasoning grows distinguishable, and eventually we have conscious induction and deduction; deliberate recollection and deliberate imagination are added to simple unguided association of ideas; more special modes of mental action, as those which result in mathematics, music, poetry, arise; and within each of these divisions the mental processes are ever being further differentiated. In definiteness it is the same. The infant makes its observations so inaccurately that it fails to distinguish individuals. The child errs continually in its spelling, its grammar, its arithmetic. The youth forms incorrect judgments on the affairs of life. Only with maturity comes that precise co-ordination in the nervous processes that is implied by a good adjustment of thoughts to things. Lastly, with the integration by which simple mental acts are combined into complex mental acts, it is so likewise. In the nursery you cannot obtain continuous attention—there is inability to form a coherent series of impressions; and there is a parallel inability to unite many co-existent impressions, even of the same order: witness the way in which a child's remarks on a picture, show that it attends only to the individual objects represented, and never to the picture as a whole. But with advancing years it becomes possible to understand an involved sentence, to follow long trains of reasoning, to hold in one mental grasp numerous concurrent circumstances. The like progressive integration takes place among the mental changes we distinguish as feelings; which in a child act singly, producing impulsiveness, but in an adult act more in concert, producing a comparatively balanced conduct.

After these illustrations supplied by individual evolution, we may deal briefly with those supplied by general evolution, which are analogous to them. A creature of very low intelligence, when aware of some large object in motion near it, makes a spasmodic movement, causing, it may be, a leap or a dart. The perceptions implied are relatively simple, homogeneous, and indefinite: the moving objects are not distinguished in their kinds as injurious or otherwise, as advancing or receding. The actions of escape are similarly all of one kind, have no adjustments of direction, and may bring the creature nearer the source of peril instead of further off. A stage higher, when the dart or the leap is away from danger, we see the nervous changes so far specialized that there results distinction of direction; indicating a greater variety among them, a greater co-ordination or integration of them in each process, and a greater definiteness. In still higher animals that discriminate between enemies and not-enemies, as a bird that flies from a man but not from a cow, the acts of perception have severally become united into more complex wholes, since cognition of certain differential attributes is implied; they have become more multiform, since each additional component impression adds to the number of possible compounds; and they have, by consequence, become more specific in their correspondences with objects— more definite. And then in animals so intelligent that they identify by sight not species only but individuals of a species, the mental changes are yet further distinguished in the same three ways. In the course of human evolution the law is equally manifested. The thoughts of the savage are nothing like so heterogeneous in their kinds as those of the civilized man, whose complex environment presents a multiplicity of new phenomena. His mental acts, too, are much less involved—he has no words for abstract ideas, and is found to be incapable of integrating the elements of such ideas. And in all but simple matters there is none of that precision in his thinking which, among civilized men, leads to the exact conclusions of science. Nor do the emotions fail to exhibit a parallel contrast.

[From *First Principles* (New York: De Witt Revolving Fund, 1958), 327, 370, 388–91.]

CHARLES DARWIN

53 The Descent of Man

There can be no doubt that the difference between the mind of the lowest man and that of the highest animal is immense. An anthropomorphous ape, if he could take a dispassionate view of his own case, would admit that though he could form an artful plan to plunder a garden—though he could use stones for fighting or for breaking open nuts, yet that the thought of fashioning a stone into a tool was quite beyond his scope. Still less, as he would admit, could he follow out a train of metaphysical reasoning, or solve a mathematical problem, or reflect on God, or admire a grand natural scene. Some apes, however, would probably declare that they could and did admire the beauty of the coloured skin and fur of their partners in marriage. They would admit, that though they could make other apes understand by cries some of their perceptions and simpler wants, the notion of expressing definite ideas by definite sounds had never crossed their minds. They might insist that they were ready to aid their fellow-apes of the same troop in many ways, to risk their lives for them, and to take charge of their orphans; but they would be forced to acknowledge that disinterested love for all living creatures, the most noble attribute of man, was quite beyond their comprehension.

Nevertheless the difference in mind between man and the higher animals, great as it is, certainly is one of degree and not of kind. We have seen that the senses and intuitions, the various emotions and faculties, such as love, memory, attention, curiosity, imitation, reason, &c., of which man boasts, may be found in an incipient, or even sometimes in a well-developed condition, in the lower animals. They are also capable of some inherited improvement, as we see in the domestic dog compared with the wolf or jackal. If it could be proved that certain high mental powers, such as the formation of general concepts, self-consciousness, &c., were absolutely peculiar to man, which seems extremely doubtful, it is not improbable that these qualities are merely the incidental results of other highly-advanced intellectual faculties; and these again mainly the result of the continued use of a perfect language. At what age does the new-born infant possess the power of abstraction, or become self-conscious, and reflect on its own existence? We cannot answer; nor can we answer in regard to the ascending organic scale. The half-art, half-instinct of language still bears the stamp of its gradual evolution. The ennobling belief in God is not universal with man; and the belief in spiritual agencies naturally follows from other mental powers. The moral sense perhaps affords the best and highest distinction between man and the lower animals; but I need say nothing on this head, as I have so lately endeavoured to shew that the social instincts,—the prime principle of man's moral constitution—with the aid of active intellectual powers and the effects of habit, naturally lead to the golden rule, 'As ye would that men should do to you, do ye to them likewise;' and this lies at the foundation of morality. [. . .]

That such evolution is at least possible, ought not to be denied, for we daily see these faculties developing in every infant: and we may trace a perfect gradation from the mind of an utter idiot, lower than that of an animal low in the scale, to the mind of a Newton.

The subjects to be discussed in this chapter are of the highest interest, but are treated by me in an imperfect and fragmentary manner. Mr Wallace, in an admirable paper, argues that man, after he had partially acquired those intellectual and moral faculties which distinguish him from the lower animals, would have been but little liable to bodily modifications through natural selection or any other means. For man is enabled through his mental faculties 'to keep with an unchanged body in harmony with the changing universe.' He has great power of adapting his habits to new conditions of life. He invents weapons, tools, and various stratagems to procure food and to defend himself. When he migrates into a colder climate he uses clothes, builds sheds, and makes fires; and by the aid of fire cooks food otherwise indigestible. He aids his fellow-men in many ways, and anticipates future events. Even at a remote period he practised some division of labour.

The lower animals, on the other hand, must have their bodily structure modified in order to survive under greatly changed conditions. They must be rendered stronger, or acquire more effective teeth or claws, for defence against new enemies; or they must be reduced in size, so as to escape detection and danger. When they migrate into a colder climate, they must become clothed with thicker fur, or have their constitutions altered. If they fail to be thus modified, they will cease to exist.

The case, however, is widely different, as Mr Wallace has with justice insisted, in relation to the intellectual and moral faculties of man. These faculties are variable; and we have every reason to believe that the variations tend to be inherited. Therefore, if they were formerly of high importance to primeval man and to his ape-like progenitors, they would have been perfected or advanced through natural selection. Of the high importance of the intellectual faculties there can be no doubt, for man mainly owes to them his predominant position in the world. We can see, that in the rudest state of society, the individuals who were the most sagacious, who invented and used the best weapons or traps, and who were best able to defend themselves, would rear the greatest number of offspring. The tribes, which included the largest number of men thus endowed, would increase in number and supplant other tribes. Numbers depend primarily on the means of subsistence, and this depends partly on the physical nature of the country, but in a much higher degree on the arts which are there practised. As a tribe increases and is victorious, it is often still further increased by the absorption of other tribes. The stature and strength of the men of a tribe are likewise of some importance for its success, and these depend in part on the nature and amount of the food which can be obtained. In Europe the men of the Bronze period were supplanted by a race more powerful, and, judging from their sword-handles, with larger hands; but their success was probably still more due to their superiority in the arts.

All that we know about savages, or may infer from their traditions and from old monuments, the history of which is quite forgotten by the present inhabitants, shew that from the remotest times successful tribes have supplanted other tribes. Relics of extinct or forgotten tribes have been discovered throughout the civilised regions of the earth, on the wild plains of America, and on the isolated islands in the Pacific Ocean. At the present day civilised nations are everywhere supplanting barbarous nations, excepting where the climate opposes a deadly barrier; and they succeed mainly, though not exclusively, through their arts, which are the products of the intellect. It is, therefore, highly probable that with mankind the intellectual faculties have been mainly and gradually perfected through natural selection; and this conclusion is sufficient for our purpose. Undoubtedly it would be interesting to trace the development of each separate faculty from the state in which it exists in the lower animals to that in which it exists in man; but neither my ability nor knowledge permits the attempt.

It deserves notice that, as soon as the progenitors of man became social (and this probably occurred at a very early period), the principle of imitation, and reason, and experience would have increased, and much modified the intellectual powers in a way, of which we see only traces in the lower animals. Apes are much given to imitation, as are the lowest savages; and the simple fact previously referred to, that after a time no animal can be caught in the same place by the same sort of trap, shews that animals learn by experience, and imitate the caution of others. Now, if some one man in a tribe, more sagacious than the others, invented a new snare or weapon, or other means of attack or defence, the plainest self-interest, without the assistance of much reasoning power, would prompt the other members to imitate him; and all would thus profit. The habitual practice of each new art must likewise in some slight degree strengthen the intellect. If the new invention were an important one, the tribe would increase in number, spread, and supplant other tribes. In a tribe thus rendered more numerous there would always be a rather greater chance of the birth of other superior and inventive members. If such men left children to inherit their mental superiority, the chance of the birth of still more ingenious members would be somewhat better, and in a very small tribe decidedly better. Even if they left no children, the tribe would still include their blood-relations; and it has been ascertained by agriculturists that by preserving and breeding from the family of an animal, which when slaughtered was found to be valuable, the desired character has been obtained.

Turning now to the social and moral faculties. In order that primeval men, or the ape-like progenitors of man, should become social, they must have acquired the same instinctive feelings, which impel other animals to live in a body; and they no doubt exhibited the same general disposition. They would have felt uneasy when separated from their comrades, for whom they would have felt some degree of love; they would have warned each other of danger, and have given mutual aid in attack or defence. All this implies some degree of sympathy, fidelity, and courage. Such social qualities, the paramount importance of which to the lower animals is disputed by no one, were no doubt acquired by the progenitors of man in a similar manner, namely, through natural selection, aided by inherited habit. When two tribes of primeval man, living in the same country, came into competition, if (other circumstances being equal) the one tribe included a great number of courageous, sympathetic and faithful members, who were always ready to warn each other of danger, to aid and defend each other, this tribe would succeed better and conquer the other. Let it be borne in mind how all-important in the never-ceasing wars of savages, fidelity and courage must be. The advantage which disciplined soldiers have over undisciplined hordes follows chiefly from the confidence which each man feels in his comrades. Obedience, as Mr Bagehot has well shewn, is of the highest value, for any form of government is better than none. Selfish and contentious people will not cohere and without coherence nothing can be effected. A tribe rich in the above qualities would spread and be victorious over other tribes: but in the course of time it would, judging from all past history, be in its turn overcome by some other tribe still more highly endowed. Thus the social and moral qualities would tend slowly to advance and be diffused throughout the world.

But it may be asked, how within the limits of the same tribe did a large number of members first become endowed with these social and moral quaiities, and how was the standard of excellence raised? It is extremely doubtful whether the offspring of the more sympathetic and benevolent parents, or of those who were the most faithful to their comrades, would be reared in greater numbers than the children of selfish and treacherous parents belonging to the same tribe. He who was ready to sacrifice his life, as many a savage has been, rather than betray his comrades, would often leave no offspring to inherit his noble nature. The bravest men, who were always willing to come to the front in war, and who freely risked their lives for others, would on an average perish in larger numbers than other men. Therefore it hardly seems probable, that the number of men gifted with such virtues, or that the standard of their excellence, could be increased through natural selection, that is, by the survival of the fittest; for we are not here speaking of one tribe being victorious over another.

Although the circumstances, leading to an increase in the number of those thus endowed within the same tribe, are too complex to be clearly followed out, we can trace some of the probable steps. In the first place, as the reasoning powers and foresight of the members became improved, each man would soon learn that if he aided his fellow-men, he would commonly receive aid in return. From this low motive he might acquire the habit of aiding his fellows; and the habit of performing benevolent actions certainly strengthens the feeling of sympathy which gives the first impulse to benevolent actions. Habits, moreover, followed during many generations probably tend to be inherited.

But another and much more powerful stimulus to the development of the social virtues, is afforded by the praise and the blame of our fellow-men. To the instinct of sympathy, as we have already seen, it is primarily due, that we habitually bestow both praises and blame on others, whilst we love the former and dread the latter when applied to ourselves; and this instinct no doubt was originally acquired, like all the other social instincts, through natural selection. At how early a period the progenitors of man in the course of their development, became capable of feeling and being impelled by, the praise or blame of their fellow-creatures, we cannot of course say. But it appears that even dogs appreciate encouragement, praise, and blame. The rudest savages feel the sentiment of glory, as they clearly show by preserving the trophies of their prowess, by their habit of excessive boasting, and even by the extreme care which they take of their personal appearance and decorations; for unless they regarded the opinion of their comrades, such habits would be senseless.

They certainly feel shame at the breach of some of their lesser rules, and apparently remorse, as shewn by the case of the Australian who grew thin and could not rest from having delayed to murder some other woman, so as to propitiate his dead wife's spirit. Though I have not met with any other recorded case, it is scarcely credible that a savage, who will sacrifice his life rather than betray his tribe, or one who will deliver himself up as a prisoner rather than break his parole, would not feel remorse in his inmost soul, if he had failed in a duty, which he held sacred.

We may therefore conclude that primeval man, at a very remote period, was influenced by the praise and blame of his fellows. It is obvious, that the members of the same tribe would approve of conduct which appeared to them to be for the general good, and would reprobate that which appeared evil. To do good unto others—to do unto others as ye would they should do unto you—is the foundation-stone of morality. It is, therefore, hardly possible to exaggerate the importance during rude times of the love of praise and the dread of blame. A man who was not impelled by any deep, instinctive feeling, to sacrifice his life for the good of others, yet was roused to such actions by a sense of glory, would by his example excite the same wish for glory in other men, and would strengthen by exercise the noble feeling of admiration. He might thus do far more good to his tribe than by begetting offspring with a tendency to inherit his own high character.

With increased experience and reason, man perceives the more remote consequences of his actions, and the self-regarding virtues, such as temperance, chastity, &c., which during early times are, as we have before seen, utterly disregarded, come to be highly esteemed or even held sacred. I need not, however, repeat what I have said on this head in the fourth chapter. Ultimately our moral sense or conscience becomes a highly complex sentiment—originating in the social instincts, largely guided by the approbation of our fellow-men, ruled by reason, self-interest, and in later times by deep religious feelings, and confirmed by instruction and habit.

It must not be forgotten that although a high standard of morality gives but a slight or no advantage to each individual man and his children over the other men of the same tribe, yet that an increase in the number of well-endowed men and an advancement in the standard of morality will certainly give an immense advantage to one tribe over another. A tribe including many members who, from possessing in a high degree the spirit of patriotism, fidelity, obedience, courage, and sympathy, were always ready to aid one another, and to sacrifice themselves for the common good, would be victorious over most other tribes; and this would be natural selection. At all times throughout the world tribes have supplanted other tribes; and as morality is one important element in their success, the standard of morality and the number of well-endowed men will thus everywhere tend to rise and increase.

[From *The Origin of Species* . . . *and The Descent of Man* (New York: The Modern Library, 1959), 494–500.]

CHARLES DARWIN

54 The Expression of the Emotions in Man and Animals

We may confidently believe that laughter, as a sign of pleasure or enjoyment, was practised by our progenitors long before they deserved to be called human; for very many kinds of monkeys, when pleased, utter a reiterated sound, clearly analogous to our laughter, often accompanied by vibratory movements of their jaws or lips, with the corners of the mouth drawn backwards and upwards, by the wrinkling of the cheeks, and even by the brightening of the eyes.

We may likewise infer that fear was expressed from an extremely remote period, in almost the same manner as it now is by man; namely, by trembling, the erection of the hair, cold perspiration, pallor, widely opened eyes, the relaxation of most of the muscles, and by the whole body cowering downwards or held motionless.

Suffering, if great, will from the first have caused screams or groans to be uttered, the body to be contorted, and the teeth to be ground together. But our progenitors will not have exhibited those highly expressive movements of the features which accompany screaming and crying until their circulatory and respiratory organs, and the muscles surrounding the eyes, had acquired their present structure. The shedding of tears appears to have originated through reflex action from the spasmodic contraction of the eyelids, together perhaps with the eyeballs becoming gorged with blood during the act of screaming. Therefore weeping probably came on rather late in the line of our descent; and this conclusion agrees with the fact that our nearest allies, the anthropomorphous apes, do not weep. But we must here exercise some caution, for as certain monkeys, which are not closely related to man, weep, this habit might have been developed long ago in a sub-branch of the group from which man is derived. Our early progenitors, when suffering from grief or anxiety, would not have made their eyebrows oblique, or have drawn down the corners of their mouth, until they had acquired the habit of endeavouring to restrain their screams. The expression, therefore, of grief and anxiety is eminently human.

Rage will have been expressed at a very early period by threatening or frantic gestures, by the reddening of the skin, and by glaring eyes, but not by frowning. For the habit of frowning seems to have been acquired chiefly from the corrugators being the first muscles to contract round the eyes, whenever during infancy pain, anger, or distress is felt, and there consequently is a near approach to screaming; and partly from a frown serving as a shade in difficult and intent vision. It seems probable that this shading action would not have become habitual until man had assumed a completely upright position, for monkeys do not frown when exposed to a glaring light. Our early progenitors, when enraged, would probably have exposed their teeth more freely than does man, even when giving full vent to his rage, as with the insane. We may, also, feel almost certain that they would have protruded their lips, when sulky or disappointed, in a greater degree than is the case with our own children, or even with the children of existing savage races.

Our early progenitors, when indignant or moderately angry, would not have held their heads erect, opened their chests, squared their shoulders, and clenched their fists, until they had acquired the ordinary carriage and upright attitude of man, and had learnt to fight with their fists or clubs. Until this period had arrived the antithetical gesture of shrugging the shoulders, as a sign of impotence or of patience, would not have been developed. From the same reason astonishment would not then have been expressed by raising the arms with open hands and extended fingers. Nor, judging from the actions of monkeys, would astonishment have been exhibited by a widely opened mouth; but the eyes would have been opened and the eyebrows arched. Disgust would have been shown at a very early period by movements round the mouth, like those of vomiting,—that is, if the view which I have suggested respecting the source of the expression is correct, namely, that our progenitors had the power, and used it, of voluntarily and quickly rejecting any food from their stomachs which they disliked. But the more refined manner of showing contempt or disdain, by lowering the eyelids, or turning away the eyes and face, as if the despised person were not worth looking at, would not probably have been acquired until a much later period.

Of all expressions, blushing seems to be the most strictly human; yet it is common to all or nearly all the races of man, whether or not any change of colour is visible in their skin. The relaxation of the small arteries of the surface, on which blushing depends, seems to have primarily resulted from earnest attention directed to the appearance of our own persons, especially of our faces, aided by habit, inheritance, and the ready flow of nerve-force along accustomed channels; and afterwards to have been extended by the power of association to self-attention directed to moral conduct. It can hardly be doubted that many animals are capable of appreciating beautiful colours and even forms, as is shown by the pains which the individuals of one sex take in displaying their beauty before those of the opposite sex. But it does not seem possible that any animal, until its mental powers had been developed to an equal or nearly equal degree with those of man, would have closely considered and been sensitive about its own personal appearance. Therefore we may conclude that blushing originated at a very late period in the long line of our descent.

From the various facts just alluded to, and given in the course of this volume, it follows that, if the structure of our organs of respiration and circulation had differed in only a slight degree from the state in which they now exist, most of our expressions would have been wonderfully different. A very slight change in the course of the arteries and veins which run to the head, would probably have prevented the blood from accumulating in our eyeballs during violent expiration; for this occurs in extremely few quadrupeds. In this case we should not have displayed some of our most characteristic expressions. [. . .]

We have seen that the study of the theory of expression confirms to a certain limited extent the conclusion that man is derived from some lower animal form, and supports the belief of the specific or sub-specific unity of the several races; but as far as my judgment serves, such confirmation was hardly needed. We have also seen that expression in itself, or the language of the emotions, as it has sometimes been called, is certainly of importance for the welfare of mankind. To understand, as far as possible, the source or origin of the various expressions which may be hourly seen on the faces of the men around us, not to mention our domesticated animals, ought to possess much interest for us. From these several causes, we may conclude that the philosophy of our subject has well deserved the attention which it has already received from several excellent observers, and that it deserves still further attention, especially from any able physiologist.

[From *The Expression of the Emotions in Man and Animals* (New York: Philosophical Library, 1871), 360–6.]

The common descent of man and all the other Mammals from one stem-form is beyond question. This long-extinct Promammal was probably evolved from Proreptiles during the Triassic period, and must certainly be regarded as the Monotreme and oviparous ancestor of *all* to Mammals.

If we hold firmly to this fundamental and most important thesis, we shall see the 'ape-question' in a very different light from that in which it is usually regarded. Little reflection is then needed to see that it is not nearly so important as it is said to be. The origin of the human race from a series of Mammal ancestors, and the historic evolution of these from an earlier series of lower Vertebrate ancestors, together with all the weighty conclusions that every thoughtful man deduces therefrom, remain untouched; as far as these are concerned, it is immaterial whether we regard true 'Apes' as our nearest ancestors or not. [. . .]

In any case, the whole of the Mammals, including man, have had a common origin; and it is equally certain that their common stem-forms were gradually evolved from a long series of lower Vertebrates.

The resistance to the theory of a descent from the Apes is clearly due in most men to feeling rather than to reason. They shrink from the notion of such an origin just because they see in the ape-organism a caricature of man, a distorted and unattractive image of themselves; because it hurts man's æsthetic complacency and self-ennoblement. It is more flattering to think we have descended from some lofty and god-like being; and so, from the earliest times, human vanity has been pleased to believe in our origin from gods or demi-gods. The Church, with that sophistic reversal of ideas of which it is a master, has succeeded in representing this ridiculous piece of vanity as 'Christian humility'; and the very men who reject with horror the notion of an animal origin, and count themselves 'children of God,' love to prate of their 'humble sense of servitude.' In most of the sermons that have poured out from pulpit and altar against the doctrine of evolution, human vanity and conceit have been a conspicuous element; and, although we have inherited this very characteristic weakness from the Apes, we must admit that we have developed it to a higher degree, which is entirely repudiated by sound and normal intelligence. We are greatly amused at all the childish follies that the ridiculous pride of ancestry has maintained from the Middle Ages to our own time; yet there is a large amount of this empty feeling in most men. Just as most people much prefer to trace their family back to some degenerate baron or some famous prince rather than to an unknown peasant, so most men would rather have as parent of the race a sinful and fallen Adam than an advancing and vigorous Ape. It is a matter of taste, and to that extent we cannot quarrel over these genealogical tendencies. Personally, the notion of ascent is more congenial to me than that of descent. It seems to me a finer thing to be the advanced offspring of a simian ancestor, which has developed progressively from the lower Mammals in the struggle for life, than the degenerate descendant of a god-like being, made from a clod, and fallen for his sins, and an Eve created from one of his ribs. Speaking of the rib, I may add to what I have said about the development of the skeleton, that the number of ribs is just the same in man and woman. In both of them the ribs are formed from the middle germlayer, and are, from the phylogenetic point of view, lower or ventral vertebral arches.

But it is said: 'That is all very well, as far as the human body is concerned; on the facts quoted it is impossible to doubt that it has really and gradually been evolved from the long ancestral series of the Vertebrates. But it is quite another thing as regards man's mind, or soul; this cannot possibly have been developed from the Vertebrate-soul.' Let us see if we cannot meet this grave stricture from the well-known facts of comparative anatomy, physiology, and embryology. It will be best to begin with a comparative study of the souls of various groups of Vertebrates. Here we find such an enormous variety of Vertebrate souls that, at first sight, it seems quite impossible to trace them all to a common 'Primitive Vertebrate.' Think of the tiny Amphioxus, with no real brain but a simple medullary tube, and its whole psychic life at the very lowest stage among the Vertebrates. The following group of the Cyclostomes are still very limited, though they have a brain. When we pass on to the Fishes, we find their intelligence remaining at a very low level. We do not see any material advance in mental development until we go on to the Amphibia and Reptiles. There is still greater advance when we come to the Mammals, though even here the minds of the Monotremes and of the stupid Marsupials remain at a low stage. But when we rise from these to the Placentals we find within this one vast group such a number of important stages of differentiation and progress that the psychic differences between the least intelligent (such as the sloths and armadillos) and the most intelligent Placentals (such as the dogs and apes) are much greater than the psychic differences between the lowest Placentals and the Marsupials or Mono-tremes. Most certainly the differences are far greater than the differences in mental power between the dog, the ape, and man. Yet all these animals are genetically-related members of a single natural class.

We see this to a still more astonishing extent in the comparative psychology of another class of animals, that is especially interesting for many reasons—the Insect class. It is well known that we find in many Insects a degree of intelligence that is found in man alone among the Vertebrates. Everybody knows of the famous communities and states of bees and ants, and of the very remarkable social arrangements in them, such as we find among the more advanced races of men, but among no other group of animals. I need only mention the social organisation and government of the monarchic bees and the republican ants, and their division into different conditions—queen, drone-nobles, workers, educators, soldiers, etc. One of the most remarkable phenomena in this very interesting province is the cattle-keeping of the ants, which rear plant-lice as milch-cows and regularly extract their honied juice. Still more remarkable is the slave-holding of the large red ants, which steal the young of the small black ants and bring them up as slaves. It has long been known that these political and social arrangements of the ants are due to the deliberate co-operation of the countless citizens, and that they understand each other. [. . .]

If we now turn from the comparative study of psychic life in different animals to the question of the organs of this function, we receive the answer that in all the higher animals they are always bound up with certain groups of cells, the ganglionic cells or neurona that compose the nervous system. All scientists without exception are agreed that the central nervous system is the organ of psychic life in the animal, and it is possible to prove this experimentally at any moment. When we partially or wholly destroy the central nervous system, we extinguish in the same proportion, partially or wholly, the 'soul' or psychic activity of the animal. We have, therefore, to examine the features of the psychic organ in man. The reader already knows the incontestable answer to this question. Man's psychic organ is, in structure and origin, just the same organ as in all the other Vertebrates. It originates in the shape of a simple medullary tube from the outer membrane of the embryo—the skin-sense-layer. The simple cerebral vesicle that is formed by the expansion of the head-part of this medullary tube divides by transverse constrictions into five, and these pass through more or less the same stages of construction in the human embryo as in the rest of the Mammals. As these are undoubtedly of a common origin, their brain and spinal cord must also have a common origin.

Physiology teaches us further, on the ground of observation and experiment, that the relation of the 'soul' to its organ, the brain and spinal cord, is just the same in man as in the other Mammals. The one cannot act at all without the other; it is just as much bound up with it as muscular movement is with the muscles. It can only develop in connection with it. If we are evolutionists at all and grant the causal connection of ontogenesis and phylogenesis, we are forced to admit this thesis: The human soul or psyche, as a function of the medullary tube, has developed along with it; and just as brain and spinal cord now develop from the simple medullary tube in every human individual, so the human mind or the psychic life of the whole human race has been gradually evolved from the lower Vertebrate-soul. [. . .]

When [. . .] dualistic philosophers are consistent they must assign a moment in the phylogeny of the human soul at which it was first 'introduced' into man's vertebrate body. Hence, at the time when the human body was evolved from the anthropoid body of the Ape (probably in the Tertiary period), a specific human psychic element—or, as people love to say, 'a spark of divinity'—must have been suddenly infused or breathed into the anthropoid brain, and been associated with the ape-soul already present in it. I need not insist on the enormous theoretical difficulties of this idea. I will only point out that this 'spark of divinity,' which is supposed to distinguish the soul of man from that of the other animals, must be itself capable of development, and has, as a matter of fact, progressively developed in the course of human history. As a rule, reason is taken to be this 'spark of divinity,' and is supposed to be an exclusive possession of humanity. But comparative psychology shows us that it is quite impossible to set up this barrier between man and the brute. Either we take the word 'reason' in the wider sense, and then it is found in the higher Mammals (ape, dog, elephant, horse) just as well as in most men; or else in the narrower sense, and then it is lacking in most men just as much as in the majority of animals. On the whole, we may still say of man's reason what Goethe's Mephistopheles said:—

> 'Life somewhat better might content him
> But for the gleam of heavenly light that Thou hast lent him.
> He calls it reason; thence his power's increased
> To be still beastlier than any beast.'

[. . .] The human 'spirit' or 'soul' is merely a force or form of energy, inseparately bound up with the material substratum of the body. The thinking force of the mind is just as much connected with the structural elements of the brain as the motor force of the muscles with their structural elements. Our mental powers are functions of the brain as much as any other force is a function of a material body. [. . .]

Thus the evolution of man is directed by the same 'eternal, iron laws' as the development of any other body. These laws always load us back to the same simple principles, the elementary principles of physics and chemistry. The various phenomena of nature differ only in the degree of complexity in which the different forces work together.

[From *The Evolution of Man*, trans. J. McCabe (London: Watts & Co., 1910), 740–9.]

GEORGE ROMANES

56 **Animal Intelligence**

Reflex actions under the influence of their appropriate stimuli may be compared to the actions of a machine under the manipulations of an operator; when certain springs of action are touched by certain stimuli, the whole machine is thrown into appropriate movement; there is no room for choice, there is no room for uncertainty; but as surely as any of these inherited mechanisms are affected by the stimulus with reference to which it has been constructed to act, so surely will it act in precisely the same way as it always has acted. But the case with conscious mental adjustment is quite different. For, without at present going into the question concerning the relation of body and mind, or waiting to ask whether cases of mental adjustment are not really quite as *mechanical* in the sense of being the necessary result or correlative of a chain of physical sequences due to a physical stimulation, it is enough to point to the variable and incalculable character of mental adjustments as distinguished from the constant and foreseeable character of reflex adjustments. All, in fact, that in an objective sense we can mean by a mental adjustment is an adjustment of a kind that has not been definitely fixed by heredity as the only adjustment possible in the given circumstances of stimulation. For were there no alternative of adjustment, the case, in an animal at least, would be indistinguishable from one of reflex action.

It is, then, adaptive action by a living organism in cases where the inherited machinery of the nervous system does not furnish data for our prevision of what the adaptive action must necessarily be—it is only here that we recognise the objective evidence of mind. The criterion of mind, therefore, which I propose, and to which I shall adhere throughout the present volume, is as follows:—Does the organism learn to make new adjustments, or to modify old ones, in accordance with the results of its own individual experience? If it does so, the fact cannot be due merely to reflex action in the sense above described. [. . .]

I may, however, here explain that in my use of this criterion I shall always regard it as fixing only the upper limit of non-mental action; I shall never regard it as fixing the lower limit of mental action. For it is clear that long before mind has advanced sufficiently far in the scale of development to become amenable to the test in question, it has probably begun to dawn as nascent subjectivity. In other words, because a lowly organised animal does *not* learn by its own individual experience, we may not therefore conclude that in performing its natural or ancestral adaptations to appropriate stimuli consciousness, or the mind-element, is wholly absent; we can only say that this element, if present, reveals no evidence of the fact. But, on the other hand, if a lowly organised animal *does* learn by its own individual experience, we are in possession of the best available evidence of conscious memory leading to intentional adaptation. Therefore our criterion applies to the upper limit of non-mental action, not to the lower limit of mental.

Of course to the sceptic this criterion may appear unsatisfactory, since it depends, not on direct knowledge, but on inference. Here, however, it seems enough to point out, as already observed, that it is the best criterion available; and further, that scepticism of this kind is logically bound to deny evidence of mind, not only in the case of the lower animals, but also in that of the higher, and even in that of men other than the sceptic himself. For all objections which could apply to the use of this criterion of mind in the animal kingdom would apply with equal force to the evidence of any mind other than that of the individual objector. This is obvious, because, as I have already observed, the only evidence we can have of objective mind is that which is furnished by objective activities; and as the subjective mind can never become assimilated with the objective so as to learn by direct feeling the mental processes which there accompany the objective activities, it is clearly impossible to satisfy any one who may choose to doubt the validity of inference, that in any case other than his own mental processes ever do accompany objective activities. Thus it is that philosophy can supply no demonstrative refutation of idealism, even of the most extravagant form. Common sense, however, universally feels that analogy is here a safer guide to truth than the sceptical demand for impossible evidence; so that if the objective existence of other organisms and their activities is granted—without which postulate comparative psychology, like all the other sciences, would be an unsubstantial dream—common sense will always and without question conclude that the activities of organisms other than our own, when analogous to those activities of our own which we know to be accompanied by certain mental states, are in them accompanied by analogous mental states.

The theory of animal automatism, therefore, which is usually attributed to Descartes (although it is not quite clear how far this great philosopher really entertained the theory), can never be accepted by common sense; and even as a philosophical speculation it will be seen, from what has just been said, that by no feat of logic is it possible to make the theory apply to animals to the exclusion of man. The expression of fear or affection by a dog involves quite as distinctive and complex a series of neuro-muscular actions as does the expression of similar emotions by a human being; and therefore, if the evidence of corresponding mental states is held to be inadequate in the one case, it must in consistency be held similarly inadequate in the other. And likewise, of course, with all other exhibitions of mental life.

It is quite true, however, that since the days of Descartes—or rather, we might say, since the days of Joule—the question of animal automatism has assumed a new or more defined aspect, seeing that it now runs straight into the most profound and insoluble problem that has ever been presented to human thought—viz. the relation of body to mind in view of the doctrine of the conservation of energy. [. . .] Here I desire only to make it plain that the mind of animals must be placed in the same category, with reference to this problem, as the mind of man; and that we cannot without gross inconsistency ignore or question the evidence of mind in the former, while we accept precisely the same kind of evidence as sufficient proof of mind in the latter.

And this proof, as I have endeavoured to show, is in all cases and in its last analysis the fact of a living organism showing itself able to learn by its own individual experience. Wherever we find an animal able to do this, we have the same right to predicate mind as existing in such an animal that we have to predicate it as existing in any human being other than ourselves. [. . .]

It becomes questionable how far analogy drawn from the activities of the insect is a safe guide to the inferring of mental states—particularly in view of the fact that in many respects, such as in the great preponderance of 'instinct' over 'reason,' the psychology of an insect is demonstrably a widely different thing from that of a man. Now it is, of course, perfectly true that the less the resemblance the less is the value of any analogy built upon the resemblance, and therefore that the inference of an ant or a bee feeling sympathy or rage is not so valid as is the similar inference in the case of a dog or a monkey. Still it *is* an inference, and, so far as it goes, a valid one—being, in fact, the only inference available. That is to say, if we observe an ant or a bee apparently exhibiting sympathy or rage, we must either conclude that some psychological state resembling that of sympathy or rage is present, or else refuse to think about the subject at all; from the observable facts there is no other inference open. Therefore, having full regard to the progressive weakening of the analogy from human to brute psychology as we recede through the animal kingdom downwards from man, still, as it is the only analogy available, I shall follow it throughout the animal series. [. . .]

Chapter XVII
Monkeys, apes, and baboons

[. . .] The intelligence of apes, monkeys, and baboons has not presented material for nearly so many observations as that of other intelligent mammals. Useless for all purposes of labour or art, mischievous as domestic pets, and in all cases troublesome to keep, these animals have never enjoyed the improving influences of hereditary domestication, while for the same reasons observation of the intelligence of captured individuals has been comparatively scant. Still more unfortunately, these remarks apply most of all to the most man-like of the group, and the nearest existing prototypes of the human race: our knowledge of the psychology of the anthropoid apes is less than our knowledge of the psychology of any other animal. But notwithstanding the scarcity of the material which I have to present, I think there is enough to show that the mental life of the *Simiadæ* is of a distinctly different type from any that we have hitherto considered, and that in their psychology, as in their anatomy, these animals approach most nearly to *Homo sapiens*.

Emotions

Affection and sympathy are strongly marked—the latter indeed more so than in any other animal, not even excepting the dog. A few instances from many that might be quoted will be sufficient to show this.

The powers of observation and readiness to establish new associations thus rendered apparent, display a high level of general intelligence. Mr Darwin further observes that Mr Belt 'likewise describes various actions of a tamed cebus, which, I think, clearly show that this animal possessed some reasoning power.' The following is the account to which Mr Darwin here refers, and I quote it *in extenso*, because, as I shall presently show, I have myself been able to confirm most of the observations on another monkey of the same genus:—

It would sometimes entangle itself round a pole to which it was fastened, and then unwind the coils again with the greatest discernment. Its chain allowed it to swing down below the verandah, but it could not reach to the ground. Sometimes, when there were broods of young ducks about, it would hold out a piece of bread in one hand, and when it had tempted a duckling within reach, seize it by the other, and kill it with a bite in the breast. There was such an uproar amongst the fowls on these occasions, that we soon knew what was the matter, and would rush out and punish Mickey (as we called him) with a switch; so that he was ultimately cured of his poultry-killing propensities. One day, when whipping him, I held up the dead duckling in front of him, and at each blow of the light switch told him to take hold of it, and at last, much to my surprise, he did so, taking it and holding it tremblingly in one hand. He would draw things towards him with a stick, and even used a swing for the same purpose. It had been put up for the children, and could be reached by Mickey, who now and then indulged himself in a swing on it. One day I had put down some bird-skins on a chair to dry, far beyond, as I thought, Mickey's reach; but, fertile in expedients, he took the swing and launched it towards the chair, and actually managed to knock the skins off in the return of the swing, so as to bring them within his reach. He also procured some jelly that was set out to cool in the same way. Mickey's actions were very human-like. When any one came near to fondle him, he never neglected the opportunity of pocket-picking. He would pull out letters, and quickly take them from their envelopes.[1]

The orang which Cuvier had used to draw a chair from one end to the other of a room, in order to stand upon it so as to reach a latch which it desired to open; and in this we have a display of rationally adaptive action which no dog has equalled, although, as in the case before given of the dog dragging the mat, it has been closely approached. Again, Rengger describes a monkey employing a stick wherewith to prise up the lid of a chest, which was too heavy for the animal to raise otherwise. This use of a lever as a mechanical instrument is an action to which no animal other than a monkey has ever been known to attain; and, as we shall subsequently see, my own observation has fully corroborated that of Rengger in this respect. More remarkable still, as we shall also subsequently see, the monkey to which I allude as having myself observed, succeeded also by methodical investigation, and without any assistance, in discovering for himself the mechanical principle of the screw; and that monkeys well understand how to use stones as hammers is a matter of common observation since Dampier and Wafer first described this action as practised by these animals in the breaking open of oyster-shells. The additional observation of Gernelli Carreri of monkeys thrusting stones into the open valves of oysters so as to save themselves the trouble of smashing the shells, though not incredible, requires confirmation. But Mr Haden, of Dundee, has communicated to me the following very remarkable appreciation of mechanical principles which he himself observed in a monkey (species not noted), and which would certainly be beyond the mental powers of any other animal:—

'A large monkey, confined alone in a large cage, had its sleeping-place in the form of a kind of hut in the centre of the cage. Springing near the hut was a tree, or imitation tree, the main branch of which ascended over the top of the hut, and then came forwards away from it. Whether the roof of the hut enabled this animal to gain any part of this branch, I did not observe, but only remarked its method at the time of gaining the part of the branch which led frontwards, and away from the hut. This could be done by means of the hut door, which, when opened, swung beneath this part of the branch. The door, either by accident or by the design of its construction, *swung to* each time the animal opened it to mount upon its top edge. After one or two efforts to mount by it in spite of its immediate swinging to, the creature procured a thick blanket which lay in the cage, and threw it over the door, having opened the same, so that its complete swinging to was prevented sufficiently for the creature to mount upon its free edge, and so gain that part of the branch which ran above it.'

The following, which I quote from 'Nature' (vol. xxiii., p. 533), also displays high intelligence:—

One of the large monkeys at the Alexandra Palace had been for some time suffering from the decay of the right lower canine, and an abscess, forming a large protuberance on the jaw, had resulted. The pain seemed so great, it was decided to consult a dentist as to what should be done; and, as the poor creature was at times very savage, it was thought that if the tooth had to be extracted, gas should be used for the safety of the operation. Preparations were made accordingly, but the behaviour of the monkey was quite a surprise to all who were concerned. He showed great fight on being taken out of the cage, and not only struggled against being put into a sack prepared with a hole cut for his head, but forced one of his hands out, and snapped and screamed, and gave promise of being very troublesome. Directly, however, Mr Lewin Moseley, who had undertaken the operation, managed to get his hand on the abscess and gave relief, the monkey's demeanour changed entirely. He laid his head down quietly for examination, and, without the use of the gas, submitted to the removal of a stump of a tooth as quietly as possible.

According to D'Osbonville, certain monkeys that he observed in the wild state were in the habit of administering corporal chastisement to their young. After suckling and cleansing them, the mothers used to sit down and watch the youngsters play. These would wrestle, throw and chase each other, &c.; but if any of them grew malicious, the dams would spring up, and, seizing their offspring by the tail with one hand, correct them severely with the other.

We have already seen that dogs and cats display the idea of maintaining discipline among their progeny.

According to Houzeau the sacred monkey of India (*Semnopithecus entellus*) is very clever in catching snakes, and in the case of poisonous species destroy the fangs by breaking them against stones.

Of the fact that monkeys act in co-operation, many proofs might be given, but one will suffice.

Lieutenant Schipp, in his Memoirs, says:—

A Cape baboon having taken off some clothes from the barracks, I formed a party to recover them. With twenty men I made a circuit to cut them off from the caverns, to which they always fled for shelter. They observed my movements, and detaching about fifty to guard the entrance, the others kept their post. We could see them collecting large stones and other missiles. One old grey-headed one, who had often paid us a visit at the barracks, was seen distributing his orders, as if a general. We rushed on to the attack, when, at a scream from him, they rolled down enormous stones on us, so that we were forced to give up the contest.

I shall here bring to a close my selections from the literature of monkey psychology.

[From *Animal Intelligence* (New York: Appleton, 1883), 4–9, 479–83.]

C. LLOYD MORGAN

57 **Introduction to Comparative Psychology**

A distinguishing feature of modern psychology is the employment of the comparative method. So long as the psychologist restricts himself to the introspective study of the workings of his own consciousness, his conclusions rest on a basis which, however sure it may appear to himself, must be limited by the inevitable restrictions of his own individuality. When he compares and correlates his own results with those of other introspective observers, he becomes so far a comparative psychologist, and by widening his basis renders his conclusions more comprehensive. A further stage of the comparative method is reached, when he endeavours to correlate the results of introspective psychology with the conclusions reached by the physiological study of those nervous processes which are the concomitants of psychical states. On the hypothesis of monism, he is thus comparing two wholly different aspects of the same natural occurrences; on the hypothesis of dualism, two wholly different occurrences, which are nevertheless invariably associated. In any case, by proceeding to this comparison, he links his subject with the science of biology in a way that has proved eminently helpful to his own branch of study. Now, the keynote of modern biology is evolution; and on the hypothesis of scientific monism here adopted, though not necessarily on that of empirical dualism, we are not only logically justified in extending our comparative psychology so as to include within its scope the field of zoological psychology, but we are logically bound to regard psychological evolution as strictly co-ordinate with biological evolution.

I propose to consider in this chapter what we can know of other minds than ours, and how we may gain this knowledge. It follows from what has just been said, that since biological evolution has given rise to individuals of divergent types of organic structure, there may be—nay, there must be—in these divergent biological individuals divergent types of mind, using the word 'mind' in the widest and most comprehensive sense as embracing all modes of psychical activity. The question arises, however, how we are to gain acquaintance with these divergent types of mind. And here we are met by the fundamental difficulty which comparative psychology, both human and zoological, encounters when it leaves the broad field of general considerations, to enter upon the more particular study of individual and concrete cases with divergent possibilities of interpretation. For we have direct and immediate acquaintance with no other psychical processes than those which we can study by the introspective method in ourselves. Hence introspective study must inevitably be the basis and foundation of all comparative psychology.

I will endeavour to illustrate the fundamental difficulty of comparative psychology by means of an analogy. Suppose that a chronometer were gifted with intelligence and reason, and were to enter upon the study of other timepieces, all access to their works being inexorably denied it. It would be able to observe the motions of the hands over the dial-plate, and perhaps gain some information by attentively listening to the internal sounds. But when it came to the interpretation of these observed phenomena, and when it attempted to explain their inner causes, the chronometer would be forced to frame all such interpretation and such explanation in terms of its own works. With no other works would it have any acquaintance. It would infer, and justly infer under the circumstances, that the works of other timepieces were, on the whole, of like nature with those which actuated the movements of its own hands over the dial-face. There can be no question, moreover, that the more thorough and accurate the acquaintance of the chronometer with its own works, the more valid would be its inferences with regard to the hidden works of other timepieces. For example, it might learn by introspection that it possessed a mechanism of compensation for changes of temperature; and noticing that in other timepieces the rate of movement of the hands varied with the rise or fall of the thermometer, it might infer that in them such mechanism was absent. It is probable, however, that the chronometer would interpret all the phenomena as due to the action of a mainspring, since it would necessarily be unacquainted with the impelling motive power derived from the descent of heavy weights; and the outflow of energy from the spring would, in its interpretation, be regulated by some sort of balance-wheel, since the principle of the pendulum would nowhere be found through introspection of its works. Thus there would be for the chronometer inevitable possibilities of error. And although it could do little more than speculate concerning these possibilities, it would certainly be wise in refraining from anything like dogmatism concerning the insides of other timepieces which it must interpret, if it interpret at all, in terms of its own chronometer works, but which might not impossibly, could it only get at them, exhibit the application of other mechanical principles.

Now this analogy must certainly not be pressed too far. It is here adduced to illustrate the fact that just as the supposed chronometer would be forced to interpret the mechanism of other timepieces in terms of its own mechanism, so man is forced to interpret the psychology of animals in terms of human psychology, since with this alone he has first-hand acquaintance through the study of the nature and sequence of his own mental processes. But it will perhaps be said that the analogy is invalidated on the principles I have myself adopted, by the fact that in animals a knowledge of the organic mechanism, the functional activity of which is the objective aspect or correlate of psychical processes, is not beyond our reach, but is attainable through physiological research. Access to the works of other timepieces, at any rate from the objective side, is, it may be said, *not* inexorably denied to man the investigating chronometer. So far from this being the case, it is the comparative study of other 'works,' taken in connection with the comparative study of the life-activities effected through their means, that affords the justification of *inferential* conclusions concerning the psychical processes of animals. This view of the matter, in which I concur, does not seem to me wholly to invalidate the chronometer analogy; but it does suggest a modification, and further development of the analogy.

The chronometer, we will suppose, is acquainted through introspection with its own psychology, and is able to take to pieces the works of other timepieces. It finds a number of chronometers whose works are all practically identical, and as it believes, but cannot demonstrate without taking itself to pieces, just like its own; and it is led to the inference that their psychology is similar to its own. It finds also a number of other timepieces whose works are constructed on similar principles, and differ chiefly in their being less highly finished and somewhat less complex; and it is led to the inference that their psychology, though less developed and less complex than its own, has probably been evolved on similar lines. But when it comes to the kitchen clock, it finds certain general similarities, cog-wheels and chains and so forth, but it also discovers principles of construction so different, the weights and the pendulum being so unlike its own balance-wheel and escapement, that it hesitates to draw any positive and definite conclusions. It sees that though the psychology of the kitchen clock may be closely analogous to its own, it may be quite different. It refuses to express a definite opinion on the psychology of the kitchen clock.

To apply the analogy in this modified form. Man, by anatomical and physiological research, has found in other men cerebral hemispheres with sensory-centres, control-centres, and so forth, similar to those which he believes that he individually possesses; and he infers that their psychology is of like nature to his own. He also finds in other vertebrates cerebral hemispheres, with sensory-centres and so forth, differing from man's chiefly in mass and complexity; and he infers that their psychology, though less developed and less complex than his own, has probably been evolved on similar lines. But when he comes to the insect, the crustacean, the mollusc, not to mention the worms, the sea-anemone, or the amæba, he finds nervous systems so different in types of structure from his own, that he hesitates to draw any definite and positive conclusions concerning the psychical states of these animals. It is true that there are nerve-fibres and nerve-cells; but the manner of their arrangement is so different from that of the vertebrates to which he belongs, that the careful student of zoological psychology is forced to conclude, that though the psychical states of insects and crustacea may be similar to those of man, they may be markedly dissimilar.

It may indeed be contended that community of environment—the joint-tenancy of the same world—must necessarily beget community of psychical faculty to meet the requirements of that environment. But while admitting the soundness of this argument so far as it goes, I venture to submit that it does not go far. For why should the community of psychical nature be greater than that of physical nature? The anatomy or the physiology of insects, for example, differs tolerably widely from that of man; why then should he suppose that their *psychical* endowments are more closely similar? Both physical nature and psychical nature are so to speak moulded in accordance with the environment. To both the argument of a joint-tenancy of the world applies. The physical nature being widely divergent from that of man, is it not reasonable to suppose that the psychical nature is, or at least may be, also widely divergent?

No one can study with any attention and care the habits and activities of such insects as ants and bees, without feeling convinced that they profit by experience and that their actions are under control. It is true that at present we know little about the physiology of this control, and of the relation of control centres to automatic centres. But this may sooner or later be remedied by an extension of our knowledge of the nerve-physiology of insects. I am the last to think of counselling any abatement of zeal in the fascinating study of the activities, and of the minute anatomy and physiology of the higher invertebrate forms of life. But I am of opinion that students in this department of investigation may do well to lay to heart the lesson conveyed by the analogy of the chronometer and the kitchen clock. In any case, in an introduction to comparative psychology, I feel bound to lay stress on the necessity for the greatest caution in the psychical interpretation of insect activities; and I feel justified in restricting myself, in this work, to a consideration of the psychical states which we may infer to be associated with the functional activity of the cerebral hemispheres in the higher vertebrates.

[From *An Introduction to Comparative Psychology* (London: Walter Scott Ltd., 1894), 36–41.]

JAMES SULLY

58 Studies of Childhood

The most obvious source of interest in the doings of infancy lies in its primitiveness. At the cradle we are watching the beginnings of things, the first tentative thrustings forward into life. Our modern science is before all things historical and genetic, going back to beginnings so as to understand the later and more complex phases of things as the outcome of these beginnings. The same kind of curiosity which prompts the geologist to get back to the first stages in the building up of the planet, or the biologist to search out the pristine forms of life, is beginning to urge the student of man to discover by a careful study of infancy the way in which human life begins to take its characteristic forms.

The appearance of Darwin's name among those who have deemed the child worthy of study suggests that the subject is closely connected with natural history. However man in his proud maturity may be related to Nature, it is certain that in his humble inception he is immersed in Nature and saturated with her. As we all know, the lowest races of mankind stand in close proximity to the animal world. The same is true of the infants of civilised races. Their life is outward and visible, forming a part of nature's spectacle; reason and will, the noble prerogatives of humanity, are scarce discernible; sense, appetite, instinct, these animal functions seem to sum up the first year of human life.

To the evolutionist, moreover, the infant exhibits a still closer kinship to the natural world. In the successive stages of fœtal development he sees the gradual unfolding of human lineaments out of a widely typical animal form. And even after birth he can discern new evidences of this genealogical relation of the 'lord' of creation to his inferiors. How significant, for example, is the fact recently established by a medical man, Dr Louis Robinson, that the new-born infant is able just like the ape to suspend his whole weight by grasping a small horizontal rod.[1]

Yet even as nature-object for the biologist the child presents distinctive attributes. Though sharing in animal instinct, he shares in it only to a very small extent. The most striking characteristic of the new-born offspring of man is its unpreparedness for life. Compare with the young of other animals the infant so feeble and incapable. He can neither use his limbs nor see the distance of objects as a new-born chick or calf is able to do. His brain-centres are, we are told, in a pitiable state of undevelopment—and are not even securely encased within their bony covering. Indeed, he resembles for all the world a public building which has to be opened by a given date, and is found when the day arrives to be in a humiliating state of incompleteness.

This fact of the special helplessness of the human off spring at birth, of its long period of dependence on parental or other aids—a period which, probably, tends to grow longer as civilisation advances—is rich in biological and sociological significance. For one thing, it presupposes a specially high development of the protective and fostering instincts in the human parents, and particularly the mother—for if the helpless wee thing were not met by these instincts, what would become of our race? It is probable, too, as Mr Spencer and others have argued, that the institution by nature of this condition of infantile weakness has reacted on the social affections of the race, helping to develop our pitifulness for all frail and helpless things.

Nor is this all. The existence of the infant, with its large and imperative claims, has been a fact of capital importance in the development of social customs. Ethnological researches show that communities have been much exercised with the problem of infancy, have paid it the homage due to its supreme sacredness, girding it about with a whole group of protective and beneficent customs.[2]

Enough has been said, perhaps, to show the far-reaching significance of babyhood to the modern savant. It is hardly too much to say that it has become one of the most eloquent of nature's phenomena, telling us at once of our affinity to the animal world, and of the forces by which our race has, little by little, lifted itself to so exalted a position above this world; and so it has happened that not merely to the perennial baby-worshipper, the mother, and not merely to the poet touched with the mystery of far-off things, but to the grave man of science the infant has become a centre of lively interest.

Nevertheless, it is not to the mere naturalist that the babe reveals all its significance. Physical organism as it seems to be more than anything else, hardly more than a vegetative thing indeed, it carries with it the germ of a human consciousness, and this consciousness begins to expand and to form itself into a truly human shape from the very beginning. And here a new source of interest presents itself. It is the human psychologist, the student of those impalpable, unseizable, evanescent phenomena which we call 'state of consciousness,' who has a supreme interest, and a scientific property in these first years of a human existence. What is of most account in these crude tentatives at living after the human fashion is the play of mind, the first spontaneous manifestations of recognition, of reasoning expectation, of feelings of sympathy and antipathy, of definite persistent purpose.

Rude, inchoate, vague enough, no doubt, are these first groping movements of a human mind: yet of supreme value to the psychologist just because they are the first. If, reflects the psychologist, he can only get at this baby's consciousness so as to understand what is passing there, he will be in an infinitely better position to find his way through the intricacies of the adult consciousness. It may be, as we shall see by-and-by, that the baby's mind is not so perfectly simple, so absolutely primitive as it at first looks. Yet it is the simplest type of human consciousness to which we can have access. The investigator of this consciousness can never take any known sample of the animal mind as his starting point if for no other reason for this, that while possessing many of the elements of the human mind, it presents these in so unlike, so peculiar a pattern.

In this genetic tracing back of the complexities of man's mental life to their primitive elements in the child's consciousness, questions of peculiar interest will arise. A problem which though having a venerable antiquity is still full of meaning concerns the precise relation of the higher forms of intelligence and of sentiment to the elementary facts of the individual's life-experience. Are we to regard all our ideas, even those of God, as woven by the mind out of its experiences, as Locke thought, or have we certain 'innate ideas' from the first? Locke thought he could settle this point by observing children. To-day, when the philosophic emphasis is laid not on the date of appearance of the 'innate' intuition, but on its originality and spontaneity, this method of interrogating the child's mind may seem less promising. Yet if of less philosophical importance than was once supposed, it is of great psychological importance. There are certain questions, such as that of how we come to see things at a distance from us, which can be approached most advantageously by a study of infant movements. In like manner I believe the growth of a moral sentiment, of that feeling of reverence for duty to which Kant gave so eloquent an expression, can only be understood by the most painstaking observation of the mental activities of the first years.

There is, however, another, and in a sense a larger, source of psychological interest in studying the processes and development of the infant mind. It was pointed out above that to the evolutional biologist the child exhibits man in his kinship to the lower sentient world. This same evolutional point of view enables the psychologist to connect the unfolding of an infant's mind with something which has gone before, with the mental history of the race. According to this way of looking at infancy the successive phases of its mental life are a brief *resumé* of the more important features in the slow upward progress of the species. The periods dominated successively by sense and appetite, by blind wondering and superstitious fancy, and by a calmer observation and a juster reasoning about things, these steps mark the pathway both of the child-mind and of the race-mind. [. . .]

There are evolutionists who hold that in the early manifested tendencies of the child, we can discern signs of a hereditary transmission of the effects of ancestral experiences and activities. His first manifestations of rage, for example, are a survival of actions of remote ancestors in their life and death struggles. The impulse of obedience, which is as much a characteristic of the child as that of disobedience, may in like manner be regarded as a transmitted rudiment of a long practised action of socialised ancestors. This idea of an increment of intelligence and moral disposition, earned for the individual not by himself but by his ancestors, has its peculiar interest. It gives a new meaning to human progress to suppose that the dawn of infant intelligence, instead of being a return to a primitive darkness, contains from the first a faint light reflected on it from the lamp of racial intelligence which has preceded that instead of a return to the race's starting point, the lowest form of the school of experience, it is a start in a higher form, the promotion being a reward conferred on the child for the exertions of his ancestors. Psychological observation will be well employed in scanning the features of the infant's mind in order to see whether they yield evidence of such ancestral dowering.

So much with respect to the rich and varied scientific interest attaching to the movements of the child's mind. [. . .]

Children are quite capable of finding their way, partly at least, to the idea that the soul has its lodgment in the head. But it is long before this thought grows clear. This may be seen in children's talk, as when a girl of four spoke of her dolly as having no sense in her *eyes*. Even when a child learns from others that we think with our brains he goes on supposing that our thoughts travel down to the mouth when we speak.

Very interesting in connexion with the first stages of development of the idea of self is the experience of the mirror. It would be absurd to expect a child when first placed before a mirror to recognise his own face. He will smile at the reflexion as early as the tenth week, though this is probably merely an expression of pleasure at the sight of a bright object. If held in the nurse's or father's arms to a glass when about six months old a baby will at once show that he recognises the image of the familiar face of the latter by turning round to the real face, whereas he does not recognise his own. He appears at first and for some months to take it for a real object, sometimes smiling to it as to a stranger and even kissing it, or, as in the case of a little girl (fifteen months old), offering it things and saying 'Ta' (sign of acceptance). In many cases curiosity prompts to an attempt to grasp the mirror-figure with the hand, to turn up the glass, or to put the hand behind it in order to see what is really there. This is very much like the behaviour of monkeys before a mirror, as described by Darwin and others. Little by little the child gets used to the reflexion, and then by noting certain agreements between his bodily self and the image, as the movement of his hands when he points, and partly, too, by a kind of inference of analogy from the doubling of other things by the mirror, he reaches the idea that the reflexion belongs to himself. By the sixtieth week Preyer's boy had associated the name of his mother with her image, pointing to it when asked where she was. By the twenty-first month he did the same thing in the case of his own image. [. . .]

The child of six, with his shock of curls, refuses to believe that he is the same as the hairless baby whose photograph the mother shows him. How different, how new, a being a child feels on a Sunday morning after the extra weekly cleansing and brushing and draping. The bodily appearance is a very big slice of the content of most people's self-consciousness, and to the child it is almost everything.

But in time the conscious self, which thinks and suffers and wills, comes to be dimly discerned. I believe that a real advance towards this true self-consciousness is marked by the appropriation and use of the difficult forms of language, 'I,' 'me,' 'mine'. [. . .]

The mystery of self-existence has probably been a puzzle to many a thoughtful child. A lady, a well-known writer of fiction, sends me the following recollection of her early thought on this subject: 'The existence of other people seemed natural: it was the "I" that seemed so strange to me. That I should be able to perceive, to think, to cause other people to act, seemed to me quite to be expected, but the power of feeling and acting and moving about myself, under the guidance of some internal self, amazed me continually.'

It is of course hard to say how exactly the child thinks about this inner self. It seems to me probable that, allowing for the great differences in reflective power, children in general, like uncivilised races, tend to materialise it, thinking of it dimly as a film-like shadow-like likeness of the visible self.

[From *Studies of Childhood* (New York: Appleton, 1896), 4–9, 112–15.]

59 **Evolutionary Psychology Demands a Mind-Dust**

In a general theory of evolution the inorganic comes first, then the lowest forms of animal and vegetable life, then forms of life that possess mentality, and finally those like ourselves that possess it in a high degree. As long as we keep to the consideration of purely outward facts, even the most complicated facts of biology, our task as evolutionists is comparatively easy. We are dealing all the time with matter and its aggregations and separations; and although our treatment must perforce be hypothetical, this does not prevent it from being *continuous*. The point which as evolutionists we are bound to hold fast to is that all the new forms of being that make their appearance are really nothing more than results of the redistribution of the original and unchanging materials. The self-same atoms which, chaotically dispersed, made the nebula, now, jammed and temporarily caught in peculiar positions, form our brains; and the 'evolution' of the brains, if understood, would be simply the account of how the atoms came to be so caught and jammed. In this story no new *natures*, no factors not present at the beginning, are introduced at any later stage.

But with the dawn of consciousness an entirely new nature seems to slip in, something whereof the potency was *not* given in the mere outward atoms of the original chaos.

The enemies of evolution have been quick to pounce upon this undeniable discontinuity in the data of the world, and many of them, from the failure of evolutionary explanations at this point, have inferred their general incapacity all along the line. Everyone admits the entire incommensurability of feeling as such with material motion as such. 'A motion became a feeling!'—no phrase that our lips can frame is so devoid of apprehensible meaning. Accordingly, even the vaguest of evolutionary enthusiasts, when deliberately comparing material with mental facts, have been as forward as anyone else to emphasize the 'chasm' between the inner and the outer worlds.

'Can the oscillation of a molecule,' says Mr Spencer, 'be represented side by side with a nervous shock [he means a mental shock], and the two be recognized as one? No effort enables us to assimilate them. That a unit of feeling has nothing in common with a unit of motion, becomes more than ever manifest when we bring the two into juxtaposition.'[1] [. . .]

We forget that in the absence of some such superadded commenting intelligence (whether it be that of the animal itself, or only ours or Mr Darwin's), the reactions cannot be properly talked of as 'useful' or 'hurtful' at all. Considered merely physically, all that can be said of them is that *if* they occur in a certain way survival will as a matter of fact prove to be their incidental consequence. The organs themselves, and all the rest of the physical world, will, however, all the time be quite indifferent to this consequence, and would quite as cheerfully, the circumstances changed, compass the animal's destruction. In a word, survival can enter into a purely physiological discussion only as an *hypothesis made by an onlooker* about the future. But the moment you bring a consciousness into the midst, survival ceases to be a mere hypothesis. No longer is it, '*if* survival is to occur, then so and so must brain and other organs work.' It has now become an imperative decree: 'Survival *shall* occur, and therefore organs *must* so work!' *Real* ends appear for the first time now upon the world's stage. The conception of consciousness as a purely cognitive form of being, which is the pet way of regarding it in many idealistic schools, modern as well as ancient, is thoroughly anti-psychological, as the remainder of this book will show. Every actually existing consciousness seems to itself at any rate to be a *fighter for ends*, of which many, but for its presence, would not be ends at all. Its powers of cognition are mainly subservient to these ends, discerning which facts further them and which do not.

Now let consciousness only be what it seems to itself, and it will help an instable brain to compass its proper ends. The movements of the brain *per se* yield the means of attaining these ends mechanically, but only out of a lot of other ends, if so they may be called, which are not the proper ones of the animal, but often quite opposed. The brain is an instrument of possibilities, but of no certainties. But the consciousness, with its own ends present to it, and knowing also well which possibilities lead thereto and which away, will, if endowed with causal efficacy, reinforce the favorable possibilities and repress the unfavorable or indifferent ones. The nerve-currents, coursing through the cells and fibres, must in this case be supposed strengthened by the fact of their awaking one consciousness and dampened by awaking another. *How* such reaction of the consciousness upon the currents may occur must remain at present unsolved: it is enough for my purpose to have shown that it may not uselessly exist, and that the matter is less simple than the brain-automatists hold.

All the facts of the natural history of consciousness lend color to this view. Consciousness, for example, is only intense when nerve-processes are hesitant. In rapid, automatic, habitual action it sinks to a minimum. Nothing could be more fitting than this, if consciousness have the teleological function we suppose; nothing more meaningless, if not. Habitual actions are certain, and being in no danger of going astray from their end, need no extraneous help. In hesitant action, there seem many alternative possibilities of final nervous discharge. The feeling awakened by the nascent excitement of each alternative nerve-tract seems by its attractive or repulsive quality to determine whether the excitement shall abort or shall become complete. Where indecision is great, as before a dangerous leap, consciousness is agonizingly intense. Feeling, from this point of view, may be likened to a cross-section of the chain of nervous discharge, ascertaining the links already laid down, and groping among the fresh ends presented to it for the one which seems best to fit the case.

[From *The Principles of Psychology* (1890) (Cambridge, Mass.: Harvard University Press, 1981).]

ALFRED RUSSEL WALLACE

60 **Darwinism**

The Origin of the Moral and Intellectual Nature of Man

THE ARGUMENT FROM CONTINUITY

Mr Darwin's mode of argument consists in showing that the rudiments of most, if not of all, the mental and moral faculties of man can be detected in some animals. The manifestations of intelligence, amounting in some cases to distinct acts of reasoning, in many animals, are adduced as exhibiting in a much less degree the intelligence and reason of man. Instances of curiosity, imitation, attention, wonder, and memory are given; while examples are also adduced which may be interpreted as proving that animals exhibit kindness to their fellows, or manifest pride, contempt, and shame. Some are said to have the rudiments of language, because they utter several different sounds, each of which has a definite meaning to their fellows or to their young; others the rudiments of arithmetic, because they seem to count and remember up to three, four, or even five. A sense of beauty is imputed to them on account of their own bright colours or the use of coloured objects in their nests; while dogs, cats, and horses are said to have imagination, because they appear to be disturbed by dreams. Even some distant approach to the rudiments of religion is said to be found in the deep love and complete submission of a dog to his master.[1]

Turning from animals to man, it is shown that in the lowest savages many of these faculties are very little advanced from the condition in which they appear in the higher animals; while others, although fairly well exhibited, are yet greatly inferior to the point of development they have reached in civilised races. In particular, the moral sense is said to have been developed from the social instincts of savages, and to depend mainly on the enduring discomfort produced by any action which excites the general disapproval of the tribe. Thus, every act of an individual which is believed to be contrary to the interests of the tribe, excites its unvarying disapprobation and is held to be immoral; while every act, on the other hand, which is, as a rule, beneficial to the tribe, is warmly and constantly approved, and is thus considered to be right or moral. From the mental struggle, when an act that would benefit self is injurious to the tribe, there arises conscience; and thus the social instincts are the foundation of the moral sense and of the fundamental principles of morality.[2]

The question of the origin and nature of the moral sense and of conscience is far too vast and complex to be discussed here, and a reference to it has been introduced only to complete the sketch of Mr Darwin's view of the continuity and gradual development of all human faculties from the lower animals up to savages, and from savage up to civilised man. The point to which I wish specially to call attention is, that to prove continuity and the progressive development of the intellectual and moral faculties from animals to man, is not the same as proving that these faculties have been developed by natural selection; and this last is what Mr Darwin has hardly attempted, although to support his theory it was absolutely essential to prove it. Because man's physical structure has been developed from an animal form by natural selection, it does not necessarily follow that his mental nature, even though developed *pari passu* with it, has been developed by the same causes only. [. . .]

Independent Proof that the Mathematical, Musical, and Artistic Faculties have not been Developed under the Law of Natural Selection

The law of Natural Selection or the survival of the fittest is, as its name implies, a rigid law, which acts by the life or death of the individuals submitted to its action. From its very nature it can act only on useful or hurtful characteristics, eliminating the latter and keeping up the former to a fairly general level of efficiency. Hence it necessarily follows that the characters developed by its means will be present in all the individuals of a species, and, though varying, will not vary very widely from a common standard. The amount of variation we found, in our third chapter, to be about one-fifth or one-sixth of the mean value—that is, if the mean value were taken at 100, the variations would reach from 80 to 120, or somewhat more, if very large numbers were compared. In accordance with this law we find, that all those characters in man which were certainly essential to him during his early stages of development, exist in all savages with some approach to equality. In the speed of running, in bodily strength, in skill with weapons, in acuteness of vision, or in power of following a trail, all are fairly proficient, and the differences of endowment do not probably exceed the limits of variation in animals above referred to. So, in animal instinct or intelligence, we find the same general level of development. Every wren makes a fairly good nest like its fellows; every fox has an average amount of the sagacity of its race; while all the higher birds and mammals have the necessary affections and instincts needful for the protection and bringing-up of their offspring.

But in those specially developed faculties of civilised man which we have been considering, the case is very different. They exist only in a small proportion of individuals, while the difference of capacity between these favoured individuals and the average of mankind is enormous. Taking first the mathematical faculty, probably fewer than one in a hundred really possess it, the great bulk of the population having no natural ability for the study, or feeling the slightest interest in it.[3] And if we attempt to measure the amount of variation in the faculty itself between a first-class mathematician and the ordinary run of people who find any kind of calculation confusing and altogether devoid of interest, it is probable that the former could not be estimated at less than a hundred times the latter, and perhaps a thousand times would more nearly measure the difference between them.

The artistic faculty appears to agree pretty closely with the mathematical in its frequency. The boys and girls who, going beyond the mere conventional designs of children, draw what they *see*, not what they *know* to be the shape of things; who naturally sketch in perspective, because it is thus they see objects; who see, and represent in their sketches, the light and shade as well as the mere outlines of objects; and who can draw recognisable sketches of every one they know, are certainly very few compared with those who are totally incapable of anything of the kind. From some inquiries I have made in schools, and from my own observation, I believe that those who are endowed with this natural artistic talent do not exceed, even if they come up to, one per cent of the whole population.

The variations in the amount of artistic faculty are certainly very great, even if we do not take the extremes. The gradations of power between the ordinary man or woman 'who does not draw,' and whose attempts at representing any object, animate or inanimate, would be laughable, and the average good artist who, with a few bold strokes, can produce a recognisable and even effective sketch of a landscape, a street, or an animal, are very numerous; and we can hardly measure the difference between them at less than fifty or a hundred fold.

The musical faculty is undoubtedly, in its lower forms, less uncommon than either of the preceding, but it still differs essentially from the necessary or useful faculties in that it is almost entirely wanting in one-half even of civilised men. For every person who draws, as it were instinctively, there are probably five or ten who sing or play without having been taught and from mere innate love and perception of melody and harmony.[4] On the other hand, there are probably about as many who seem absolutely deficient in musical perception, who take little pleasure in it, who cannot perceive discords or remember tunes, and who could not learn to sing or play with any amount of study. The gradations, too, are here quite as great as in mathematics or pictorial art, and the special faculty of the great musical composer must be reckoned many hundreds or perhaps thousands of times greater than that of the ordinary 'unmusical' person above referred to.

It appears then, that, both on account of the limited number of persons gifted with the mathematical, the artistic, or the musical faculty, as well as from the enormous variations in its development, these mental powers differ widely from those which are essential to man, and are, for the most part, common to him and the lower animals; and that they could not, therefore, possibly have been developed in him by means of the law of natural selection. [. . .]

The Interpretation of the Facts

The facts now set forth prove the existence of a number of mental faculties which either do not exist at all or exist in a very rudimentary condition in savages, but appear almost suddenly and in perfect development in the higher civilised races. These same faculties are further distinguished by their sporadic character, being well developed only in a very small proportion of the community; and by the enormous amount of variation in their development, the higher manifestations of them being many times—perhaps a hundred or a thousand times—stronger than the lower. Each of these characteristics is totally inconsistent with any action of the law of natural selection in the production of the faculties referred to; and the facts, taken in their entirety, compel us to recognise some origin for them wholly distinct from that which has served to account for the animal characteristics— whether bodily or mental—of man.

[From *Darwinism* (London: Macmillan, 1912), 461–3, 469–73.]

DANIEL DENNETT

61 The Role of Language in Intelligence

> When ideas fail, words come in very handy.
> —ANONYMOUS

We are not like other animals; our minds set us off from them. That is the claim that inspires such passionate defense. It is curious that people who want so much to defend this difference should be so reluctant to examine the evidence in its favor coming from evolutionary biology, ethology, primatology, and cognitive science. Presumably, they are afraid they might learn that, although we are different, we aren't different *enough* to make the life-defining difference they cherish. For Descartes, after all, the difference was absolute and metaphysical: animals were just mindless automata; *we* have souls. Descartes and his followers have suffered calumny over the centuries at the hands of animal-lovers who have deplored his claim that animals have no souls. More theoretically minded critics have deplored his faintheartedness from the opposite pole: how could such a sound, ingenious mechanist flinch so badly when it came to making an exception for humanity? *Of course* our minds are our brains, and hence are ultimately just stupendously complex 'machines'; the difference between us and other animals is one of huge degree, not metaphysical kind. It is no coincidence, I have shown, that those who deplore Artificial Intelligence are also those who deplore evolutionary accounts of human mentality: if human minds are nonmiraculous products of evolution, then they are, in the requisite sense, artifacts, and all their powers must have an ultimately 'mechanical' explanation. We are descended from macros and made of macros, and nothing we can do is anything beyond the power of huge assemblies of macros (assembled in space and time).

Still, there is a huge difference between our minds and the minds of other species, a gulf wide enough even to make a moral difference. It is—it must be—due to two intermeshed factors, each of which requires a Darwinian explanation: (1) the brains we are born with have features lacking in other brains, features that have evolved under selection pressure over the last six million years or so, and (2) these features make possible an enormous elaboration of powers that accrue from the sharing of Design wealth through cultural transmission. [. . .]

I want to propose a framework in which we can place the various design options for brains, to see where their power comes from. It is an outrageously oversimplified structure, but idealization is the price one should often be willing to pay for synoptic insight. I call it the Tower of Generate-and-Test; as each new floor of the Tower gets constructed, it empowers the organisms at that level to find better and better moves, and find them more efficiently.

In the beginning—once the pump had been primed—there was Darwinian evolution of species by natural selection. A variety of candidate organisms were blindly generated by more or less arbitrary processes of recombination and mutation of genes. These organisms were field-tested, and only the best designs survived. This is the ground floor of the Tower. Let us call its inhabitants *Darwinian creatures*.

This process went through many millions of cycles, producing many wonderful designs, both plant and animal, and eventually among its novel creations were some designs with the property of phenotypic plasticity. The individual candidate organisms were not wholly designed at birth, or, in other words, there were elements of their design that could be adjusted by events that occurred during the field tests. [. . .] Some of these candidates,

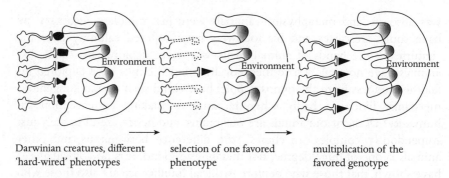

Darwinian creatures, different 'hard-wired' phenotypes   selection of one favored phenotype   multiplication of the favored genotype

Figure 1

we may suppose, were no better off than their hard-wired cousins, since they had no way of favoring (selecting for an encore) the behavioral options they were equipped to 'try out,' but others, we may suppose, were fortunate enough to have wired-in 'reinforcers' that happened to favor Smart Moves, actions that were better for their agents. These individuals thus confronted the environment by generating a variety of actions, which they tried out, one by one, until they found one that worked. We may call this subset of Darwinian creatures, the creatures with conditionable plasticity, *Skinnerian creatures*, since, as B. F. Skinner was fond of pointing out, operant conditioning is not just analogous to Darwinian natural selection; it is continuous with it. [. . .]

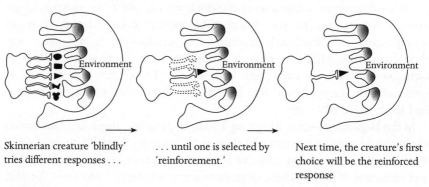

Skinnerian creature 'blindly' tries different responses . . .   . . . until one is selected by 'reinforcement.'   Next time, the creature's first choice will be the reinforced response

Figure 2

Skinnerian conditioning is a fine capacity to have, so long as you are not killed by one of your early errors. A better system involves *preselection* among all the possible behaviors or actions, weeding out the truly stupid options before risking them in the harsh world. We human beings are creatures capable of this third refinement, but we are not alone. We may call the beneficiaries of this third story in the Tower *Popperian creatures*, since, as Sir

Karl Popper once elegantly put it, this design enhancement 'permits our hypotheses to die in our stead.' Unlike the merely Skinnerian creatures, many of whom survive only because they make lucky first moves, Popperian creatures survive because they're smart enough to make better-than-chance first moves. Of course, they're just lucky to be smart, but that's better than just being lucky.

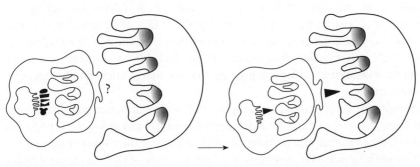

Popperian creature has an inner selective environment that previews candidate acts.

First time, the creature acts in a foresightful way (better than chance)

Figure 3

But how is this preselection in Popperian agents to be done? Where is the feedback to come from? It must come from a sort of *inner environment*—an inner something-or-other that is structured in such a way that the surrogate actions it favors are more often than not the very actions the real world would also bless, if they were actually performed. In short, the inner environment, whatever it is, must contain lots of *information* about the outer environment and its regularities. Nothing else (except magic) could provide preselection worth having. Now, here we must be very careful not to think of this inner environment as simply a replica of the outer world, with all its physical contingencies reproduced. (In such a miraculous toy world, the little hot stove in your head would be hot enough actually to burn the little finger in your head that you placed on it!) The information about the world has to be there, but it also has to be structured in such a way that there is a nonmiraculous explanation of how it got there, how it is maintained, and how it actually achieves the preselective effects that are its *raison d'être*.

Which animals are Popperian creatures, and which are merely Skinnerian? Pigeons were Skinner's favorite experimental animals, and he and his followers developed the technology of operant conditioning to a very sophisticated level, getting pigeons to exhibit quite bizarre and sophisticated learned behaviors. Notoriously, the Skinnerians never succeeded in proving that pigeons were *not* Popperian creatures, and research on a host of different species, from octopuses to fish to mammals, strongly suggests that if there are any purely Skinnerian creatures, capable only of blind trial-and-error learning, they are to be found among the simple invertebrates. The sea slug *Aplysia* has more or less replaced the pigeon as the focus of attention among those who study the mechanisms of simple conditioning. (Researchers unhesitatingly and uncontroversially rank species in terms of how intelligent they are. This involves no myopic endorsement of the Great Chain of Being, no unwarranted assumptions about climbing the ladder of progress. It depends on objective measures of cognitive competence. The octopus, for instance, is stunningly smart, a fact that would not be available to surprise us if there weren't ways of measuring intelligence that are independent of phylogenetic chauvinism.)

We do not differ from all other species in being Popperian creatures, then. Far from it; mammals and birds and reptiles and fish all exhibit the capacity to use information from their environments to presort their behavioral options before striking out. We have now reached the story of the Tower on which I want to build. Once we get to Popperian creatures, creatures whose brains have the potential to be shaped into inner environments with preselective prowess, what happens next? How does new information about the outer environment get incorporated into these brains? This is where *earlier* design decisions come back to haunt—to constrain—the designer. [. . .]

The successors to mere Popperian creatures are those whose inner environments are informed by the *designed* portions of the outer environment. We may call this sub-sub-subset of Darwinian creatures *Gregorian creatures*, since the British psychologist Richard Gregory is to my mind the pre-eminent theorist of the role of information (or, more exactly, what Gregory calls Potential Intelligence) in the creation of Smart Moves (or what Gregory calls Kinetic Intelligence). Gregory observes that a pair of scissors, as a well-designed artifact, is not just a result of intelligence, but an endower of intelligence (external Potential Intelligence), in a very straight-forward and intuitive sense: when you give someone a pair of scissors, you enhance his potential to arrive more safely and swiftly at Smart Moves. [. . .]

Anthropologists have long recognized that the advent of tool use accompanied a major increase in intelligence. Chimpanzees in the wild fish for termites with crudely prepared fishing sticks. This fact takes on further significance when we learn that not all chimpanzees have hit upon the trick; in some chimpanzee 'cultures,' termites are a present but unexploited food source. That reminds us that tool use is a two-way sign of intelligence; not only does it *require* intelligence to recognize and maintain a tool (let alone fabricate one), but tool use *confers* intelligence on those who are lucky enough to be given the tool. The better designed the tool (the more information embedded in its fabrication), the more Potential Intelligence it confers on its user. And among the pre-eminent tools, Gregory reminds us, are what he calls 'mind-tools': words.

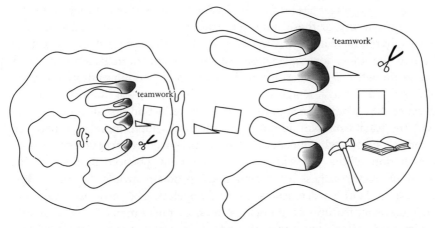

Gregorian creature imports mind-tools from the (cultural) environment; these improve both the generators and the testers.

Figure 4

Words and other mind-tools give a Gregorian creature an inner environment that permits it to construct ever more subtle move-generators and move-testers. Skinnerian creatures ask themselves, 'What do I do next?' and haven't a clue how to answer until they have taken some hard knocks. Popperian creatures make a big advance by asking themselves, 'What should I think about next?' before they ask themselves, 'What should I do next?' Gregorian creatures take a further big step by learning how to think better about what they should think about next—and so forth, a tower of further internal reflections with no fixed or discernible limit.

[From *Darwin's Dangerous Idea* (New York: Simon & Schuster, 1995), 370, 374–8.]

THOMAS NAGEL
....
62   What is it Like to be a Bat?

Consciousness is what makes the mind–body problem really intractable. Perhaps that is why current discussions of the problem give it little attention or get it obviously wrong. The recent wave of reductionist euphoria has produced several analyses of mental phenomena and mental concepts designed to explain the possibility of some variety of materialism, psychophysical identification, or reduction. 'But the problems dealt with are those common to this type of reduction and other types, and what makes the mind–body problem unique, [. . .] is ignored.

Every reductionist has his favorite analogy from modern science. It is most unlikely that any of these unrelated examples of successful reduction will shed light on the relation of mind to brain. But philosophers share the general human weakness for explanations of what is incomprehensible in terms suited for what is familiar and well understood, though entirely different. This has led to the acceptance of implausible accounts of the mental largely because they would permit familiar kinds of reduction. I shall try to explain why the usual examples do not help us to understand the relation between mind and body—why, indeed, we have at present no conception of what an explanation of the physical nature of a mental phenomenon would be. Without consciousness the mind–body problem would be much less interesting. With consciousness it seems hopeless. The most important and characteristic feature of conscious mental phenomena is very poorly understood. Most reductionist theories do not even try to explain it. And careful examination will show that no currently available concept of reduction is applicable to it. Perhaps a new theoretical form can be devised for the purpose, but such a solution, if it exists, lies in the distant intellectual future.

Conscious experience is a widespread phenomenon. It occurs at many levels of animal life, though we cannot be sure of its presence in the simpler organisms, and it is very difficult to say in general what provides evidence of it. (Some extremists have been prepared to deny it even of mammals other than man.) No doubt it occurs in countless forms totally unimaginable to us, on other planets in other solar systems throughout the universe. But no matter how the form may vary, the fact that an organism has conscious experience at all means, basically, that there is something it is like to be that organism. There may be further implications about the form of the experience; there may even (though I doubt it) be implications about the behavior of the organism. But fundamentally an organism has conscious mental states if and only if there is something that it is like to be that organism—something it is like for the organism.

We may call this the subjective character of experience. It is not captured by any of the familiar, recently devised reductive analyses of the mental, for all of them are logically compatible with its absence. It is not analyzable in terms of any explanatory system of functional states, or intentional states, since these could be ascribed to robots or automata that behaved like people though they experienced nothing. [. . .] It is useless to base the defense of materialism on any analysis of mental phenomena that fails to deal explicitly with their subjective character. For there is no reason to suppose that a reduction which seems plausible when no attempt is made to account for consciousness can be extended to include consciousness. Without some idea, therefore, of what the subjective character of experience is, we cannot know what is required of a physicalist theory.

While an account of the physical basis of mind must explain many things, this appears to be the most difficult. [. . .] If physicalism is to be defended, the phenomenological features must themselves be given a physical account. But when we examine their subjective character it seems that such a result is impossible. The reason is that every subjective phenomenon is essentially connected with a single point of view, and it seems inevitable that an objective, physical theory will abandon that point of view.

Let me first try to state the issue somewhat more fully than by referring to the relation between the subjective and the objective, or between the *pour-soi* and the *en-soi*. This is far from easy. Facts about what it is like to be an *X* are very peculiar, so peculiar that some may be inclined to doubt their reality, or the significance of claims about them. To illustrate the connection between subjectivity and a point of view, and to make evident the importance of subjective features, it will help to explore the matter in relation to an example that brings out clearly the divergence between the two types of conception, subjective and objective.

I assume we all believe that bats have experience. After all, they are mammals, and there is no more doubt that they have experience than that mice or pigeons or whales have experience. I have chosen bats instead of wasps or flounders because if one travels too far down the phylogenetic tree, people gradually shed their faith that there is experience there at all. Bats, although more closely related to us than those other species, nevertheless present a range of activity and a sensory apparatus so different from ours that the problem I want to pose is exceptionally vivid (though it certainly could be raised with other species). Even without the benefit of philosophical reflection, anyone who has spent some time in an enclosed space with an excited bat knows what it is to encounter a fundamentally *alien* form of life.

I have said that the essence of the belief that bats have experience is that there is something that it is like to be a bat. Now we know that most bats (the microchiroptera, to be precise) perceive the external world primarily by sonar, or echolocation, detecting the reflections, from objects within range, of their own rapid, subtly modulated, high-frequency shrieks. Their brains are designed to correlate the outgoing impulses with the subsequent echoes, and the information thus acquired enables bats to make precise discriminations of distance, size, shape, motion, and texture comparable to those we make by vision. But bat sonar, though clearly a form of perception, is not similar in its operation to any sense that we possess, and there is no reason to suppose that it is subjectively like anything we can experience or imagine. This appears to create difficulties for the notion of what it is like to be a bat. We must consider whether any method will permit us to extrapolate to the *particular*

inner life of the bat from our own case,[1] and if not, what alternative methods there may be for understanding the notion.

Our own experience provides the basic material for our imagination, whose range is therefore limited. It will not help to try to imagine that one has webbing on one's arms, which enables one to fly around at dusk and dawn catching insects in one's mouth; that one has very poor vision, and perceives the surrounding world by a system of reflected high-frequency sound signals; and that one spends the day hanging upside down by one's feet in an attic. In so far as I can imagine this (which is not very far), it tells me only what it would be like for *me* to behave as a bat behaves. But that is not the question. I want to know what it is like for a *bat* to be a bat. Yet if I try to imagine this, I am restricted to the resources of my own mind, and those resources are inadequate to the task. I cannot perform it either by imagining additions to my present experience, or by imagining segments gradually subtracted from it, or by imagining some combination of additions, subtractions, and modifications.

To the extent that I could look and behave like a wasp or a bat without changing my fundamental structure, my experiences would not be anything like the experiences of those animals. On the other hand, it is doubtful that any meaning can be attached to the supposition that I should possess the internal neurophysiological constitution of a bat. Even if I could by gradual degrees be transformed into a bat, nothing in my present constitution enables me to imagine what the experiences of such a future stage of myself thus metamorphosed would be like. The best evidence would come from the experiences of bats, if we only knew what they were like.

So if extrapolation from our own case is involved in the idea of what it is like to be a bat, the extrapolation must be incompletable. We cannot form more than a schematic conception of what it *is* like. For example, we may ascribe general *types* of experience on the basis of the animal's structure and behavior. Thus we describe bat sonar as a form of three-dimensional forward perception; we believe that bats feel some versions of pain, fear, hunger, and lust, and that they have other, more familiar types of perception besides sonar. But we believe that these experiences also have in each case a specific subjective character, which it is beyond our ability to conceive. And if there is conscious life else where in the universe, it is likely that some of it will not be describable even in the most general experiential terms available to us. [. . .]

If anyone is inclined to deny that we can believe in the existence of facts like this whose exact nature we cannot possibly conceive, he should reflect that in contemplating the bats we are in much the same position that intelligent bats or Martians would occupy if they tried to form a conception of what it was like to be us. The structure of their own minds might make it impossible for them to succeed, but we know they would be wrong to conclude that there is not anything precise that it is like to be us: that only certain general types of mental state could be ascribed to us (perhaps perception and appetite would be concepts common to us both; perhaps not). We know they would be wrong to draw such a skeptical conclusion because we know what it is like to be us. And we know that while it includes an enormous amount of variation and complexity, and while we do not possess the vocabulary to describe it adequately, its subjective character is highly specific, and in some respects describable in terms that can be understood only by creatures like us. The fact that we cannot expect ever to accommodate in our language a detailed description of Martian or bat phenomenology should not lead us to dismiss as meaningless the claim that bats and Martians have experiences fully comparable in richness of detail to our own. It would be fine if someone were to develop concepts and a theory that enabled us to think about those things; but such an understanding may be permanently denied to us by the limits of our nature. [. . .]

This bears directly on the mind–body problem. For if the facts of experience—facts about what it is like *for* the experiencing organism—are accessible only from one point of view, then it is a mystery how the true character of experiences could be revealed in the physical operation of that organism. The latter is a domain of objective facts *par excellence*—the kind that can be observed and understood from many points of view and by individuals with differing perceptual systems. There are no comparable imaginative obstacles to the acquisition of knowledge about bat neurophysiology by human scientists, and intelligent bats or Martians might learn more about the human brain than we ever will.

This is not by itself an argument against reduction. A Martian scientist with no understanding of visual perception could understand the rainbow, or lightning, or clouds as physical phenomena, though he would never be able to understand the human concepts of rainbow, lightning, or cloud, or the place these things occupy in our phenomenal world. The objective nature of the things picked out by these concepts could be apprehended by him because, although the concepts themselves are connected with a particular point of view and a particular visual phenomenology, the things apprehended from that point of view are not: they are observable from the point of view but external to it; hence they can be comprehended from other points of view also, either by the same organisms or by others. Lightning has an objective character that is not exhausted by its visual appearance, and this can be investigated by a Martian without vision. To be precise, it has a *more* objective character than is revealed in its visual appearance. [. . .]

In the case of experience, on the other hand, the connection with a particular point of view seems much closer. It is difficult to understand what could be meant by the *objective* character of an experience, apart from the particular point of view from which its subject apprehends it. After all, what would be left of what it was like to be a bat if one removed the viewpoint of the bat? But if experience does not have, in addition to its subjective character, an objective nature that can be apprehended from many different points of view, then how can it be supposed that a Martian investigating my brain might be observing physical processes which were my mental processes (as he might observe physical processes which were bolts of lightning), only from a different point of view? How, for that matter, could a human physiologist observe them from another point of view?

[From 'What is it Like to be a Bat', *Philosophical Review*, 83 (1975), 435–44.]

ROGER PENROSE

63   Natural Selection of Algorithms?

If we suppose that the action of the human brain, conscious or otherwise, is merely the acting out of some very complicated algorithm, then we must ask how such an extraordinarily effective algorithm actually came about. The standard answer, of course, would be 'natural selection'. As creatures with brains evolved, those with the more effective algorithms would have a better tendency to survive and therefore, on the whole, had more progeny. These progeny also tended to carry more effective algorithms than their cousins, since they inherited the ingredients of these better algorithms from their parents; so gradually the algorithms improved—not necessarily steadily, since there could have been considerable fits and starts in their evolution—until they reached the remarkable status that we (would apparently) find in the human brain. [. . .]

Even according to my own viewpoint, there would have to be *some* truth in this picture, since I envisage that much of the brain's action is indeed algorithmic, and—as the reader will have inferred from the above discussion—I am a strong believer in the power of natural selection. But I do not see how natural selection, in itself, can evolve algorithms which could have the kind of conscious judgements of the *validity* of other algorithms that we seem to have.

Imagine an ordinary computer program. How would *it* have come into being? Clearly not (directly) by natural selection! Some human computer programmer would have conceived of it and would have ascertained that it correctly carries out the actions that it is supposed to. (Actually, most complicated computer programs contain errors—usually minor, but often subtle ones that do not come to light except under unusual circumstances. The presence of such errors does not substantially affect my argument.) Sometimes a computer program might itself have been 'written' by another, say a 'master' computer program, but then the master program itself would have been the product of human ingenuity and insight; or the program might well be pieced together from ingredients some of which were the products of other computer programs. But in all cases the validity and the very conception of the program would have ultimately been the responsibility of (at least) one human consciousness.

One can imagine, of course, that this need not have been the case, and that, given enough time, the computer programs might somehow have evolved spontaneously by some process of natural selection. [. . .]

One [. . .] might imagine some kind of natural selection process being effective for producing *approximately* valid algorithms. Personally, I find this very difficult to believe, however. Any selection process of this kind could act only on the *output* of the algorithms and not directly on the ideas underlying the actions of the algorithms. This is not simply extremely in efficient; I believe that it would be totally unworkable. In the first place, it is not easy to ascertain what an algorithm actually is, simply by examining its output. (It would be an easy matter to construct two quite different simple Turing machine actions for which the output tapes did not differ until, say, the 2^{65536} place—and this difference could never be spotted in the entire history of the universe!) Moreover, the slightest 'mutation' of an algorithm (say a slight change in a Turing machine specification, or in its input tape) would tend to render it totally useless, and it is hard to see how actual *improvements* in algorithms could ever arise in this random way. (Even *deliberate* improvements are difficult without 'meanings' being available. This is particularly borne out by the not-infrequent circumstances when an inadequately documented and complicated computer program needs to be altered or corrected; and the original programmer has departed or perhaps died. Rather than try to disentangle all the various meanings and intentions that the program implicitly depended upon, it is probably easier just to scrap it and start all over again!)

Perhaps some much more 'robust' way of specifying algorithms could be devised, which would not be subject to the above criticisms. In a way, this is what I am saying myself. The 'robust' specifications are the *ideas* that underlie the algorithms. But ideas are things that, as far as we know, need conscious minds for their manifestation. We are back with the problem of what consciousness actually is, and what it can actually do that unconscious objects are incapable of—and how on earth natural selection has been clever enough to evolve *that* most remarkable of qualities.

The products of natural selection are indeed astonishing. The little knowledge that I have myself acquired about how the human brain works—and, indeed, any other living thing—leaves me almost dumbfounded with awe and admiration. The working of an individual neuron is extraordinary, but the neurons themselves are organized together in a quite remarkable way, with vast numbers of connections wired up at birth, ready for all the tasks that will be needed later on. It is not just consciousness itself that is remarkable, but all the paraphernalia that appear to be needed in order to support it!

If we ever do discover in detail what quality it is that allows a physical object to become conscious, then, conceivably, we might be able to construct such objects for ourselves—though they might not qualify as 'machines' in the sense of the word that we mean it now. One could imagine that these objects could have a tremendous advantage over us, since they could be designed *specifically* for the task at hand, namely to *achieve consciousness*. They would not have to grow from a single cell. They would not have to carry around the 'baggage' of their ancestry (the old and 'useless' parts of the brain or body that survive in ourselves only because of the 'accidents' of our remote ancestry). One might imagine that, in view of these advantages, such objects could succeed in *actually* superseding human beings, where (in the opinions of such as myself) the algorithmic computers are doomed to subservience.

But there may well be more to the issue of consciousness than this. Perhaps, in some way, our consciousness does depend on our heritage, and the thousands of millions of years of *actual* evolution that lie behind us. To my way of thinking, there is still something mysterious about evolution [. . .] 'groping' towards some future purpose. Things at least *seem* to organize themselves somewhat better than they 'ought' to, just on the basis of blind-chance evolution and natural selection. It may well be that such appearances are quite deceptive. There seems to be something about the way that the laws of physics work, which allows natural selection to be a much more effective process than it would be with just arbitrary laws.

[From *The Emperor's New Mind* (New York: Vantage, 1990), 534–8.]

....

Mind and Self: Divided, Constructed, and Multiplied

....

INTRODUCTION

The mythic origins of Athenian independence include the legendary hero Theseus who made his way to Crete, descended into the bowels of the Labyrinth, and killed the Minotaur. This half-man, half-bull monster had long been fed innocent Athenian youth as an annual sacrifice exacted by King Minos, whose daughter, Ariadne, gave Theseus the golden cord by which he could retrace his steps and escape from the Labyrinth. Every year Greek cities would celebrate the triumph of Theseus, whose ship would make the rounds from port to port. Routine maintenance of this worthy craft required the removal of rotten planks and the addition of new wood to keep it afloat. Over the course of time virtually all of the original wood had been replaced, leading to one of those intriguing philosophical questions: is it still the Ship of Theseus? One might even ask whether—had the rotten planks been refinished and then used to fabricate yet another ship—the newly fashioned vessel was the 'real' Ship of Theseus.

One of the defining features of mind is that its contents are uniquely owned in that every idea or feeling or desire is *someone's*. The contents of consciousness can be expressed but, it was long thought, not relocated. One can describe one's toothache, but not give it to another. Even if Smith and Jones both have toothaches of identical intensity and even felt in precisely the same part of the left incisor, each nonetheless has a uniquely possessed sensation. In other words, no principle or law of identities can collapse the sensations (thoughts, desires, feelings) experienced by two persons into one. Mental contents, on this understanding, are unlike pencils, peaches, or prawns. It is in the very nature of 'mind' that each mind is someone's and no other's, and that its contents are authoritatively known by that someone and only non-authoritatively if at all by any other. Moreover, the arena of experience is one that it is unstable from moment to moment, as is every feature of body and brain. Nonetheless, one remains one's *self* through it all. Like the Ship of Theseus, it would seem that there is some sort of continuing identity even as the physical composition is radically altered.

How might the dominant theories of mind address the foregoing? When the ancient philosophers asked whether Socrates seated and Socrates standing are the same the question was understood as addressing the nature of essence (*ousia*) or just what it is that makes something what it is. The Aristotelian claim that the form of a thing is what makes it the kind of thing it is is an early version of this *essentialism*. Descartes's claim that he is a *res cogitans*—a *thinking thing*—is another version. But, as we have seen in earlier sections, notions of 'essences' and 'substances' are problematic, at least to the extent they are accorded real existence apart from the sensible attributes by which they can be known. Ryle's 'category mistake' points to the problem of disembodied 'essences' in much the way that Ockham pointed to the incoherence of medieval *realist* theories of the universal.

Common-sense or 'folk' conceptions of minds and persons persist in affirming one or another form of essentialism. The common-sense under-standing is that one must have a mind for experiences to be had; that even though one's body and brain are in constant flux, there is an 'essential' or 'substantial' *self* that endures through all such (merely) physical transforma-tions; that not only is Socrates the same when seated or when standing, but is the same Socrates when sleeping as when debating Protagoras. One retains one's defining and 'essential' nature even as one matures, learns things, moves to a new house.

What, then, of total amnesia? What, then, of insanity? If there is this inextricable relationship between mind and one's *essential* nature, must the latter not be subject to profound transformations once the mental domain is itself thus transformed? John Locke's answer was a decisive and highly controversial *Yes*, as it had to be in light of the empiricistic theory of mind advanced in his *Essay*. If, indeed, the mind is furnished solely by experience, then it follows that one's very identity is forged out of one's experiences. Locke illustrates the point with the thought-experiment involving the Prince and the Cobbler. In the course of sleep each has the contents of mind relocated into the mind of the other. It is clear to Locke that on arising the next day each would be the same man but not the same *person*. Although their corporeal identities would remain unchanged, their *personal identity* would now have been entirely transformed. We would have a prince in cobbler's clothing. It is the content of consciousness itself that makes one the person one is. The content is the accumulation of experiences over the course of a lifetime. The 'self' or one's personal identity, then, is constructed out of these experiences and is simply a non-entity in their absence.

As might be expected, Locke's theory would endure attacks from the exquisite wits of early eighteenth-century England. An actual club was formed to hold up to mirthful criticism what was taken to be the nonsensical productions of the philosophical mind. Taking their name from Arbuthnot's famous Dr Scriblerus, this group of Scriblerians set out to save the ordinary citizen from the confusions spawned by science and metaphysics. Swift was the most famous member of the group. In *Gulliver's Travels* he presents the airborne island of Laputa, operated by a scientific elite, busily extracting sunshine from green plants and promising to perfect the technique so that sunlight will soon be sold at a more reasonable price. The target, of course, was the Royal Society, founded in 1660, and, by Swift's time, already enjoying an authority the Scriblerians judged to be excessive and dangerous. With Locke's account of the Prince and the Cobbler, the Scriblerians had a field day, concluding with the assurance that there never could be another criminal prosecution: by the time the defendant was brought to trial, he would no longer be the same *person* who had committed the act.

David Hume did not underestimate the cogency of criticisms based on the fact that one's personal identity survives intact even as experiences become ever more numerous, various, and replaced. He, too, was sceptical of essentialism and committed to an empiricistic theory of mental life. He leaves no doubt about his own metaphysical attachments when he owns that in every search for his 'self' he can find nothing but a *bundle of sensations*. How, then, is this 'self' continuous, even as the sensations vary? Hume's theory of mind is associationistic. It is by way of the laws of association that ideas become joined into trains and ensembles. Chief among the laws is that of *cause and effect*, itself reducible to *constant conjunctions* of events or objects in experience. Once formed, however, the chains or bundles retain their character even as one item or link is removed and replaced by another. The metaphor of the parade formation is illustrative. Hume reasons that, just as the parade formation remains intact when one marcher is removed and replaced by another, so the continuity of 'self'—as but a bundle of perceptions—is preserved even when one or another element is jettisoned and another is put in its place. No separate 'self' need be posited, for the 'self'—far from being some mysterious substance that ideas inhere in—is no more than the bundles of ideas held together by association.

Thomas Reid rejects both the Lockian and the Humian accounts, but for somewhat different reasons. In the passages reprinted here, taken from the third of his *Essays on the Intellectual Powers of Man*, he understands Locke to be contending that one's personal identity is no more than what is stored in the mind, thus equating personal identity with memory. Reid finds this both logically and psychologically absurd. First the logical defect, which was anticipated by George Berkeley in his *Alciphron*: imagine an officer decorated for valour and recalling the time he had been chastised for stealing fruit from the orchard. Call the officer 'B' and the punished young boy 'A'. On Locke's account, A and B are identical owing to the shared contents of consciousness. Now consider the aged general who well remembers the day of his decoration but has no recollection whatever of the young boy. Call the aged general 'C'. What we now have is, 'A is identical to B', and 'B is identical to C' but 'A is *not* identical to C'. The principles of associativity and commutativity being violated, the identity simply fails. This, however, is only at the level of logic. The manifest defect of the Lockian account is that it seems to establish one's identity on the grounds of one's memory, where memory itself might be delusional and insane. Recalling oneself to have lost a decisive battle at Waterloo cannot constitute one as Napoleon no matter how vivid the recollection might be.

The Humian theory also fails, according to Reid, but for reasons rather more subtle. A summary should be sufficient. Locke had accepted the reality of a 'self' in whom various experiences inhere, the identity of that 'self' being determined by the conscious contents of these experiences. Hume's theory of personal identity is more radical in that it accepts only the experiences themselves; the 'bundle of perceptions' knitted together by the laws of association and surviving not *in* some self but *as* a self. Reid in his *Inquiry* had found in this account 'an odd strain of humour' in the author, for Hume certainly seems to be addressing actual persons and also would hope to enjoy credit himself for writing such deathless prose. For there to be treason, says Reid, there must be a traitor; and for Hume to look for his *self*, there must be a Hume doing the looking.

There is much more to the criticism than this, however. Hume's theory of personal identity depends utterly on his theory of *cause and effect* and, more generally, his associationistic theory of mind. Elsewhere in his *An Inquiry into the Human Mind* Reid had challenged Hume's account of causal concepts. To the extent that Reid had successfully refuted the Humian theory of causation in that work—and to the extent that that theory is the linchpin of the theory of 'self'—Reid can claim to make short work of the latter.

Hume's theory of causation is a psychological theory about the manner in which we come to consider events or objects as causing anything. It is important to keep in mind that Hume is (almost certainly) not sceptical about events in the world being caused; rather, he is at pains to establish the only grounds on which we ever arrive at the *concept* of causation. As he will not accept it as in any sense innate or intuitive, he must explain it in terms consistent with his overall empiricistic philosophy. The explanation is this: we come to regard any event or object as the cause of another when the two have been 'constantly conjoin'd' in experience. All other factors being equal, 'A' is the cause of 'B' when (*a*) A and B have occurred together reliably, (*b*) they have been contiguous in time and place, and (*c*) they share with other such pairings the property of similarity or resemblance. Thus, the chain of thoughts and the construction of ideas in the mind come about through that principle of cause and effect understood as a product of past experience.

Reid rejects this theory on several grounds. First, there are many events that are constantly conjoined but where 'no man come of age' regards them as causally related. No two events, says Reid, have been as constantly conjoined as day and night, yet we never regard one as the 'cause' of the other. Second, no one must engage repetitively in an action in order to determine that he, in fact, is the source of the effects thereupon brought about. Furthermore, were the mind possessed of no resources beyond that by which it can record temporal coincidences, it would never attain the idea of one of the terms being the *cause* of the other. Rather, argues Reid, our concept of causation is an inference drawn from our direct awareness of our own *active powers*. From the knowledge we have of ourselves as the cause of our intended actions, we then infer that regular occurrences in the external world must also be brought about by some sort of power or agency. Had we not this intuitive recognition of ourselves as the source of such effects we would never conclude that anything external to ourselves had causal efficacy. But to recognize ourselves as having such powers presupposes our *selves* in the root-intuitive sense. Reid concludes that the 'self' is not derived from experience but is at once the necessary, irreducible, underived, and unanalysable entity, absent which there cannot be experience. Does this cast him as a defender of the dreaded 'substance' theories of old? Yes and no. Reid finds no more in the word 'substance' than what he calls elsewhere in his writings *an unchanging object of thought*.

William James was quite content to accept that a person has as many social selves as there are persons who recognize him! James also saw fit to distinguish between the material, social, spiritual, and 'pure Ego' senses of self, finding more than humour in the old chestnut according to which 'the human person is composed of . . . soul, body and clothes'. One's identity is socially constructed as well as corporeally defined. But parents and possessions and neighbourhoods, too, are parts of the *self*, and when these are removed so much of the self is thus modified.

The spiritual self is the term James employs to cover 'the most enduring and intimate part of the self, that which we most verily seem to be'. Here he is referring to one's conscience, one's moral values, one's will and purpose. Where these are altered, one may truly be said to be alienated from oneself: *alienatus a se*. More fundamental, however, seems to be '*this self of all the other selves*', which for James is a kind of feeling, a genuine sensation of sorts utterly distinct from rational or cognitive operations; in James's own case, feelings associated with 'cephalic movements' of some sort. He will not vote in this case either for empiricist or transcendentalist, but will (as usual) permit his own unfailing experiences to dispose of the matter. He can't find or sense a spirit, but he is sure of the sensible occurrences within his body that seem to ground 'this self of all the other selves'.

John Dewey's pragmatic and sociological position on mind and conscious-ness is something of a middle course between a self that is known intuitively and one that is no more than a bundle of connected experiences. For Dewey, 'mind' represents the various modes of activity and concern that fill out the actually lived lives of persons. Memory, attention, purpose, solicitude, anxiety, and all the other words idiomatically used to describe the moment-to-moment cares of life exhaust the content of 'mind' as such. Dewey concludes that, 'Mind is primarily a verb', which denotes our adjustments to and dealings with the situations in which we find ourselves. The linguistic nuances applied to things mental record no more (and no less) than the great variety of such situations: scientific, executive, artistic, commercial. It is proper, then, to deconstruct mind in such a way as to respect the range and depth of its performances, but at the same time to eliminate anything suggesting an existence independent from these actual practices.

With greater philosophical originality but also more elusively does Ludwig Wittgenstein develop this same understanding. *The Blue and Brown Books* are notes dictated to his Cambridge students in the 1930s. They are cited less now than his *Philosophical Investigations*, though his thought is more accessible than in the *Investigations*. Given the homiletic nature of his writing, Wittgenstein lends himself to a variety of interpretations but there is a central core to his works on which there is no disagreement; viz. the grounding of meaning in *praxis*. When Wittgenstein modestly summarized his philosophical aims as no more than 'showing the fly the way out of the bottle', he was like Theseus himself, aided by Ariadne's golden cord, and extricating himself from the Labyrinth. For Wittgenstein, the labyrinth is of our own making, however, and its dead-ends are invariably linguistic in origin. Philosophical problems, at least the enduring metaphysical problems, call less for 'solution' than for a kind of grammatical parsing. In this, Wittgenstein is very much in the tradition of Socrates: how we answer a question (e.g. 'Can virtue be taught?') depends on how we mean its major terms to be taken.

Had Wittgenstein said no more than that one must define one's terms if one is to be understood, his contribution would have been true and trite. How does one *define* a term? Whether by dictionary or consensus, at the end of the day it is the manner in which the term is used in practice that defines it. 'The meaning of a phrase for us is characterized by the use we make of it'. Nor are the plural noun-forms accidental, for only by way of a *shared* or cooperative enterprise can meaning be established. This includes such indexicals as 'I' and 'he' and accounts, according to Wittgenstein, for the now unsurprising fact that when Smith says, 'I have a toothache', Smith can't be wrong. No more could 'one moan with pain by mistake'.

If propositions about minds or selves are to be meaningful, their meaning must arise from the cultural practices, aims, and understandings by which any sign comes to signify anything. Orange-coloured octagonal figures are only STOP signs under a specified set of cultural conditions. The same is true of such signs as the utterance, 'I have a toothache'. What this utterance signifies is what, earlier in life, was signified by the holding of one's jaw, the release of tears, and the production of audible crying. Presumably, these latter natural signs could have been replaced by very different words or gestures. On these grounds Wittgenstein is able to reflect on such enduring problems of as that of personal identity, 'unconscious thought', and 'other minds'. The Wittgensteinian mind is constructed out of social practices. As such it is a cultural artefact expressive of a given form of life and understanding itself in terms that have been authenticated by the culture itself. There is no private screen or private language by which one gains privileged access to one's 'own' mind; only actions and statements the meaning of which comes about through collaborative engagement. Little if anything mental is, as it were, *given*.

It is doubtful, however, that Freud would have accepted Wittgenstein's neatly grammatical answer to the question of whether there are unconscious thoughts. Nor, a century after Sigmund Freud's first published book, are readers likely to settle for Thomas Reid's Common Sense account of identity and selfhood or John Dewey's pragmatic account of mind. They may be only slightly less reluctant to accept Lockian and Humian alternatives which seem to regard mind and consciousness as more or less synonymous. It seems nearly ironic these days to read in Hume that, when he is asleep, his 'self' no longer exists; ironic in a post-Freudian age in which the occurrences in sleep may reveal more of the 'self' than anything discoverable through a study of conscious content.

The unprecedented influence Freudian thought has had on both popular and scholarly conceptions of the mind should not obscure the modest and conservative motives that guided Freud's earliest theoretical efforts. Trained as a neurologist, he had the usual share of 'hysterical' patients in his Viennese practice; patients displaying neurological symptoms, but at the same time symptoms that could not be reconciled to the known functional anatomy of the nervous system. The patient complaining of a loss of sensation in one hand, from finger tips to wrist—the so-called 'glove anaesthesia'—is illustrative. Neuropathies can result in diminished or lost sensitivity in circumscribed areas of the body, but not an area marked out by the contours of a glove.

As a good clinician Freud followed promising medical leads wherever they might take him. Learning that the celebrated Dr Charcot was reporting success with the use of hypnosis in diagnosing and treating hysterics, Freud took himself to Paris and attended Charcot's lecture-demonstrations. Freud would write years later that he abandoned the method for several reasons: not all patients could be brought under hypnosis; the symptomatic relief it produced was typically short-lived; and (revealingly) the entire process struck him as mysterious and superstitious. It is worth noting this to underscore Freud's enduring loyalty to that scientific, positivistic world-view that had come to dominate medicine and the biological sciences in the second half of the nineteenth century. It was this very perspective that resulted in Freud's own dismissal by much of the medical fraternity when the details of psychoanalytic theory began to appear in Freud's works.

In 1896 he collaborated with fellow psychiatrist Joseph Breuer in the publication of *Studies of Hysteria*, the work that introduced the Freudian theory of hysteria as a 'conversion reaction' resulting from *repression*. The hysteric's symptoms, on this account, are the physical manifestation of what, at the level of the unconscious, is the blockage of the movement or discharge of psychical energy. The theory was explicitly beholden to the newly discovered and developed laws of conservation in thermodynamics and classical physics. In a closed system energy is neither created nor destroyed, though it may manifest itself in different form; mechanical energy might be transformed into heat, electricity into light, etc. Thus, the physical symptoms arising in hysteria exemplify another closed system in which the normal energy exchanges become blocked, the 'work' of repression now 'converted' into the hysterical reaction.

The theory of repression would become enlarged and variegated into the theory of *unconscious motivation* by which even the most developed features of social life and civilization come to be understood in psychoanalytic terms. In the pages reproduced in this Section, taken from Freud's *Introductory Lectures*, the sources and purposes of the *id* are discussed. It operates at the level of the unconscious, but 'unconscious' now referring not simply to things out of mind that can be called up; rather, 'unconscious' as '*withdrawn from the ego's knowledge*' and functioning in a dynamic fashion. It is *alien* to the ego. The domain of mind is no longer to be understood as a unified space in which ideas and experiences inhere in a conscious being. Rather, it is a tripartite and ceaselessly active collection of processes standing in essentially competing relation to each other. The mind is the house divided in which one is fated to serve two masters, each having claims against the other. The id, this 'dark, inaccessible part of our personality', is, Freud says, 'a chaos, a cauldron full of seething excitations . . . taking up into itself instinctual needs'. Logic has no force here; only the *pleasure principle*. The gratification of the id is the means by which survival itself is secured; it is secured through instinctual self-defence, sexuality, destructive self-assertion, rapaciousness —all on which the ultimate success of a *species* comes to depend. The wishes that have their grounding here 'are virtually immortal; after the passage of decades they behave as though they had just occurred'. It is only though psychoanalysis that these can be brought to consciousness and dealt with, but chiefly by redirection rather than elimination.

For the id itself to survive, in the face of society's formidable powers, there must be some unsteady peace established between the *pleasure principle* and the *reality principle*. In the socialization of the young society develops a conscience or *superego* in each of its members such that the instinctual impulses of the id are provided with incomplete but permissible modes of expression. Dreams, rituals, rites of passage, social institutions, forms of humour, slips of the tongue—the full panoply of the lesser vices and villainies—provide ample evidence of the ways the ego sets about to defend itself against the instinctual urges. The task is impossible, however, so the achievement must be limited and transient. 'The poor ego . . . serves three severe masters . . . the external world, the super-ego, and the id . . . It feels hemmed in on three sides, threatened by three kinds of danger, to which, if it is hard pressed, it reacts by generating anxiety.' 'Life is not easy', he says.

It was surely not easy for Oliver Sacks's patient, 'The Disembodied Lady', suffering from an acute polyneuritis that stripped her of all proprioception. She could not sense her body at all, her very *embodiment*. Sacks underscores the relevance of this case to Wittgenstein's philosophy. The practices in which Christina can no longer participate—even at the level of sensation— become increasingly meaningless to her, even as her sense of her *self* progressively changes. Bereft of all bodily sensations her sense of individuality becomes degraded, for she has no feeling of that individuated body that is her own. On the other hand, Christina's own confusion and understandable distress leave no doubt but that her personal identity has been preserved even in the course of this extraordinary loss of self-sensation, otherwise there would be neither confusion nor distress.

Sacks respects the important function of the patient's will, not to mention that wisdom of the body by which compensatory adjustments are made in the face of seemingly insuperable odds. Christina's sense of her *self* is clearly but not totally tied to her proprioceptive sense. That her personal identity endures establishes only that proprioception is not a necessary condition for it. Suppose, however, that she also suffered from a memory-deficit proposed by Wittgenstein as a thought-experiment: she could recall only events occurring on the odd days of the week rather than the even ones. Might *two* minds thus arise, and as a result two distinguishable personal identities? Is the Lockian memory-theory worth reviving?

These questions are addressed directly by Derek Parfit in his *Reasons and Persons* in the context of research on patients whose inter-cerebral connections have been surgically severed. The pathways joining the two halves of the brain are referred to generically as commissures and the severing of such pathways as commissurotomies. The commissure joining the two cerebral hemispheres is the *corpus callosum*. This is not the only pathway by which one side of the brain might influence the other, for there are other connecting pathways that are sub-cortical; e.g. the *massa intermedia* which forms a bridge at the level of the thalamus.

Parfit summarizes studies of patients who have undergone commissuro-tomies as a means by which to control otherwise intractable epileptic seizures. He recognizes the relevance of such research to the overall question of mind/body reductionism and to the related question of personal identity and 'persons'. Parfit's thought-experiment begins with his adopting the cognitive non-dominance of the two halves of his brain. He thereby is able to devote each half to a divided problem-set, later uniting the two into a single stream of consciousness. It may be argued that he has begged the question when he says that, the work now over, 'I am about to reunite my mind', for, as with Reid's criticism of Hume, there seems to be an undivided Parfit doing this uniting. But Parfit rejects the requirement of a unified consciousness. He takes it as factually established that commissurotomized patients 'have two separate streams of consciousness' with each unaware of the other.

This leads directly to the argument favouring the continuation of a given personal identity as a brain is moved from one body into another of the right sort. What it means to be Smith-as-person is to have the conscious contents by which Smith is identifiable and by which he knows himself to be the person he is. These contents are possible in virtue of the functions of the brain and are coextensive with its proper performance. If the undamaged brain of one victim of an accident (whose body has been destroyed) replaces the dead brain of another victim (whose body has been spared), who can doubt but that the brain-recipient is now the *person* whose brain it was? Commissurotomies yield results that challenge the notion of the unity of consciousness. The scientifically warranted expectations of what would happen when brains are transplanted challenge the Cartesian notion of a (substantial) 'Self'. Together, the findings and expected findings sustain the principal claims of the reductionist.

Do they? Recall Wittgenstein's reflections on the person who has two distinct sets of memories—one for events that happen on the even days of the week and the other for those taking place on the odd days.

Are we bound to say that here two persons are inhabiting the same body? That is, is it right to say that there are, and wrong to say that there aren't, or vice versa? Neither. For the *ordinary* use of the word 'person' is what one might call a composite use suitable under the ordinary circumstances . . . One might say in such a case that the term 'personality' hasn't got one legitimate heir only. (*Blue Book*, 62)

Grant Gillett considers Parfit's arguments and finds them wanting. He accepts that personal identity is not some disembodied Cartesian essence, but insists that it depends on a fully integrated nervous system that has successfully recorded and processed the complex flow of information received in the course of actual living. On Gillett's reading, the reductionism that must fail is at the informational and experiential level. Parfit's argument holds only at that level of abstraction at which neither persons nor brains actually function.

The final article in this Section returns to the question of the unity of self and the extent to which 'split brain' patients challenge this notion. As it happens, a wide variety of experimental and real-life conditions can produce just those states of *epistemic contradiction* on which the claimed division or multiplication of mental lives depends. Hypnosis, experiments in vision and auditory research, studies of cued retrieval in memory, clinical findings in neurology and psychoanalysis, cases of multiple-personality, temporary insanity, pseudo-reminiscence—a great number and variety of conditions have been employed and cases discovered in which persons simultaneously or successively affirm and deny a given state of affairs. Binet's century-old research on automatic writing and related findings led him to write a book-length treatise on so-called double-consciousness. In light of the evidence perhaps the greater mystery is not that mental life is divisible but that it is ever unified.

JOHN LOCKE

64 The Idea of Personal Identity

To find wherein personal identity consists, we must consider what *person* stands for;—which, I think, is a thinking intelligent being, that has reason and reflection, and can consider itself as itself, the same thinking thing, in different times and places; which it does only by that consciousness which is inseparable from thinking, and, as it seems to me, essential to it: it being impossible for any one to perceive without *perceiving* that he does perceive. When we see, hear, smell, taste, feel, meditate, or will anything, we know that we do so. Thus it is always as to our present sensations and perceptions: and by this every one is to himself that which he calls *self:*—it not being considered, in this case, whether the same self be continued in the same or divers substances. For, since consciousness always accompanies thinking, and it is that which makes every one to be what he calls self, and thereby distinguishes himself from all other thinking things, in this alone consists personal identity, i.e. the sameness of a rational being: and as far as this consciousness can be extended backwards to any past action or thought, so far reaches the identity of that person; it is the same self now it was then; and it is by the same self with this present one that now reflects on it, that that action was done.

But it is further inquired, whether it be the same identical substance. This few would think they had reason to doubt of, if these perceptions, with their consciousness, always remained present in the mind, whereby the same thinking thing would be always consciously present, and, as would be thought, evidently the same to itself. But that which seems to make the difficulty is this, that this consciousness being interrupted always by forgetfulness, there being no moment of our lives wherein we have the whole train of all our past actions before our eyes in one view, but even the best memories losing the sight of one part whilst they are viewing another; and we sometimes, and that the greatest part of our lives, not reflecting on our past selves, being intent on our present thoughts, and in sound sleep having no thoughts at all, or at least none with that consciousness which remarks our waking thoughts,—I say, in all these cases, our consciousness being interrupted, and we losing the sight of our past selves, doubts are raised whether we are the same thinking thing, i.e. the same *substance* or no. Which, however reasonable or unreasonable, concerns not *personal* identity at all. The question being what makes the same person; and not whether it be the same identical substance, which always thinks in the same person, which, in this case, matters not at all: different substances, by the same consciousness (where they do partake in it) being united into one person, as well as different bodies by the same life are united into one animal, whose identity is preserved in that change of substances by the unity of one continued life. For, it being the same consciousness that makes a man be himself to himself, personal identity depends on that only, whether it be annexed solely to one individual substance, or can be continued in a succession of several substances. For as far as any intelligent being *can* repeat the idea of any past action with the same consciousness it had of it at first, and with the same consciousness it has of any present action; so far it is the same personal self. For it is by the consciousness it has of its present thoughts and actions, that it is *self to itself* now, and so will be the same self, as far as the same consciousness can extend to actions past or to come, and would be by distance of time, or change of substance, no more two persons, than a man be two men by wearing other clothes to-day than he did yesterday, with a long or a short sleep between: the same consciousness uniting those distant actions into the same person, whatever substances contributed to their production.

That this is so, we have some kind of evidence in our very bodies, all whose particles, whilst vitally united to this same thinking conscious self, so that *we feel* when they are touched, and are affected by, and conscious of good or harm that happens to them, are a part of ourselves; i.e. of our thinking conscious self. Thus, the limbs of his body are to every one a part of himself; he sympathizes and is concerned for them. Cut off a hand, and thereby separate it from that consciousness he had of its heat, cold, and other affections, and it is then no longer a part of that which is himself, any more than the remotest part of matter. Thus, we see the *substance* whereof personal self consisted at one time may be varied at another, without the change of personal identity; there being no question about the same person, though the limbs which but now were a part of it, be cut off.

But the question is, Whether if the same substance which thinks be changed, it can be the same person; or, remaining the same, it can be different persons?

And to this I answer: First, This can be no question at all to those who place thought in a purely material animal constitution, void of an immaterial substance. For, whether their supposition be true or no, it is plain they conceive personal identity preserved in something else than identity of substance; as animal identity is preserved in identity of life, and not of substance. And therefore those who place thinking in an immaterial substance only, before they can come to deal with these men, must show why personal identity cannot be preserved in the change of immaterial substances, or variety of particular immaterial substances, as well as animal identity is preserved in the change of material substances, or variety of particular bodies: unless they will say, it is one immaterial spirit that makes the same life in brutes, as it is one immaterial spirit that makes the same person in men; which the Cartesians at least will not admit, for fear of making brutes thinking things too.

But next, as to the first part of the question, Whether, if the same thinking substance (supposing immaterial substances only to think) be changed, it can be the same person? I answer, that cannot be resolved but by those who know what kind of substances they are that do think; and whether the consciousness of past actions can be transferred from one thinking substance to another. I grant were the same consciousness the same individual action it could not: but it being a present representation of a past action, why it may not be possible, that that may be represented to the mind to have been which really never was, will remain to be shown. And therefore how far the consciousness of past actions is annexed to any individual agent, so that another cannot possibly have it, will be hard for us to determine, till we know what kind of action it is that cannot be done without a reflex act of perception accompanying it, and how performed by thinking substances, who cannot think without being conscious of it. But that which we call the same consciousness, not being the same individual act, why one intellectual substance may not have represented to it, as done by itself, what *it* never did, and was perhaps done by some other agent—why, I say, such a representation may not possibly be without reality of matter of fact, as well as several representations in dreams are, which yet whilst dreaming we take for true—will be difficult to conclude from the nature of things. And that it never is so, will by us, till we have clearer views of the nature of thinking substances, be best resolved into the goodness of God; who, as far as the happiness or misery of any of his sensible creatures is concerned in it, will not, by a fatal error of theirs, transfer from one to another that consciousness which draws reward or punishment with it. How far this may be an argument against those who would place thinking in a system of fleeting animal spirits, I leave to be considered. But yet, to return to the question before us, it must be allowed, that, if the same consciousness (which, as has been shown, is quite a different thing from the same numerical figure or motion in body) can be transferred from one thinking substance to another, it will be possible that two thinking substances may make but one person. For the same consciousness being preserved, whether in the same or different substances, the personal identity is preserved.

As to the second part of the question, Whether the same immaterial substance remaining, there may be two distinct persons; which question seems to me to be built on this,—Whether the same immaterial being, being conscious of the action of its past duration, may be wholly stripped of all the consciousness of its past existence, and lose it beyond the power of ever retrieving it again: and so as it were beginning a new account from a new period, have a consciousness that *cannot* reach beyond this new state. All those who hold pre-existence are evidently of this mind; since they allow the soul to have no remaining consciousness of what it did in that pre-existent state, either wholly separate from body, or informing any other body; and if they should not, it is plain experience would be against them. So that personal identity, reaching no further than consciousness reaches, a pre-existent spirit not having continued so many ages in a state of silence, must needs make different persons. [. . .]

And thus may we be able, without any difficulty, to conceive the same person at the resurrection, though in a body not exactly in make or parts the same which he had here,—the same consciousness going along with the soul that inhabits it. But yet the soul alone, in the change of bodies, would scarce to any one but to him that makes the soul the man, be enough to make the same man. For should the soul of a prince, carrying with it the consciousness of the prince's past life, enter and inform the body of a cobbler, as soon as deserted by his own soul, every one sees he would be the same *person* with the prince, accountable only for the prince's actions: but who would say it was the same *man*? The body too goes to the making the man, and would, I guess, to everybody determine the man in this case, wherein the soul, with all its princely thoughts about it, would not make another man: but he would be the same cobbler to every one besides himself. I know that, in the ordinary way of speaking, the same person, and the same man, stand for one and the same thing. And indeed every one will always have a liberty to speak as he pleases, and to apply what articulate sounds to what ideas he thinks fit, and change them as often as he pleases. But yet, when we will inquire what makes the same *spirit, man*, or *person*, we must fix the ideas of spirit, man, or person in our minds; and having resolved with ourselves what we mean by them, it will not be hard to determine, in either of them, or the like, when it is the same, and when not. [. . .]

Self is that conscious thinking thing,—whatever substance made up of, (whether spiritual or material, simple or compounded, it matters not)— which is sensible or conscious of pleasure and pain, capable of happiness or misery, and so is concerned for itself, as far as that consciousness extends. Thus every one finds that, whilst comprehended under that consciousness, the little finger is as much a part of himself as what is most so. Upon separation of this little finger, should this consciousness go along with the little finger, and leave the rest of the body, it is evident the little finger would be the person, the same person; and self then would have nothing to do with the rest of the body. As in this case it is the consciousness that goes along with the substance, when one part is separate from another, which makes the same person, and constitutes this inseparable self: so it is in reference to substances remote in time. That with which the consciousness of this present thinking thing *can* join itself, makes the same person, and is one self with it, and with nothing else; and so attributes to itself, and owns all the actions of that thing, as its own, as far as that consciousness reaches, and no further; as every one who reflects will perceive. [. . .]

This may show us wherein personal identity consists: not in the identity of substance, but, as I have said, in the identity of consciousness, wherein if Socrates and the present mayor of Queinborough agree, they are the same person: if the same Socrates waking and sleeping do not partake of the same consciousness, Socrates waking and sleeping is not the same person. And to punish Socrates waking for what sleeping Socrates thought, and waking Socrates was never conscious of, would be no more of right—than to punish one twin for what his brother-twin did, whereof he knew nothing, because their outsides were so like, that they could not be distinguished; for such twins have been seen.

[From *An Essay Concerning Human Understanding*, ed. A. C. Fraser, 2 vols. (New York: Dover Books, n.d.), i. 448–60.]

DAVID HUME

65 Of Personal Identity

There are some philosophers, who imagine we are every moment intimately conscious of what we call our SELF; that we feel its existence and its continuance in existence; and are certain, beyond the evidence of a demonstration, both of its perfect identity and simplicity. The strongest sensation, the most violent passion, say they, instead of distracting us from this view, only fix it the more intensely, and make us consider their influence on *self* either by their pain or pleasure. To attempt a farther proof of this were to weaken its evidence; since no proof can be deriv'd from any fact, of which we are so intimately conscious; nor is there any thing, of which we can be certain, if we doubt of this.

Unluckily all these positive assertions are contrary to that very experience, which is pleaded for them, nor have we any idea of *self*, after the manner it is here explain'd. For from what impression cou'd this idea be deriv'd? This question 'tis impossible to answer without a manifest contradiction and absurdity; and yet 'tis a question, which must necessarily be answer'd, if we wou'd have the idea of self pass for clear and intelligible. It must be some one impression, that gives rise to every real idea. But self or person is not any one impression, but that to which our several impressions and ideas are suppos'd to have a reference. If any impression gives rise to the idea of self, that impression must continue invariably the same, thro' the whole course of our lives; since self is suppos'd to exist after that manner. But there is no impression constant and invariable. Pain and pleasure, grief and joy, passions and sensations succeed each other, and never all exist at the same time. It cannot, therefore, be from any of these impressions, or from any other, that the idea of self is deriv'd; and consequently there is no such idea.

But farther, what must become of all our particular perceptions upon this hypothesis? All these are different, and distinguishable, and separable from each other, and may be separately consider'd, and may exist separately, and have no need of any thing to support their existence. After what manner, therefore, do they belong to self; and how are they connected with it? For my part, when I enter most intimately into what I call *myself*, I always stumble on some particular perception or other, of heat or cold, light or shade, love or hatred, pain or pleasure. I never can catch *myself* at any time without a perception, and never can observe any thing but the perception. When my perceptions are remov'd for any time, as by sound sleep; so long am I insensible of *myself*, and may truly be said not to exist. And were all my perceptions remov'd by death, and cou'd I neither think, nor feel, nor see, nor love, nor hate after the dissolution of my body, I shou'd be entirely annihilated, nor do I conceive what is farther requisite to make me a perfect non-entity. If any one upon serious and unprejudic'd reflexion, thinks he has a different notion of *himself*, I must confess I can reason no longer with him. All I can allow him is, that he may be in the right as well as I, and that we are essentially different in this particular. He may, perhaps, perceive something simple and continu'd, which he calls *himself*; tho' I am certain there is no such principle in me.

But setting aside some metaphysicians of this kind, I may venture to affirm of the rest of mankind, that they are nothing but a bundle or collection of different perceptions, which succeed each other with an inconceivable rapidity, and are in a perpetual flux and movement. Our eyes cannot turn in their sockets without varying our perceptions. Our thought is still more variable than our sight; and all our other senses and faculties contribute to this change; nor is there any single power of the soul, which remains unalterably the same, perhaps for one moment. The mind is a kind of theatre, where several perceptions successively make their appearance; pass, re-pass, glide away, and mingle in an infinite variety of postures and situations. There is properly no *simplicity* in it at one time, nor *identity* in different; whatever natural propension we may have to imagine that simplicity and identity. The comparison of the theatre must not mislead us. They are the successive perceptions only, that constitute the mind; nor have we the most distant notion of the place, where these scenes are represented, or of the materials, of which it is compos'd.

What then gives us so great a propension to ascribe an identity to these successive perceptions, and to suppose ourselves possest of an invariable and uninterrupted existence thro' the whole course of our lives? In order to answer this question, we must distinguish betwixt personal identity, as it regards our thought or imagination, and as it regards our passions or the concern we take in ourselves. The first is our present subject; and to explain it perfectly we must take the matter pretty deep, and account for that identity, which we attribute to plants and animals; there being a great analogy betwixt it, and the identity of a self or person.

We have a distinct idea of an object, that remains invariable and uninterrupted thro' a suppos'd variation of time; and this idea we call that of *identity* or *sameness*. We have also a distinct idea of several different objects existing in succession, and connected together by a close relation; and this to an accurate view affords as perfect a notion of *diversity*, as if there was no manner of relation among the objects. But tho' these two ideas of identity, and a succession of related objects be in themselves perfectly distinct, and even contrary, yet 'tis certain, that in our common way of thinking they are generally confounded with each other. That action of the imagination, by which we consider the uninterrupted and invariable object, and that by which we reflect on the succession of related objects, are almost the same to the feeling, nor is there much more effort of thought requir'd in the latter case than in the former. The relation facilitates the transition of the mind from one object to another, and renders its passage as smooth as if it contemplated one continu'd object. This resemblance is the cause of the confusion and mistake, and makes us substitute the notion of identity, instead of that of related objects. However at one instant we may consider the related succession as variable or interrupted, we are sure the next to ascribe to it a perfect identity, and regard it as invariable and uninterrupted. Our propensity to this mistake is so great from the resemblance above-mention'd, that we fall into it before we are aware; and tho' we incessantly correct ourselves by reflexion, and return to a more accurate method of thinking, yet we cannot long sustain our philosophy, or take off this biass from the imagination. Our last resource is to yield to it, and boldly assert that these different related objects are in effect the same, however interrupted and variable. In order to justify to ourselves this absurdity, we often feign some new and unintelligible principle, that connects the objects together, and prevents their interruption or variation. Thus we feign the continu'd

304 OF PERSONAL IDENTITY

existence of the perceptions of our senses, to remove the interruption; and run into the notion of a *soul*, and *self*, and *substance*, to disguise the variation. But we may farther observe, that where we do not give rise to such a fiction, our propension to confound identity with relation is so great, that we are apt to imagine something unknown and mysterious, connecting the parts, beside their relation; and this I take to be the case with regard to the identity we ascribe to plants and vegetables. And even when this does not take place, we still feel a propensity to confound these ideas, tho' we are not able fully to satisfy ourselves in that particular, nor find any thing invariable and uninterrupted to justify our notion of identity.

Thus the controversy concerning identity is not merely a dispute of words. For when we attribute identity, in an improper sense, to variable or interrupted objects, our mistake is not confin'd to the expression, but it is commonly attended with a fiction, either of something invariable and uninterrupted, or of something mysterious and inexplicable, or at least with a propensity to such fictions. What will suffice to prove this hypothesis to the satisfaction of every fair enquirer, is to shew from daily experience and observation, that the objects, which are variable or interrupted, and yet are suppos'd to continue the same, are such only as consist of a succession of parts, connected together by resemblance, contiguity, or causation. For as such a succession answers evidently to our notion of diversity, it can only be by mistake we ascribe to it an identity; and as the relation of parts, which leads us into this mistake, is really nothing but a quality, which produces an association of ideas, and an easy transition of the imagination from one to another, it can only be from the resemblance, which this act of the mind bears to that, by which we contemplate one continu'd object, that the error arises. Our chief business, then, must be to prove, that all objects, to which we ascribe identity, without observing their invariableness and uninterrupt-edness, are such as consist of a succession of related objects.

In order to this, suppose any mass of matter, of which the parts are contiguous and connected, to be plac'd before us; 'tis plain we must attribute a perfect identity to this mass, provided all the parts continue uninterruptedly and invariably the same, whatever motion or change of place we may observe either in the whole or in any of the parts. But supposing some very *small* or *inconsiderable* part to be added to the mass, or substracted from it; tho' this absolutely destroys the identity of the whole, strictly speaking; yet as we seldom think so accurately, we scruple not to pronounce a mass of matter the same, where we find so trivial an alteration. The passage of the thought from the object before the change to the object after it, is so smooth and easy, that we scarce perceive the transition, and are apt to imagine, that 'tis nothing but a continu'd survey of the same object.

There is a very remarkable circumstance, that attends this experiment; which is, that tho' the change of any considerable part in a mass of matter destroys the identity of the whole, yet we must measure the greatness of the part, not absolutely, but by its *proportion* to the whole. The addition or diminution of a mountain wou'd not be sufficient to produce a diversity in a planet; tho' the change of a very few inches wou'd be able to destroy the identity of some bodies. 'Twill be impossible to account for this, but by reflecting that objects operate upon the mind, and break or interrupt the continuity of its actions not according to their real greatness, but according to their proportion to each other: And therefore, since this interruption makes an object cease to appear the same, it must be the uninterrupted progress of the thought, which constitutes the imperfect identity.

This may be confirm'd by another phænomenon. A change in any considerable part of a body destroys its identity; but 'tis remarkable, that where the change is produc'd *gradually* and *insensibly* we are less apt to ascribe to it the same effect. The reason can plainly be no other, than that the mind, in following the successive changes of the body, feels an easy passage from the surveying its condition in one moment to the viewing of it in another, and at no particular time perceives any interruption in its actions. From which continu'd perception, it ascribes a continu'd existence and identity to the object.

But whatever precaution we may use in introducing the changes gradually, and making them proportionable to the whole, 'tis certain, that where the changes are at last observ'd to become considerable, we make a scruple of ascribing identity to such different objects. There is, however, another artifice, by which we may induce the imagination to advance a step farther; and that is, by producing a reference of the parts to each other, and a combination to some *common end* or purpose. A ship, of which a considerable part has been chang'd by frequent reparations, is still consider'd as the same; nor does the difference of the materials hinder us from ascribing an identity to it. The common end, in which the parts conspire, is the same under all their variations, and affords an easy transition of the imagination from one situation of the body to another.

But this is still more remarkable, when we add a *sympathy* of parts to their *common end*, and suppose that they bear to each other, the reciprocal relation of cause and effect in all their actions and operations. This is the case with all animals and vegetables; where not only the several parts have a reference to some general purpose, but also a mutual dependance on, and connexion with each other. The effect of so strong a relation is, that tho' every one must allow, that in a very few years both vegetables and animals endure a *total* change, yet we still attribute identity to them, while their form, size, and substance are entirely alter'd. An oak, that grows from a small plant to a large tree, is still the same oak; tho' there be not one particle of matter, or figure of its parts the same. An infant becomes a man, and is sometimes fat, sometimes lean, without any change in his identity. [. . .]

We now proceed to explain the nature of *personal identity*, which has become so great a question in philosophy, especially of late years in *England*, where all the abstruser sciences are study'd with a peculiar ardour and application. And here 'tis evident, the same method of reasoning must be continu'd, which has so successfully explain'd the identity of plants, and animals, and ships, and houses, and of all the compounded and changeable productions either of art or nature. The identity, which we ascribe to the mind of man, is only a fictitious one, and of a like kind with that which we ascribe to vegetables and animal bodies. It cannot, therefore, have a different origin, but must proceed from a like operation of the imagination upon like objects.

But lest this argument shou'd not convince the reader; tho' in my opinion perfectly decisive; let him weigh the following reasoning, which is still closer and more immediate. 'Tis evident, that the identity, which we attribute to the human mind, however perfect we may imagine it to be, is not able to run the several different perceptions into one, and make them lose their characters of distinction and difference, which are essential to them. 'Tis still true, that every distinct perception, which enters into the composition of the mind, is a distinct existence, and is different, and distinguishable, and separable from every other perception, either contemporary or successive. But, as, notwithstanding this distinction and separability, we suppose the whole train of perceptions to be united by identity, a question naturally arises concerning this relation of identity; whether it be something that really binds our several perceptions together, or only associates their ideas in the imagination. That is, in other words, whether in pronouncing concerning the identity of a person, we observe some real bond among his perceptions, or only feel one among the ideas we form of them. This question we might easily decide, if we wou'd recollect what has been already prov'd at large, that the understanding never observes any real connexion among objects, and that even the union of cause and effect, when strictly examin'd, resolves itself into a customary association of ideas. For from thence it evidently follows, that identity is nothing really belonging to these different perceptions, and uniting them together; but is merely a quality, which we attribute to them, because of the union of their ideas in the imagination, when we reflect upon them. Now the only qualities, which can give ideas an union in the imagination, are these three relations above-mention'd. These are the uniting principles in the ideal world, and without them every distinct object is separable by the mind, and may be separately consider'd, and appears not to have any more connexion with any other object, than if disjoin'd by the greatest difference and remoteness. 'Tis, therefore, on some of these three relations of resemblance, contiguity and causation, that identity depends; and as the very essence of these relations consists in their producing an easy transition of ideas; it follows, that our notions of personal identity, proceed entirely from the smooth and uninterrupted progress of the thought along a train of connected ideas, according to the principles above-explain'd.

The only question, therefore, which remains, is, by what relations this uninterrupted progress of our thought is produc'd, when we consider the successive existence of a mind or thinking person. And here 'tis evident we must confine ourselves to resemblance and causation, and must drop contiguity, which has little or no influence in the present case.

To begin with *resemblance*; suppose we cou'd see clearly into the breast of another, and observe that succession of perceptions, which constitutes his mind or thinking principle, and suppose that he always preserves the memory of a considerable part of past perceptions; 'tis evident that nothing cou'd more contribute to the bestowing a relation on this succession amidst all its variations. For what is the memory but a faculty, by which we raise up the images of past perceptions? And as an image necessarily resembles its object, must not the frequent placing of these resembling perceptions in the chain of thought, convey the imagination more easily from one link to another, and make the whole seem like the continuance of one object? In this particular, then, the memory not only discovers the identity, but also contributes to its production, by producing the relation of resemblance among the perceptions. The case is the same whether we consider ourselves or others.

As to *causation*; we may observe, that the true idea of the human mind, is to consider it as a system of different perceptions or different existences, which are link'd together by the relation of cause and effect, and mutually produce, destroy, influence, and modify each other. Our impressions give rise to their correspondent ideas; and these ideas in their turn produce other impressions. One thought chaces another, and draws after it a third, by which it is expell'd in its turn. In this respect, I cannot compare the soul more properly to anything than to a republic or commonwealth, in which the several members are united by the reciprocal ties of government and subordination, and give rise to other persons, who propagate the same republic in the incessant changes of its parts. And as the same individual republic may not only change its members, but also its laws and constitutions; in like manner the same person may vary his character and disposition, as well as his impressions and ideas, without losing his identity. Whatever changes he endures, his several parts are still connected by the relation of causation. And in this view our identity with regard to the passions serves to corroborate that with regard to the imagination, by the making our distant perceptions influence each other, and by giving us a present concern for our past or future pains or pleasures.

As memory alone acquaints us with the continuance and extent of this succession of perceptions, 'tis to be consider'd, upon that account chiefly, as the source of personal identity. Had we no memory, we never shou'd have any notion of causation, nor consequently of that chain of causes and effects, which constitute our self or person. But having once acquir'd this notion of causation from the memory, we can extend the same chain of causes, and consequently the identity of our persons beyond our memory, and can comprehend times, and circumstances, and actions, which we have entirely forgot, but suppose in general to have existed.

[From *A Treatise of Human Nature*, ed. L. A. Selby-Bigge (Oxford: Oxford University Press, 1978), 251–62.]

THOMAS REID

66   Of Mr Locke's Account of Personal Identity

In a long chapter upon identity and diversity, Mr Locke has made many ingenious and just observations, and some which, I think, cannot be defended. I shall only take notice of the account he gives of our own personal identity. His doctrine upon this subject has been censured by bishop Butler, in a short essay subjoined to his Analogy, with whose sentiments I perfectly agree.

Identity, as was observed chap. 4, of this Essay, supposes the continued existence of the being of which it is affirmed, and therefore can be applied only to things which have a continued existence. While any being continues to exist, it is the same being; but two beings which have a different beginning or a different ending of their existence, cannot possibly be the same. To this I think Mr Locke agrees.

He observes very justly, that to know what is meant by the same person, we must consider what the word *person* stands for; and he defines a person to be an intelligent being, endowed with reason and with consciousness, which last he thinks inseparable from thought.

From this definition of a person, it must necessarily follow, that while the intelligent being continues to exist and to be intelligent, it must be the same person. To say that the intelligent being is the person, and yet that the person ceases to exist, while the intelligent being continues, or that the person continues while the intelligent being ceases to exist, is, to my apprehension, a manifest contradiction.

One would think that the definition of a person should perfectly ascertain the nature of personal identity, or wherein it consists, though it might still be a question how we come to know and be assured of our personal identity.

Mr Locke tells us, however, 'that personal identity, that is, the sameness of a rational being, consists in consciousness alone; and, as far as this consciousness can be extended backward to any past action or thought, so far reaches the identity of that person. So that whatever has the consciousness of present and past actions, is the same person to whom they belong.'

This doctrine has some strange consequences, which the author was aware of. Such as, that if the same consciousness can be transferred from one intelligent being to another, which he thinks we cannot show to be impossible, then two or twenty intelligent beings may be the same person. And if the intelligent being may lose the consciousness of the actions done by him, which surely is possible, then he is not the person that did those actions; so that one intelligent being may be two or twenty different persons, if he shall so often lose the consciousness of his former actions.

There is another consequence of this doctrine, which follows no less necessarily, though Mr Locke probably did not see it. It is, that a man may be, and at the same time not be, the person that did a particular action.

Suppose a brave officer to have been flogged when a boy at school, for robbing an orchard, to have taken a standard from the enemy in his first campaign, and to have been made a general in advanced life. Suppose also, which must be admitted to be possible, that when he took the standard, he was conscious of his having been flogged at school; and that when made a general, he was conscious of his taking the standard, but had absolutely lost the consciousness of his flogging.

These things being supposed, it follows, from Mr Locke's doctrine, that he who was flogged at school is the same person who took the standard; and that he who took the standard is the same person who was made a general. Whence it follows, if there be any truth in logic, that the general is the same person with him who was flogged at school. But the general's consciousness does not reach so far back as his flogging, therefore, according to Mr Locke's doctrine, he is not the person who was flogged. Therefore the general is, and at the same time is not, the same person with him who was flogged at school.

Leaving the consequences of this doctrine to those who have leisure to trace them, we may observe, with regard to the doctrine itself;

1st, That Mr Locke attributes to consciousness the conviction we have of our past actions, as if a man may now be conscious of what he did twenty years ago. It is impossible to understand the meaning of this, unless by consciousness be meant memory, the only faculty by which we have an immediate knowledge of our past actions.

Sometimes, in popular discourse, a man says he is conscious that he did such a thing, meaning that he distinctly remembers that he did it. It is unnecessary, in common discourse, to fix accurately the limits between consciousness and memory. This was formerly shown to be the case with regard to sense and memory: and therefore distinct remembrance is sometimes called sense, sometimes consciousness, without any inconvenience.

But this ought to be avoided in philosophy, otherwise we confound the different powers of the mind, and ascribe to one what really belongs to another. If a man can be conscious of what he did twenty years, or twenty minutes ago, there is no use for memory, nor ought we to allow that there is any such faculty. The faculties of consciousness and memory are chiefly distinguished by this, that the first is an immediate knowledge of the present, the second an immediate knowledge of the past.

When, therefore, Mr Locke's notion of personal identity is properly expressed, it is, that personal identity consists in distinct remembrance: for, even in the popular sense, to say that I am conscious of a past action, means nothing else than that I distinctly remember that I did it.

2dly, It may be observed, that in this doctrine, not only is consciousness confounded with memory, but, which is still more strange, personal identity is confounded with the evidence which we have of our personal identity.

It is very true, that my remembrance that I did such a thing is the evidence I have that I am the identical person who did it. And this, I am apt to think, Mr Locke meant: but to say that my remembrance that I did such a thing, or my consciousness, makes me the person who did it, is, in my apprehension, an absurdity too gross to be entertained by any man who attends to the meaning of it: for it is to attribute to memory or consciousness, a strange magical power of producing its object, though that object must have existed before the memory or consciousness which produced it.

Consciousness is the testimony of one faculty; memory is the testimony of another faculty: and to say that the testimony is the cause of the thing testified, this surely is absurd, if any thing be, and could not have been said by Mr Locke, if he had not confounded the testimony with the thing testified. [. . .]

As our consciousness sometimes ceases to exist, as in sound sleep, our personal identity must cease with it. Mr Locke allows, that the same thing cannot have two beginnings of existence, so that our identity would be irrecoverably gone every time we cease to think, if it was but for a moment.

[From *An Inquiry into the Human Mind* (1st US edn., Charlestown: Samuel Etheridge, 1814), 356–9, 362.]

WILLIAM JAMES

67   **The Consciousness of Self**

Let us begin with the Self in its widest acceptation, and follow it up to its most delicate and subtle form, advancing from the study of the empirical, as the Germans call it, to that of the pure, Ego.

The Empirical Self or Me

The Empirical Self of each of us is all that he is tempted to call by the name of *me*. But it is clear that between what a man calls *me* and what he simply calls *mine* the line is difficult to draw. We feel and act about certain things that are ours very much as we feel and act about ourselves. Our fame, our children, the work of our hands, may be as dear to us as our bodies are, and arouse the same feelings and the same acts of reprisal if attacked. And our bodies themselves, are they simply ours, or are they *us*? Certainly men have been ready to disown their very bodies and to regard them as mere vestures, or even as prisons of clay from which they should some day be glad to escape.

We see then that we are dealing with a fluctuating material; the same object being sometimes treated as a part of me, at other times as simply mine, and then again as if I had nothing to do with it at all. *In its widest possible sense, however, a man's Self is the sum total of all that he CAN call his*, not only his body and his psychic powers, but his clothes and his house, his wife and children, his ancestors and friends, his reputation and works, his lands and horses, and yacht and bank-account. All these things give him the same emotions. If they wax and prosper, he feels triumphant; if they dwindle and die away, he feels cast down,—not necessarily in the same degree for each thing, but in much the same way for all. Understanding the Self in this widest sense, we may begin by dividing the history of it into three parts, relating respectively to—

1. Its constituents;
2. The feelings and emotions they arouse,—*Self-feelings*;
3. The actions to which they prompt,—*Self-seeking* and *Self-preservation*.

1. *The constituents of the Self* may be divided into two classes, those which make up respectively—

(*a*) The material Self;
(*b*) The social Self;
(*c*) The spiritual Self; and
(*d*) The pure Ego.

(*a*) The body is the innermost part of *the material Self* in each of us; and certain parts of the body seem more intimately ours than the rest. The clothes come next. The old saying that the human person is composed of three parts—soul, body and clothes—is more than a joke. We so appropriate our clothes and identify ourselves with them that there are few of us who, if asked to choose between having a beautiful body clad in raiment perpetually shabby and unclean, and having an ugly and blemished form always spotlessly attired, would not hesitate a moment before making a decisive reply. Next, our immediate family is a part of ourselves. Our father and mother, our wife and babes, are bone of our bone and flesh of our flesh.

When they die, a part of our very selves is gone. If they do anything wrong, it is our shame. If they are insulted, our anger flashes forth as readily as if we stood in their place. Our home comes next. Its scenes are part of our life; its aspects awaken the tenderest feelings of affection; and we do not easily forgive the stranger who, in visiting it, finds fault with its arrangements or treats it with contempt. All these different things are the objects of instinctive preferences coupled with the most important practical interests of life. We all have a blind impulse to watch over our body, to deck it with clothing of an ornamental sort, to cherish parents, wife and babes, and to find for ourselves a home of our own which we may live in and 'improve.'

An equally instinctive impulse drives us to collect property; and the collections thus made become, with different degrees of intimacy, parts of our empirical selves. The parts of our wealth most intimately ours are those which are saturated with our labor. There are few men who would not feel personally annihilated if a lifelong construction of their hands or brains—say an entomological collection or an extensive work in manuscript—were suddenly swept away. The miser feels similarly towards his gold; and although it is true that a part of our depression at the loss of possessions is due to our feeling that we must now go without certain goods that we expected the possessions to bring in their train, yet in every case there remains, over and above this, a sense of the shrinkage of our personality, a partial conversion of ourselves to nothingness, which is a psychological phenomenon by itself. We are all at once assimilated to the tramps and poor devils whom we so despise, and at the same time removed farther than ever away from the happy sons of earth who lord it over land and sea and men in the full-blown lustihood that wealth and power can give, and before whom, stiffen ourselves as we will by appealing to anti-snobbish first principles, we cannot escape an emotion, open or sneaking, of respect and dread.

(b) *A man's Social Self* is the recognition which he gets from his mates. We are not only gregarious animals, liking to be in sight of our fellows, but we have an innate propensity to get ourselves noticed, and noticed favorably, by our kind. No more fiendish punishment could be devised, were such a thing physically possible, than that one should be turned loose in society and remain absolutely unnoticed by all the members thereof. If no one turned round when we entered, answered when we spoke, or minded what we did, but if every person we met 'cut us dead,' and acted as if we were non-existing things, a kind of rage and impotent despair would ere long well up in us, from which the cruellest bodily tortures would be a relief; for these would make us feel that, however bad might be our plight, we had not sunk to such a depth as to be unworthy of attention at all.

Properly speaking, *a man has as many social selves as there are individuals who recognize him* and carry an image of him in their mind. To wound any one of these his images is to wound him. [. . .]

The most peculiar social self which one is apt to have is in the kind of the person one is in love with. The good or bad fortunes this self cause the most intense elation and dejection—unreasonable enough as measured by every other standard than that of the organic feeling of the individual. To his own consciousness he *is* not, so long as this particular social self fails to get recognition, and when it is recognized his contentment passes all bounds.

A man's *fame*, good or bad, and his *honor* or dishonor, are names of one of his social selves. The particular social self of a man called his honor is usually the result of one of those splittings of which we have spoken. It is his image in the eyes of his own 'set,' which exalts or condemns him as he conforms or not to certain requirements that may not be made of one in another walk of life. [. . .]

What may be called 'club-opinion' is one of the very strongest forces in life. The thief must not steal from other thieves; the gambler must pay his gambling-debts, though he pay no other debts in the world. The code of honor of fashionable society has throughout history been full of permissions as well as of vetoes, the only reason for following either of which is that so we best serve one of our social selves. You must not lie in general, but you may lie as much as you please if asked about your relations with a lady; you must accept a challenge from an equal, but if challenged by an inferior you may laugh him to scorn: these are examples of what is meant.

(*c*) By the Spiritual Self, so far as it belongs to the Empirical Me, I mean a man's inner or subjective being, his psychic faculties or dispositions, taken concretely; not the bare principle of personal Unity, or 'pure' Ego, which remains still to be discussed. These psychic dispositions are the most enduring and intimate part of the self, that which we most verily seem to be. We take a purer self-satisfaction when we think of our ability to argue and discriminate, of our moral sensibility and conscience, of our indomitable will, than when we survey any of our other possessions. Only when these are altered is a man said to be *alienatus a se*.

Now this spiritual self may be considered in various ways. We may divide it into faculties, as just instanced, isolating them one from another, and identifying ourselves with either in turn. This is an *abstract* way of dealing with consciousness, in which, as it actually presents itself, a plurality of such faculties are always to be simultaneously found; or we may insist on a concrete view, and then the spiritual self in us will be either the entire stream of our personal consciousness, or the present 'segment' or 'section' of that stream, according as we take a broader or a narrower view—both the stream and the section being concrete existences in time, and each being a unity after its own peculiar kind. But whether we take it abstractly or concretely, our considering the spiritual self at all is a reflective process, is the result of our abandoning the outward-looking point of view, and of our having become able to think of subjectivity as such, *to think ourselves as thinkers*. [. . .]

Now this subjective life of ours, distinguished as such so clearly from the objects known by its means, may, as aforesaid, be taken by us in a concrete or in an abstract way. Of the concrete way I will say nothing just now, except that the actual 'section' of the stream will ere long, in our discussion of the nature of the principle of *unity* in consciousness, play a very important part. The abstract way claims our attention first. If the stream as a whole is identified with the Self far more than any outward thing, a *certain portion of the stream abstracted from the rest* is so identified in an altogether peculiar degree, and is felt by all men as a sort of innermost centre within the circle, of sanctuary within the citadel, constituted by the subjective life as a whole. Compared with this element of the stream, the other parts, even of the subjective life, seem transient external possessions, of which each in turn can be disowned, whilst that which disowns them remains. Now, *what is this self of all the other selves?*

Probably all men would describe it in much the same way up to a certain point. They would call it the *active* element in all consciousness; saying that whatever qualities a man's feelings may possess, or whatever content his thought may include, there is a spiritual something in him which seems to *go out* to meet these qualities and contents, whilst they seem to *come in* to be received by it. It is what welcomes or rejects. It presides over the perception of sensations, and by giving or withholding its assent it influences the movements they tend to arouse. It is the home of interest,—not the pleasant or the painful, not even pleasure or pain, as such, but that within us to which pleasure and pain, the pleasant and the painful, speak. It is the source of effort and attention, and the place from which appear to emanate the fiats of the will. A physiologist who should reflect upon it in his own person could hardly help, I should think, connecting it more or less vaguely with the process by which ideas or incoming sensations are 'reflected' or pass over into outward acts. Not necessarily that it should *be* this process or the mere feeling of this process, but that it should be in some close way *related* to this process; for it plays a part analogous to it in the psychic life, being a sort of junction at which sensory ideas terminate and from which motor ideas proceed, and forming a kind of link between the two. Being more incessantly there than any other single element of the mental life, the other elements end by seeming to accrete round it and to belong to it. It becomes opposed to them as the permanent is opposed to the changing and inconstant.

[From *The Principles of Psychology* (1890) (Cambridge, Mass.: Harvard University Press, 1981), 279–83.]

Popular psychology and much so-called scientific psychology have been pretty thoroughly infected by the idea of the separateness of mind and body. This notion of their separation inevitably results in creating a dualism between 'mind' and 'practice,' since the latter must operate through the body. The idea of the separation perhaps arose, in part at least, from the fact that so much of mind at a given time is aloof from action. The separation, when it is once made, certainly confirms the theory that mind, soul, and spirit can exist and go through their operations without any interaction of the organism with its environment. The traditional notion of leisure is thoroughly infected by contrast with the character of onerous labor.

It seems to me, accordingly, that the idiomatic use of the word 'mind' gives a much more truly scientific, and philosophic, approach to the actual facts of the case than does the technical one. For in its non-technical use, 'mind' denotes every mode and variety of interest in, and concern for, things: practical, intellectual, and emotional. It never denotes anything self-contained, isolated from the world of persons and things, but is always used with respect to situations, events, objects, persons and groups. Consider its inclusiveness. It signifies memory. We are reminded of this and that. Mind also signifies attention. We not only keep things in mind, but we bring mind to bear on our problems and perplexities. Mind also signifies purpose; we have a mind to do this and that. Nor is mind in these operations something purely intellectual. The mother minds her baby; she cares for it with affection. Mind is care in the sense of solicitude, anxiety, as well as of active looking after things that need to be tended; we mind our step, our course of action, emotionally as well as thoughtfully. From giving heed to acts and objects, mind comes also to signify, to obey—as children are told to mind their parents. In short 'to mind' denotes an activity that is intellectual, to *note* something; affectional, as caring and liking, and volitional, practical, acting in a purposive way.

Mind is primarily a verb. It denotes all the ways in which we deal consciously and expressly with the situations in which we find ourselves. Unfortunately, an influential manner of thinking has changed modes of action into an underlying substance that performs the activities in question. It has treated mind as an independent entity *which* attends, purposes, cares, notices, and remembers. This change of ways of responding to the environment into an entity from which actions proceed is unfortunate, because it removes mind from necessary connection with the objects and events, past, present and future, of the environment with which responsive activities are inherently connected. Mind that bears only an accidental relation to the environment occupies a similar relation to the body. In making mind purely immaterial (isolated from the organ of doing and undergoing), the body ceases to be living and becomes a dead lump. This conception of mind as an isolated being underlies, for example, the conception that esthetic experience is merely something 'in mind,' and strengthens the conception which isolates the esthetic from those modes of experience in which the body is actively engaged with the things of nature and life. It takes art out of the province of the live creature.

In the idiomatic sense of the word 'substantial,' as distinct from the metaphysical sense of a substance, there is something substantial about mind. Whenever anything is undergone in consequence of a doing, the self is modified. The modification extends beyond acquisition of greater facility and skill. Attitudes and interests are built up which embody in themselves some deposit of the meaning of things done and undergone. These funded and retained meanings become a part of the self. They constitute the capital with which the self notes, cares for, attends, and purposes. In this substantial sense, mind forms the background upon which every new contact with surroundings is projected; yet 'background' is too passive a word, unless we remember that it is active and that, in the projection of the new upon it, there is assimilation and reconstruction both of background and of what is taken in and digested.

This active and eager background lies in wait and engages whatever comes its way so as to absorb it into its own being. Mind as background is formed out of modifications of the self that have occurred in the process of prior interactions with environment. Its animus is toward further interactions. Since it is formed out of commerce with the world and is set toward that world nothing can be further from the truth than the idea which treats it as something self-contained and self-enclosed. When its activity is turned upon itself, as in meditation and reflective speculation, its withdrawal is only from the immediate scene of the world during the time in which it turns over and reviews material gathered from that world.

Different kinds of minds are named from the different interests that actuate the gathering and assemblage of material from the encompassing world: the scientific, the executive, the artistic, the business mind. In each there is a preferential manner of selection, retention, and organization. These inherent impulses become mind when they fuse with a particular background of experience.

[From 'Mind and Consciousness', in *Intelligence in the Modern World; John Dewey's Philosophy*, ed. J. Ratner (New York: The Modern Library, 1939), 811–13.]

I shall try to elucidate the problem discussed by realists, idealists, and solipsists by showing you a problem closely related to it. It is this: 'Can we have unconscious thoughts, unconscious feelings, etc.?' The idea of there being unconscious thoughts has revolted many people. Others again have said that these were wrong in supposing that there could only be conscious thoughts, and that psychoanalysis had discovered unconscious ones. The objectors to unconscious thought did not see that they were not objecting to the newly discovered psychological reactions, but to the way in which they were described. The psychoanalysts on the other hand were misled by their own way of expression into thinking that they had done more than discover new psychological reactions; that they had, in a sense, discovered conscious thoughts which were unconscious. The first could have stated their objection by saying 'We don't wish to use the phrase "unconscious thoughts"; we wish to reserve the word "thought" for what you call "conscious thoughts"'. They state their case wrongly when they say: 'There can only be conscious thoughts and no unconscious ones'. For if they don't wish to talk of 'unconscious thought' they should not use the phrase 'conscious thought', either.

But is it not right to say that in any case the person who talks both of conscious and unconscious thoughts thereby uses the word 'thoughts' in two different ways?—Do we use a hammer in two different ways when we hit a nail with it and, on the other hand, drive a peg into a hole? And do we use it in two different ways or in the same way when we drive this peg into this hole and, on the other hand, another peg into another hole? Or should we only call it different uses when in one case we drive something into something and in the other, say, we smash something? Or is this all using the hammer in one way and is it to be called a different way only when we use the hammer as a paper weight?—In which cases are we to say that a word is used in two different ways and in which that it is used in one way? To say that a word is used in two (or more) different ways does in itself not yet give us any idea about its use. It only specifies a way of looking at this usage by providing a schema for its description with two (or more) subdivisions. It is all right to say: 'I do *two* things with this hammer: I drive a nail into this board and one into that board'. But I could also have said: 'I am doing only one thing with this hammer; I am driving a nail into this board and one into that board'. There can be two kinds of discussions as to whether a word is used in one way or in two ways: (*a*) Two people may discuss whether the English word 'cleave' is only used for chopping up something or also for joining things together. This is a discussion about the facts of a certain actual usage.

(b) They may discuss whether the word 'altus', standing for both 'deep' and 'high', is *thereby* used in two different ways. This question is analogous to the question whether the word 'thought' is used in two ways or in one when we talk of conscious and unconscious thought. The man who says 'surely, these are two different usages' has already decided to use a two-way schema, and what he said expressed this decision.

Now when the solipsist says that only his own experiences are real, it is no use answering him: 'Why do you tell us this if you don't believe that we really hear it?' Or anyhow, if we give him this answer, we mustn't believe that we have answered his difficulty. There is no common sense answer to a philosophical problem. One can defend common sense against the attacks of philosophers only by solving their puzzles, i.e., by curing them of the temptation to attack common sense; not by restating the views of common sense. A philosopher is not a man out of his senses, a man who doesn't see what everybody sees; nor on the other hand is his disagreement with common sense that of the scientist disagreeing with the coarse views of the man in the street. That is, his disagreement is not founded on a more subtle knowledge of fact. We therefore have to look round for the *source* of his puzzlement. And we find that there is puzzlement and mental discomfort, not only when our curiosity about certain facts is not satisfied or when we can't find a law of nature fitting in with all our experience, but also when a notation dissatisfies us—perhaps because of various associations which it calls up. Our ordinary language, which of all possible notations is the one which pervades all our life, holds our mind rigidly in one position, as it were, and in this position sometimes it feels cramped, having a desire for other positions as well. Thus we sometimes wish for a notation which stresses a difference more strongly, makes it more obvious, than ordinary language does, or one which in a particular case uses more closely similar forms of expression than our ordinary language. Our mental cramp is loosened when we are shown the notations which fulfil these needs. These needs can be of the greatest variety. [. . .]

There are many uses of the word 'personality' which we may feel inclined to adopt, all more or less akin. The same applies when we define the identity of a person by means of his memories. Imagine a man whose memories on the even days of his life comprise the events of all these days, skipping entirely what happened on the odd days. On the other hand, he remembers on an odd day what happened on previous odd days, but his memory then skips the even days without a feeling of discontinuity. If we like we can also assume that he has alternating appearances and characteristics on odd and even days. Are we bound to say that here two persons are inhabiting the same body? That is, is it right to say that there are, and wrong to say that there aren't, or vice versa? Neither. For the *ordinary* use of the word 'person' is what one might call a composite use suitable under the ordinary circumstances. If I assume, as I do, that these circumstances are changed, the application of the term 'person' or 'personality' has thereby changed; and if I wish to preserve this term and give it a use analogous to its former use, I am at liberty to choose between many uses, that is, between many different kinds of analogy. One might say in such a case that the term 'personality' hasn't got one legitimate heir only. (This kind of consideration is of importance in the philosophy of mathematics. Consider the use of the words 'proof', 'formula', and others. Consider the question: 'Why should what we do here be called "philosophy"? Why should it be regarded as the only legitimate heir of the different activities which had this name in former times?')

Now let us ask ourselves what sort of identity of personality it is we are referring to when we say 'when anything is seen, it is always I who see'. What is it I want all these cases of seeing to have in common? As an answer I have to confess to myself that it is not my bodily appearance. I don't always see part of my body when I see. And it isn't essential that my body, if seen amongst the things I see, should always look the same. In fact I don't mind how much it changes. And I feel the same way about all the properties of my body, the characteristics of my behaviour, and even about my memories.—— When I think about it a little longer I see that what I wished to say was: 'Always when anything is seen, something is seen'. I.e., that of which I said it continued during all the experiences of seeing was not any particular entity 'I', but the experience of seeing itself. This may become clearer if we imagine the man who makes our solipsistic statement to point to his eyes while he says 'I'. (Perhaps because he wishes to be exact and wants to say expressly which eyes belong to the mouth which says 'I' and to the hands pointing to his own body). But what is he pointing to? These particular eyes with the identity of physical objects? (To understand this sentence, you must remember that the grammar of words of which we say that they stand for physical objects is characterized by the way in which we use the phrase 'the *same* so-and-so', or 'the identical so-and-so', where 'so-and-so' designates the physical object.) We said before that he did not wish to point to a particular physical object at all. The idea that he had made a significant statement arose from a confusion corresponding to the confusion between what we shall call 'the geometrical eye' and 'the physical eye'. I will indicate the use of these terms: If a man tries to obey the order 'Point to your eye', he may do many different things, and there are many different criteria which he will accept for having pointed to his eye. If these criteria, as they usually do, coincide, I may use them alternately and in different combinations to show me that I have touched my eye. If they don't coincide, I shall have to distinguish between different senses of the phrase 'I touch my eye' or 'I move my finger towards my eye'. If, e.g., my eyes are shut, I can still have the characteristic kinaesthetic experience in my arm which I should call the kinaesthetic experience of raising my hand to my eye. That I had succeeded in doing so, I shall recognize by the peculiar tactile sensation of touching my eye. But if my eye were behind a glass plate fastened in such a way that it prevented me from exerting a pressure on my eye with my finger, there would still be a criterion of muscular sensation which would make me say that now my finger was in front of my eye. As to visual criteria, there are two I can adopt. There is the ordinary experience of seeing my hand rise and come towards my eye, and this experience, of course, is different from seeing two things meet, say, two finger tips. On the other hand, I can use as a criterion for my finger moving towards my eye, what I see when I look into a mirror and see my finger nearing my eye. If that place on my body which, we say, 'sees' is to be determined by moving my finger towards my eye, according to the second criterion, then it is conceivable that I may see with what according to other criteria is the tip of my nose, or places on my forehead; or I might in this way point to a place lying outside my body. If I wish a person to point to his eye (or his eyes) according to the second criterion *alone*, I shall express my wish by saying: 'Point to your geometrical eye (or eyes)'. The grammar of the word 'geometrical eye' stands in the same relation to the grammar of the word 'physical eye' as the grammar of the expression 'the visual sense datum of a tree' to the grammar of the expression 'the physical tree'. In either case it confuses everything to say 'the one is a *different kind* of object from the other'; for those who say that a sense datum is a different kind of object from a physical object misunderstand the grammar of the word 'kind', just as those who say that a number is a different kind of object from a numeral. They think they are making such a statement as 'A railway train, a railway station, and a railway car are different kinds of objects', whereas their statement is analogous to 'A railway train, a railway accident, and a railway law are different kinds of objects'.

What tempted me to say 'it is always I who see when anything is seen', I could also have yielded to by saying: 'whenever anything is seen, it is *this* which is seen', accompanying the word 'this' by a gesture embracing my visual field (but not meaning by 'this' the particular objects which I happen to see at the moment). One might say, 'I am pointing at the visual field as such, not at anything in it'. And this only serves to bring out the senselessness of the former expression.

Let us then discard the 'always' in our expression. Then I can still express my solipsism by saying, 'Only what *I* see (or: see now) is really seen'. And here I am tempted to say: 'Although by the word "I" I don't mean L.W., it will do if the others understand "I" to mean L.W., if just now I am in fact L.W.' I could also express my claim by saying: 'I am the vessel of life'; but mark, it is essential that everyone to whom I say this should be unable to understand me. It is essential that the other should not be able to understand 'what I really *mean*', though in practice he might do what I wish by conceding to me an exceptional position in his notation. But I wish it to be *logically* impossible that he should understand me, that is to say, it should be meaningless, not false, to say that he understands me. Thus my expression is one of the many which is used on various occasions by philosophers and supposed to convey something to the person who says it, though essentially incapable of conveying anything to anyone else. Now if for an expression to convey a meaning means to be accompanied by or to produce certain experiences, our expression may have all sorts of meanings, and I don't wish to say anything about them. But we are, as a matter of fact, misled into thinking that our expression has a meaning in the sense in which a non-metaphysical expression has; for we wrongly compare our case with one in which the other person can't understand what we say because he lacks a certain information. (This remark can only become clear if we understand the connection between grammar and sense and nonsense.)

The meaning of a phrase for us is characterized by the use we make of it. The meaning is not a mental accompaniment to the expression. Therefore the phrase 'I think I mean something by it', or 'I'm sure I mean something by it', which we so often hear in philosophical discussions to justify the use of an expression is for us no justification at all. We ask: 'What do you mean?', i.e., 'How do you use this expression?' If someone taught me the word 'bench', and said that he sometimes or always put a stroke over it thus: 'bench', and that this meant something to him, I should say: 'I don't know what sort of idea you associate with this stroke, but it doesn't interest me unless you show me that there is a use for the stroke in the kind of calculus in which you wish to use the word "bench" '.—I want to play chess, and a man gives the white king a paper crown, leaving the use of the piece unaltered, but telling me that the crown has a meaning to him in the game, which he can't express by rules. I say: 'as long as it doesn't alter the use of the piece, it hasn't what I call a meaning'.

One sometimes hears that such a phrase as 'This is here', when while I say it I point to a part of my visual field, has a kind of primitive meaning to me, although it can't impart information to anybody else.

When I say 'Only this is seen', I forget that a sentence may come ever so natural to us without having any use in our calculus of language. Think of the law of identity, 'a = a', and of how we sometimes try hard to get hold of its sense, to visualize it, by looking at an object and repeating to ourselves such a sentence as 'This tree is the same thing as this tree'. The gestures and images by which I apparently give this sentence sense are very similar to those which I use in the case of 'Only this is really seen'. (To get clear about philosophical problems, it is useful to become conscious of the apparently unimportant details of the particular situation in which we are inclined to make a certain metaphysical assertion. Thus we may be tempted to say 'Only this is really seen' when we stare at unchanging surroundings, whereas we may not at all be tempted to say this when we look about us while walking.)

There is, as we have said, no objection to adopting a symbolism in which a certain person always or temporarily holds an exceptional place. And therefore, if I utter the sentence 'Only I really see', it is conceivable that my fellow creatures thereupon will arrange their notation so as to fall in with me by saying 'so-and-so is really seen' instead of 'L.W. sees so-and-so', etc., etc. What, however, is wrong, is to think that I can *justify* this choice of notation. When I said, from my heart, that only I see, I was also inclined to say that by 'I' I didn't really mean L.W., although for the benefit of my fellow men I might say 'It is now L.W. who really sees' though this is not what I really mean. I could almost say that by 'I' I mean something which just now inhabits L.W., something which the others can't see. (I meant my mind, but could only point to it via my body.) There is nothing wrong in suggesting that the others should give me an exceptional place in their notation; but the justification which I wish to give for it: that this body is now the seat of that which really lives—is senseless. For admittedly this is not to state anything which in the ordinary sense is a matter of experience. (And don't think that it is an experiential proposition which only I can know because only I am in the position to have the particular experience.) Now the idea that the real I lives in my body is connected with the peculiar grammar of the word 'I', and the misunderstandings this grammar is liable to give rise to. There are two different cases in the use of the word 'I' (or 'my') which I might call 'the use as object' and 'the use as subject'. Examples of the first kind of use are these: 'My arm is broken', 'I have grown six inches', 'I have a bump on my forehead', 'The wind blows my hair about'. Examples of the second kind are: '*I* see so-and-so', '*I* hear so-and-so', '*I* try to lift my arm', '*I* think it will rain', '*I* have toothache'. One can point to the difference between these two categories by saying: The cases of the first category involve the recognition of a particular person, and there is in these cases the possibility of an error, or as I should rather put it: The possibility of an error has been provided for. The possibility of failing to score has been provided for in a pin game. On the other hand, it is not one of the hazards of the game that the balls should fail to come up if I have put a penny in the slot. It is possible that, say in an accident, I should feel a pain in my arm, see a broken arm at my side, and think it is mine, when really it is my neighbour's. And I could, looking into a mirror, mistake a bump on his forehead for one on mine. On the other hand, there is no question of recognizing a person when I say I have toothache. To ask 'are you sure that it's *you* who have pains?' would be nonsensical. Now, when in this case no error is possible, it is because the move which we might be inclined to think of as an error, a 'bad move', is no move of the game at all. (We distinguish in chess between good and bad moves, and we call it a mistake if we expose the queen to a bishop. But it is no mistake to promote a pawn to a king.) And now this way of stating our idea suggests itself: that it is as impossible that in making the statement 'I have toothache' I should have mistaken another person for myself, as it is to moan with pain by mistake, having mistaken someone else for me. To say, 'I have pain' is no more a statement *about* a particular person than moaning is. 'But surely the word "I" in the mouth of a man refers to the man who says it; it points to himself; and very often a man who says it actually points to himself with his finger'. But it was quite superfluous to point to himself. He might just as well only have raised his hand. It would be wrong to say that when someone points to the sun with his hand, he is pointing both to the sun and himself because it is *he* who points; on the other hand, he may by pointing attract attention both to the sun and to himself.

The word 'I' does not mean the same as 'L.W.' even if I am L.W., nor does it mean the same as the expression 'the person who is now speaking'. But that doesn't mean: that 'L.W.' and 'I' mean different things. All it means is that these words are different instruments in our language.

[From *The Blue and Brown Books* (New York: Harper Torchbooks, 1958), 57–67.]

SIGMUND FREUD

70   Dissection of the Personality

There is no need to discuss what is to be called conscious: it is removed from all doubt. The oldest and best meaning of the word 'unconscious' is the descriptive one; we call a physical process unconscious whose existence we are obliged to assume—for some such reason as that we infer it from its effects—, but of which we know nothing. In that case we have the same relation to it as we have to a psychical process in another person, except that it is in fact one of our own. If we want to be still more correct, we shall modify our assertion by saying that we call a process unconscious if we are obliged to assume that it is being activated *at the moment*, though *at the moment* we know nothing about it. This qualification makes us reflect that the majority of conscious processes are conscious only for a short time; very soon they become *latent*, but can easily become conscious again. We might also say that they had become unconscious, if it were at all certain that in the condition of latency they are still something psychical. So far we should have learnt nothing new; nor should we have acquired the right to introduce the concept of an unconscious into psychology. But then comes the new observation that we were already able to make in parapraxes. In order to explain a slip of the tongue, for instance, we find ourselves obliged to assume that the intention to make a particular remark was present in the subject. We infer it with certainty from the interference with his remark which has occurred; but the intention did not put itself through and was thus unconscious. If, when we subsequently put it before the speaker, he recognizes it as one familiar to him, then it was only temporarily unconscious to him; but if he repudiates it as something foreign to him, then it was permanently unconscious. From this experience we retrospectively obtain the right also to pronounce as something unconscious what had been described as latent. A consideration of these dynamic relations permits us now to distinguish two kinds of unconscious—one which is easily, under frequently occurring circumstances, transformed into something conscious, and another with which this transformation is difficult and takes place only subject to a considerable expenditure of effort or possibly never at all. In order to escape the ambiguity as to whether we mean the one or the other unconscious, whether we are using the word in the descriptive or in the dynamic sense, we make use of a permissible and simple way out. We call the unconscious which is only latent, and thus easily becomes conscious, the 'preconscious' and retain the term 'unconscious' for the other. We now have three terms, 'conscious', 'preconscious' and 'unconscious', with which we can get along in our description of mental phenomena. Once again: the preconscious is also unconscious in the purely descriptive sense, but we do not give it that name, except in talking loosely or when we have to make a defence of the existence in mental life of unconscious processes in general.

You will admit, I hope, that so far that is not too bad and allows of convenient handling. Yes, but unluckily the work of psycho-analysis has found itself compelled to use the word 'unconscious' in yet another, third, sense, and this may, to be sure, have led to confusion. Under the new and powerful impression of there being an extensive and important field of mental life which is normally withdrawn from the ego's knowledge so that the processes occurring in it have to be regarded as unconscious in the truly dynamic sense, we have come to understand the term 'unconscious' in a topographical or systematic sense as well [. . .] and have used the word more and more to denote a mental province rather than a quality of what is mental. [. . .]

Following a verbal usage of Nietzsche's [. . .] we will in future call it the 'id'. This impersonal pronoun seems particularly well suited for expressing the main characteristic of this province of the mind—the fact of its being alien to the ego. The super-ego, the ego and the id—these, then, are the three realms, regions, provinces, into which we divide an individual's mental apparatus, and with the mutual relations of which we shall be concerned in what follows. [. . .]

You will not expect me to have much to tell you that is new about the id apart from its new name. It is the dark, inaccessible part of our personality; what little we know of it we have learnt from our study of the dream-work and of the construction of neurotic symptoms, and most of that is of a negative character and can be described only as a contrast to the ego. We approach the id with analogies: we call it a chaos, a cauldron full of seething excitations. We picture it as being open at its end to somatic influences, and as there taking up into itself instinctual needs which find their psychical expression in it, but we cannot say in what substratum. It is filled with energy reaching it from the instincts, but it has no organization, produces no collective will, but only a striving to bring about the satisfaction of the instinctual needs subject to the observance of the pleasure principle. The logical laws of thought do not apply in the id, and this is true above all of the law of contradiction. Contrary impulses exist side by side, without cancelling each other out or diminishing each other: at the most they may converge to form compromises under the dominating economic pressure towards the discharge of energy. There is nothing in the id that could be compared with negation; and we perceive with surprise an exception to the philosophical theorem that space and time are necessary forms of our mental acts. There is nothing in the id that corresponds to the idea of time; there is no recognition of the passage of time, and—a thing that is most remarkable and awaits consideration in philosophical thought—no alteration in its mental processes is produced by the passage of time. Wishful impulses which have never passed beyond the id, but impressions, too, which have been sunk into the id by repression, are virtually immortal; after the passage of decades they behave as though they had just occurred. They can only be recognized as belonging to the past, can only lose their importance and be deprived of their cathexis of energy, when they have been made conscious by the work of analysis, and it is on this that the therapeutic effect of analytic treatment rests to no small extent.

We can best arrive at the characteristics of the actual ego, in so far as it can be distinguished from the id and from the super-ego, by examining its relation to the outermost superficial portion of the mental apparatus. [. . .] The relation to the external world has become the decisive factor for the ego; it has taken on the task of representing the external world to the id—fortunately for the id, which could not escape destruction if, in its blind efforts for the satisfaction of its instincts, it disregarded that supreme external power. In accomplishing this function, the ego must observe the external world, must lay down an accurate picture of it in the memory-traces of its perceptions, and by its exercise of the function of 'reality-testing' must put aside whatever in this picture of the external world is an addition derived from internal sources of excitation. The ego controls the approaches to motility under the id's orders; but between a need and an action it has interposed a postponement in the form of the activity of thought, during which it makes use of the mnemic residues of experience. In that way it has dethroned the pleasure principle which dominates the course of events in the id without any restriction and has replaced it by the reality principle, which promises more certainly and greater success. [. . .]

To adopt a popular mode of speaking, we might say that the ego stands for reason and good sense while the id stands for the untamed passions.

So far we have allowed ourselves to be impressed by the merits and capabilities of the ego; it is now time to consider the other side as well. The ego is after all only a portion of the id, a portion that has been expediently modified by the proximity of the external world with its threat of danger. From a dynamic point of view it is weak, it has borrowed its energies from the id, and we are not entirely without insight into the methods—we might call them dodges—by which it extracts further amounts of energy from the id. [. . .]

We are warned by a proverb against serving two masters at the same time. The poor ego has things even worse: it serves three severe masters and does what it can to bring their claims and demands into harmony with one another. These claims are always divergent and often seem incompatible. No wonder that the ego so often fails in its task. Its three tyrannical masters are the external world, the super-ego and the id. When we follow the ego's efforts to satisfy them simultaneously—or rather, to obey them simultaneously—we cannot feel any regret at having personified this ego and having set it up as a separate organism. It feels hemmed in on three sides, threatened by three kinds of danger, to which, if it is hard pressed, it reacts by generating anxiety. Owing to its origin from the experiences of the perceptual system, it is earmarked for representing the demands of the external world, but it strives too to be a loyal servant of the id, to remain on good terms with it, to recommend itself to it as an object and to attract its libido to itself. In its attempts to mediate between the id and reality, it is often obliged [. . .] to conceal the id's conflicts with reality, to profess, with diplomatic disingenuousness, to be taking notice of reality even when the id has remained rigid and unyielding. On the other hand it is observed at every step it takes by the strict super-ego, which lays down definite standards for its conduct, without taking any account of its difficulties from the direction of the id and the external world, and which, if those standards are not obeyed, punishes it with tense feelings of inferiority and of guilt. Thus the ego, driven by the id, confined by the super-ego, repulsed by reality, struggles to master its economic task of bringing about harmony among the forces and influences working in and upon it; and we can understand how it is that so often we cannot suppress a cry: 'Life is not easy!' If the ego is obliged to admit its weakness, it breaks out in anxiety—realistic anxiety regarding the external world, moral anxiety regarding the super-ego and neurotic anxiety regarding the strength of the passions in the id.

[From *New Introductory Lectures on Psycho-Analysis and other works*, in *The Standard Edition of the Complete Psychological Works of Sigmund Freud*, ed. J. Strachey, vol. xxii (London: Hogarth Press, 1962), 70–8.]

71 The Disembodied Lady

> The aspects of things that are most important for us are hidden because
> of their simplicity and familiarity. (One is unable to notice something
> because it is always before one's eyes.) The real foundations of his
> enquiry do not strike a man at all.
>
> —Wittgenstein

What Wittgenstein writes here, of epistemology, might apply to aspects of
one's physiology and psychology—especially in regard to what Sherrington
once called 'our secret sense, our sixth sense'—that continuous but
unconscious sensory flow from the movable parts of our body (muscles,
tendons, joints), by which their position and tone and motion are continually
monitored and adjusted, but in a way which is hidden from us because it is
automatic and unconscious.

Our other senses—the five senses—are open and obvious; but this—our
hidden sense—had to be discovered, as it was, by Sherrington, in the 1890s.
He named it 'proprioception', to distinguish it from 'exteroception' and
'interoception', and, additionally, because of its indispensability for our sense
of *ourselves*; for it is only by courtesy of proprioception, so to speak, that we
feel our bodies as proper to us, as our 'property', as our own. [. . .]

Christina was a strapping young woman of twenty-seven, given to hockey
and riding, self-assured, robust, in body and mind. She had two young
children, and worked as a computer programmer at home. She was
intelligent and cultivated, fond of the ballet, and of the Lakeland poets (but
not, I would think, of Wittgenstein). She had an active, full life—had scarcely
known a day's illness. Somewhat to her surprise, after an attack of abdominal
pain, she was found to have gallstones, and removal of the gall-bladder was
advised.

She was admitted to hospital three days before the operation date, and
placed on an antibiotic for microbial prophylaxis. This was purely routine, a
precaution, no complications of any sort being expected at all. Christina
understood this, and being a sensible soul had no great anxieties.

The day before surgery Christina, not usually given to fancies or dreams,
had a disturbing dream of peculiar intensity. She was swaying wildly, in her
dream, very unsteady on her feet, could hardly feel the ground beneath her,
could hardly feel anything in her hands, found them flailing to and fro, kept
dropping whatever she picked up.

She was distressed by this dream. ('I never had one like it,' she said. 'I can't
get it out of my mind.')—so distressed that we requested an opinion from the
psychiatrist. 'Pre-operative anxiety,' he said. 'Quite natural, we see it all the
time.'

But later that day *the dream came true*. Christina did find herself very unsteady on her feet, with awkward flailing movements, and dropping things from her hands.

The psychiatrist was again called—he seemed vexed at the call, but also, momentarily, uncertain and bewildered. 'Anxiety hysteria,' he now snapped, in a dismissive tone. 'Typical conversion symptoms—you see them all the while.'

But the day of surgery Christina was still worse. Standing was impossible—unless she looked down at her feet. She could hold nothing in her hands, and they 'wandered'—unless she kept an eye on them. When she reached out for something, or tried to feed herself, her hands would miss, or overshoot wildly, as if some essential control or coordination was gone.

She could scarcely even sit up—her body 'gave way'. Her face was oddly expressionless and slack, her jaw fell open, even her vocal posture was gone.

'Something awful's happened,' she mouthed, in a ghostly flat voice. 'I can't feel my body. I feel weird—disembodied.'

This was an amazing thing to hear, confounded, confounding. 'Disembodied'—was she crazy? But what of her physical state then? The collapse of tone and muscle posture, from top to toe; the wandering of her hands, which she seemed unaware of; the flailing and overshooting, as if she were receiving no information from the periphery, as if the control loops for tone and movement had catastrophically broken down.

'It's a strange statement,' I said to the residents. 'It's almost impossible to imagine what might provoke such a statement.'

'But it's hysteria, Dr Sacks—didn't the psychiatrist say so?'

'Yes, he did. But have you ever seen a hysteria like this? Think phenomenologically—take what you see as genuine phenomenon, in which her state-of-body and state-of-mind are not fictions, but a psychophysical whole. Could anything give such a picture of undermined body and mind?

'I'm not testing you,' I added. 'I'm as bewildered as you are. I've never seen or imagined anything quite like this before . . .'

I thought, and they thought, we thought together.

'Could it be a biparietal syndrome?' one of them asked.

'It's an "as if",' I answered: '*as if* the parietal lobes were not getting their usual sensory information. Let's *do* some sensory testing—and test parietal lobe function, too.'

We did so, and a picture began to emerge. There seemed to be a very profound, almost total, proprioceptive deficit, going from the tips of her toes to her head—the parietal lobes were working, *but had nothing to work with*. Christina might have hysteria, but she had a great deal more, of a sort which none of us had ever seen or conceived before. We put in an emergency call now, not to the psychiatrist, but to the physical medicine specialist, the physiatrist.

He arrived promptly, responding to the urgency of the call. He opened his eyes very wide when he saw Christina, examined her swiftly and comprehensively, and then proceeded to electrical tests of nerve and muscle function. 'This is quite extraordinary,' he said. 'I have never seen or read about anything like this before. She has lost all proprioception—you're right—from top to toe. She has no muscle or tendon or joint sense whatever. There is slight loss of other sensory modalities—to light touch, temperature, and pain, and slight involvement of the motor fibres, too. But it is predominantly position-sense—proprioception—which has sustained such damage.'

'What's the cause?' we asked.

'You're the neurologists. You find out.'

By afternoon, Christina was still worse. She lay motionless and toneless; even her breathing was shallow. Her situation was grave—we thought of a respirator—as well as strange. [. . .]

'What's the verdict?' Christina asked, with a faint voice and fainter smile, after we had checked her spinal fluid.

'You've got this inflammation, this neuritis . . .' we began, and told her all we knew. When we forgot something, or hedged, her clear questions brought us back.

'Will it get better?' she demanded. We looked at each other, and at her: 'We have no idea.'

The sense of the body, I told her, is given by three things: vision, balance organs (the vestibular system), and proprioception—which she'd lost. Normally all of these worked together. If one failed, the others could compensate, or substitute—to a degree. In particular, I told of my patient Mr MacGregor, who, unable to employ his balance organs, used his eyes instead. And of patients with neurosyphilis, *tabes dorsalis*, who had similar symptoms, but confined to the legs—and how they too had to compensate by use of their eyes [. . .] And how, if one asked such a patient to move his legs, he was apt to say: 'Sure, Doc, as soon as I find them.'

Christina listened closely, with a sort of desperate attention.

'What I must do then,' she said slowly, 'is use vision, use my eyes, in every situation where I used—what do you call it?—proprioception before. I've already noticed,' she added, musingly, 'that I may "lose" my arms. I think they're one place, and I find they're another. This "proprioception" is like the eyes of the body, the way the body sees itself. And if it goes, as it's gone with me, *it's like the body's blind*. My body can't "see" itself if it's lost its eyes, right? So *I* have to watch it—be its eyes. Right?'

'Right,' I said, 'right. You could be a physiologist.'

'I'll *have* to be a sort of physiologist,' she rejoined, 'because my physiology has gone wrong, and may never *naturally* go right . . .'

It was as well that Christina showed such strength of mind, from the start, for, though the acute inflammation subsided, and her spinal fluid returned to normal, the damage it did to her proprioceptive fibres persisted—so that there was no neurological recovery a week, or a year, later. Indeed there has been none in the eight years that have now passed—though she has been able to lead a life, a sort of life, through accommodations and adjustments of every sort, emotional and moral no less than neurological.

That first week Christina did nothing, lay passively, scarcely ate. She was in a state of utter shock, horror and despair. What sort of a life would it be, if there was not natural recovery? What sort of a life, every move made by artifice? What sort of a life, above all, if she felt disembodied?

Then life reasserted itself, as it will, and Christina started to move. She could at first do nothing without using her eyes, and collapsed in a helpless heap the moment she closed them. She had, at first, to monitor herself by vision, looking carefully at each part of her body as it moved, using an almost painful conscientiousness and care. Her movements, consciously monitored and regulated, were at first clumsy, artificial, in the highest degree. But then—and here both of us found ourselves most happily surprised, by the power of an ever-increasing, daily increasing, automatism—then her movements started to appear more delicately modulated, more graceful, more natural (though still wholly dependent on use of the eyes).

Increasingly now, week by week, the normal, unconscious feedback of proprioception was being replaced by an equally unconscious feedback by vision, by visual automatism and reflexes increasingly integrated and fluent. Was it possible, too, that something more fundamental was happening? That the brain's visual model of the body, or body-image—normally rather feeble (it is, of course, absent in the blind), and normally subsidiary to the proprioceptive body-model—was it possible that *this*, now the proprioceptive body model was lost, was gaining, by way of compensation or substitution, an enhanced, exceptional, extraordinary force? [. . .]

Thus at the time of her catastrophe, and for about a month afterwards, Christina remained as floppy as a ragdoll, unable even to sit up. But three months later, I was startled to see her sitting very finely—too finely, statuesquely, like a dancer in mid-pose. And soon I saw that her sitting was, indeed, a pose, consciously or automatically adopted and sustained, a sort of forced or wilful or histrionic posture, to make up for the continuing lack of any genuine, natural posture. Nature having failed, she took to 'artifice', but the artifice was suggested by nature, and soon became 'second nature'. Similarly with her voice—she had at first been almost mute.

This too was projected, as to an audience from a stage. It *was* a stagey, theatrical voice—not because of any histrionism, or perversion of motive, but because there was still no natural vocal posture. And with her face, too—this still tended to remain somewhat flat and expressionless (though her inner emotions were of full and normal intensity), due to lack of proprioceptive facial tone and posture,[1] unless she used an artificial enhancement of expression (as patients with aphasia may adopt exaggerated emphases and inflections).

But all these measures were, at best, partial. They made life possible—they did not make it normal. Christina learned to walk, to take public transport, to conduct the usual business of life—but only with the exercise of great vigilance, and strange ways of doing things—ways which might break down if her attention was diverted. Thus if she was eating while she was talking, or if her attention was elsewhere, she would grip the knife and fork with painful force—her nails and fingertips would go bloodless with pressure; but if there was any lessening of the painful pressure, she might nervelessly drop them straightaway—there was no in-between, no modulation, whatever.

Thus, although there was not a trace of neurological recovery (recovery from the anatomical damage to nerve fibres), there was, with the help of intensive and varied therapy—she remained in hospital, on the rehabilitation ward, for almost a year—a very considerable functional recovery, i.e., the ability to function using various substitutions and other such tricks. It became possible, finally, for Christina to leave hospital, go home, rejoin her children. She was able to return to her home-computer terminal, which she now learned to operate with extraordinary skill and efficiency, considering that everything had to be done by vision, not feel. She had learned to operate—but how did she feel? Had the substitutions dispersed the disembodied sense she first spoke of?

The answer is—not in the least. She continues to feel, with the continuing loss of proprioception, that her body is dead, not-real, not-hers—she cannot appropriate it to herself. She can find no words for this state, and can only use analogies derived from other senses: 'I feel my body is blind and deaf to itself . . . it has no sense of itself'—these are her own words. She has no words, no direct words, to describe this bereftness, this sensory darkness (or silence) akin to blindness or deafness. She has no words, and we lack words too. And society lacks words, and sympathy, for such states. The blind, at least, are treated with solicitude—we can imagine their state, and we treat them accordingly. But when Christina, painfully, clumsily, mounts a bus, she receives nothing but uncomprehending and angry snarls: 'What's wrong with you, lady? Are you blind—or blind-drunk?' What can she answer—'I have no proprioception'? The lack of social support and sympathy is an additional trial: disabled, but with the nature of her disability not clear—she is not, after all, manifestly blind or paralysed, manifestly anything—she tends to be treated as a phoney or a fool. This is what happens to those with disorders of the hidden senses (it happens also to patients who have vestibular impairment, or who have been labyrinthectomised).

Christina is condemned to live in an indescribable, unimaginable realm— though 'non-realm', 'nothingness', might be better words for it. At times she breaks down—not in public, but with me: 'If only I could *feel!*' she cries. 'But I've forgotten what it's like . . . I *was* normal, wasn't I? I *did* move like everyone else?'

'Yes, of course.'

'There's no "of course". I can't believe it. I want proof.'

I show her a home movie of herself with her children, taken just a few weeks before her polyneuritis. [. . .]

For Christina there is this general feeling—this 'deficiency in the egoistic sentiment of individuality'—which has become less with accommodation, with the passage of time. And there is this specific, organically based, feeling of disembodiedness, which remains as severe, and uncanny, as the day she first felt it. This is also felt, for example, by those who have high transections of the spinal cord—but they of course, are paralysed; whereas Christina, though 'bodiless', is up and about.

There are brief, partial reprieves, when her skin is stimulated. She goes out when she can, she loves open cars, where she can feel the wind on her body and face (superficial sensation, light touch, is only slightly impaired). 'It's wonderful,' she says. 'I feel the wind on my arms and face, and then I know, faintly, I *have* arms and a face. It's not the real thing, but it's something—it lifts this horrible, dead veil for a while.'

But her situation is, and remains, a 'Wittgensteinian' one. She does not know 'Here is one hand'—her loss of proprioception, her de-afferentation, has deprived her of her existential, her epistemic, basis—and nothing she can do, or think, will alter this fact. She cannot be certain of her body—what would Wittgenstein have said, in her position?

[From *The Man Who Mistook His Wife for a Hat* (New York: Harper & Row, 1970), 43–53.]

DEREK PARFIT

72   Why Our Identity is not What Matters

Divided Minds

Some recent medical cases provide striking evidence in favour of the Reductionist View. Human beings have a lower brain and two upper hemispheres, which are connected by a bundle of fibres. In treating a few people with severe epilepsy, surgeons have cut these fibres. The aim was to reduce the severity of epileptic fits, by confining their causes to a single hemisphere. This aim was achieved. But the operations had another unintended consequence. The effect, in the words of one surgeon, was the creation of 'two separate spheres of consciousness'.

This effect was revealed by various psychological tests. These made use of two facts. We control our right arms with our left hemispheres, and vice versa. And what is in the right halves of our visual fields we see with our left hemispheres, and vice versa. When someone's hemispheres have been disconnected, psychologists can thus present to this person two different written questions in the two halves of his visual field, and can receive two different answers written by this person's two hands.

Here is a simplified version of the kind of evidence that such tests provide. One of these people is shown a wide screen, whose left half is red and right half is blue. On each half in a darker shade are the words, 'How many colours can you see?' With both hands the person writes, 'Only one'. The words are now changed to read: 'Which is the only colour that you can see?' With one of his hands the person writes 'Red', with the other he writes 'Blue'.

If this is how this person responds, there seems no reason to doubt that he is having visual sensations—that he does, as he claims, see both red and blue. But in seeing red he is not aware of seeing blue, and vice versa. This is why the surgeon writes of 'two separate spheres of consciousness'. In each of his centres of consciousness the person can see only a single colour. In one centre, he sees red, in the other, blue.

The many actual tests, though differing in details from the imagined test that I have just described, show the same two essential features. In seeing what is in the left half of his visual field, such a person is quite unaware of what he is now seeing in the right half of his visual field, and vice versa. And in the centre of consciousness in which he sees the left half of his visual field, and is aware of what he is doing with his left hand, this person is quite unaware of what he is doing with his right hand, and vice versa.

One of the complications in the actual cases is that for most people, in at least the first few weeks after the operation, speech is entirely controlled by the right-handed hemisphere. As a result, 'if the word "hat" is flashed on the left, the left hand will retrieve a hat from a group of concealed objects if the person is told to pick out what he has seen. At the same time he will insist verbally that he saw nothing.' Another complication is that, after a certain time, each hemisphere can sometimes control both hands. Nagel quotes an example of the kind of conflict which can follow:

A pipe is placed out of sight in the patient's left hand, and he is then asked to write with his left hand what he was holding. Very laboriously and heavily, the left hand writes the letters P and I. Then suddenly the writing speeds up and becomes lighter, the I is converted to an E, and the word is completed as PENCIL. Evidently the left hemisphere has made a guess based on the appearance of the first two letters, and has interfered . . . But then the right hemisphere takes over control of the hand again, heavily crosses out the letters ENCIL, and draws a crude picture of a pipe.

Such conflict may take more sinister forms. One of the patients complained that sometimes, when he embraced his wife, his left hand pushed her away.

Much has been made of another complication in the actual cases, hinted at in Nagel's example. The left hemisphere typically supports or 'has' the linguistic and mathematical abilities of an adult, while the right hemisphere 'has' these abilities at the level of a young child. But the right hemisphere, though less advanced in these respects, has greater abilities of other kinds, such as those involved in pattern recognition, or musicality. It is assumed that, after the age of three or four, the two hemispheres follow a 'division of labour', with each developing certain abilities. The lesser linguistic abilities of the right hemisphere are not intrinsic, or permanent. People who have had strokes in their left hemispheres often regress to the linguistic ability of a young child, but with their remaining right hemispheres many can re-learn adult speech. It is also believed that, in a minority of people, there may be no difference between the abilities of the two hemispheres.

Suppose that I am one of this minority, with two exactly similar hemispheres. And suppose that I have been equipped with some device that can block communication between my hemispheres. Since this device is connected to my eyebrows, it is under my control. By raising an eyebrow I can divide my mind. In each half of my divided mind I can then, by lowering an eyebrow, reunite my mind.

This ability would have many uses. Consider

My Physics Exam. I am taking an exam, and have only fifteen minutes left in which to answer the last question. It occurs to me that there are two ways of tackling this question. I am unsure which is more likely to succeed. I therefore decide to divide my mind for ten minutes, to work in each half of my mind on one of the two calculations, and then to reunite my mind to write a fair copy of the best result. What shall I experience?

When I disconnect my hemispheres, my stream of consciousness divides. But this division is not something that I experience. Each of my two streams of consciousness seems to have been straightforwardly continuous with my one stream of consciousness up to the moment of division. The only changes in each stream are the disappearance of half my visual field and the loss of sensation in, and control over, one of my arms.

Consider my experiences in my 'right-handed' stream. I remember deciding that I would use my right hand to do the longer calculation. This I now begin. In working at this calculation I can see, from the movements of my left hand, that I am also working at the other. But I am not aware of working at the other. I might, in my right-handed stream, wonder how, in my left-handed stream, I am getting on. I could look and see. This would be just like looking to see how well my neighbour is doing, at the next desk. In my right-handed stream I would be equally unaware both of what my neighbour is now thinking and of what I am now thinking in my left-handed stream. Similar remarks apply to my experiences in my left-handed stream.

My work is now over. I am about to reunite my mind. What should I, in each stream, expect? Simply that I shall suddenly seem to remember just having worked at two calculations, in working at each of which I was not aware of working at the other. This, I suggest, we can imagine. And, if my mind had been divided, my apparent memories would be correct.

In describing this case, I assumed that there were two separate series of thoughts and sensations. If my two hands visibly wrote out two calculations, and I also claimed later to remember two corresponding series of thoughts, this is what we ought to assume. It would be most implausible to assume that either or both calculations had been done unconsciously.

It might be objected that my description ignores 'the necessary unity of consciousness'. But I have not ignored this alleged necessity. I have denied it. What is a fact must be possible. And it is a fact that people with disconnected hemispheres have two separate streams of consciousness—two series of thoughts and experiences, in having each of which they are unaware of having the other. Each of these two streams separately displays unity of consciousness. This may be a surprising fact. But we can understand it. We can come to believe that a person's mental history need not be like a canal, with only one channel, but could be like a river, occasionally having separate streams. I suggest that we can also imagine what it would be like to divide and reunite our minds. My description of my experiences in my Physics Exam seems both to be coherent and to describe something that we can imagine. [. . .]

What Explains the Unity of Consciousness?

Suppose that, because we are not yet Reductionists, we believe that there must be a true answer to the question, 'Who has each stream of consciousness?' And suppose that, for the reasons just given, we believe that this case involves only a single person: me. We believe that for ten minutes I have a divided mind.

Remember next the view that psychological unity is explained by ownership. On this view, we should explain the unity of a person's consciousness, at any time, by ascribing different experiences to this person, or 'subject of experiences'. What unites these different experiences is that they are being had by the same person. This view is held both by those who believe that a person is a separately existing entity, and by some of those who reject this belief. And this view also applies to the unity of each life.

When we consider my imagined Physics Exam, can we continue to accept this view? We believe that, while my mind is divided, I have two separate series of experiences, in having each of which I am unaware of having the other. At any time in one of my streams of consciousness I am having several different thoughts and sensations. I might be aware of thinking out some part of the calculation, feeling writer's cramp in one hand, and hearing the squeaking of my neighbour's old-fashioned pen. What unites these different experiences?

On the view described above, the answer is that these are the experiences being had by me at this time. This answer is incorrect. I am not just having these experiences at this time. I am also having, in my other stream of consciousness, several other experiences. We need to explain the unity of consciousness within each of my two streams of consciousness, or in each half of my divided mind. We cannot explain these two unities by claiming that all of these experiences are being had by me at this time. This makes the two unities one. It ignores the fact that, in having each of these two sets of experiences, I am unaware of having the other.

Suppose that we continue to believe that unity should be explained by ascribing different experiences to a single subject. We must then believe that this case involves at least two different subjects of experiences. What unites the experiences in my left-handed stream is that they are all being had by one subject of experiences. What unites the experiences in my right-handed stream is that they are all being had by another subject of experiences. We must now abandon the claim that 'the subject of experiences' is the person. On our view, I am a subject of experiences. While my mind is divided there are two different subjects of experiences. These are not the same subject of experiences, so they cannot both be me. Since it is unlikely that I am one of the two, given the similarity of my two streams of consciousness, we should probably conclude that I am neither of these two subjects of experiences. The whole episode therefore involves three such entities. And two of these entities cannot be claimed to be the kind of entity with which we are all familiar, a person. I am the only person involved, and two of these subjects of experiences are *not* me. Even if we assume that I *am* one of these two subjects of experiences, *the other* cannot be me, and is therefore not a person. [. . .]

What Happens when I Divide?

I shall now describe another natural extension of the actual cases of divided minds. Suppose first that I am one of a pair of identical twins, and that both my body and my twin's brain have been fatally injured. Because of advances in neuro-surgery, it is not inevitable that these injuries will cause us both to die. We have between us one healthy brain and one healthy body. Surgeons can put these together.

This could be done even with existing techniques. Just as my brain could be extracted, and kept alive by a connection with an artifical heart-lung machine, it could be kept alive by a connection with the heart and lungs in my twin's body. The drawback, today, is that the nerves from my brain could not be connected with the nerves in my twin's body. My brain could survive if transplanted into his body, but the resulting person would be paralysed.

Even if he is paralysed, the resulting person could be enabled to communicate with others. One crude method would be some device, attached to the nerve that would have controlled this person's right thumb, enabling him to send messages in Morse Code. Another device, attached to some sensory nerve, could enable him to receive messages. Many people would welcome surviving, even totally paralysed, if they could still communicate with others. The stock example is that of a great scientist whose main aim in life is to continue thinking about certain abstract problems.

Let us suppose, however, that surgeons are able to connect my brain to the nerves in my twin's body. The resulting person would have no paralysis, and would be completely healthy. Who would this person be?

This is not a difficult question. It may seem that there is a disagreement here between the Physical and Psychological Criteria. Though the resulting person will be psychologically continuous with me, he will not have the whole of my body. But, as I have claimed, the Physical Criterion ought not to require the continued existence of my whole body.

If all of my brain continues both to exist and to be the brain of one living person, who is psychologically continuous with me, I continue to exist. This is true whatever happens to the rest of my body. When I am given someone else's heart, I am the surviving recipient, not the dead donor. When my brain is transplanted into someone else's body, it may seem that I am here the dead donor. But I am really still the recipient, and the survivor. Receiving a new skull and a new body is just the limiting case of receiving a new heart, new lungs, new arms, and so on.

It will of course be important what my new body is like. If my new body is quite unlike my old body, this would affect what I could do, and might thus indirectly lead to changes in my character. But there is no reason to suppose that being transplanted into a very different body would disrupt my psychological continuity.

[From *Reasons and Persons* (Oxford: Clarendon Press, 1984), 245–9, 253.]

It has been argued that 'brain bisection' data leads us to abandon our traditional conception of personal identity. Nagel has remarked:

The ultimate account of the unity of what we call a single mind consists of an enumeration of the types of functional integration that typify it. We know that these can be eroded in different ways and to different degrees. The belief that even in their complete version they can be explained by the presence of a numerically single subject is an illusion.[1]

Parfit has adopted a similar position, contending that patients with 'split brains' become two separate 'streams of consciousness' and thus that our normal sense of personal identity, or at least 'what matters' about personal identity is constituted by psychological relations between connected conscious experiences.[2] It is claimed that in 'split brain' patients certain of the relations are disrupted and that we thus see clearly that the nature of the unity that is normally present does not reside in a single subject with a given identity, but in the connectedness and continuity that normally obtains. Parfit draws on two sources of support for these contentions: the first is the actual events that transpire after a human being is submitted to the operation of sectioning the corpus callosum (or 'brain bisection'), and the second is the imaginative consideration of various scenarios involving graded mental and physical discontinuity, and the 'fission' and 'fusion' of persons. I shall do little more than argue that the actual data will not sustain the interpretation put on them.

We must first note that none of these patients have bisected brains; rather, they have had a limited operation in which most of the fibres between the two hemispheres of the forebrain have been divided. The forebrain comprises the diencephalon, a central processing area which relays information to the cerebral cortex and the two hemispheres with their covering of cerebral cortex. The cortex is that part of the brain which subserves the most complex integration and patterning of neural excitation. Functions affected by cortical damage include language, visual pattern recognition, tactile identification of objects, and so on. The data we have available on patients who have had such operations indicate that, under certain conditions, they can be induced to make disparate responses to information which is delivered separately to each cerebral hemisphere. This effect may be produced, for example, by momentarily flashing visual cues on to a screen or by allowing only one hand to feel an object. There are problems with auditory cues due to bilaterality of connections in the brain stem (which is not divided). In the visual case, the cues are so arranged that differing content is 'perceived' in each half of the visual field and so is directly available to only one hemisphere. In this way each hemisphere can be differently informed. The right hemisphere almost exclusively controls the left hand and the left hemisphere the right hand. The left hand cannot respond adequately to information delivered to the left hemisphere as the interhemispheric connections, or most of them, have been severed. This means that each hand can be used to respond in a way opposite to the other in certain simple tasks. There is no question that each hemisphere 'performs' tasks which show a degree of informational complexity. The behaviour produced would normally be considered the conscious performance of an intelligent person. There is also no question that each hemisphere is unable to use some of the information given to the person involved.

What observers found surprising was that, in everyday life, there was no fragmentation of abilities, despite rare occasions on which different tendencies were evinced by left and right hands to the same external object. One patient, for example, both embraced and pushed away his wife with different hands, and another had occasional difficulties as right and left hands chose different clothes for him to wear for the day. These exceptions aside, it was noted that, even in an experimental situation (where information was carefully split between hemispheres), the patients used 'self-cueing' techniques to achieve correct responses; for example, if the left hand were asked to perform an 'object choice', the information for which had been given to the left hemisphere, the person might grimace each time the left hand tended toward an incorrect object and smile when it finally chose the correct object. Sperry remarks:

The observed disconnection effects as in the forgoing examples do not show up readily in ordinary behaviour. They have to be demonstrated by flashing the visual material fast enough so that eye movements cannot be used to sneak the answers into the wrong hemisphere.[3]

Here we see the patient attempting to integrate information which has been fragmented due to the disruption of the normal causal conditions which enable him to make full cognitive use of it.

Similar devices are employed by patients where their mental functions are disrupted by some other kind of 'disconnection syndrome' produced by a brain lesion. In a certain kind of dyslexia, resulting from damage to the posterior part of the dominant (or language mediating) hemisphere, the patient cannot read words or sentences but can spell words, read letters, and recognise words spelt out to him. When testing such a patient it is necessary to ensure that, when one shows him a written word such as INK, he does not, overtly or *sotto voce*, spell out I . . . N . . . K . . . and give you the answer 'Ink'. If one allows this sort of subterfuge, real disabilities may well go unnoticed. In this case and in the case of the 'brain bisection' patient, it seems far more reasonable to look at the person who is aware of the incongruity between the required response and his own performance than to leap into an hypothesis about separate 'spheres' or 'streams' of consciousness. Sperry writes:

Everything we have seen so far indicates that the surgery has left these people with two separate minds, that is, two separate spheres of consciousness.[4]

Parfit uncritically accepts this conclusion but I argue that we should not.

In real life the state of informational disruption is a transient phenomenon and the patients tend to 'get their act back together again' albeit gradually. If such people do function in such a remarkably integrated way, surely we should ask 'Who is performing these tasks?', or, 'Is there a single subject of experience who is making and is aware of making these mistakes?' rather than 'How many separate streams of consciousness are there here?'. The fact is that the person realises that *he* has made a mistake, not that someone, perhaps contingently related to him, has made a mistake which he has the knowledge to correct. As far as he is concerned, the person in error and the person who is not are he, himself, one person and one mind, but he is not functioning properly.

Luria writes about a man who survived a penetrating missile injury to the brain which left him with severely fragmented thoughts:

. . . this is a book about a person who fought with the tenacity of the damned to recover the use of his damaged brain. Though in many respects he remained as helpless as before, in the long run he won his fight.[5]

Again, in the face of severe disconnexion and disruption of mental functions or 'conscious experience', the person preserves a unity in his thought life and a sense of personal identity which is a crucial factor in his rehabilitation.

In the 'brain bisection' cases, we have a serious problem for the conception of a person as a 'rational' agent. The individual patient receives certain information and may, on the basis of that, form two different intentions, which could be contradictory. Parfit writes:

here is a simplified version of the kind of evidence that such tests provide. One of these people is shown a wide screen, whose left half is red and right half is blue. On each half in a darker shade are the words 'How many colours can you see?'. With both hands the person writes 'Only one'. The words are now changed to read 'Which is the only colour that you can see?'. With one of his hands the person writes 'Red', with the other he writes 'Blue'.[6]

We must first note that this example is untrue to the facts in that it violates the constraints on information presentation noted by Sperry above. The information here envisaged is too complex to ensure 'perceptual splitting'.

If we respect this and focus on a simpler case, we shall have a more secure basis for discussion. Take the situation where, after a visual 'message' which gives the names of different shapes to each hemisphere, the left hand picks out a square object and the right hand picks out a round object. We can give an explanation of these events in terms of brain function but what is less clear is whether we can say what the agent is thinking in this situation. He can select a square object but not say that what he has selected is square. He can both select a round object and say that it is round. What thoughts can be attributed? Several points need to be made about the ascription of conscious thoughts to him:

1. I cannot say how I do many of the things that I know how to do; tying a knot would be one example, recognizing a colour as red or responding to the grammatical structure of a sentence would be others. Some of these abilities enable me to think as I do, but they do not themselves constitute thought and they are not attributable to me as part of my conscious experience. The patients with brain bisection can do a number of things with objects, try to draw them, mime their use, and so on, but often only with one hand. By the very nature of their lesions they are precluded from saying what they are doing. Why then should we not say that the mute hemisphere is fully conscious of the objects and is merely unable to use language. The point is one made by Davidson (elaborated from Wittgenstein) that in the absence of language certain detailed propositional attitudes and consequently certain conscious thoughts cannot be justifiably ascribed. A 'tighter' or more austere set of information processing abilities will do.[7]

Consider, for instance, the patient whose two hands evinced different reactions to his wife. It would be implausible, on a moment's reflection, to claim that one of his hemispheres loved his wife and the other one hated her. We would want to know about beliefs, intentions, commitments, expectations, and a great number of 'propositional attitudes' held by any candidate for these ascriptions.

2. In order to determine a person's thought content, we must take note of the structural patterns (or 'generality constraints') which it shows and certain inferential connections which it has. The concepts involved must be available to enter a variety of structurally related thoughts and the thoughts themselves must be available to be used in a variety of ways. If these determinacy conditions are not met, we do not know what it means to ascribe, or self-ascribe, a given thought.

3. It is his suitability as a subject of thought ascriptions that constitutes a person as being a conscious rational thinker, i.e. as having a mind. Thoughts which can be determinately and fully ascribed in accordance with these constraints can be understood as being part of the conscious thought of the thinker. The situation is less than clear in these experiments. The subjects are conscious and often conscious of an internal conflict, so that they try to overcome the conflict (for example by 'tipping themselves off'). Because

they do try to reintegrate their information, or make best use of their disrupted brain function in tackling the tasks they are set, they can properly be said to be struggling with certain confusions to which they find themselves subject rather than to have become two mutually independent streams of consciousness which are in no more than a contingent relation to each other.

What cautious conclusions are warranted by Sperry's data?

1. We can conclude that human cognition is dependent upon the intact function of the brain, and is not carried out in some immaterial, inner, cognitive substance or mental self.

2. We can conclude that persons, thinking subjects, are *essentially* constituted in the way that they are.

There is a person, with a certain identity, who is involved in the events surrounding a 'brain bisection'; he tries to perform the tasks he is set; he makes mistakes and is conscious of doing so. There are manifestly not two separate 'streams of consciousness' each carrying on as it pleases. We all, in various ways and at various times, get our information processing a bit messed up and most of us do not have to contend with surgeons doing it for us. For these unfortunate patients the latter situation does occur. Given that *they* do not have problems about their own identity it seems a little perverse to imply that these should be added to the considerable burden they are already obliged to carry.

Parfit extends the intuitions, aroused by 'brain bisection' cases and suggests certain fantasies including the replication of persons, graded psychological and physical discontinuities of personal constitution, and the idea of 'fission' and 'fusion' of persons. The problems with brain bisection data affect some of these scenarios.

In one type of thought experiment I am replaced piecemeal, either mental link by mental link, or cell by cell, so that in the most radical example envisaged I lose all resemblance to my original self.

Another scenario represents me as having had my brain divided and placed in two different bodies, each of which comes to live a normal life. Here again I would be unable to claim the one-to-one relation of identity with either resultant person and yet I have a very important connection with both. Surely living as two people is not the same as dying, so it cannot be identity which really matters here. Predictably, what matters is claimed to be mental connectedness and continuity.

In considering these imagined situations, we have a right to ask whether the mental concepts used have retained their meaning, which they have in virtue of the interpersonal relations (involving reciprocity and mutual interpretation) between human beings. Human beings are born with a certain biological potential and, through the many and varied experiences they undergo, develop into adults who have a certain conceptual repertoire, character, set of memories, self-image, emotionality, set of aspirations, abilities, eccentricities, and so on, all of which are holistically connected. To call a human person a person is to refer to him as an entity whom we implicitly take to be constituted in this kind of way. We thus are able to apply the concepts we use to think about this kind of thing. Events and their complex interactions over time form the identity of a person from its crude biological beginnings. The nature of this process and the complex interrelation between history and brain structure and function mean that a person cannot be simply replicated, replaced, or divided, so it is less than obvious that one can elucidate what matters about the nature of a person by discussing the kinds of things which could.

Consider some facts about persons and their brains. Some patients have strokes or hemispherectomy operations in which the cerebral cortex and a variable amount of underlying white matter is destroyed on one side. This may occur in patients with cerebro-vascular disease or in children with epilepsy. The person in this case has not lost half of his brain but 'merely' the superficial parts of one hemisphere (of the forebrain) and yet he suffers severe physical and mental disabilities. There is no blithe continuation of personal life with largely intact psychological function here despite the impression created by Parfit and others.

Parfit further considers the fusion of persons:

We can imagine a world in which fusion was a natural process. Two people come together. While they are unconscious, their two bodies grow into one. One person then wakes up.[8]

It ought to be obvious by now that whether we *can* imagine what is described here is not all clear. What exactly are we imagining? Are one person's cells going to destroy the other's? What about the brain cells; how many neural interconnections will be displaced or disrupted? What will happen to the exquisitely intricate connections by which the hypothalamus and limbic system integrate the higher level 'stimulus analysing' functions with the more primitive 'affective-appetitive' centres? These have never been significantly disrupted in any patient who has then gone on to exercise coherent conscious rational thought. If we take any concept, say 'hard', and consider the myriad different interactions and experiences which have secured its role in our conceptual system, what are we to say about this concept in the 'fused' individual? Can he think? Can he know what he thinks? There is nothing we can do with this putative notion of fusion; we do not quite know what we are saying.

The same indeterminacy applies to every situation that Parfit urges us to imagine with cavalier disregard for the facts. To move from the highly circumscribed anomalies in the neuropsychology of patients with hemi-spheric disconnection to a discussion of persons dividing and fusing abandons not only the constraints of actuality, but also the normal content which we bring to the use of the concepts concerned.

In talking of 'my division', Parfit says:

My brain is divided, and each half is successfully transplanted into the body of one of my brothers. Each of the resulting people believes that he is me, seems to remember living my life, has my character, and is in every other way psychologically continuous with me.[9]

What this person has is the integrity that is found in the life of a human being, which is dependent on the activity of a fully functioning brain. There may be psychological entities somewhere in the universe who have two half brains which can continue to function in separate bodies but it is quite indeterminate whether they would be persons and what their mental lives would be like.

This is not a stipulation concerning real possibilities and thought experiments. If it were so, it would be open to Parfit to reply that he is not concerned with what is possible but rather wishes to bring into sharp focus what *matters* to us about our mental lives. I have argued that the terms which are used to describe what matters have complex conceptual connections, which determine their content and thus our grasp of what we are thinking. These involve the ways in which integrated human beings function, unify their thought life, and develop and refine their thought and actions. These functions alone would seem to require, as Kant so shrewdly noted, a principle of unity in the thinker concerned. These points could be argued in more detail, but I shall not do so in this short discussion of what the case is in 'brain bisection' and what its relevance is for personal identity.

['Brain Bisection and Personal Identity', *Mind*, 378 (1986), 224–9.]

DANIEL N. ROBINSON

74 Cerebral Plurality and the Unity of Self

The *unity of self* is both a persistent fact of daily life and an enduring dilemma in philosophical psychology. The concept goes by several names: the unity of conscious experience, the indivisibility of the person, the uniqueness of the soul. Indeed, the claimed unicity is an essential feature of psychology's notion of personality, of the moral concept of responsibility, and of religious belief in personal immortality. Traditionally, personality has referred to the remarkably stable ensemble of emotional and attitudinal attributes that persist throughout life's seasonal challenges and upheavals. This view implies that these attributes inhere in a continuous psychological being—a self—whose identity is established and conveyed by this personality. The same commitment to the reality of a unified self exists at the level of moral philosophy and jurisprudence. To judge a person in a moral way, one must establish that the actions in question proceeded from that person's intentions and no other's. Finally, the entire history of Judeo-Christian religious teaching is animated by the same theory of individual responsibility, personal identity, and the irreducibility of the unique self.

In light of this, it should not be surprising that historical challenges to this concept have been met with incredulity and alarm. Not only do such challenges go to the heart of basic religious and institutional principles, but they also collide with the common citizens' least doubted assumption—that they are who they are and are not anyone else!

Philosophy's abiding mission, of course, is to raise questions about all of our assumptions, including, if not especially, those that enjoy the nearly universal approval of the human race. In modern times (although there are ample ancient and medieval precedents) Descartes was the first to submit this assumption to sustained conceptual analysis. His celebrated statement, *cogito, ergo sum*, was the triumphant deduction of a great rationalist unwilling to accept his own existence until he had found a good argument for it.

With no less an authority than Descartes insisting that the issue was worthy of attention, it was inevitable that the 18th century would savor it. This, after all, was the century that would force itself to choose between 'Cartesianism' and 'Newtonianism,' often bending and distorting the views of both geniuses just to make the debate more lively. Locke, as might be expected, had prepared the way by attempting to absorb the issue into his larger empiricistic philosophy. Thus, he took *self* to be no more than the contents of memory or, more generally, of consciousness. According to Locke,[1] the defining identity of the person is entirely explained by what that person knows and recalls of current and past experiences. To the extent that the person's consciousness,

can be extended backwards to any past action or thought, so far reaches the identity of that person . . . so that whatever has the consciousness of the present and past actions, is the same person to whom they both belong. (pp. 130–135)

David Hume[2] was even more summary in his dismissal of overly metaphysical or rationalistic conceptions of the self:

For my part, when I enter most intimately into what I call *myself*, I always stumble on some particular perception or other. . . . When my perceptions are remov'd for any time, as by sound sleep; so long am I insensible of *myself*, and may truly be said not to exist. (p. 252)

The debate may be said to have reached its first modern philosophical plateau with the incisive critique developed by Thomas Reid, Hume's less renowned contemporary and the man most psychologists know as the father of the 'Common Sense' school. Reid's criticism of Locke's theory of the self was entirely successful, although his more oblique attack on Hume's thesis proved to be less convincing.[3] Briefly, Reid's demolition of the Lockean thesis proceeds as follows: Take an adult (*A*) who is conscious (has the memory) of once having been punished as a small boy (call the boy *B*). Now consider *A* years hence, an aged person (call him *C*) vividly aware of having been *A* but having no recollection at all of *B*. Reid took Locke's theory as asserting that the contents of consciousness are identical to 'self.' But in this illustration we discover that although $A = B$ and $A = C$, $B \neq C$. Thus, the property of transitivity is not preserved, and accordingly, the identity collapses. More to the point, the recollection of having done something does not establish that, in fact, one has done it, and the mere failure to be 'conscious' of a past action does not prove that one did not perform it.

The Humean 'bundle of perceptions' account is part of Hume's overall epistemology, and since Reid was satisfied that the latter was defective, he found little reason to dwell on that Humean theory of self implied by it. Reid was satisfied that, for Hume to search for himself, there must have been a self doing the searching. In any case, Reid judged that, 'A man that disbelieves his own existence, is surely as unfit to be reasoned with, as a man that believes he is made of glass'.[4] However, as the Enlightenment dissolved into the 19th century, any number of traditional philosophical debates were declared to be within the province of science; no longer needing comments from the armchair.

Phrenology and the Multiplicity of Selves

We still await a definitive biography of Franz Joseph Gall, a work that will do much to unravel that knotted epoch in which philosophy, science, politics and faith sought their legitimate positions. But we need not know the whole of Gall's story to be confident in at least this appraisal: He was one of the chief architects of some of the most important of the modern neural sciences. He surely has the status of a pioneer in comparative neuroanatomy, fetal neuroanatomy, human histo-pathological anatomy, and that part of psychobiology most dependent on findings from the clinic. None of the silliness of his 'bumpology' can cancel these contributions.

As is widely known, however, Gall's difficulties with his scientific (and religious) contemporaries predated the 'bumpology' cult—a cult that was thriving years after Gall's death and one that seldom troubled itself with Gall's own cautions, his *science*. The real trouble began for Gall when his theory of separate brain 'organs' clearly implied a *multiplicity of selves*. Referring to Gall's thesis, his famous adversary, Pierre Flourens[5] had this to say:

The consciousness tells me that I am *one*, and Gall insists that I am *multiple*; that consciousness tells me that I am *free*, and Gall avers that there is no moral liberty . . . Philosophers will talk. (pp. 123–124)

Flourens marshalled the authority of Descartes against these views even before he began to challenge them experimentally. From Descartes Flourens borrowed the thesis that consciousness allows not only 'the *unity* of the *moi*' but also 'the *continuity* of the *moi*.' He noted that from this fact Descartes was able to reason 'still more admirably, to the immortality of the soul' (p. 123).

Gall was not only convinced that his critics were moved by utterly nonscientific considerations, but that their objections were invariably grounded in systematic (deliberate?) misunderstandings of his argument. In proposing to offer a scientific account of the 'moral and intellectual faculties,' Gall had to remind his detractors that he took the various regions and processes of the cerebrum not as the *causes* but as the *conditions* of mental life. Thus, he was not defending a radical form of reductive materialism, if only because he never doubted the existence of genuinely *mental* processes and phenomena. It was not Descartes' dualism he opposed but Descartes' denial of the dependence of our rational nature on our cerebral organization.

Historians who are apt to spend more time reading Gall's critics than his works can claim continuing responsibility for the caricatures that would pass for critical appraisals of this work. Gall never proposed, for example, that there was a 'reasoning center' or an 'intelligence center' or a 'felony center' in the cerebrum. He did argue that there were as many distinct cerebral *organs* as there are distinct mental *faculties*, but he was quick to disavow the view that complex psychological functions arose from a single 'faculty': 'An organ of intellect or understanding is as entirely inadmissable as an organ of instinct'.[6] His point is that when such terms as *intellect* or *understanding* or *reason* are used by philosophers, the actual processes involved are manifold and interdependent, often engaging the perceptual, motivational, emotional, and attentional 'faculties' simultaneously. This theory therefore implies the awareness that an apparently rational or cognitive deficit may well depend on sensory or affective indispositions of the relevant cerebral 'organs.' His clinical findings turned up many such instances. Yet.

It is vain that we demonstrate to the adversaries of the plurality of organs that, from the lowest species . . . up to man, the cerebrum becomes more and more complicated . . . Obstinately bent on explaining the simplicity of the *moi*, they see in all these incontestable facts nothing but a diminution of the simple cerebral mass. (p. 87)

The Gall–Flourens debate early in the 19th century permanently inscribed the problem of localization of function on the map of what we now call psychobiology. The received history casts Flourens as an early Lashley, staunchly defending the law of mass action and proudly admitting failure in his own 'search for the engram.' But of course, it was Flourens himself who performed brilliant experiments confirming the cerebral localization of certain functions, and it was Gall who relentlessly contended that complex psychological functions could only be explained through an examination of numerous and broadly distributed cerebral 'organs.'

As the glamour and the clamor surrounding phrenology subsided, the 'unity of self' debate was consigned to the footnotes of the more influential scientific treatises. At midcentury there were signs that the controversy was still alive, but for the seasoned perspective on it, we can consult Griesinger, who was described by his British translators as 'the acknowledged leader of the modern German school of Medical Psychology':[7]

The opinions of Wigan ('Duality of Mind', London, 1844), who assumes a complete duality of mind in the two cerebral hemispheres; the conjecture of Holland[8] ('On the Brain as a double organ, Chapters on Mental Physiology,' 2d Ed., London, 1858, p. 179), that many mental disorders, especially the states of mental disunity and internal contradiction, depend upon a disharmony in the functions of both hemispheres; and lastly, the recent attempt of Follet to refer mental aberrations to 'disturbance in the equilibrium of the innervation of the two hemispheres,' are wanting in sufficient proof. (pp. 18–19)

Thus, although Wigan, Holland, Follet, and others agreed with the notion of mental duality within the scientific context of cerebral function, the leaders of scientific thought were demanding a much broader data base. The scientific community had by now divorced itself from anything bearing the slightest trace of 'metaphysics.' And the issue of self, now parading in the heroic raiment of Fichte's and Hegel's *das Ich*, had become so thoroughly 'metaphysical' that few beyond the duchy of Weimar were willing to touch it.

The dominant philosophical circles had transcendentalized the self beyond recognition. In the patrimony of Hegel the leaders of Romantic Idealism had so removed the absolute ego from the realm of experience as to make the very concept indistinguishable from arrant superstition. William James chided those who 'act, in short, as if they were going up in a balloon, whenever the notion of it [ego] crossed their mind'.[9] Thus did the 'unity of self' thesis almost disappear from the scientific arena.

Clinical Psychology's Turn

That the notion of ego did not disappear is due largely to the interest aroused among the late 19th-century clinical psychologists. The issue was revived in a setting that was clearly not metaphysical, but one that was also far from entirely scientific. Those who brought it back to life were the French doctors and psychologists who came to play such a leading part in the founding of clinical psychology: Ribot, Charcot, Janet, Féré, Binet. This group refused to adopt either the essentially speculative psychology of England or the sensory–experimental psychology of Germany. Janet,[10] with England in mind but remaining politely mute on the matter of nationality, put it this way: 'Instead of accidentally connecting the description of patients with the study of philosophic problems, we wish to describe the patient in and by himself' (p. xiv). Alfred Binet[11] was more explicit: 'With relatively few exceptions, the psychologists of my country have left the investigations of psychophysics to the Germans' (p. 12).

Both were intrigued by clinical signs of mental 'disunity.' Janet wrote at length on 'automatic writing,' and Binet (ibid.) devoted an entire volume to 'double consciousness.' Both also took a somewhat neutral position on possible neurophysiological determinants, calmly advising that the phenomena must be understood in *psychological* terms no matter what the neural correlates might be.[12]

As for the phenomena themselves, the descriptions by Janet and Binet will repay the modern reader's attention. Somnambulism, anesthesia, automatic writing, multiple personality, and the like are presented in great detail and discussed with sober ingenuity. Binet, in his *Alterations of Personality*,[13] summarized a typical experiment germane to the issue of the 'unity of consciousness':

I have sometimes made use of the following device, which puzzles a great many patients: Any number whatever, say three, is written on a piece of paper, which is folded up and given to the patient, who is asked to choose any number he likes and to think of it for a few moments. While the patient is determining . . . his anaesthetic hand is pricked three times, which obliges him to think of the figure 3. Then when he announces this three that he believes he has chosen at random, he is told to unfold the paper and is shown that his thought was foreseen. The success of this little experiment is almost certain. (pp. 211–212)

Binet himself was persuaded that such phenomena were best understood as the result of distraction, of alterations in the processes of attention. He treated forms of multiple personality as instances of 'vigiambulism' in which a new and 'complete psychological existence' comes into being of which the patient is completely oblivious (ibid. pp. 3–4). On these and numerous similar clinical grounds Binet rejected the metaphysical theory of a consciousness that defines itself and that cannot be divided. A scientific psychology, according to Binet, must not take the constructions of philosophers for its subject but must confine itself to observations of actual human beings. Such observations, he declared, have already disconfirmed the 'unity of self' thesis by showing that the *actual* self is a dynamic composite of complex psychological states.

Binet and his contemporaries saw the matter as one to be settled on the basis of evidence and not one to be used as part of a polemic against an ideological antagonist. By the end of the 19th century, the ideological sides of such disputes had run their course in France. Since the middle of the 18th century, with La Mettrie's *l'Homme Machine*, and through successive decades, the writings of Cabanis, Gall, Flourens, Magendie, Destutt Tracy, Main de Biran, Ribot—a veritable legion of savants—had placed French psychology squarely in the court of natural science. By Binet's time France had a long tradition of immunizing scientific scholarship against threats from beyond the scientific establishment. This, of course, did not eliminate the imposition of fashion from within the community of scientists, but it allowed metaphysical neutrality to prosper as something more useful than veiled hostility.

In England during the second half of the 19th century the division of intellectual labor was not quite as neat. There is, for example, a stridency in Maudsley's (1867) *Physiology and Pathology of the Mind* and in Huxley's (1874). 'On the Hypothesis that Animals are Automata, and Its History' that had already become passé in French scientific circles. Moreover, but for reasons that cannot be explored here, modern psychology came into the province of medicine more quickly and fully in France than anywhere else. Within this province the facts of *mind* could be dealt with in the same way as all other clinical data and did not have to conform to some larger political or religious sectarianism. Accordingly, writers such as Janet and Binet could resist the temptation to 'physiologize' psychological processes without fear of rebuke. For them, physiological theories of mental function were scientific theories to be accepted or rejected according to specific clinical and experimental findings. To the extent that such theories were merely modes of philosophical rhetoric, however, these leaders of French psychology found no reason to consider them.

If only for this reason, however, the great clinicians did not bring much order to the issue. Whatever virtue may attach to the scientific commitment to unedited observation, it is not a method for settling fundamental conceptual problems. Binet, Janet, and their contemporaries were satisfied that the usual signs of conscious unity could be disrupted in many different ways in both healthy and mentally disturbed persons. The evidence was clear and consistent enough to reject the traditional arguments offered by philosophy and religion in defense of the unity of self. Although Binet was sternly critical of British associationistic psychology, he was very much in the empiricistic tradition of French thought. Accordingly, he was satisfied (like Hume) that *self* and the *evidence of self* referred to the same condition of mind. Having observed in the clinic and the laboratory any number of variations in the evidence, as this evidence was accessible to the patient's consciousness, he was drawn directly to the conclusion that the 'unity of self' dogma was false.

As I shall attempt to show in the final pages of this essay, Binet underestimated the subtlety of the issue, in part because he thought of it as a scientific problem and in part because he brought an inadequate (empiricistic) theory to bear on it. As with his fellow scientists throughout the Western world, he thought of 'metaphysics' as something to be shunned rather than as the necessary foundation for all serious inquiry, including scientific inquiry. To be sure, his age was led to this unfortunate position by the tragicomic excesses of 19th-century philosophers of neo-Hegelian persuasion. It would be many years before the developed sciences shed their aversion to metaphysics and resumed the essential task of conceptual and linguistic analysis and the analysis of *explanation* itself. Psychology's resumption of this has remained truant, and I submit that this is why we are inclined to 'stop the presses' each time a novel finding is reported. Let me turn, then, to such a finding which is widely and, I suggest, wrongly thought to require a reassessment of the concept of the 'unity of self.'

Commissurotomy and the 'Two Selves' Thesis

The most current and dramatic version of this historic controversy has been aroused by experiments on patients who have undergone a surgical 'deconnection' of the cerebral hemispheres.[14] Each year seems to bring a number of qualifications of claims made about these patients, and it is therefore too early to say which of the empirical claims might be taken as final. Nevertheless, the evidence is quite consistent in pointing to some form of psychological 'deconnection' as a corollary of commissural sectioning. The commissurotomized patient fails to identify *verbally* readily perceived stimuli that are projected to the non-dominant hemisphere. This and a variety of similar deficits have been taken as evidence of 'two minds' or 'two selves' residing within a single body. Philosophers have been alert in recognizing the implications of these findings to the issue of personal identity,[15] and the scientific community seems generally convinced that the findings are revolutionary. We now routinely read descriptions of 'the speaking hemisphere,' 'the self-conscious hemisphere,' 'the side consciousness is on,' and so on. Suggestions for restraint[16] have been greeted with gracious indifference.

It is fair to say that, although the scientific dimensions of the issue have undergone the inevitable technical refinements, the conceptual aspects are as cluttered as ever. Ignoring the specific findings—which as I have noted, appear to be in a state of flux—we might profitably confine attention to what seems to be characteristic of all of them, a personal state of epistemic contradiction.[17] The same patient, often at nearly the same time, will assert and deny a specific empirical claim or fact of memory. The left hand, as the expression goes, may not know what the right one is doing, or as today's commentator would say, the left brain doesn't know what the right one is saying, because the right one cannot speak.

Amid the welter of findings and revised findings, this condition of epistemic contradiction stands in defense of the notion of the disunity or multiplicity of self. Indeed, the convention that has recently come into being phrases the defense in terms of the *duality* of self, apparently because there happen to be two hemispheres. If we are to assess the merits of this defense, we must ask whether there is anything unique about the commissuroto-mized patient with respect to this state of epistemic contradiction.

The plain fact, as has been discussed elsewhere,[18] is that any number of experimental operations produce just this state in perfectly normal observers. Under conditions of visual metacontrast, for example, observers will respond just as quickly to a flash they never 'see' as to the same flash when it is presented alone;[19] observers under conditions of cued retrieval will 'recall' a number or letter which, after the array had initially been presented, they had not recognized at all;[20] 'hysterical' patients will adopt entirely distinct identities; somnambulists will complete (with subsequent amnesia) elaborate actions; hypnotic subjects will deny what they know. This list can, of course, be extended considerably, with each entry qualifying as an instance of epistemic contradiction—an instance of paired knowledge-claims, one of which contradicts the other.

For those who would use such findings as proof of a multiplicity of selves, there is an embarrassment of riches to which commissurotomies add very little, but for those committed to the duality thesis, the findings are actually too good for the thesis to be true. States of epistemic contradiction are, as it happens, not limited to two per person. Recall Eve's *three* faces, and Binet turned up cases involving many more. Needless to say, however, none of these cases included any evidence of more than two hemispheres.

In referring to these clinical and experimental instances of epistemic contradiction, I am not suggesting that they are somehow like the effects of commissurotomy.[21] Indeed, there are few similarities displayed by any pair of such findings. To underscore this point, let me say that I do not oppose the usual claim that nothing in the clinical literature mimics the symptoms and characteristics of patients who have been commissurotomized.

However, the results of commissurotomies have not been introduced in discussions of the 'unity of self' merely because they are novel. Their inclusion in these discussions is based on the claim that they are *relevantly* novel. The question, then, is just what is relevant about these admittedly novel findings. There is, for example, nothing novel about cerebral lateralization of speech and language mechanisms or about the failure of intercerebral transfer of information in commissurotomized animals. What is relevant (or is alleged to be relevant) to the issue at hand is the class of phenomena I have labeled epistemic contradictions. These phenomena, since they can be produced in various ways, are not likely to be explained according to precisely the same principles. It is safe to doubt, for example, that the mechanisms responsible for reaction time under conditions of metacontrast are the same ones that give rise to vigiambulism, multiple personality, and 'automatic writing.' On this basis, there would seem to be no a priori grounds for challenging the claim that the *processes* affected by commissurotomies are unique. But then so are those that regulate or participate in the other conditions of epistemic contradiction discussed above.

One conclusion that plausibly flows from this is that we now have overwhelming evidence to disconfirm the 'unity of self' thesis and that, although commissurotomies do not provide anything relevantly novel, they do add to the already thick folio of data. But let me offer a competing conclusion that may be even more plausible.

The 'Moi' Reconsidered

The current literature is infected by a version of what William James meant by 'the psychologist's fallacy'.[22] Words that have quite different meanings are used interchangeably, leading not only to confusion but to subtle deceptions.

Let us take the following terms illustratively, for they are the ones that come to the surface most frequently when this issue is treated in both the historical and the contemporary journals and treatises: (a) *self*, (b) *self-identity*, (c) *personal identity*, (d) *person*.

What is ordinarily meant by a *person* is a human being, often of unknown identity, possessing certain intellectual, moral, and social attributes not present to the same degree in the balance of the animal kingdom. Used this way, *person* refers to a collection of attributes shared by entities of a certain kind. It is not an answer to the question of *who*, but rather to the question of *what*.

Personal identity, however, is an answer to the first of these questions. We can observe someone doing a variety of things and decide, in the absence of any biographical data, that the actor is a person. But to know *who* that person is we must go beyond the attributes that establish personhood. Thus, we will inquire as to name and occupation, address, social security number, fingerprints, credit cards, and so on. Following this investigation, which may move deeply into the details of this actor's life, we are prepared to assert that we now know the actual identity of the person—the personal identity. Note, however, that the person thus identified may be totally amnesic and therefore ignorant of the very identity we have established. In such a case, we would say that the person has a personal identity, but not *self-identity*. Nonetheless, the amnesic is not doubtful of existing (*cogito, ergo sum*). This person surely must be granted a self, and will claim as much whether we grant it or not.

Much of the trouble Flourens had with Gall and that Reid had with both Locke and Hume appears to have been caused by this conflation of terms.

Locke's memory theory of self was actually a theory of self-identity and not a theory of self at all. Hume, too, could come up with no identity other than that confirmed by his perceptions and recognized that this identity was inaccessible during states of sleep. But those who would defend the unity of the 'moi' were referring not to the identity of the self but to *selfhood*: the irreducible conscious awareness of unified being.

What, then, is to be said of the epistemic contradictions committed by the split-brain patient? Or the multiple and independent personalities revealed in cases of hysteria? Or, for that matter, the epistemic contradictions so easily secured in ordinary psychophysical settings? The most that can be said is that some of these effects are little more than signs of what Binet had in mind when he wrote of 'distraction' and what we would explain in the new language of information-processing. The rest of the effects *may* be taken as evidence of multiple personal identities and even multiple self-identities, but in no case as evidence of multiple selves. The separate personal identities and the different self-identities ascribed to and adopted by a person may be shocking to that person when subsequently discovered. But the basic fact of existence as a conscious entity cannot be shocking, for this is never news. As of now logic, language, and data leave the 'moi' intact and preserve the unity of self as an issue of continuing interest, and even of mystery.

['Cerebral Plurality and the Unity of Self', *American Psychologist*, 37 (1982), 904–9.]

Section 6

Epilogue: The Mind of the Poets

INTRODUCTION

This *Epilogue* is intended less as an addition or complement to the scientific and philosophical pages of earlier sections than as something of a retreat from them. The record of progress and clarification compiled by the disciplines of philosophy, science, and medicine needs little defence, even if the preceding pages keep one alert to the distance still to be travelled. But there are parallel understandings of life and mind, no less worthy for adopting modes of expression different from the established disciplinary forms of enquiry. Then, too, the aesthetic mind is a restless and often rebellious one, sometimes presciently withholding its allegiance, even as the popular enthusiasm eagerly attaches itself to the flavour of the month.

Needless to say, poets have written more about matters of the heart than of the brain or the mind. To be sure, the literature of sentiment is no less mental for its evocative power. But an anthology devoted to the mind must draw the line somewhere, and these days all might agree that that should be at the high cervical level, if not somewhere in the forebrain. So in these final pages the passages are chosen to match up with issues and tensions treated in the previous sections.

Although these few specimens of the poetic imagination are offered to keep the reader mindful of the aesthete's reluctance to turn too much over to science or philosophy, there is one significant exception: it is Lucretius, whose *De Rerum Natura* is a poetical summary of the atomistic natural philosophy of Epicurus. There is no surviving complete work by Epicurus, but there is this classic by an avid disciple. What had been expressed as matter of dry clinical fact in the Hippocratic medical works is now given poetic and rhetorical impetus, but all to the same effect: 'Mind' is a product of natural, corporeal processes, coming into being with the body and ending with its death, either flourishing or foundering depending on the condition of the body itself. In the passages copied here Lucretius declares that the mind grows and ages with the body, gets sick with it, and 'can be healed and changed by medicine'. There can be no doubt, then, but that 'the mind has a mortal life'.

Neither Andrew Marvell nor Lord Tennyson concurs, the latter taking himself to be more than brain and rejecting as meaningless any theory that declares otherwise. It is generally best, however, to let the poets speak for themselves. It is enough to note that in a volume that includes the question, 'What is it like to be a bat', Richard Wilbur's *The Mind* hazards an answer worth pondering.

LUCRETIUS

75 On the Nature of Things

Listen now: that you may be able to recognize that the minds and light spirits of living creatures are born and are mortal, I shall proceed to set forth verses worthy of your character, long sought out and found with delightful toil. Be so good as to apply both these names to one thing; and when for example I speak of spirit, showing it to be mortal, believe me to speak also of mind, inasmuch as it is one thing and a combined nature. [. . .]

Besides, we feel that the mind is begotten along with the body, and grows up with it, and with it grows old. For as toddling children have a body infirm and tender, so a weak intelligence goes with it. Next, when their age has grown up into robust strength, the understanding too and the power of the mind is enlarged. Afterwards, when the body is now wrecked with the mighty strength of time, and the frame has succumbed with blunted strength, the intellect limps, the tongue babbles, the intelligence totters, all is wanting and fails at the same time. It follows therefore that the whole nature of the spirit is dissolved abroad, like smoke, into the high winds of the air, since we see it begotten along with the body, and growing up along with it, and as I have shown, falling to pieces at the same time worn out with age.

Add to this that, just as the body itself is liable to awful diseases and harsh pain, so we see the mind liable to carking care and grief and fear; therefore it follows that the mind also partakes of death.

Moreover, in bodily diseases the mind often wanders astray; for it is demented and talks deliriously, and at times is carried by heavy lethargy into the deep everlasting sleep with eyes drooping and dejected head, from which it can neither catch the voices nor recognize the looks of those who stand round calling it back to life, their faces and cheeks bedewed with tears. Therefore you must confess that the mind also is dissolved, since the contagion of disease penetrates within it; for both pain and disease are makers of death, as we have been well taught by the perishing of many before now. [. . .]

And since we see that the mind, like a sick body, can be healed and changed by medicine, this also foreshows that the mind has a mortal life. For it is necessary to add parts or transpose them or draw away at least some tittle from the whole, whenever anyone attempts and begins to alter the mind or indeed to change any other nature whatever. But that which is immortal does

not permit its parts to be transposed, or anything to be added, or one jot to
ebb away; for whatever by being changed passes outside its own boundaries,
at once that is death for that which was before. Therefore, if the mind is sick,
it gives indications of mortality, as I have shown, or if it is changed by
medicine: so completely is the truth seen to combat false reasoning, and to
cut off its retreat as it flies, and to convict falsehood by a double refutation.

[From *De Rerum Natura*, trans. W. H. D. Rouse, rev. M. F. Smith, Loeb Classics edn.
(Cambridge, Mass.: Harvard University Press, 1975), 221–9.]

ANDREW MARVELL

76   A Dialogue between the Soul and Body

Soul

O who shall, from this Dungeon, raise
A Soul inslav'd so many wayes?
With bolts of Bones, that fetter'd stands
In Feet; and manacled in Hands.
Here blinded with an Eye; and there
Deaf with the drumming of an Ear.
A Soul hung up, as 'twere, in Chains
Of Nerves, and Arteries, and Veins.
Tortur'd, besides each other part,
In a vain Head, and double Heart.

Body

O who shall me deliver whole,
From bonds of this Tyrannic Soul?
Which, stretcht upright, impales me so,
That mine own Precipice I go;
And warms and moves this needless Frame:
(A Fever could but do the same.)
And, wanting where its spight to try,
Has made me live to let me dye.
A Body that could never rest,
Since this ill Spirit it possest.

Soul

What Magick could me thus confine
Within anothers Grief to pine?

Where whatsover it complain,
I feel, that cannot feel, the pain.
And all my Care its self employes,
That to preserve, which me destroys:
Constrain'd not only to indure
Diseases, but, whats worse, the Cure:
And ready oft the Port to gain,
Am Shipwrackt into Health again.

Body

But Physick yet could never reach
The Maladies Thou me dost teach;
Whom first the Cramp of Hope does Tear:
And then the Palsie Shakes of Fear.
The Pestilence of Love does heat:
Or Hatred's hidden Ulcer eat.
Joy's chearful Madness does perplex:
Or Sorrow's other Madness vex.
Which Knowledge forces me to know;
And Memory will not foregoe.
What but a Soul could have the wit
To build me up for Sin so fit?
So Architects do square and hew,
Green Trees that in the Forest grew.

[From *Poems and Letters*, ed. H. Margoliouth (Oxford: Clarendon Press, 1927).]

PHINEAS FLETCHER

77   The All-Seeing Intellect

The Island's Prince, of frame more than celestial,
Is rightly called the all-seeing Intellect:
All glorious bright, such nothing is terrestrial,
Whose sun-like face and most divine aspect
  No human sight may ever hope descry,
  For when himself on's self reflects his eye
Dull and amazed he stands as so bright majesty.

Look as the sun, whose ray and searching light
Here, there, and everywhere itself displays,

No nook or corner flies his piercing sight;
Yet on himself when he reflects his rays
   Soon back he flings the too bold venturing gleam,
   Down to the earth the flames all broken stream:
Such is this famous Prince, such his unpierced beam.

His strangest body is not bodily,
But matter without matter; never filled,
Nor filling; though within his compass high
All heaven and earth, and all in both, are held,
   Yet thousand thousand heavens he could contain,
   And still as empty as at first remain,
And when he takes in most, readiest to take again.

Though travelling all places, changing none:
Bid him soar up to heaven, and thence down throwing
The centre search, and Dis dark realm: he's gone,
Returns, arrives, before thou saw'st him going;
   And while his weary kingdom safely sleeps,
   All restless night he watch and warding keeps,
Never his careful head on resting pillow steeps.

In every quarter of this blessed Isle
Himself both present is, and President;
Nor once retires (ah happy realm the while,
That by no officer's lewd ravishment
   With greedy lust and wrong consumed art!).
   He all in all, and all in every part,
Does share to each his due, and equal dole impart.

He knows nor death, nor years, nor feeble age,
But as his time, his strength and vigour grows:
And when his kingdom by intestine rage
Lies broke and wasted, open to his foes,
   And battered sconce now flat and even lies,
   Sooner than thought to that great Judge he flies,
Who weighs him just reward of good or injuries.

For he the Judge's viceroy here is placed,
Where if he live as knowing he may die,
He never dies, but with fresh pleasures graced
Bathes his crowned head in soft eternity,

Where thousand joys, and pleasures ever new,
And blessings thicker than the morning dew,
With endless sweets rain down on that immortal crew.

There golden stars set in the crystal snow;
There dainty joys laugh at white-headed caring;
There day no night, delight no end shall know;
Sweets without surfeit, fullness without sparing,
　And by its spending, growing happiness.
　There God Himself in glories lavishness
Diffused in all, to all, is all full blessedness.

But if he here neglect his master's law,
And with those traitors 'gainst his Lord rebels,
Down to the deeps ten thousand fiends him draw:
Deeps where night, death, despair and horror dwells,
　And in worst ills, still worse expecting fears;
　Where fell despite for spite his bowels tears,
And still increasing grief, and torment never wears.

Prayers there are idle, death is wooed in vain;
In midst of death, poor wretches long to die;
Night without day or rest, still doubling pain,
Woes spending still, yet still their end less nigh;
　The soul there restless, helpless, hopeless lies,
　The body frying roars, and roaring fries:
There's life that never lives, and death that never dies.

Hence while unsettled here, he fighting reigns,
Shut in a tower where thousand enemies
Assault the fort; with wary care and pains
He guards all entrance, and by divers spies
　Searches into his foes' and friends' designs,
　For most he fears his subjects' wavering minds:
This tower then only falls when treason undermines.

[From *The Purple Island, or The Isle of Man* (1633), in *Jacobean and Caroline Poetry*, ed. T. G. S.
Cain (London: Methuen, 1981).]

L

Be near me when my light is low,
     When the blood creeps, and the nerves prick
     And tingle; and the heart is sick,
And all the wheels of being slow.

Be near me when the sensuous frame
     Is rack'd with pangs that conquer trust;
     And Time, a maniac scattering dust,
And Life, a Fury slinging flame.

Be near me when my faith is dry,
     And men the flies of latter spring,
     That lay their eggs, and sting and sing
And weave their petty cells and die.

Be near me when I fade away,
     To point the term of human strife,
     And on the low dark verge of life
The twilight of eternal day. [. . .]

CXX

I trust I have not wasted breath:
     I think we are not wholly brain,
     Magnetic mockeries; not in vain,
Like Paul with beasts, I fought with Death;

Not only cunning casts in clay:
     Let Science prove we are, and then
     What matters Science unto men,
At least to me? I would not stay.

Let him, the wiser man who springs
     Hereafter, up from childhood shape
     His action like the greater ape,
But I was *born* to other things.

79 **The Mind**

Mind in its purest play is like some bat
That beats about in caverns all alone.
Contriving by a kind of senseless wit
Not to conclude against a wall of stone.

It has no need to falter or explore;
Darkly it knows what obstacles are there,
And so may weave and flitter, dip and soar
In perfect courses through the blackest air.

And has this simile a like perfection?
The mind is like a bat. Precisely. Save
That in the very happiest intellection
A graceful error may correct the cave.

[From *New and Collected Poems* (New York, 1988).]

Notes

Extract 10

GEORGE BERKELEY: *On the Principles of Human Knowledge*
  1. To be convinced of which, the reader need only reflect and try to separate in his own thoughts the being of a sensible thing from its being perceived.

Extract 24

WILLIAM JAMES: *Does 'Consciousness' Exist?*
  1. Articles by Baldwin, Ward, Bawden, King, Alexander and others. Dr Perry is frankly over the border.

Extract 32

JULIEN OFFRAY DE LA METTRIE: *Man a Machine*
  1. There are peoples, even to-day, who, through lack of a greater number of signs, can count only to 20.

Extract 36

PIERRE FLOURENS: *Phrenology Examined*
  1. See my Recherches Expérimentales sur les propriétés et les fonctions du Système Nerveux.
  2. Ibid.
  3. See my Recherches Expérimentales sur les propriétés et les fonctions du Système Nerveux.
  4. 'From what I have now said, it clearly follows that the aperceptive faculty, the faculty of reminiscence, and that of memory, are nothing but attributes common to all the fundamental faculties.'—Gall, [*On the Functions of the Brain*,] t. iv. p. 319. 'All that I have just said, is also applicable to the judgment and the imagination,' &c.—Ibid. p. 325. 'the sentiments and the propensities also have their judgment, their imagination, their recollection, and their memory.'—Ibid. p. 327.
  5. Ibid. 328.
  6. Ibid. 327.
  7. Gall, t. iv. p. 339.
  8. Ibid. p. 341.
  9. 'The *intellectual faculty* and all its subdivisions, such as perception, recollection, memory, judgment, imagination, &c. are not fundamental faculties, but merely general attributes of them.'—Gall, t. iv. p. 327.
  10. 'Reason,' says Gall, 'is the result of the simultaneous action of all the intellectual faculties.' Gall, t. iv. p. 341.

Extract 39

THOMAS HENRY HUXLEY: *On the Hypothesis that Animals are Automata*
1. 'Essai de Psychologie,' chap. xxvii.

Extract 40

THOMAS ERSKINE: *The Trial of Hadfield*
1. Mr Erskine put his hand to the prisoner's head, who stood by him at the bar of the Court.

Extract 41

HENRY MAUDSLEY: *Responsibility in Mental Disease*
1. Mind may be defined physiologically as a general term denoting the sum total of those functions of the brain which are known as thought, feeling, and will. By disorder of mind is meant disorder of those functions.

Extract 42

J. J. C. SMART: *Sensations and Brain Processes*
1. This is a very slightly revised version of a paper which was first published in the *Philosophical Review*, LXVIII (1959), 141–56. Since that date there have been criticisms of my paper by J. T. Stephenson, *Philosophical Review*, LXIX (1960), 505–10, to which I have replied in *Philosophical Review*, LXX (1961), 406–7, and by G. Pitcher and by W. D. Joske, *Australasian Journal of Philosophy*, XXXVIII (1960), 150–60, to which I have replied in the same volume of the journal, pp. 252–54.
2. *British Journal of Psychology*, XLVII (1956), 44–50.
3. *Minnesota Studies in the Philosophy of Science*, Vol. II (Minneapolis: University of Minnesota Press, 1958), pp. 370–497.
4. Some philosophers of my acquaintance, who have the advantage over me in having known Wittgenstein, would say that this interpretation of him is too behavioristic. However, it seems to me a very natural interpretation of his printed words, and whether it is not Wittgenstein's real view it is certainly an interesting and important one. I wish to consider it here as a possible rival both to the 'brain-process' thesis and to straight-out old-fashioned dualism.
5. See Ryle, *The Concept of Mind* (London: Hutchinson's University Library, 1949), p. 93.
6. On this point see Paul Oppenheim and Hilary Putnam, 'Unity of Science as a Working Hypothesis,' in *Minnesota Studies in the Philosophy of Science*, Vol. II (Minneapolis: University of Minnesota Press, 1958), pp. 3–36.
7. Feigl, op. cit., p. 428. Feigl uses the expression 'nomological danglers' for the laws whereby the entities dangle: I have used the expression to refer to the dangling entities themselves.
8. Wittgenstein did not like the word 'disposition.' I am using it to put in a nutshell (and perhaps inaccurately) the view which I am attributing to Wittgenstein. I should like to repeat that I do not wish to claim that my interpretation of Wittgenstein is correct. Some of those who knew him do not interpret him in this

way. It is merely a view which I find myself extracting from his printed words and which I think is important and worth discussing for its own sake.

9. See Place, op. cit., p. 102, and Feigl, op. cit., p. 390, near top.

10. See J. H. Woodger, *Theory Construction*, International Encyclopedia of Unified Science, II, No. 5 (Chicago: University of Chicago Press, 1939), 38. I here permit myself to speak loosely. For warnings against possible ways of going wrong with this sort of talk, see my note 'Spatialising Time,' *Mind*, LXIV (1955), 239–41.

11. Cf. Feigl, op. cit., p. 439.

12. See Place, op. cit., p. 106; also Feigl, op. cit., p. 438.

13. I think this objection was first put to me by Professor Max Black. I think it is the most subtle of any of those I have considered, and the one which I am least confident of having satisfactorily met.

14. See B. A. Farrell 'Experience,' *Mind*, LIX (1959), 170–98; reprinted in this volume, pp. 23–48 above; see especially p. 27 (of this volume).

Extract 56

GEORGE ROMANES: *Animal Intelligence*
1. *Naturalist in Nicaragua*, p. 119.

Extract 58

JAMES SULLY: *Studies of Childhood*
1. The *Nineteenth Century* (1891). Cf. the somewhat fantastic and not too serious paper by S. S. Buckman on 'Babies and Monkeys' in the same journal (1894).
2. See, for example, the works of H. Ploss, *Das Kind in Branch und Sitte*, and *Das kleine Kind*.

Extract 59

WILLIAM JAMES: *Evolutionary Psychology Demands a Mind-Dust*
1. *Psychology*, § 62.

Extract 60

ALFRED RUSSEL WALLACE: *Darwinism*
1. For a full discussion of all these points, see *Descent of Man*, chap. iii.
2. *Descent of Man*, chap. iv.
3. This is the estimate furnished me by two mathematical masters in one of our great public schools of the proportion of boys who have any special taste or capacity for mathematical studies. Many more, of course, can be drilled into a fair knowledge of elementary mathematics, but only this small proportion possess the natural faculty which renders it possible for them ever to rank high as mathematicians, to take any pleasure in it, or to do any original mathematical work.
4. I am informed, however, by a music master in a large school that only about one per cent have real or decided musical talent, corresponding curiously with the estimate of the mathematicians.

Extract 62

THOMAS NAGEL: *What is it Like to be a Bat?*

1. By 'our own case' I do not mean just 'my own case,' but rather the mentalistic ideas that we apply unproblematically to ourselves and other human beings.

Extract 71

OLIVER SACKS: *The Disembodied Lady*

1. Purdon Martin, almost alone of contemporary neurologists, would often speak of facial and vocal 'posture', and their basis, finally, in proprioceptive integrity. He was greatly intrigued when I told him about Christina and showed him some films and tapes of her—many of the suggestions and formulations here are, in fact, his.

Extract 73

GRANT GILLETT: *Brain Bisection and Personal Identity*

1. T. Nagel, 'Brain Bisection and the Unity of Consciousness', *Mortal Questions*, Cambridge, Cambridge University Press, 1979.
2. D. Parfit, *Reasons and Persons*, Oxford, Oxford University Press, 1983.
3. R. Sperry, 'Brain Bisection and the Mechanisms of Consciousness', in J. C. Eccles, ed., *The Brain and Conscious Experience*, New York, Springer-Verlag, 1965.
4. Ibid., p. 299.
5. A. R. Luria, *The Man with the Shattered World*, Basic Books, USA, 1972.
6. Parfit, op. cit., p. 245.
7. C. Peacock, *Sense and Content*, Oxford, Clarendon Press, 1983.
8. Parfit, op. cit.
9. Parfit, op. cit., p. 254.

Extract 74

DANIEL N. ROBINSON: *Cerebral Plurality and the Unity of Self*

1. J. Locke, *An essay concerning human understanding*. Chicago: Regnery, 1956. (Originally published, 1690.)
2. *A treatise of human nature*, ed. L. A. Selby-Bigge. New York: Dover, 1965. (Originally published, 1740.)
3. D. Robinson, *Systems of modern psychology: A critical sketch*. New York: Columbia University Press, 1979. D. Robinson and T. Beauchamp, 'Personal identity: Reid's answer to Hume', *The Monist*, 61 (1978), 326–339.
4. *An inquiry into the human mind*, ed. T. Duggan. Chicago: University of Chicago Press, 1970. (Originally published, 1764.)
5. *Phrenology examined*, trans. C. Meigs. Philadelphia: Hogan & Thompson, 1846.
6. F. J. Gall, *On the functions of the brain and each of its parts* (6 vols.), trans. Winslow Lewis, Jr. Boston: Marsh, Capon & Lyon, 1835, pp. 265–266.
7. W. Griesinger, *Mental pathology and therapeutics*, trans. C. L. Robertson and J. Rutherford. New York: Wood, 1882, p. iii.
8. Sir Henry Holland (1788–1873) is referred to here. His *Chapters on Mental Physiology*

NOTES 367

was first published in 1852, the year he became physician to Queen Victoria.

9. *Principles of psychology.* New York: Holt, 1890, p. 365.
10. P. Janet, *The mental state of hystericals*, trans. C. R. Corson. New York: Putnam, 1901.
11. *On double consciousness.* Chicago: Open Court, 1890.
12. D. Robinson, *The mind unfolded: Essays on psychology's historic texts.* Washington, DC: University Publications of America, 1978.
13. Trans. H. Baldwin. New York: Appleton, 1896.
14. M. Gazzaniga, *The bisected brain.* New York: Appleton-Century-Crofts, 1970. R. Sperry, M. Gazzaniga, and J. Bogen, 'Interhemispheric relationships: the neocortical commisures: Syndromes of hemispheric deconnection'. In P. J. Vinken and G. W. Bruyn (eds.), *Handbook of clinical neurology* (Vol. 4). Amsterdam: North Holland, 1969.
15. R. Puccetti, 'Brain bisection and personal identity', *British Journal for the Philosophy of Science*, 24 (1973), 339–355.
16. D. Robinson, 'What sort of persons are hemispheres? Another look at the "split-brain" man', *British Journal for the Philosophy of Science*, 27 (1976), 73–78.
17. D. Robinson, 'Neurometaphorology: The new faculty psychology, *Behaviour and Brain Science*, 4 (1981), 112–113.
18. Robinson, 'What sort of persons are hemispheres?'.
19. D. H. Raab, 'Backward masking', *Psychological Bulletin*, 60 (1963), 118–129.
20. G. Sperling, 'The information available in brief visual presentations', *Psychological Monographs*, 74 (1960) (11, Whole No. 498).
21. In the most recent decade there have been numerous and interesting studies conducted on commissurotomized patients and on a wide variety of 'laterality' phenomena. The evidence is now quite strong that each cerebral hemisphere takes the lion's share of certain cognitive or symbolic functions, a possibility that was not explored a century ago. Thanks to Broca, scientists in the 1870s were alert to the fact that specific linguistic functions were largely confined to the 'dominant' hemisphere. Nonetheless, contemporary research has turned up many utterly new findings and theories regarding the lateralization of psychological processes. It is, however, one of the burdens of my essay to argue that notwithstanding the scientific merits of this work, the basic *metaphysical* issue is largely undisturbed.
22. In its first coining, the 'psychologist's fallacy' referred to the tendency on the part of the researcher to consider the actual mental processes to be identical to the ones assumed by the experimenter and isolated by a certain procedure. Thus, in requiring the observer to arrive at a complex idea by stringing together simpler 'elements,' the experimenter moves (fallaciously) to the conclusion that thought is comprised of such elements.

Select Bibliography

1. THE TRANSCENDENT MIND

BARNES, J. (ed.), *The Complete Works of Aristotle*. Princeton, 1984.
BERKELEY, G., *A Treatise Concerning the Principles of Human Knowledge* (1710). La Salle, Ill., 1963.
BRICKHOUSE, T., and Smith, N., *Plato's Socrates*. Oxford, 1994.
BRODIE, S., *Ethics with Aristotle*. Oxford, 1991.
DESCARTES, R., *The Philosophical Writings of Descartes*, 2 vols., ed. J. Cottingham, *et al.* Cambridge, 1984.
GAUKROGER, S., *Descartes: An Intellectual Biography*. Oxford, 1996.
GILSON, E., *The Christian Philosophy of St Thomas Aquinas*. New York, 1956.
JOWETT, B. (trans.), *The Dialogues of Plato*, Oxford, edition of 1953.
KANT, I., *Critique of Pure Reason*, trans. N. K. Smith. London, 1929.
KENNY, A., *Aristotle on the Perfect Life*. Oxford, 1992.
KINGSLEY, P., *Ancient Philosophy, Mystery and Magic*. Oxford, 1995.
KITCHER, P., *Kant's Transcendental Psychology*. Oxford, 1990.
LUCE, A. A., *The Works of George Berkeley*, 4 vols. London, 1949.
MATES, B., *The Philosophy of Leibniz*. Oxford, 1986.
PEGIS, A., *The Basic Writings of Saint Thomas Aquinas*, 2 vols. New York, 1945.
RADHAKRISHNAN, S., *The Principal Upanisads*. London, 1953.
ROBINSON, D. N., *Aristotle's Psychology*. New York, 1989.
ROZEMOND, M., *Descartes' Dualism*. Cambridge, Mass., 1996.
RYLE, G., 'Plato', in *The Encyclopedia of Philosophy*, vol. vi, ed. Paul Edwards. New York, 1967.
VAILATI, E., *Leibniz and Clarke: A Study of their Correspondence*. Oxford, 1997.
WARNOCK, J. G., *Berkeley*. London, 1953.
WINKLER, K., *Berkeley: An Interpretation*. Oxford, 1989.
WOLFF, R., *Kant's Theory of Mental Activity*. Cambridge, 1963.
WOOLHOUSE, R., and Francks, R. (eds.), *Leibniz's 'New System' and Associated Contemporary Texts*. Oxford, 1997.
ZAEHNER, R., *Hinduism*. London, 1962.

2. THE MIND AS SPECTATOR

AUGUSTINE, St, *Confessions*, 3 vols., ed. J. O'Donnell. Oxford, 1992.
BARNES, J. (ed.), *The Complete Works of Aristotle*. Princeton, 1984.
BOEHNER, P. (ed.), *Ockham: Philosophical Writings*. Edinburgh, 1957.
BRODIE, S., *Ethics with Aristotle*. Oxford, 1991.
GILSON, E., *The Christian Philosophy of St Augustine*. London, 1961.
—— *The Christian Philosophy of St Thomas Aquinas*. New York, 1956.
HOBBES, T., *Leviathan*. ed. J. Gaskin. Oxford, 1996.
HUME, D., *An Enquiry Concerning Human Understanding* (1748). Indianapolis, 1955.

JAMES, W., *The Varieties of Religious Experience*. New York, 1902.
—— *Pragmatism: A New Name for Some Old Ways of Thinking*. New York, 1907.
KENNY, A., *Aristotle on the Perfect Life*. Oxford, 1992.
LOCKE, J., *An Essay Concerning the Human Understanding* (1690), 2 vols., ed. J. Yolton. Oxford, 1961.
MARROU, J., *St Augustine*. London, 1958.
MARTIN, T., *The Instructed Vision*. Bloomington, 1961.
MILL, J. S., *An Examination of Sir William Hamilton's Philosophy*. London; 6th edition, 1889.
PEARS, D., *Hume's System*. Oxford, 1991.
PEGIS, A., *The Basic Writings of Saint Thomas Aquinas*, 2 vols. New York, 1945.
PERRY, R., *The Thought and Character of William James*, 2 vols. Boston, 1935.
REID, T., *Works*, 2 vols., ed. William Hamilton. Edinburgh, 1846–63.
ROBINSON, D. N., *Aristotle's Psychology*. New York, 1989.
—— *Toward a Science of Human Nature: Essays on the Psychologies of Hegel, Mill, Wundt and James*. New York, 1982; ch. 2.
ROGERS, G. (ed.), *Locke's Philosophy: Content and Context*. Oxford, 1994.
RYLE, G., *The Concept of Mind*. London, 1949.
—— *Dilemmas*. Cambridge, 1954.
WATKINS, J., *Hobbes's System of Ideas*. London, 1965.

3. MIND, BRAIN, AND MODULES

BEACH, F. *et al.* (eds.), *The Neuropsychology of Karl Lashley*. New York, 1960.
CABANIS, P., *On the Relationship between the Moral and the Physical. Preface*, trans. F. S. Robinson; and *Tenth Memoire*, trans. M. Heliotis. In *Significant Contributions to the History of Psychology* (in 28 vols.), ed. D. N. Robinson, Series E, Vol. i (pp. 373–476). Washington, DC, 1978.
CHURCHLAND, P., and Churchland, P. S., 'Could Machines Think?', in E. Dietrich (ed.), *Thinking Computers and Virtual Persons*. Boston, 1994.
DAVIDSON, W., 'Professor Bain's Philosophy'. *Mind*, 13 (1904) 161–79.
FLOURENS, P., *Phrenology Examined*, trans. Charles Meigs. Philadelphia, 1846.
GALEN, *On the Natural Faculties*, trans. A. Brock. New York, 1928.
—— *On the Usefulness of the Parts of the Body*, 2 vols., trans. M. May. Ithaca, 1968.
GASSENDI, P., 'Fifth Set of Objections' to Descartes' *Meditations*, in *The Philosophical Writings of Descartes*, ed. J. Cottingham *et al.*, Vol. ii Cambridge, 1984.
HARTLEY, D., *Observations on Man, His Frame, His Duty and His Expectations*. London, 1749 (and in several later editions).
HIPPOCRATES, *Works*, 4 vols., ed. W. Jones and E. Withington. Cambridge, 1948–53.
HUXLEY, T., *Man's Place in Nature*. London, 1864.
IRVINE, W., *Thomas Henry Huxley*. London, 1960.
JACOBI, J., *The Psychology of C. G. Jung*. New Haven, 1962.
JUNG, C. G., *Basic Writings*, ed. V. de Laszlo. New York 1993.
LA METTRIE, J., *Man a Machine*, trans. G. Bussey. Chicago, 1912.
MARTIN, T., *The Instructed Vision*. Bloomington, 1961.
MAUDSLEY, H., *The Physiology and Pathology of the Mind*. New York, 1867.

PENFIELD, W., *The Mystery of the Mind: A Critical Study of Consciousness in the Human Brain*. Princeton, 1975.

REID, T., *Works*, 2 vols., ed. William Hamilton. Edinburgh, 1846–63.

ROBINSON, D. N., *An Intellectual History of Psychology* (3rd edn.). Wisconsin, 1995; ch. 10.

—— *Wild Beasts & Idle Humours: The Insanity Defense from Antiquity to the Present.* Cambridge, 1996; ch. 5 and notes.

SEARLE, J. *Minds, Brains and Science*. Cambridge, 1984.

—— *The Rediscovery of Mind*. Cambridge, 1992.

SMART, J. J. C. 'Sensations and brain processes', in V. C. Chappell (ed.), *The Philosophy of Mind*, Englewood Cliffs, NS, 1962.

SPURZHEIM, J., *Outlines of Phrenology*. London, 1832.

STRAWSON, G., *Mental Reality*. Cambridge, 1994.

4. THE EVOLUTION OF MIND

BARNES, J. (ed.), *The Complete Works of Aristotle*. Princeton, 1984.

BRODIE, S., *Ethics with Aristotle*. Oxford, 1991.

DARWIN, C., *Autobiography*, ed. N. Barlow. London, 1958.

—— *Life and Letters of Charles Darwin*, ed. F. Darwin. New York, 1959.

—— *The Descent of Man*. London, 1871 (and in many editions).

DENNETT, D., *Brainstorms: Philosophical Essays on Mind and Psychology*. Cambridge, Mass., 1978.

—— *Darwin's Dangerous Idea: Evolution and the Meaning of Life*. New York, 1995.

EISLEY, L., *Darwin's Century*. New York, 1958.

HAECKEL, E., *The Evolution of Man*, trans. J. McCabe, New York, 1910.

—— *Last Words on Evolution*, trans. J. McCabe. London, 1906.

JAMES, W., *Principles of Psychology*, 2 vols. New York, 1890; (available as a single volume paperback from Harvard University Press).

KENNY, A., *Aristotle on the Perfect Life*. Oxford, 1992.

MORGAN, C. L., *An Introduction to Comparative Psychology*. London, 1894.

—— *The Animal Mind*. London, 1930.

NAGEL, T., 'What is it like to be a bat?' *Philosophical Review*, 83 (1974), 435–50.

—— *The View from Nowhere*. Oxford, 1986.

—— *The Last Word*. Oxford, 1997.

PENROSE, R., *The Emperor's New Mind*. Oxford, 1989.

—— *Shadows of the Mind: A Search for the Missing Science of Consciousness*. Oxford, 1994.

ROBINSON, D. N., *Aristotle's Psychology*. New York, 1989.

ROMANES, G., *Animal Intelligence*. London, 1881.

SPENCER, H., *Man vs. State*. London, 1884.

—— *Autobiography*. London, 1904.

SULLY, J., *Studies of Childhood* (2nd edn.). London, 1896.

WALLACE, A. R., *Darwinism*. London, 1889.

5. MIND AND SELF: DIVIDED, CONSTRUCTED, AND MULTIPLIED

DEWEY, J., 'The Reflex Arc Concept in Psychology'. *Psychological Review*, 3 (1896), 357–70.

FREUD, S., *Complete Psychological Works*, 24 vols., ed. James Strachey. London, 1953–64.

GILLETT, G., *Brain Bisection and Personal Identity, Mind*, 378 (1986), 224–9.

HOOK, S., *John Dewey: An Intellectual Portrait*. New York, 1939.

HUME, D., *A Treatise of Human Nature*, ed. L. A. Selby-Bigge (2nd edn.). Oxford, 1978.

JAMES, W., *Principles of Psychology*, 2 vols. New York, 1890; (available as a single-volume paperback from Harvard University Press).

JONES, E., *The Life and Work of Sigmund Freud*, 3 vols. London, 1957.

LOCKE, J., *An Essay Concerning the Human Understanding* (1690), 2 vols., ed. J. Yolton. Oxford, 1961.

MARTIN, T., *The Instructed Vision*. Bloomington, 1961.

PARFIT, D., *Reasons and Persons*. Oxford, 1984.

REID, T., *Works*, 2 vols., ed. William Hamilton. Edinburgh, 1846–63.

ROGERS, G. (ed.), *Locke's Philosophy: Content and Context*. Oxford, 1994.

SACKS, O., *The Man Who Mistook his Wife for a Hat*. New York, 1983.

SCHLIPP, P. (ed.), *The Philosophy of John Dewey*. Chicago, 1939.

STERN, D., *Wittgenstein on Mind and Language*. Oxford, 1995.

WITTGENSTEIN, L., *Philosophical Investigations*, ed. G. Anscombe, *et al*. Oxford, 1953.

6. EPILOGUE: THE MIND OF THE POETS

BRADLEY, A. C., *A Commentary on Tennyson's 'In Memorian'*. London, 1925.

FLETCHER, P., *The Purple Island, or the Isle of Man* (in various editions).

LUCRETIUS, *On the Nature of the Universe*, trans. R. Melville. Oxford, 1997.

MARVELL, A., *Poems and Letters*, ed. H. Margoliouth. Oxford, 1927.

WILBUR, R., *New and Collected Poems*. New York, 1988.

WINSPEAR, A., *Lucretius and his Scientific Thought*. Montreal, 1963.

Biographical Notes

ARISTOTLE (384–322 BC) was born into a respectable family in the Ionian city of Stagira, and studied in Plato's academy for twenty years (367–347 BC). He founded his own school, the Lyceum (335 BC), after some years of travel, which included the tutoring of Alexander, then the 13-year-old son of Philip II, king of Macedon. Aristotle's scholarship ranged over all academic subjects and would exert an unequalled influence on scientific and philosophical thought until the seventeenth century.

ST AUGUSTINE (354–430), also 'Aurelius Augustinus', was born in North Africa and would finally appease his Roman Catholic mother's anxieties after he had devoted his early years to the widest range of pleasures. He became a Christian in 386, drawn first to Manichaeanism, but then turning to Christian Neoplatonism. With the possible exception of Thomas Aquinas—himself much the 'Augustinian'—he would compose the most influential treatises in the history of Roman Catholicism.

ALEXANDER BAIN (1818–1903) was a close friend of John Stuart Mill and other leading 'radical' reformers. He wrote influentially in the field of psychology and in 1876 founded the journal *Mind*. He defended associationistic theories of mental life and physiological approaches to explanation in psychology. His most widely cited works were *The Senses and the Intellect* (1851) and *The Emotions and the Will* (1855).

GEORGE BERKELEY (1685–1753) was an Irish Anglican bishop who had mastered the mathematics and optical sciences of his age. He made a seminal contribution to the field of visual perception with his *An Essay Towards a New Theory of Vision* (1709). A Fellow of Trinity College, Dublin, he ranks as the most celebrated philosopher Ireland would produce. With Locke before him and Hume after, he is one of the major architects of British philosophical empiricism. Nonetheless, his willingness to draw out what he took to be the central implications of empiricism led him to reject the possibility of matter having existence independent of mind. His aborted plan to establish a college in Bermuda found him settling for a time in Rhode Island.

PIERRE-JEAN GEORGE CABANIS (1757–1808) was intimately associated with such figures of the French Enlightenment as 'Baron' Holbach and Condillac, the latter having done much to promulage Lockian philosophy in France. Holbach's was perhaps the most materialistic of prevailing philosophies of mind, and Cabanis's training in medicine made him especially receptive to this approach. With Destutt de Tracy he developed the philosophy of *Idéologie*, an empiricistic and rigorously scientific perspective on mind. His other acquaintances included both Benjamin Franklin and Thomas Jefferson.

PAUL CHURCHLAND is Professor of Philosophy at the University of California, San Diego. He and Patricia Churchland have written forcefully in defence of eliminative materialism, arguing that mentalistic terms are residuals of pre-scientific thought.

CHARLES DARWIN (1809–82) chose against both medicine at Edinburth and theology at Cambridge, and was finally drawn to the naturalistic studies on which his fame would ultimately rest. As the unsalaried naturalist on the *HMS Beagle* (1831–6) he made observations that would culminate in his revolutionary theories. On issues of mind and mental life, his most important works are *The Descent of Man* (1871) and *The Expression of the Emotions in Animals and Man* (1870).

DANIEL DENNETT is Professor of Psychology at Tufts University in Massachusetts. He is the author of many books in which he examines the arguments for and against computational models of mind and the prospects for a developed and defensible artificial intelligence.

RENÉ DESCARTES (1596–1650) is widely regarded as the first of the truly modern philosophers, owing in large part to his official scepticism toward older modes of enquiry. Educated by the Jesuits, he had a firm grounding in logic. It was in a dream (10 November 1619) that he was instructed to devise a comprehensive natural science based on mathematics. He invented analytical geometry and his *Discourse on Method* and *Meditations* put in place a variety of abiding problems, including problems of explanation and the mind/body problem. His insistence that non-human ('non-rational') creatures lacked a defining mental life would enable many later experimentalists to practise vivisection without ethical scruple.

JOHN DEWEY (1859–1952) was an important figure in American education and social criticism, and, with William James, the most important American philosopher of the later nineteenth century. His academic years at the University of Chicago and then at Columbia University exposed him as well to the social problems of urban life and aroused in him deep interest in child rearing and early education. His thought was enriched by the integration of classical sources and modern experimental science, the former stressing the social and cultural forces that shape experience itself.

THOMAS ERSKINE (1750–1823), a native Scot and Edinburgh educated, was the greatest trial lawyer of his age. His long and not untroubled life would find him both a member of Parliament and Lord Chancellor of England. His defence of James Hadfield did much to transform legal thinking on the matter of criminal responsibility. He also served as defence counsel to Thomas Paine, tried *in absentia* (1792) for sedition. His earlier defence of Lord George Gordon (1781) essentially eliminated the doctrine of constructive treason.

PHINEAS FLETCHER (1582–1650), brother of Giles the younger, was educated at Eton and Cambridge and spent most of his life as a cleric in Hilgay, Norfolk. The anatomical detail of *The Purple Island* may be indebted to first-hand observations of human dissections performed at Cambridge by Harvey.

PIERRE FLOURENS (1794–1867) earned his MD at Montpellier. In 1822 he published his *Experimental Research on the Properties and Functions of the Nervous System of Vertebrates*, a pioneering work in experimental neurosurgery. He was named Perpetual Secretary of the Academy of Sciences in 1833, a member of the French Academy in 1838, and a Peer of France in 1846. In 1847 he introduced the use of chloroform to anaesthetize animal subjects, this however after more than two decades of surgery on non-anaesthetized dogs and cats.

SIGMUND FREUD (1856–1939), the father of psychoanalytic theory and practice, received his medical degree from the University of Vienna, working productively with the leading neurophysiologist, Ernst Brucke. His private practice as a consulting neurologist brought him into contact with patients suffering from a variety of 'hysterical' symptoms calling for explanation and treatment not to be found in standard neurological texts. With Joseph Breuer, Freud came to regard such symptoms as the outcome of psychodynamic processes, chiefly that of *repression*. The skeleton of the theory was presented in S. Freud and J. Breuer, *Studien über Hysterie* (1896). Over the next forty years Freud would write volumes of books and articles, developing and defending the Freudian theory of unconscious motivation, neurosis, dreams, religion, and art.

GALEN (129–99) was a Greek physician whose works would influence the theory and practice of medicine for a thousand years. He insisted that the competent physician would be well trained in philosophy and mathematics, but would rely on experimental demonstrations. Influenced as much by Plato as by Aristotle and Theophrastus in his psychological studies, Galen held to a fairly strict hereditarianism.

PIERRE GASSENDI (1592–1655) was a contemporary and critic of Descartes and a celebrated philosopher and scientist in his own right. His writings did much to revive a modified form of ancient Epicurean (atomistic) philosophy and to cast doubt on the adequacy of Aristotelianism. He was ordained into the priesthood in 1616, but found no inconsistency between his religious convictions and a consistently materialistic perspective on mind and body.

ERNST HAECKEL (1834–1919) studied with both Johannes Müller and with Rudolf Virchow and came to be a tireless defender of evolutionary theory as applicable to every aspect of life, human and animal. *The Riddle of the Universe* (1899) attracted a wide readership, recording Haeckel's conviction that all 'riddles', including consciousness, finally evaporate when their utterly material composition is understood. An essentially atheistic result was readily derived from this ontology.

DAVID HARTLEY (1705–57) produced one of the earliest associationistic psychologies based on physiological processes. His *Observations on Man* was in the patrimony of Newtonian science and Locke's (Newtonian) philosophy of mind. It greatly impressed Joseph Priestley, who published an abridgement of it in 1775. Hartley also contributed to the development of mathematical probability theory.

HIPPOCRATES of Cos (460–380 BC) is the eponymous founder of ancient Greek's most celebrated 'school' of medicine. There are scant references to him in Plato's *Phaedrus* but, by the Hellenistic age many books attributed to him and his teaching began to appear. The collection of all 'Hippocratic' writings is vast. The four-volume edition in the Loeb Classics series provides instructive introductions including datings and likely sources.

THOMAS HOBBES (1588–1679) was a vicar's son, taking five years at Oxford to receive his degree (1608). His classical education prepared him for the major project of translating Thucydides, as travel abroad disabused him of the authority of Aristotelian science. It was on the Continent that he was won over fully to the new mechanistic science of Galileo. He formed friendships with the best minds in Europe, including

Pierre Gassendi and Abbé Marsenne, whom he joined in the celebrated critique of Cartesian philosophy. In the politically turbulent period of his life his writings on law and politics would earn him both friends and enemies. His *Leviathan* (1651) made out a strong case for an absolute sovereign monarch, but based on the needs and expectations of those who would surrender to such rule.

DAVID HUME (1711–76), arguably the most influential English-speaking philosopher, was a central figure in the Scottish Enlightenment. His *A Treatise of Human Nature* (1739) suffered neglect and incomprehension by a small readership, but his later works (*An Enquiry Concerning the Principles of Morals*, 1748; *An Enquiry Concerning Human Understanding*, 1758) would come to be the subject of great debate and consternation, casting Hume as the textbook 'sceptic' on matters moral and metaphysical. In these works, intended partly to oppose scepticism, he defends empiricism against the claims of rationalism, insisting that the source of all knowledge is perception, just as the source of morality is sentiment.

THOMAS HUXLEY (1825–95) was a self-educated Londoner who would befriend and effectively defend Charles Darwin over a course of turbulent years following the publication of *The Origin of Species* and of *The Descent of Man*. His 'epiphenomenalism' was a common-sense 'solution' to the mind/body problem; one designed to accept the validity of mental states but only as a by-product of the complex operations of the brain. He was, as one critic noted, a 'prince of debaters' and one of the most effective defenders of science and science education that the Victorian world would produce.

WILLIAM JAMES (1842–1910) was, with Dewey, America's most influential philosopher. His *Principles of Psychology* (1890) remains the most interesting textbook ever written on the subject. His 'radical empiricism' and pragmatism were replies to transcendentalisms of all forms, whether by way of Hegel or Royce. His was a down-to-earth and open-ended philosophy, hostile to the 'nothing-but' and block-universe schools. He introduced experimental psychology to the Harvard curriculum as early as 1875, giving him at least arguable claims to priority over Wundt. Still, it was the human experience as lived—not as contracted and caricatured in laboratories—that he took to be the subject of 'that nasty little subject' of psychology.

CARL GUSTAV JUNG (1875–1961) was a Swiss-educated physician who helped to found the psychoanalytical movement until his break with Freud. Jung had studied with Pierre Janet in France and then was attracted to Freud's works. He was the first president of the International Psychoanalytic Society (1911). His theory of ancestral archetypes and the collective unconscious enriched analytical psychology with research and theory in mythology, anthropology, and cultural history.

IMMANUEL KANT (1724–1804) was educated and lived his entire life in Königsberg, finally receiving the chair in Logic at the University in 1750. Though instructed and deeply interested in the natural sciences, his reputation was earned chiefly through the publication of the famous trio of 'critiques': *Critique of Pure Reason* (1781), *Critique of Practical Reason* (1788), and *Critique of Judgment* (1790). The first critique sought to establish the necessary conditions for all experience and knowledge; the second, the foundational precepts of ethics; the third, the quasi-rational and ultimately non-rational framework of aesthetics. In his *Religion within the Bounds of Mere Reason* (1793) he would derive whatever is of value in religion from morals, dismissing the rest as essentially superstitious.

JULIEN OFFRAY DE LA METTRIE (1709–51) was a controversial physician born in St Malo who completed his medical education at Rheims (1733). He translated and published works by the great Boerhaave. His *Natural History of the Soul* (1745) offered a preview of his radically materialistic psychology and resulted in official censure. Self-exiled in Holland he had published his *Man a Machine* (1747), requiring him to seek sanctuary in the court of Frederick the Great, who would write and read La Mettrie's eulogy.

KARL LASHLEY (1890–1958), after receiving his doctorate in the field of anatomy, turned to psychology and became the leading physiological psychologist of the first half of the twentieth century. His use of experimental surgery to identify brain–behaviour relationships placed him at the forefront of scientists in the field. He opposed the mechanistic principles of Pavlov and drew attention to the integrative nature of brain function; the brain's more or less total involvement in complex cognitive tasks, and its great plasticity in compensating for injury.

GOTTFRIED LEIBNIZ (1646–1716) is one of the most original minds in recorded history. His contributions range over philosophy, mathematics and probability theory, history, moral and legal thought. He was barred from sitting the examination for the doctoral degree in law (1666) because he was simply too young! Independently of Newton, he devised a system of calculus for which he was later falsely and scandalously charged with plagiarism. He was a welcome guest at court, where the young queen of Prussia, Sophie Charlotte, would engage him in theological colloquy. In 1700, he was made life-president of the newly formed Berlin Society (Prussian Royal Academy).

JOHN LOCKE (1632–1704) received his BA from Oxford in 1656, remaining there as a teacher for several years where he was influenced by the scientific endeavours of Robert Boyle. By 1664 he had earned a medical degree and later would work with no less than Thomas Sydenham. Though Locke never actually practised medicine, he did take up residence with his old Oxford friend, now Lord Shaftesbury, a relationship that excited Locke's interests in politics and government. But the most profound influence on his thought came from the extraordinary achievements of Isaac Newton, whom Locke would come to befriend. In his *Essay Concerning the Human Understanding* he makes clear that it is a *Newtonian* science of the mind that needs cultivating. His philosophy would come to strongly influence the thought of Enlightenment France and colonial America. More narrowly, it imposed an empiricistic character on psychological enquiry that persists to the present time.

LUCRETIUS (*c*.99–55 BC) attempted to recover the essence of Epicurean teaching and to render it memorable by casting it in a didactic poem of more than 7,000 lines. Just as Plato surely added originally to the thought of Socrates, Lucretius offers a work that is more than a mere poetical summary of another's thought. A thoroughgoing sensationist psychology is defended and is assumed to be grounded in the purely material interactions between the senses and the external world. There is sufficient indeterminacy (the 'swerve') in the atomic motions to permit moral freedom, which arises from an inborn power in the actor. It was Gassendi's revival of Epicureanism that restored this estimable work to the attention of scholars.

ANDREW MARVELL (1621–78) was born in Yorkshire, educated at Cambridge, and evolved into a Puritan poet who had nonetheless great esteem for the doomed Charles I. His friendships included Milton, and his service included that of tutor to the ward of Cromwell. His satirical verse and prose earned him many enemies—and admirers, of whom Swift was in the front ranks.

HENRY MAUDSLEY (1835–1918) was trained in medicine and developed an interest in psychiatric problems through the writings of Prichard, Griesinger, and Equirol. He served on the staff of the Manchester Asylum, then as Professor of Medical Jurisprudence at University College, London. His philanthropy endowed a psychiatric facility in London that would evolve into the famous Maudsley Hospital. His books and articles on medical jurisprudence did much to establish the field itself.

JOHN STUART MILL (1806–73) was widely regarded as the greatest philosopher of the English-speaking world of the nineteenth century. His writings became so popular that, as his friend and eulogist John Morely said, they sold for the price 'of a railway novel'. He carried forward the empiricistic tradition of Locke, Hume, and Hartley, avoiding both a premature biological psychology and a retrograde introspective psychology. His political writings (e.g. *On Liberty*) are informed by the empiricistic 'authority of experience', as are his works in logic and economics. His defence and development of utilitarianism marks a major chapter in ethical thought.

C. LLOYD MORGAN (1852–1936) was trained in metallurgy but developed a passionate interest, cultivated by his teacher, T. H. Huxley, in the relationship between science and philosophy. After a stint in South Africa, he earned a position at University College, Bristol, where he undertook research on animal behaviour. His theory of 'emergents', and thus *emergent evolution* was intended to improve the Darwinian account by allowing for sudden and progressive discontinuities.

THOMAS NAGEL is Professor of Philosophy at New York University. He has written widely in philosophy, with influential contributions to the philosophy of mind and to political philosophy.

DEREK PARFIT is Reader in Philosophy at the University of Oxford and the author of major works on philosophy of mind and personal identity.

WILDER PENFIELD (1891–1976) was American born, a Rhodes Scholar who worked in the laboratory of Sir Charles Sherrington, and then for forty years in Canada as one of the premier neurosurgeons in the world. His surgical skills and his writings helped bring fame to the Montreal Neurological Institute.

ROGER PENROSE, Fellow of All Souls, Oxford, is a theoretical mathematician whose interest in the philosophy of mind has resulted in a number of influential and provocative publications. He has offered both technical and formal arguments against the view that mental life is adequately modelled by any computational system.

PLATO (c.428–c.348 BC) is the veritable father of philosophy, as it would come to be known, his dialogues covering the full range of metaphysical, scientific, ethical, political, and psychological issues that define scholarly enquiry. His thought develops over a course of years and reveals if not distinct stages at least discernible shifts in emphasis. Nonetheless, his theory of mind retains a transcendentalist core throughout. Plato never married and, though tempted, never committed himself to positions of political power that were offered to him. He was but 31 when Socrates died and it would be years before Plato would compose many of the dialogues featuring Socrates and his circle of friends and friendly antagonists.

PYTHAGORAS (*c*.570 BC–?) was the first to call himself a philosopher and was judged by Heraclitus as possessed of the most enquiring mind. Born on the island of Samos, in the Ionian world that invented philosophy, he journeyed to the Nile valley and learned from the scholars and mathematicians of that region. But his own mathematical and kindred achievements outstripped all others. He is credited with discovering the musical scale of harmonies, is famous for the theorem that bears his name, and developed philosophical conceptions of knowledge and of the soul that would greatly influence Socrates and generations of Platonists.

THOMAS REID (1710–96) was educated at Aberdeen, where he then taught until 1764 when he took the chair at Glasgow recently vacated by Adam Smith. Reid is regarded as the father of Scottish 'Common Sense' philosophy and most effective of Hume's contemporary critics. His *An Inquiry into the Human Mind* (1764) is one of the most skilful philosophical executions in the English language, its sprightliness sometimes concealing its very deep profundity. Reid's influence in colonial America was great, as it was in France and Germany, notwithstanding Kant's intemperate (and probably politically prompted) attack on him, Ostwald, and Beattie. He would also enjoy the praise of both William James and C. S. Peirce, whose works have Reidian resonances. An undeviating defender of the methods of Bacon and Newton—ever suspicious of mere philosophical speculation—Reid advanced a 'faculty' theory of mind and mental life that would be revived by the phrenologists of the early nineteenth century, and then again by the 'modularity' theorists of the late twentieth.

GEORGE ROMANES (1848–94) was born in Canada but moved to London in childhood and graduated from Cambridge in 1870. He was a friend of Darwin's and was encouraged by the master to apply evolutionary theory to psychology. His *Mental Evolution in Man* (1888) is a derived but important contribution to what would emerge as 'sociobiology'.

GILBERT RYLE (1900–82) was classically educated at Oxford and maintained a lifelong interest in classical philosophy. He served long and with great distinction as the editor of *Mind*, and with comparable distinction as Waynflete Professor of Metaphysical Philosophy at Oxford, where he was the grey eminence behind that institution's celebrated B. Phil. He is best known for *The Concept of Mind* (1949), a recognized classic in philosophy which did much to bring mentalistic (Cartesian) ontologies into view. His behaviouristic programme of reform is not of the simplistic (Skinnerian) stripe, but it presses relentlessly for observable referents for all psychological terms.

OLIVER SACKS is a practising neuropsychiatrist who has derived from a wide variety of clinical cases any number of examples of the dependence of mental life on the physiological integrity of the nervous system. His patients include those whose presenting symptoms are not simply sensory, motor, or cognitive; but include utterly lost senses of their own body and still more mystifying alterations of selfhood.

JOHN SEARLE is Professor of Philosophy at the University of California, Berkeley, and a major contributor to the field of philosophy of mind and philosophy of language. He has criticized the strong Artificial Intelligence thesis and has argued that much of contemporary cognitive science is based on mistaken notions about the nature of consciousness and the nature of computers. His famous 'Chinese Room' exemplifies his doubts about the relevance of computer science to an understanding of mind.

J. J. C. SMART is Professor of Philosophy at the University of New South Wales. He has refined and defended so-called mind/body 'identity' theories in a number of influential publications.

HERBERT SPENCER (1820–1903) was the quintessential 'social Darwinist'. The son of a Quaker teacher, Spencer first prepared himself for an engineering career, but then became increasingly interested in political philosophy and social issues. His editorial services to *The Economist* (1848) drew him into a circle of influential social commentators, including Carlyle and Huxley. His *Social Statics* (1850) anticipated much that would be found nearly a decade later in *Origin of Species*. The latter work spurred Spencer on to yet other volumes in which evolutionary ideas were applied across the social and moral spectrum. At once utilitarian and positivistic, Spencer advocated a rigorous education in the sciences and, like Huxley, thought the classics in education were simply a waste of effort. Like Mill, he was a staunch defender of the individual against the collective, finding in the freest exchange of ideas the means by which error is uncovered and truth found.

JOHANN G. SPURZHEIM (1776–1832) closely collaborated with Franz Gall in furthering the pseudoscience of phrenology, which Spurzheim himself named on the suggestion of T. Forster in 1815. Gall's earliest lectures on the subject were given in Vienna in 1776, but there was not a major publication until Gall and Spurzheim collaborated on their *Research on the Nervous System in General* . . . in 1809. By 1813 the two had parted, Spurzheim going on to lecture and write for another twenty years.

GALEN STRAWSON is Tutor in Philosophy and Fellow of Jesus College, Oxford. In his *Mental Reality* he offers a critical appraisal of major approaches to the mind/body problem, displaying a healthy if uncommon confidence in the validity of 'folk psychology' as the proper starting point for any serious scientific or philosophical enquiry. His 'agnostic materialism' is subtle in that it accepts as primitive the knowledge that might now be claimed as to the essential properties and possibilities of physical reality.

JAMES SULLY (1842–1923) late in life finally enjoyed appointment as Grote Professor of Mind and Logic at the University of London. His textbooks were well received (by both Darwin and Wundt, for example) and he formed associations with major figures in England and on the Continent. In his *Studies of Childhood* he brings the Darwinian, 'natural history' method to bear on developmental studies of human psychology.

ALFRED LORD TENNYSON (1809–92) was reared in the natural beauty of Lincolnshire and drawn early to poetry; his 'whole world seemed to be darkened' by the news of Byron's death. Yet another death, years later—this time his intimate friend, Hallam—preceded the composition of *In Memoriam*, a work in which the poet must believe that he, like his lost friend, is more than brain.

ST THOMAS AQUINAS (1224–74) is the leading religious philosopher of Roman Catholicism and one of the great commentators on Aristotle, 'The Philosopher'. His early education was by way of the Benedictines, after which he completed a course of study in the liberal arts at Naples. In 1244 he entered the Dominican order, studying at Paris and then under Albertus Magnus at Cologne. His psychological theories are characterized by both a moderate empiricism and a moderate rationalism, not unlike Aristotle's own. Reasoning that 'If our nature were different, our duties would be different', Thomas attempted to ground moral and social precepts in what he took to be the essentially universal features of humanity.

UPANIṢADS is a term whose literal meaning pertains to a 'sitting next to' which, in this case, refers to a master or teacher of the meaning of the *Brahamanas* or rituals. The Upaniṣads arose from these enquiries in the ninth century BC and were refined for centuries thereafter. The central query has to do with the deeper meaning and nature of *Brahman*, the power or wisdom that holds things together.

ALFRED RUSSEL WALLACE (1823–1913) co-discovered with Charles Darwin the theory of evolution by natural selection. Well read and self-educated, he became a celebrated naturalist and defender of Darwinian theory. Indeed, his *Darwinism* (1889) did much to silence critics of the theory, owing to Wallace's systematic, balanced, and scientifically informed arguments. But Wallace found in human abstract rationality and morality, as well as in aesthetics and religous belief, features that could not be absorbed into the general theory. His *Darwinism* concludes with expressions of these principled reservations. His reputation among scientists suffered as a result of his interest in the occult; William James invited comparable criticism for this same interest. Darwin, however, respected him deeply, writing to him on one occasion that the thought of disagreeing with Wallace caused him sleepless nights.

RICHARD WILBUR is the Pulitzer Prize-winning American poet.

WILLIAM OF OCKHAM (1285–1349) came to play a leading part in the emergence of an independent mode of scientific enquiry (natural philosophy), liberated from theological attachments and methods. At both Oxford and Paris Ockham's devastating critique of 'realist' theories, his insistence that universals are class *terms* rather then entities, and his requirement that explanations include the fewest causal principles sufficient to account for events would all serve as rallying points for the next generation of progressive thinkers.

LUDWIG WITTGENSTEIN (1889–1951) was born in Vienna to a father who was a self-made man and a cultivated mother whose regular guests included Johannes Brahms. Wittgenstein was educated at home until he was 14, then sent to Linz and thereafter to Berlin for specialized study in mathematics and engineering. In England at the University of Manchester (1908) his interests moved from engineering to mathematics and was drawn to Cambridge by Russell's writings. At Cambridge he immersed himself in philosophical and logical studies, even attempting hypnosis as a means by which to solve logical conundrums. Over a course of many years, and battling his own eccentricities, Wittgenstein moved between Cambridge and a number of unlikely outposts, serving as a hospital orderly at St Guys during the Second World War and a 'lab boy' in Newcastle. Wittgenstein's *Tractatus* and *Philosophical Investigations* reveal the wide arc of his philosophical thought developed over a course of years; the former adopting something of a 'picture' theory of meaning, whereas the latter penetrates to the very cultural and practical core of linguistic expressions.

Source Acknowledgements

AQUINAS, T., *Summa Theologiae*. Excerpts from *The Basic Writings of Saint Thomas Aquinas*, edited by Anton C. Pegis, 1943, repr. by permission of Hackett Publishing Company. All rights reserved.

ARISTOTLE (trans. H. Tredennick), *Metaphysics*, in *Aristotle*, vol. xvii, Harvard University Press, Cambridge, Massachusetts, 1933. Reprinted by permission of the publishers and the Loeb Classical Library.

ARISTOTLE (trans. W. Hett), *On the Soul*, in *Aristotle*, vol. viii, Harvard University Press, Cambridge, Massachusetts, 1936. Reprinted by permission of the publishers and the Loeb Classical Library.

ARISTOTLE, *Posterior Analytics; On the Soul; Parts of Animals; History of Animals*, in J. Barnes (ed.), *The Complete Works of Aristotle*, Princeton University Press, Princeton. Copyright © 1984, repr. by permission of Princeton University Press.

AUGUSTINE (trans. T. Williams), *On the Free Choice of the Will*, Hackett, Cambridge, 1993, repr. with permission. Copyright © 1993 by Hackett Publishing Company. All rights reserved.

BAIN, A., *The Senses and the Intellect*, Parker & Son, London, 1855.

BERKELEY, G., *A Treatise Concerning the Principles of Human Knowledge* (1710).

CABANIS, P. (trans. F. Robinson), *Preface to 'On the Relationship between the Moral and the Physical'*, Greenwood Publishing Co., Connecticut.

CHURCHLAND, P., *Eliminative Materialism and the Propositional Attitudes* (ed. W. Lycan), Basil Blackwell, Oxford, 1990.

DARWIN, C., *The Expression of the Emotions in Man and Animals* (1871), Philosophical Library, New York.

DARWIN, C., *The Origin of Species* (1859), Modern Library edn., New York.

DE LA METTRIE, J. O. (trans. M. W. Calkins), *Man a Machine*, Open Court, La Salle, Illinois, 1912. Reprinted by permission of Open Court Publishing Company, a division of Carus Publishing Company, Peru, Illlinois.

DENNETT, D., *Darwin's Dangerous Idea*, Simon & Schuster, New York, 1995.

DESCARTES, R., *Meditations on the First Philosophy*, in *The Philosophical Writings of Descartes*, vol. ii (ed. J. Cottingham and others), Cambridge University Press, Cambridge, 1984. Reprinted by permission of the editor and publishers.

DESCARTES, R. (trans. J. Cottingham and others), *Principles of Philosophy*, in *The Philosophical Writings of Descartes*, vol. i (ed. and trans. J. Cottingham and others), Cambridge University Press, Cambridge, 1984. Reprinted by permission of the editor and publishers.

DEWEY, J., 'Mind and Consciousness', in Dewey, *Intelligence in the Modern World* (ed. J. Ratner), Modern Library, New York, 1939.

ERSKINE, T., *The Trial of Hadfield*, Howelle's State Trials, 1800.

FLETCHER, P., 'The Purple Island', in T. G. S. Cain (ed.), *Jacobean and Caroline Poetry, an Anthology*, Methuen, London and New York, 1981.

FLOURENS, P. (trans. C. Meigs), *Phrenology Examined*, Philadelphia, Hogan & Thompson, 1846.

FREUD, S. (trans. J. Strachey), *New Introductory Lectures on Psycho-Analysis*, Standard Edition vol. xxii, Hogarth Press, London.

GALEN (trans. M. T. May), *On the Usefulness of the Parts of the Body*, Cornell University Press, Ithaca, New York, 1969. Copyright © 1968 by Cornell University, repr. by permission of the publisher.

GALEN (trans. P. N. Singer), *Selected Works*, Oxford World's Classics, Oxford University Press, Oxford, 1997.

GILLETT, G., 'Brain Bisection and Personal Identity', *Mind*, 378 (1986), 224–9. Reprinted by permission of the publishers, Oxford University Press, Oxford, and the author.

GUTHRIE, K. S., *The Pythagorean Sourcebook and Library*, Phanes Press, Grand Rapids, Michigan, 1987.

HAECKEL, E. (trans. J. McCabe), *The Evolution of Man*, Watts & Co., London, 1910.

HARTLEY, D., *Observations on Man*, Scholars' Facsimile Edition, Gainesville, Florida, 1966.

HIPPOCRATES (trans. W. H. S. Jones), *Ancient Medicine*, in *Hippocrates*, vol. i, Harvard University Press, Cambridge, Massachusetts. Reprinted by permission of the publishers and the Loeb Classical Library.

HOBBES, T., *Leviathan* (1651 edn.), Penguin, Harmondsworth, 1974.

HUME, D., *An Enquiry Concerning Human Understanding* (ed. L. A. Selby-Bigge), Oxford University Press, Oxford, 3rd edn., 1975.

HUXLEY, T. H., 'On the Hypothesis that Animals are Automata', *Fortnightly Review*, 1874.

JAMES, W., *Does Consciousness Exist?* (1904). In *The Writings of William James* (ed. J. McDermott), Chicago University Press, Chicago, 1967.

JAMES, W., *The Principles of Psychology* (1890), Harvard University Press, Cambridge, Massachusetts. Copyright © 1981 by the President and Fellows of Harvard College, repr. by permission of the publishers.

JUNG, C. G., *Basic Postulates of Analytical Psychology* (trans. R. Hull), in *The Structure and Dynamics of the Psyche*, Princeton University Press, Princeton. Copyright © 1970, repr. by permission of Princeton University Press.

KANT, I. (trans. J. M. Meiklejohn), *Critique of Pure Reason*, Willey Book Co., New York, 1943.

LASHLEY, K., *The Neuropsychology of Lashley: Selected Papers* (ed. F. Beach), New York, McGraw-Hill, 1960.

LEIBNIZ, G. W. F. (trans. G. Montgomery), *Monadology*, Doubleday & Co., New York, 1960.

LEIBNIZ, G. W. F. (trans. P. Remnant and J. Bennett), *New Essays on Human Understanding*, Cambridge University Press, Cambridge, 1982. Reproduced by permission of the publishers and the translators.

LLOYD MORGAN, C., *An Introduction to Comparative Psychology*, Walter Scott Ltd., London, 1894.

LOCKE, J., *An Essay Concerning Human Understanding* (ed. A. C. Fraser), Dover Books, New York, 1959.

LUCRETIUS (trans. W. H. D. Rouse), *On the Nature of Things*, Harvard University Press, Cambridge, Massachusetts. Reprinted by permission of the publishers and the Loeb Classical Library, 1975.

MARVELL, A., 'A Dialogue between the Soul and the Body', in *Anchor Anthology of Seventeenth-Century Verse*, Doubleday, New York, 1969.

MAUDSLEY, H., *Responsibility in Mental Disease*, D. Appleton & Co., New York, 1876.

MILL, J. S., *A System of Logic Ratiocinative and Inductive*, Longmans, Green, London, 1990.

NAGEL, T., 'What is it Like to be a Bat?', *Philosophical Review*, 83 (1975), 435–44.

OCKHAM, WILLIAM OF (trans. P. Boehner), *Philosophical Writings*, Bobbs-Merrill, Indianapolis, 1964.

OLIVELLE, P. (trans.), *Upaniṣads* (Oxford World's Classics, Oxford University Press, Oxford and New York, 1996).

PARFIT, D., *Reasons and Persons*, Oxford University Press, Oxford, 1984, revised paperback 1989. Reprinted by permission of the publishers.

PENFIELD, W., *The Mystery of the Mind*, Princeton University Press, Princeton. Copyright © 1972, repr. by permission of Princeton University Press.

PENROSE, R., *The Emperor's New Mind*, Oxford University Press, Oxford, 1990.

PLATO (trans. H. N. Fowler), *Phaedo*, in *Plato*, vol. i, Harvard University Press, Cambridge, Massachusetts, 1914. Reprinted by permission of the publishers and the Loeb Classical Library.

PLATO (trans. W. R. M. Lamb), *Meno*, Heinemann, London, 1924.

REID, T., *An Inquiry into the Human Mind* (1813 edn.).

ROBINSON, D., 'Cerebral Plurality and the Unity of Self', *American Psychologist* (1990).

ROMANES, G., *Animal Intelligence*, Appleton, New York, 1883.

RYLE, G., *The Concept of Mind*, Routledge (Unwin Hyman), London, 1949. With permission of the Principal Fellow and Scholars of Hertford College in the University of Oxford.

SACKS, O., 'The Disembodied Lady', repr. with permission of Simon & Schuster from *The Man who Mistook his Wife for a Hat and Other Clinical Tales*. Copyright © 1970, 1981, 1983, 1984, 1985.

SEARLE, J., *The Rediscovery of the Mind*, MIT Press, Cambridge, Massachusetts, and London, England, 1992. Reprinted by permission of the publishers.

SMART, J. J. C., 'Sensations and Brain Processes', in V. C. Chappell (ed.), *The Philosophy of Mind*, Prentice Hall, New Jersey, 1962.

SPENCER, H., *First Principles*, De Witt Revolving Fund, New York, 1958.

SPURZHEIM, G., *Outlines of Phrenology*, Marsh, Capen & Lyon, Boston, 1832.

STRAWSON, G., *Mental Reality*, MIT Press, Cambridge, Massachusetts, and London, 1994. Reprinted by permission of the publishers.

SULLY, J., *Studies of Childhood*, Appleton, New York, 1896.

TURING, A. N., 'Computing, Machinery and Intelligence', *Mind*, 59 (1950), 433–60.

WALLACE, A. R., *Darwinism*, Macmillan, London, 1912.

WILBUR, R., 'The Mind'.

WITTGENSTEIN, L., *The Blue and Brown Books*, Harper Torchbooks, New York, 1958.

Index